Immoral Memories

Immoral

A sketch by Eisenstein for "Alexander Nevsky"

Memories

An Autobiography
by Sergei M. Eisenstein

Translated by Herbert Marshall

Houghton Mifflin Company   Boston   1983

Library of Congress Cataloging in Publication Data

Eisenstein, Sergei, 1898–1948.
　Immoral memories.

　Includes index.
　1. Eisenstein, Sergei, 1898–1948.　2. Moving-picture
producers and directors—Soviet Union—Biography.
I. Marshall, Herbert, date.　II. Title.
PN1998.A3E519　1983　　　791.43′0233′0924 [B]　　　83-8417
ISBN 0-395-33101-3

Printed in the United States of America

V 10 9 8 7 6 5 4 3 2 1

Book design by Roy Brown

All illustrations are from the Herbert Marshall Archives
unless otherwise credited.

Contents

Photographs follow pages 68, 132, and 196

Preface

TO ME, EISENSTEIN was distinguished by a great leonine head and exceedingly delicate hands. His psychological presence was such that his height seemed irrelevant. The noble forehead became even more noble as he aged, but his eyes always retained a quizzical expression. Throughout the nine years I knew him, I could never tell whether he was laughing with someone or at someone, for he possessed a perpetual Mona Lisa smile. And that was appropriate, since Leonardo da Vinci was his ideal man — one who blended art and science.

When I consider his personality, however, I have to say he always seemed like a Russian *matriushka* — the famous carved wooden doll, hiding within it another doll, hiding another doll, and so ad infinitum. Outside he was a Soviet Russian; inside, according to some, he was a Christian. According to others, he was a Jew; to yet others, a homosexual; to a few, a cynical critic . . . and what else? It was difficult to know what he was fundamentally. He never expressed it verbally. Still, there was one medium through which he expressed his innermost feelings — his drawings and caricatures.

Whatever unpleasantness may have taken place outside the class where I studied with him in Moscow, he never vented it on the students. One time, when Eisenstein arrived at class from the Moscow Film Studios, he was in a subdued mood, saying nothing, not even his usual greetings. The students were at once apprehensive. Something was up. He went straight to the blackboard, picked up a piece of chalk, and rapidly started sketching — first a tree trunk, then a dachshund, which encircled the tree twice with its elongated sausagelike body, until its nose was brought round to face its own behind. He then added a subtitle (like one in a silent film): "Twenty years I've worked in the Moscow Film Studios, but it's the first time I've seen *that* director!"

That was all. He never explained what or whom he had in mind, and he picked up his lecture where he had left off at the last meeting.

Later we learned the reason for that drawing: the first film he was making in Russia in six years, *Bezhin Meadow*, had been stopped and he had been condemned. He stated this had been one of the worst experiences of his life.

Throughout that life Eisenstein was always a lonely figure. His nearest neighbor was his childhood friend from Riga, Maxim Shtraukh, the actor, who lived in the flat next door with his wife, Judith Glizer. His closest associates were his cameraman, Eduard Tisse, and his assistant and wife, Pera Attasheva. But he was never on an intimate basis even with Tisse, and Pera was a wife in name only. Above all, Pera was his bulwark, his defender. She was utterly in love with him. When her love proved impossible of fulfillment, she never had another man in her life. Her last years, after Eisenstein's death, were totally dedicated to perpetuating his memory and seeing his unpublished works published; they had all been suppressed by Stalin. Pera suffered from diabetes and heart and kidney trouble; when my wife and I saw her, she had not long to live. But she told us she was determined not to die until Sergei Mikhailovich's works were in print.

"It could come back!" she said, referring to the repressions of the Stalin years.

At that time Russia was replete with the euphoria of Khrushchev's liberalism, de-Stalinization, and the renaissance of Soviet art, which had been crushed under Stalin. We were still romantics, I suppose; we did not dream Stalinism "could come back."

Pera had no illusions, and before her death she supervised the publication of four volumes of Eisenstein's *Collected Works*, which were later followed by another two. And so the volumes remain — for the seventh has been withheld by Soviet authorities, as has a major monograph on his life. In addition, access to Eisenstein's archives has been forbidden to researchers from outside the Soviet Union. Pera was right to be in such a hurry.

She kept a brave front before strangers during her illness, but, to my wife and me, at times she would give way and cry out: "Fredda — Gerbert — *Ya tak bolna!*" ("Fredda — Herbert — I am so ill!") All we could do was to mourn with her, embrace her stricken body, and weep.

In those final days my wife made a beautiful portrait sculpture of her, for which she posed patiently. She was very pleased with it and hoped that one day it would hang beside the magnificent portrait Fredda had made of Eisenstein.

It is not generally known that Eisenstein was very superstitious. That was made clear one day when a group of students came out of the film institute with him. The institute was then in the old building on Leningradskoye Chaussee, once famous as the former Tsigane restaurant. Tales were told that Rasputin had held his orgies here, but the only remnants of those days were the brass figure of a sphinx at the base of the main staircase and great ornamental mirrors in our classroom. As we strode toward Tverskaya (now Gorky Street), a black cat suddenly crossed our path. Eisenstein shrieked like a girl and jumped back. He refused to take another step in the direction we were going and resolutely turned round and walked in the opposite direction. We all followed, somewhat taken aback by the vehemence of his reaction. But even though we joked about it, he would not turn back until we came to the next crossing; then he turned left across the street and left again down the other side of the Chaussee. He admitted that he reacted the same way to a nun or priest, which had caused him some trouble in France, but he conceded that in the Soviet Union there were now more black cats than nuns or priests!

As the following pages reveal, this erudite intellectual had a taste for thrillers and detective stories. He was also fond of such American film stars as Deanna Durbin, Judy Garland, and Elizabeth Taylor. During the wartime alliance he borrowed films and books from the American Office of War Information in Moscow, which was headed by Miss Elizabeth Eagan. When he was hospitalized, he wrote to her: "I want to thank you so much for the enormous pleasure you provided in sending me the *National Velvet* and Louis Jacob's book . . . Let Arthur bring me the picture *Meet Me in St. Louis*. I'm terribly fond of Judy Garland! And also if you have by any chance a copy of *Forever Amber*? I'd like to read that very much, and, P.S., Is there no way to find Agatha Christie's *Murder of Roger Ackroyd* in Moscow?"

Eisenstein's first film, made in 1923 when he was twenty-four, was the visualization of a character's diary in his production of Ostrovsky's drawing room drama *Enough Simplicity in Every Wise Man*. This play was adapted "futuristically" by his friend Sergei Tretiakov (later imprisoned and murdered by the KGB) and produced by Eisenstein in the Moscow Proletcult Theater.

As far as I know, this was the first time film was blended into a theatrical production. Eisenstein also anticipated Orson Welles by projecting a film clip of himself bowing to the audience at the end of the stage performance, and though this first film was in the nature of a gimmick, it was the start of Eisenstein's path into cinema history.

His next film, *Strike* (made in 1924–1925 and based on a Proletcult dramatization), introduced all the stylistic motifs that were to evolve and flower in his later films. *Strike* also reflected the influence of his film mentor, the American cinematic genius D. W. Griffith. Eisenstein, along with other Soviet film directors, always gave full credit to Griffith's masterpieces — *Intolerance*, *The Birth of a Nation*, and *Way Down East* — and their importance to Soviet cinema.

When I was a fellow at the Woodrow Wilson Center for International Studies, I was able to compare the films of Griffith and Eisenstein and at one time ran them in parallel on a two-screen movieola. The influence of *Intolerance* was clear not only in *Strike*, but in *Alexander Nevsky* and *Ivan the Terrible*. What also emerged as noteworthy was that the presentation of the class struggle by the arch-conservative aristocratic Southerner, Griffith, was more truthful in retrospect than that of the Marxist dialectician and revolutionary, Eisenstein. Where

Griffith treated the classes objectively, Eisenstein caricatured the capitalists and the petit bourgeois and idealized the workers. What remains realistic and convincing in Griffith's films is exaggerated and unconvincing in Eisenstein's.

Tragically, this tendency to falsification is inherent in works of art produced under Communist Party dictatorship, particularly its films. When Eisenstein was finishing his epic film of the Russian Revolution *October* (or *Ten Days That Shook the World*), he was forced by Stalin to cut out all shots and references to Trotsky, Zinoviev, and Kamenev.

Thus in the next film, about the agricultural "revolution," *The General Line* (or *The Old and the New*), Eisenstein could not show the true nature of the "liquidation of the kulaks as a class" (virtually a second civil war), the deliberate starving out of millions of those middle peasants, nor their eventual herding into Gulag prison camps and use as forced labor to build the Socialist five-year plan. But still Stalin didn't like the film.[1]

The General Line also introduced Eisenstein's use of religious symbolism, for the newly acquired cream-separator machine was the holy grail of the collective farm. His use of such symbolism reached its apotheosis in his aborted film *Que Viva Mexico!* and is graphically shown in his book *Mexican Drawings*.

Eisenstein's intention in *Que Viva Mexico!* was to surpass Griffith's *Intolerance*. But, alas, that film also came to naught because of Stalin.

When Eisenstein and Grisha Alexandrov, his closest co-worker, returned from Mexico in disgrace, Alexandrov broke off all contact with Eisenstein. By opting for safety and making only comedies, which became the favorites of Stalin, Alexandrov managed to ingratiate himself with Stalin. But, as Pera Attasheva noted, though Alexandrov had access and influence, he refused to help his former comrade and friend. After Stalin's death Alexandrov was ostracized by the Soviet film industry.

In the 1930s the Soviet film industry was put in the charge of one organization, the Committee for Cinematography of the USSR, and Stalin appointed one Boris Shumyatsky as chairman. In reality, Shumyatsky was one of the tools Stalin used to frustrate every attempt by Eisenstein to continue his creative work.

Eisenstein had got on the wrong side of Stalin by overstaying his leave while trying to finish his Mexican film. He was ordered back to Moscow but disobeyed, and Stalin sent a telegram to Upton Sinclair (who had backed the film), calling Eisenstein "a deserter." In consequence, from the time he returned in 1931, he was not allowed to make any films of his choosing for seven years but was allowed to teach.

---

1. I worked with the Dutch film-maker Joris Ivens on a film about Soviet youth in industry, *The Song of Heroes*. In it, we showed the construction of the vast iron and steel foundries at Magnitogorsk, but we left out completely the American engineers and technicians who designed them and the former kulaks, now prisoners in Magnitogorsk's own Gulag, who built the giant blast furnaces.

Still, in 1934 Shumyatsky proposed (on behalf of Stalin, of course) that Eisenstein make a film on collectivization and the transformation of the Soviet village. Eisenstein chose a story by Rzheshevsky, based on Turgenev's *Bezhin Meadow*, in which the hero, Pavel Morozov, clashes with his father over collectivization and is shot by him. But production was halted when the film was half-completed. Eisenstein was ordered to remake it according to the new Party line. In his effort to comply, he called in an old friend, the writer Isaac Babel, to help him rescript it.

I remember at the time thinking this somewhat incongruous, as Babel was a specialist in the Yiddish life of Odessa and the Red Cavalry, not in collectivization in the countryside. But despite the reshooting and re-editing, the film was ruthlessly criticized as showing the struggle of "good and evil" and not "the class struggle," with the father as Abraham, the son as Isaac, and other such images. Finally, the film was banned and then destroyed. Within three years the original script writer, Rzheshevsky, and his successor, Babel, were arrested as "enemies of the people" and imprisoned in the Gulag without trial. After the death of Stalin, Rzheshevsky was released and rehabilitated, but died soon after from the privations of his imprisonment. The great writer Isaac Babel did not survive. No one has revealed where he lies buried, but he too has been "rehabilitated," albeit posthumously.

To compound tragedy with irony, Boris Shumyatsky, Stalin's tried and trusted emissary, who tried desperately to fulfill every whim of the dictator, was also arrested and disappeared into the Gulag, never to emerge.

Following the banning of *Bezhin Meadow*, Eisenstein was attacked on all fronts, by film critics, fellow film directors, and Party theoreticians. The witch-hunt reached its climax in a special Conference of Cinema Workers in January 1935.

I was present and heard it all — and despite all that happened there, all the insinuations and deprecations — it was obvious that Eisenstein's intellectual brilliance and erudition outshone them all. But of course it didn't help. Stalin had chosen a worthy opponent to head the conference. He was Sergei Dynamov, a Marxist philosopher from the agit-prop department of the Central Committee of the Communist Party. A brilliant intellectual, he led the attack on Eisenstein's theory of intellectual cinema as "bourgeoisie-influenced formalism." But later he too was to meet the same fate as Shumyatsky: execution as an enemy of the people.

Other film directors criticized Eisenstein; the criticism was typified by Alexander Dovzhenko: "I'm convinced in more ways than one that his erudition is killing him." Later this brilliant Ukrainian director was mercilessly attacked by Stalin and Lavrenti Beria for Ukrainian "nationalism" and was banned from working in his own Ukrainian studios in Kiev. Now that he is dead, the studios are named after him!

Only one man defended Eisenstein, though he himself was in deep trouble.

This was Lev Kuleshov, a pioneer of film theory and one of my teachers at the institute. He summed up all the attacks on Eisenstein: "Dovzhenko said that one can burst from too much knowledge and he was afraid that would happen to you. Dear Sergei Mikhailovich, no one ever burst from too much knowledge but from too much envy. That is all I have to say."

Brave Lev Kuleshov! To go against Stalin and the Party! After that, his path was to oblivion, although he continued to teach at the institute until his death.

That about sums it up: envy of Eisenstein by all his contemporaries in the USSR still haunts him long after his death. For twenty-five years many of Eisenstein's works remained unpublished. After his death his teachings were forbidden in his own institute, and his early films were not shown to the new generations of students. Some other director-teachers, like Yutkevich, were expelled for endeavoring to expound his formalistic theories, and some students were arrested.

In contrast to their treatment in the Soviet Union, Eisenstein's works were translated and published in English, French, German, Italian, Spanish, Japanese, and other languages. In this autobiography he notes that in the American Film Index of 1941 he occupies fourth place in cinema history for the quantity of work written about him.

As one reads *Immoral Memories*, one must remember that these autobiographical notes were started only after Eisenstein had had a very serious heart attack, on February 2, 1946, and was confined to the Kremlin Hospital. He never expected them to be published in his lifetime — or in Stalin's — and they weren't! But even so, he still does not reveal his innermost feelings, as did Dovzhenko and Vertov, his fellow film directors, in their posthumous diaries.

Dovzhenko openly cursed Stalin, Beria, and their *apparachiki*; Vertov cursed the *apparachiki*, but did not realize Stalin was behind the slow death of his creative work. But never once did Eisenstein curse any of them openly.

Only in three places in this autobiography does he let go. The first is his account of his grief over the fate of his beloved master, Vsevelod Meyerhold (who, at the time he was writing, was a "nonperson").

He wrote: "I must say that I never loved, idolized, worshiped anyone as much as I did my teacher, and to extreme old age I shall consider myself unworthy to kiss the dust from his feet." Meyerhold was still "an enemy of the people": all his works were banned, his theater was closed; all information about him was deleted from reference books and encyclopedias; the new theater he designed was renamed the Tchaikovsky Concert Hall; his wife was butchered; and Meyerhold himself was murdered in the cellars of the KGB.

Then, in Khrushchev's day, it was learned that Meyerhold's archives had not been destroyed by the KGB (as everyone assumed) but had been hidden by

Eisenstein and Pera Attasheva in their *dacha* and so preserved for posterity. Under Stalin that was a brave act.

The second instance occurs when he pinpoints the three most tragic periods of his life: the abortion of *Que Viva Mexico!*; the suppression of *Bezhin Meadow*; and the condemnation and suppression of *Ivan the Terrible*, Part II. All of these happened because of Stalin, but he never openly says so.

The third place is where he uses allegorical means to express his fate: he reveals that in his films is "the implacable image of relentless fate" that stalked him all his life — from the jackboots of the soldiers down the Odessa steps (in *Potemkin*), the overwhelming charge of the Teutonic knights in armor with implacable blind snouts (in *Alexander Nevsky*), and the oncoming mass of black cowls of Ivan's bodyguards, hidden in monks' black habits. About these he writes: "Later, I myself fell into the tenacious clutches of the image, now come alive."

That was in 1946, which he said was "the worst autumn of his life," when the decree of the Central Committee of the Communist Party damned him and Part II of *Ivan*. Yet his comrade Ivor Montagu wrote of this same decree "that every word of it was just."

However, following the empty years after *Que Viva Mexico!*, Eisenstein finally had to submit to Stalin's will by accepting the subject of Alexander Nevsky, though in the twenties Eisenstein had intended to "debunk" Nevsky as a vassal of the Moguls. He had also to submit to the imposition of political commissars placed right by his side throughout the production. This was to make sure there would be no more improvisations such as those that had produced the classic "Odessa Steps" sequence in his masterpiece *Potemkin*. He had to abide by what was called "the cast-iron scenario" and not diverge from what had been approved on high. Thus for *Alexander Nevsky*, he was given Peter Pavlenko as co-writer and D. I. Vasiliev as co-director. Both were Stalin-appointed hard-liners. Indeed, Pavlenko wrote the grotesque glorification of Stalin in the Soviet feature films *The Vow* and *The Fall of Berlin* (in which Stalin alone won the war), later devastatingly castigated by Khrushchev and withdrawn. Such were the people Eisenstein was forced to work with. Despite this, Eisenstein managed to inject his own formal approach and at the same time please Stalin. For this he was granted the medal and title hitherto withheld — the Order of Lenin and the degree of doctor of arts.

His next film, in the autumn of 1939, was to be about the building of the Ferghana Canal in Soviet Central Asia. Here again he hoped to parallel Griffith's *Intolerance*. He planned three parallel histories: the original building of the canals and irrigation, which made the whole desert area fertile and prosperous; then their utter destruction by the ruthless conqueror Tamerlaine the Great, and finally their resurrection under Soviet power, when the desert would once again blossom. Eisenstein studied the domain, which included the exotic cities of Bokhara and Samarkand and the tomb of Tamerlaine. Then suddenly it was stopped — again obviously by Stalin. It seemed that, as with Ivan the Terrible, the tyrant and destroyer Tamerlaine was a hero to Stalin. But the parallel was too close, for on top of everything else Tamerlaine had a defect in his leg, as Stalin had in his arm. I learned from Pera Attasheva that this blow reduced Eisenstein to despair and the serious contemplation of suicide, from which only Pera and his students saved him.

To cap this, at the end of December 1939 came the Hitler-Stalin pact, for which Eisenstein again had to debase himself. He was "asked" to broadcast over the Comintern radio "greetings to his German cultural brother," and then to produce, at the Bolshoi Opera House, *Die Walküre*, by Wagner, Hitler's favorite composer. Obviously a sop to Hitler from Stalin.

However, only two years later Eisenstein was asked to sign an appeal from Soviet Jews to the Jews of the world to mobilize all help to fight the "Fascist barbarians." For the first time Eisenstein declared himself a Jew, along with many other distinguished people, such as Ilya Ehrenberg and Hans Richter. Although of Jewish descent, Eisenstein had been baptized a Christian, but outsiders may not know that in reality he was imbued with *Yiddishkeit* (Jewishness).

Once, coming into the classroom after an English-language class, Eisenstein happened to glance at a textbook belonging to a student, Kolya Rozhkov. It gave the names in English of various kitchen utensils headed *Pots and Pans*. With a quick gesture of his pencil, he encircled the word *Pots* and then the word *Pans*, and just said: "That's what I think of them!" Kolya grinned, but wouldn't explain afterward, although it was clear that he understood.

Later I found out. Eisenstein knew Kolya was Jewish and understood Yiddish slang, as well as some Polish. *Pots* is close to a Yiddish slang word for penis, and *pan* is the Polish title for mister or gentleman, equivalent to the old Russian title of *gospodin*, replaced since the Revolution by the title *tovarish* (comrade). Now it seems Eisenstein was saying that the comrades were *pots* and had become *pans* once again.

Following the success of *Alexander Nevsky*, Eisenstein contemplated shooting various subjects. Some were just talked about; others had treatments or even scripts, which he prepared. But in the end, none was produced. However varied they were, not one was acceptable to Stalin. Then came the dictator's decision — that Eisenstein should make *Ivan the Terrible*, but as the story of a positive historical character, despite the fact that up to the Stalin era, Ivan had been portrayed by all Marxist historians — let alone others — as a cruel tyrant, a fratricidal murderer, a ruler *not* to be emulated. Eisenstein now had to portray the opposite, which he proceeded to do in Part I.

Having faithfully followed the Party line, he continued and completed Part II of *Ivan*. When he submitted it to the Ministry of Cinematography, there was consternation and fear. It was clear that Eisenstein had shown Ivan as a paranoiac murderer and drawn the parallel with Stalin. The inevitable happened: a condemnatory decree from the Central Committee descended like a plague on leading Soviet film directors: Pudovkin, Kozintsev, and Trauberg, as well as Eisenstein. They were castigated for the "fictitious" representation of the history they were portraying in their productions. So "Ivan the Terrible — the mighty leader, diplomat, and statesman, creator of a multinational Russian state, the forerunner of Peter the Great" — is linked with "the theme of a Hamlet-like despot, of a historical bloodthirsty tyrant with a shattered conscience and sick will."

Following the completion of Part II of *Ivan*, Eisenstein had a severe heart attack. In order not to exacerbate this condition, his friends tried to prevent him from learning of the terrible attack on him by the Central Committee. But of course he eventually learned the truth. He promised Stalin he would remake Part II and complete Part III, some of which he had shot. But, alas, he was never able to; his heart was too weak.

I asked Pera Attasheva how he had managed to make such an extraordinary image of Stalin and get away with it. She said it was the luck of the whole Moscow film studios' being evacuated to Alma-Ata in Uzbekistan, at the height of the war, thousands of miles from the Kremlin, with Stalin obviously too busy with the war to deal with his recalcitrant film director.

I am sure too that Eisenstein, fully aware of his heart condition, "decided to go the whole hog" (in the words of his fellow film director Mikhail Romm) when he presented the finished film *Ivan the Terrible* Part II to the Ministry of Cinematography.

Eighteen months later he died of heart failure.

This, his last film, was banned under Stalin and not released until fifteen years after his death. The world recognized it at once as a masterpiece.

To help the reader find his way in this autobiography I have appended a chronology of events to show what was happening to Eisenstein at any particular time. But to appreciate this book fully, one needs some knowledge of the Russian Revolution and its eventual history and transformation.

Eisenstein's films are, in themselves, a reflection of this transformation — from the staccato dynamic montage of his early documentary-style films (*Potemkin, October,* and *The Old and the New*) to the ponderous, slow-moving, pseudoclassic operatic style of his last two films (*Alexander Nevsky* and *Ivan the Terrible*). In this change of style the imprint of Stalin's era is patently evident. Here in *Immoral Memories*, Eisenstein tells of a Persian folk legend about an epic hero who,

> in order to preserve his strength for the future, obediently spread himself out in the dust beneath the feet of his mockers. Later he succeeded in accomplishing all the unprecedented feats required of him. This episode . . . the unprecedented self-

control and sacrifice of everything, even his self-respect, to further the achievement and realization of what had been prescribed and ordered from the beginning, completely captivated me . . . accepting humiliation in the name of our most passionate aspiration.

In my personal, too personal history, I too often perpetrated this heroic deed of self-abasement. And in my personal, too personal innermost life, perhaps somewhat too often, too hurriedly, even too willingly, and also . . . as unsuccessfully.

This is the only clear indication I can find in all of Eisenstein's published works of what really went on in his "too personal history," which otherwise he never gave a clue to. How every time he was flayed by his mockers, he "obediently spread himself in the dust," wrote letters of self-abasement and humiliation, and overtly praised the tyrant — which he did "even most too willingly," but also just "as unsuccessfully."

The parallel with Galileo is obvious. As Ivor Montagu points out: "In relation to the frustrations he met over *Bezhin Meadow,* at the end of which he capitulated and renounced his theories, like Galileo and then still more like Galileo — *Eppur si muova!* (Nevertheless it moves!)."

As I have said, it was through drawings and caricatures that Eisenstein expressed his innermost feelings. Much has been heard of his pornographic drawings (which I have seen and which so upset Upton Sinclair and the American customs officials in 1931), but even some of his published Mexican drawings give a taste of his grotesque and blasphemous treatment of religious themes.

At boring meetings Eisenstein was always doodling, and his fellow film director Gregory Roshal preserved many of the doodles, one of which is a striking example of how he really felt. It is a caricature of a man, obviously Stalin, dressed as a surgeon-butcher at the operating table, cutting up a helpless victim with a great carving knife, while his other hand is thrust deep into a gaping wound.

Moments of despair came more frequently to Eisenstein in his later years. During the shooting of *Ivan the Terrible* in Alma-Ata, Eisenstein was to lose his closest friend and faithful comrade, the crack cameraman Eduard Tisse. Every Eisenstein film had been shot by Tisse, who had steadfastly stood by him in all his troubles and who refused to work with anyone else. Suddenly, to everyone's astonishment, Eisenstein hired another famous cameraman, André Moskvin, who previously had worked only for the Leningrad directors Kozintsev and Trauberg.

The standard explanation given was that Moskvin was better at interiors and Tisse at exterior shooting. This was patently absurd, since Tisse had shot everything for all of Eisenstein's masterpieces — interiors, exteriors, and trick shots. Apart from that, Tisse had already shot interiors for Part I of *Ivan.* Marie Seton asserts that Tisse had artistic disagreements with Eisenstein and hence joined Alexandrov's group.

However, the truth was revealed to me personally by Tisse's widow, Beatrice, in 1960. Through an error, Tisse's passport stated he was of German origin. When Germany was at war with the Soviet Union, all Germans and Soviet citizens of German origin were rounded up and interned. In Alma-Ata the Soviet secret police, believing Tisse to be German, put him under house arrest until they cleared his fate with Moscow. Eisenstein was told that his chief cameraman couldn't work with him and he had to find another. Eventually Beatrice Tisse was able to clear up the error and her husband was released. But by then, of course, Moskvin was already shooting Part II of *Ivan*, so some excuse was found to justify Eisenstein now having two chief cameramen: one for interiors, one for exteriors.

Mrs. Tisse, however, complained that though these facts were known to the authorities, they published a monograph on the cameraman André Moskvin in which illustrations of interiors shot by Tisse were attributed to Moskvin. They then held up the publication of a monograph on Tisse because Mrs. Tisse insisted they tell the truth. As far as I know, it has not been published to this day — just like the monograph on Eisenstein.

As to the "artistic conflict" between Eisenstein and Tisse, I was told by Pera Attasheva that it resulted because Tisse complained that Part I whitewashed Ivan the Terrible and falsified history, whereas Alexandrov took the opposite point of view. He objected to showing the negative side of Ivan, because the script "showed little but intrigue" and what, according to Marie Seton, Alexandrov characterized as "dirty family washing."

That remark typifies the whole behavior of Alexandrov in relation to the Stalinist terror. Alexandrov approved of the "whitewashing" of Ivan in Part I, but when Eisenstein in Part II exposed the behavior of a paranoiac mass murderer, Alexandrov considered this to be merely washing dirty linen in public. He warned that trouble would follow, but Eisenstein ignored him. He was burning his boats and he knew it.

Up until then — at the end of his life — Eisenstein had never overtly criticized Stalin, certainly not in his writings or speeches. A leading Soviet film critic, Zorkaya, wrote about this very book:

> Even though we had hoped these autobiographical notes would reveal the truth about its author . . . the varying expressions of the author, articles, notes, certain pages of the diary now published, *unfortunately even now cannot serve as irrefutable evidence of the true intentions and views of their author . . .* The discord between what was necessary to write and what was in reality becomes completely stabilized in Eisenstein's public statements. Here the point is not, of course, in something double-faced in him personally, but in the misfortune of a permanent moral compromise . . . which became the normal condition of man. [Italics added.]

This was the much-vaunted "new Soviet man." In the prophetic words of George Orwell, in such a society the normal condition of man is to learn double-speak and double-think. Such a condition inevitably gives birth to irreconcilable conflict in every sphere, particularly the artistic. Engendering the eternal attempt of every true artist, under tyranny and censorship, to smuggle in the truth by means of artistic images and metaphorical allegories, by double-entendre and what the Russians call *inoskazaniye* (between the lines). This moral compromise leads to the contradiction another Soviet critic, Freilich, pointed out about Eisenstein: that "to one it seemed that *Ivan the Terrible* was almost a justification for the cult of the personality. To others that *Ivan* indirectly protested against the repressions of the period of the cult of the personality, for which reason Part II was not shown on the screen during the lifetime of Stalin."

Added to this and other indiscretions of Eisenstein was the fact that, unlike his fellow film directors, he avoided any social work outside his teaching at the film institute. These other directors would visit factories and collective farms, houses of culture and schools, and take patronage over amateur cinema groups. They could serve on committees for cultural relations with foreign countries or the World Peace Council. Pudovkin was very active in the latter, together with Ivor Montagu. Both these institutions were Communist Party front organizations, under the "guidance" of the KGB.

When the Communist Party mobilized all its propagandists to put over a new zigzag in the Party line, or attack any particular "class enemy," practically every teacher in the film institute would introduce it into his class, however irrelevant it might be to his subject. I remember one foreign student telling me of such an event, even in Khruschev's days. He was in Mikhail Romm's class on film direction, when Romm suddenly gave them a brief talk on the sins of Boris Pasternak and attacked his novel *Dr. Zhivago*. Each student was asked to give his approval to this censure of the poet. However, this particular foreign student said that he had to abstain, because he hadn't read the novel in question. But, of course, neither had anyone else in the class, probably including Romm himself! Nevertheless the censure was passed "unanimously."

This of course is typical of Soviet society — as is the fact that Romm, like Eisenstein and Pasternak, was of Jewish descent and had himself been bitterly attacked as a "cosmopolitan" and *"yid"* by the Communist Party.

Eisenstein never did this kind of thing in our class. He felt he was on the level of Darwin, Marx, and da Vinci, developing Marxist philosophy and aesthetics, which were the long-term projects of the Party. Thus, he seemed to practically everyone an intellectual snob, dodging his social obligations. But despite all criticisms he continued to concentrate on preparing and expounding his intellectual theories to his students in what he called his laboratory. We were his guinea pigs, through which he would prove or disprove his theories of the synthesis of art and science. He regarded us, he said, as his "hope for the future."

But what happened to his hope for the future?

We were in all about twenty-two students — mainly Russian, but also

Ukrainian, Armenian, Georgian, one Pole, one Korean, one Englishman (myself), and, for part of the course, one American. Two were women. Six were Jews.

We graduated in 1935, and our fellow student Valya Kadochnikov drew a wonderful cartoon of the graduation, with Eisenstein as a broody hen and myself perching on his tail.

My wife and I left the Soviet Union in 1937 and did not return until after the death of Stalin, in Khrushchev's liberal days, 1960. When we tried to find our fellow students, we learned that over half of them had died in their youth. Four or five were killed as soldiers in World War II; three were imprisoned with their families in Gulag prison camps, where two died; two were killed by accidents and one by Communist Party neglect; and five died of sickness.

But that was not all. We learned that the bulk of them, though they had graduated as feature film directors, had never directed a feature film. By the time they had graduated, Stalin was planning to reduce the production of feature films from a hundred to ten a year. He decided the Soviet film industry would produce only masterpieces! This incredible concept lasted for over a decade and helped to ruin the Soviet film industry and, along with it, Eisenstein's hope for the future. I myself had been allocated to the international film studio, Mezhrabpom Film, and was preparing the production of a feature film under the artistic direction of Mikhail Romm, when it was stopped. Then a second project was shelved, and finally the studio was closed down. My hope for the future vanished, and I returned home to England.

Then I went back after twenty-three years and learned of the personal tragedies of my erstwhile fellow students.

One of my closest friends, and one of the most talented, was Valya Kadochnikov (who had drawn the graduation cartoon). He came to an untimely end because of Communist Party indifference. According to Eisenstein, his tragic and unnecessary death came about because the Communist Party "sent him on work incompatible with his health, his upbringing, and his abilities," despite all protests.

This caused Eisenstein to give vent in print to one of his rare cries of open despair at the inhumanity of the Communist Party. But it is significant that even in this published article he never dots the i's, never says what organization or persons were responsible, or what actually Kadochnikov was forced to do. It was only from Pera Attasheva I learned the facts, for she was there.

They were in evacuation in Alma-Ata and, as is customary in Soviet society, they were all expected to do what is called "social work"; that is, voluntary work on top of one's normal job. "Voluntary" means that when the Party tells you to do voluntary work, you do it. So Valya Kadochnikov was ordered to go with a brigade to cut down trees for fuel. For this he had to travel a long distance in a truck in terribly hot weather and perform hard labor, cutting and loading lumber. Despite protests from Pera and others, Valya went on working and eventually collapsed from the heat and overstrain.

Another fellow student, Valichko, died an accidental death in a film studio, which Eisenstein categorized, like that of Kadochnikov, as being "caused by carelessness and indifference to one another, which more and more begins to afflict both our studios and our collectives."

My closest student friends were a most incongruous pair. One, Joseph Skliut, was a Russian Jew. The other, Vartan Kishmishov, was an Armenian. Skliut and I became close at first because he could speak Yiddish, and I spoke some German and only elementary Russian at the time. We went everywhere together. He was a real "operator"; he could wangle anything — scarce theater tickets, entry to special showings of foreign films, or even a free holiday in the Crimean rest homes. Much later I learned he was the KGB informer in charge of me, though I didn't know it at the time. On the other hand, it was well known that my other "guard" was Vartan Kishmishov, a one-time member of the KGB Border Guards in Armenia. He had been invalided out because of wounds sustained while "liquidating kulaks as a class." His family had fled to Soviet Armenia after the massacre by the Turks. He was naturally a dedicated Communist, because he owed everything to the new Soviet state, which trained him, gave him a position of trust and authority, and, after discharge, the scholarship to the film institute that he had asked for. He would have given his life unhesitatingly for the Party and Stalin. And he did.

He was one of the group of students who were killed in action with the Soviet Home Guards defending Moscow. Three other students became civil servants, representatives abroad of Soviet Export Film. One, Altzev, apparently got into trouble in Canada. Unable to withstand the temptations of "bourgeois life," he and his wife were sentenced to three years in a Gulag prison camp. They emerged only to perish in a severe earthquake in Ashkhabad.

The only Oriental in our class was Tsoi, a Korean emigrant from Siberia. He was a very intelligent and handsome boy and was chosen by Dovzhenko to play a leading role in his film, made especially for Stalin, *Aerograd*. In this film he represented the national minorities liberated by the Soviet state; later, in real life, he was imprisoned in the Gulag, apparently as a spin-off of one of the Soviet clashes with the Japanese on the Far Eastern border. He was suspected of being a spy. However, it seemed he survived and was working as a director of an eastern theater in Siberia.

Another fellow student, a Russian Jew, now director in a national film studio, told me that during the Stalin "purges" he had waited for nearly a year with his bundle packed, waiting for that fatal knock on the door in the early hours, ready to be arrested and taken to the Gulag by the KGB. Why? Because he had been a close comrade of mine when we were students and had lived with me in the same dormitory room — and I was a foreigner! "They never came," he said, "but I was a wreck at the end of the year!"

Another Jewish friend, Grisha Lifschitz, told me that for twenty years he had tried to get transferred from the Ukraine film studios in Kiev to Moscow, because there was less anti-Semitism in Russia than in the Ukraine. He said he was never able to get a top feature-film assignment because his passport said he was a Jew, though he was completely assimilated. He had been a Red Army tank officer, had fought with his tanks all the way to victory in Berlin, had a breastful of medals and a body shot to shreds, but was never permitted to transfer to less anti-Semitic climes and died in his fifties.

Another victim was Phillipov, one of our inner student group. I accidentally met him some twenty years later in Bombay, when he was with a Soviet film delegation. But he had completely changed. Instead of the free and easy fellow of our student days, he was a taciturn, withdrawn, nervous man who didn't want to talk to me at all. Eventually I learned he was a problem for the delegation. He had a fear of foreigners, was frightened of being poisoned by foreign food, and wanted to go back to Russia. I never learned what he had gone through to reach such a state. He just wouldn't talk.

Victor Ivanov, a Ukrainian from Kiev, as a student was the life and soul of the party. We called him *rupor* (megaphone), because he had a stentorian voice and would always greet me with some odd English word in a Russian sentence, shouting: *"Gerbert, daitye mnye* pencil!"* (Herbert, give me a pencil!) In reminiscing, he mused: "You know, Herbert, it's your fault we never learned English, because you always gave us the answers to our exercises!"

Victor had been a locomotive engineer, who, on first seeing Eisenstein's classic *Battleship Potemkin*, with its rhythmic engines and pounding pistons, wanted to be a film director and study under Eisenstein. But the railways wouldn't release him. It wasn't until he did years of extra social work and became a Stakhanovite that he won a scholarship to the film institute. And it took him another ten years or more after graduation to direct his first feature film on a Ukrainian subject — and that was on a category B budget.

But he was no longer the life and soul of the party; the barren Stalinist years had taken their toll of his mind and his health.

Two of the women students came to an even more tragic end: they were arrested as "relatives of enemies of the people" and imprisoned in Gulag prison camps. One was Kira Andronnikova, wife of the famous writer Boris Pilnyak (who had been imprisoned already). She was sent to prison together with her six-year-old child. The other was Masha Pugachevskaya, a former Red Cavalry woman and a heroine of the civil war, straight out of Isaac Babel's tales. Her husband was a high-ranking officer under Marshal Tukhachevsky; the men were executed "as enemies of the people." After Stalin's death my fellow students were rehabilitated. But Masha died in prison, by what means was never learned, and Kira, who was eventually released, died from the privations she suffered while incarcerated.

Only one student escaped from the dead-end of Soviet society, and that was Isaac Schmidt. He became an official artist and caricaturist, but, though Jewish, never landed in the Gulag. Years later, I discovered why.

He had made portraits of all the Red Army marshals and generals, as well as their tzarist predecessors, all of which were on display at the Central House of the Red Army. If he had been arrested, as a matter of course the authorities would have had to remove all these portraits from the great Red Army center! So he escaped. He finally emigrated to Israel, but his health was so bad that he died before he could enjoy his new-found freedom.

Only one student achieved some significant stature as a feature film director and became an Honored Worker of Art of the Georgian Soviet Socialist Republic — that was Constantine Pepinashvili. But his best film was banned until after Stalin's death. He did manage to make a film, *The Young Mayakovsky* (which had previously been taboo under Stalin), because he was born in Georgia.

It was Constantine, because of his more privileged position, who decided to summon all the surviving students of Eisenstein to meet in Tbilisi and found a voluntary society called Rupor, to propagate the life and works of our great master. Thus my wife and I were his guests in beautiful Tbilisi, capital of Georgia. Our meeting with our fellow students after twenty-five years was most moving. It was there that I learned their tragic history. They naturally wanted to know how I survived — both the purges and the war. They could never believe all the things I had done, not only as feature-film director, but as a director in theater, radio, and TV, an author, translator, teacher, professor, as well as a director of England's National Theater. The straitjacket of Soviet society had prevented them from doing anything other than what their diplomas said, and if that was not possible, they did nothing. Though technically never unemployed, actually they had been mostly creatively unemployed. They had graduated when times were out of joint and were in the main disillusioned, disappointed, and broken-hearted men and women.

Perhaps there may be some consolation in the fact that there remains for the world what we produced as Eisenstein's guinea-pigs; his major theoretical treatises, *Montage* and *Nonindifferent Nature* (now ready for publication, translated by Herbert Marshall and Roberta Reeder); and the as yet unpublished manuscripts, as well as some fond memories of us in his autobiography and diaries. So it is to my brother and sister students, dead and alive, that I dedicate this book with love and sorrow.

— Herbert Marshall
Professor Emeritus (Performing Arts)

A Note on Eisenstein's Language and Style

EVERYONE WHO HAS attempted it knows that translating Eisenstein is a most difficult task. His subject matter is unusual, complex, and erudite in the extreme. He was an original thinker, creating new concepts that are couched in new terminology, with words often stretched to new usages, as, for instance, the words "montage" and "pathos," or with neologisms invented by Eisenstein himself. A further complication is caused by Eisenstein's fluency in four languages. He was able effortlessly to switch from one to another, writing them in the original, or absorbing them into the Russian language. Then, too, his reading was so universal and voracious that he frequently quoted from unexpected and often unknown sources, and the Russian transliteration of a foreign word sometimes makes it very difficult for the translator to find out how the original word was spelled. This applies especially to languages that depend on pronunciation, like French. And when Chinese or Japanese are quoted, the original and the English forms may be poles apart.

I have tried my best to make sure that the English forms are correct, but despite the most painstaking checking and research, there may be errors. Here is an example of such a problem: a chapter was headed, in Cyrillic, "Rue de Grenelle." Then, almost immediately following it, Eisenstein wrote, again in Cyrillic and this time in quotation marks, "Rue Grenelle." And then, still in Cyrillic, *Ulitsa Grenelle*, using the Russian word for street or road.

Why the shortened form? Is it because colloquially, in the local patois, it was so called, or was it what he and other foreigners called it? Of course, his putting it in Russian was for the convenience of most of his readers, who didn't know French.

On top of all this, his style was at times far from lucid, its significance difficult to decipher, and, when translated, after much discussion and analysis and research, it remained overly complicated and convoluted. He jumped from association to association in a myriad of directions; he partly explained this himself, saying at one point, "Here I slip into a fatal unrestricted verbiage in all directions, away from the immediate actual basis of the article," and elsewhere, "Some chapters begin with one thing. Then follows an accidentally emerging reminiscence and, finally, a whole chain of free association. Beginning a chapter, I never know where it will take off to."

Now, if this weren't enough, there is another formidable obstacle to understanding: the assumption that the reader will have a general knowledge of the complex and often confused background of Russian history in general and of certain periods in particular, for example, the reigns of Ivan the Terrible, Peter the Great, Nicholas I, and Nicholas II; the First World War; the two revolutions; the civil war; foreign intervention; the NEP (the New Economic Policy of Lenin); the nature of the Communist Party and its internal struggles, its treatment of art and culture; the internecine battles over styles of art, labelled Formalist and Socialist Realist; the aims of the Proletcult and such slogans as "the living man"; the growth of Stalinism and its totalitarian structure and terror; the growing control and total dictatorship over form and content of all the arts; the necessity for Soviet citizens to develop the "double-think" in order to survive, and the way an artist has to utilize the double-entendre, metaphor, and allegory to express what he really feels, as compared with how the Communist Party orders him to feel or think or act. Eisenstein was a master at this kind of writing: there is hardly an overt word of criticism of the Communist Party in any of his writings, but deep down it is there — as this autobiography will reveal to those who can read between the lines.

Then there is a special development of Eisenstein's style into what I call "cinematic montage" — his deliberate habit of breaking down his sentences into montage pieces of very short length. So the reader must not be surprised to find a sentence broken into several lines set, paragraph fashion, sometimes after a comma, sometimes not, and starting with a lower-case letter, then breaking off at another comma, and again a new line, and still no period or capital letter.

But that is the essence of Eisenstein's literary style — the continuity and clash of lines, as if they were film shots, to form a cinematic sequence of words. This explains why he used a great deal more inversion than is usual in prose; it is a fundamental ingredient of the structure of poetry and often the basis for bringing to the end of the line a rhyme word. Like other writing techniques, its quality depends on the skill of the writer: it can be consummately skillful, the art that conceals art; or it can be painfully awkward and obvious. Mayakovsky was a master in this respect, as was Pushkin. Mayakovsky in particular is closest to Eisenstein, who was, in fact, the Mayakovsky of cinema, as Mayakovsky was the Eisenstein of poetry.

Mayakovsky made his key word the rhyme word at the end of the line; Eisenstein did the same thing with his montage breakdown of prose, without, of course, rhyming. At times, however, this can be awkward and even Germanic.

Here is a literal translation of the Russian text, with the original punctuation. It is all one sentence!

And how much this would be in my style and to my taste! — first in the previous, color episode let flow the black color of the cassock onto the gold caftans of the *oprichniki*, the black of the cassocks of the *oprichniki* — onto the gold regalia of Vladimir, before the whole mass of the black *oprichniki* in a black lava inundates the interior of the cathedral, in which amongst them and — their still blacker shadows with a hardly heard sob chokes in the darkness of the womb of the night cathedral a helpless, pathetic, and at the same time invoking pity Vladimir . . .[1]

It is the last paragraph of the next-to-last chapter of his tragic finale *P.S. P.S. P.S.*, and it ends on the word "Vladimir," the pitiful tragic figure of the would-be tsar whom Ivan played with as a cat with a mouse, and whose murder he engineered. Here again we come across the way in which a Soviet artist expresses his true feelings under artistic images. Why end on the murder of Vladimir and with the words "helpless, pathetic, and at the same time invoking pity Vladimir . . ."? Well, those who have studied Eisenstein will know that Vladimir is an image of Eisenstein himself. This is also confirmed by Marie Seton in her biography of Eisenstein, in which she recalls personal conversations with her subject.[2] So the treatment of Vladimir by Ivan the Terrible is a parallel with the treatment of Eisenstein by Stalin the Terrible. And the black lava of Ivan's bodyguards (the *oprichniki*) that engulfs him is the parallel to Stalin's bodyguards (the *apparachiki*). Hence, the culminating word before Eisenstein's last two death cries is the image of himself.

Then he stated the superobjective (to use Stanislavsky's term) of his artistic life — the incarnation of the ultimate idea of the achievement of unity.

And his last ironic *P.S.* reminds posterity, and in particular his own countrymen, that if "a prophet is not without honor in his own country," outside the Soviet Union he is honored as *"un des plus fameux metteurs en scène de son temps . . ."* (one of the most famous film directors of his time).

---

1. *S. M. Eisenstein Collected Works* (Russian edition, 1964), Vol. I, page 536.
2. *S. M. Eisenstein*, by Marie Seton (New York: Grove Press, 1960), page 437.

Immoral Memories

Foreword

I MUST WARN YOU right away: these notes are completely immoral.

But at the same time I must disappoint those who expect them to be filled with immoral episodes, suggestive details, or salacious descriptions. They're not at all like that. In front of you is no — how shall I say — Red Casanova, nor an account of the amorous episodes in the life of a Russian film director.

In that sense the most immoral of all contemporary autobiographies is undoubtedly Frank Harris's *My Life and Loves*. This very unpleasant, importunate author described his own life and his Don Juan catalogue with the same unpleasant frankness and the same absence of tact as he did the majority of his outstanding contemporaries.

And indeed, whose name didn't fall beneath the pen of this bearded, shifty-eyed blackmailer?

I read three volumes of his autobiography in the U.S.A. — of course from under the counter — in an unexpurgated edition, where everything usually censored was printed in another type for the convenience of the reader.

And what then?

I can't remember a single one of the salacious scenes!

Indeed, of the three volumes, I can remember only one scene — and that dubious in its authenticity — about a certain person — one of the young Harris's first bosses, I think — who was attacked by nervous laughter of such force that he shook for three days on end. After which he died, as the incessant shaking caused "his flesh to come away from his bones"!

So, although hunger and love are the most powerful of instincts, it seems that in memoirs it isn't they that are the most memorable. Particularly in those cases when these feelings are sublimated. That is why there won't be much about those feelings here. Still fewer shocking details and tidbits.

The immorality of these notes will be of quite another kind. They will not moralize. They will not set themselves any moral aims nor preach any sermons.

•

They will not prove anything. Not explain anything. Not teach anything.

In my creative work throughout my life, I have been occupied with composing *á thèse*. I have proved; I have explained; I have taught. Here I simply wish to browse through my own past, as I loved to browse through the junk and antiques of Alexandrovsky Market in Petersburg, through the secondhand bookstalls of Paris's Left Bank, through nocturnal Hamburg or Marseille, through museum halls or waxwork shows.

Moreover, I now observe yet another phenomenon. In these writings one more contradiction has been resolved. They're as much reading as they are writing!

In the beginning a page, a chapter, or sometimes even a phrase, often I don't know where the continuation will lead me. Just as in turning the pages of a book I don't know what I shall find on the other side.

Let the material be drawn from the depths of my personal reserves, let the factual evidence be dug out of my personal experience, and here is a whole sphere of the unexpected and unforeseen with much that is completely new: the juxtaposition of material, conclusions drawn from these juxtapositions, fresh aspects and "revelations" stemming from these conclusions.

More often than not these pages are simply a springboard leap that, in the very process of writing, yields as much again as already exists in ready-made conclusions and intentions, when some element of the theme suddenly and insistently demands to be written down.

So this is not only an adventurous excursion through pictures and images of the past, but also the revelation, en route, of conclusions and combinations, to which odd disconnected facts and impressions — outside their juxtapositions — could have no right, no basis for a claim!

I was never fond of Marcel Proust.

Not out of snobbery — that is, a deliberate defiance of the terribly powerful fashion for Proust — but probably for the very same reason I don't like Gavarni.[1]

I am always shocked when the name Gavarni is spoken in the same breath as Daumier. Whereas Daumier is a genius, ranging alongside the greatest artists of the greatest epoch of art, Gavarni is no more than an elegant *boulevardier* of lithography, no matter how much his praises were sung by his friends the Goncourts.[2]

In the twenties and thirties the name of Proust was also announced in the same breath as James Joyce. And if Joyce is indeed a colossus, whose greatness will outlive fashion and the unhealthy success derived from the scandal over the

---

1. Paul Gavarni was the pseudonym of Sulpice Guillaume Chevalier (1804–1866), a French lithographer and caricaturist.

2. The Goncourt brothers, Jules (1830–1870), and Edmond (1822–1896), had written a book on the illustrator, *Gavarni: The Man and His Work.*

excessively frank pages of *Ulysses*, and the bans of the censors, changing fashions, and temporary indifference to his memory, Marcel Proust occupied only temporarily the place that has been taken in turn by Céline and, later, by Jean Paul Sartre.

No doubt my dislike of Proust explains why I don't remember precisely whether the critics were surprised by the unusual nature of his titles only in relation to *Du Côté de Chez Swann* and *A l'Ombre des Jeunes Filles en Fleurs* or to the general title *A la Recherche du Temps Perdu*.

Today my attitude toward Proust has hardly changed, although at this very moment I vibrate particularly sharply in response to that general title. In it is the key to that mad and ornate thoroughness with which Proust writes, describes, narrates each invariably autobiographical detail, as if groping, fondling, striving to hold in his hands the hopelessly vanishing past . . .

Suddenly, in my fiftieth year, in me too arises sharply and tormentingly the desire to catch and hold my lost time as it slips into the past.

Some Anglo-Saxon once truly said that we all live as if we had a million years ahead of us.

We all live, of course, differently. One, hoarding time within himself; another, spending it cautiously or recklessly; a third, losing it.

Our epoch has been deprived of the hackneyed *"Verweile doch, du bist so schön"*[3] more than the epoch of Goethe, in which only the insight of a genius could prophesy the central drama of the characters of the twentieth century . . .

In February of 1946 I was felled by a heart attack. For the first time in my entire life I was brought suddenly to a halt, confined to a life in bed.

Blood circulation sluggish. Thinking slow.

Ahead lay several months of absolute sameness. I was even glad.

I thought, At last I'll be able to take a look at myself, glance backward, think things over. And I'll understand everything about myself, about life, about the forty-eight years that have been lived.

Let me say at once: I understood nothing. Not about life. Not about myself. Not about the forty-eight years that had been lived.

Nothing — except perhaps for one thing.

That life had passed at a gallop, without a backward glance, in constant transit, leaving one train to chase after another. My attention riveted all the time to the second hand.

Hurrying somewhere — Not to be late. Managing to get here. Managing to get away from here.

Fragments of childhood, segments of youth, strata of maturity, flash by as from a train window. Bright, varied, whirling, full of color.

And, suddenly, an awful realization! That it hasn't all been retained, only

---

3. "Stay awhile, thou art so fair." Goethe, *Faust*.

just tasted. Nothing drunk to the dregs and rarely, only rarely, swallowed and not merely sipped at.

Somewhere ascending, with already the thought of descending the same stairs.

Unpacking a suitcase, and already the thought of packing it.

And so I was seized by an urgent desire to grasp, capture, and hold in words these moments of "lost time."

Moments that were always known, by the anticipation of them, the recollection of them, and by a certain impatient restlessness in the experience of them.

I lived in an epoch without parallel. But it is not of the epoch that I wish to write.

I want to describe how, like a completely unforeseen counterpoint, an average man passes through a time of greatness. How a man can not notice historical dates, which he brushes with his sleeve. How it is possible to be engrossed in Maeterlinck while in charge of trench work during the civil war, or in Schopenhauer while crouching in the shadow of a troop train.

I want to describe how it feels to step for the first time on the soil of the film kingdom, Hollywood. Or how you behave during an American police interrogation as contrasted with a French. How you climb the thousand-year-old pyramids of Yucatán and sit purposely at the base of the ruined Temple of a Thousand Columns in order to gaze at the familiar outline of the Great Bear, lying upside down in the Mexican sky, and wait for the moment it sinks behind the Pyramid of Warriors. And how you sit there deliberately trying to fix the memory of this moment in the future stream of recollections, much as seamen fix their course by the very same stars.

Or how the impression was engraved on the retina when you saw your first Lesbian ball in Berlin twenty years ago.

An outline of any image and type appears as if etched in your visual memory. So much so that you are almost ready to accept the absurd myth that the image of the murderer is fixed, as though on a photograph, upon the retina of his victim.

Putting books on the shelves and wondering who will take them off after my death.

Peer Gynt wandering through a storm of dry leaves — his unformulated thoughts, his unaccomplished deeds.

It is said of De Quincey that he would rent an apartment, accumulate books, then abandon everything and flee to a new place, where the same thing began all over again.

I once met King Gillette, millionaire inventor of the safety razor, when he was already in his sixties. He was obsessed with the construction of country houses in deserts. Amid arid sandy wastes a palatial structure, surrounded by gardens, would no sooner appear than the builder would race off to another desert to build another palace. In some respects there is a similarity in the way I lived these many years in relation to the events of my own life.

I have lived like the proverbial donkey that reaches for the carrot dangling from his own yoke and runs after it, uncontrollably, hopelessly, eternally.

One thing I recall from those long months in bed: an unceasing torrent of memories of endless past hours, in answer to the question I had asked myself: "Has there been any Life, or has it always been merely a travel warrant — valid for the next ten or twenty minutes, the next day, week, or month?"

It turns out there has been Life.

Life lived acutely, joyously, tormentedly, at times even sparkling, unquestionably colorful, and such a life that, I suppose, I would not exchange for another.

In Thomas Dixon's American novel *The Clansmen*, glorifying the birth of the Ku Klux Klan, this absurd idea of an image fixed in the retina is used as material evidence to prove the guilt of a Negro accused of rape. Griffith's film *The Birth of a Nation* was based on this book.

Images.

The first time in the theater — as a spectator.

The first time — as a director.

The first time — as a producer.

The first impression as a cinema spectator: in Paris in 1908 on the Boulevard des Italiens.

The famous coachman of that genius, Georges Méliès, holding the reins of a skeleton horse that is harnessed to a carriage.[4]

Mr. Hartvik, a butcher in black glistening gauntlets — the owner of the cottage my parents rented on the Riga seashore when I was a child.

Mrs. Kevich, Mrs. Koppitz, and Mrs. Klapper, owners of the summer hotels where we stayed, after my mother and father had separated.

My grandmother — like the character from Maxim Gorky's *Vassa Zheleznova*,[5] heading the Marinsky fleet of barges on the River Neva.

Childhood walks in the Alexander Nevsky Monastery.

The silver chalice of the saint whom I was destined to make a film hero, after the country had made him a national hero.[6]

The intoxicating aroma of fermenting maguey juice that rises from below, where, in the flickering candlelight of a primitive Madonna, they are making Mexican vodka — pulque. The vapors penetrate my temporary bedroom on the second floor of the Tetlapayac Hacienda[7] . . . Now a real hacienda instead of "The Hacienda of Doña Manuella," which I encountered as a child in *The World of Adventure*.

---

4. In the first animated cartoon created by Georges Méliès, there was a funeral carriage drawn by a skeleton horse.

5. *Vassa Zheleznova*, a play by Gorky, was published in 1910.

6. The reference is to the sound film *Alexander Nevsky*, with music by Prokofiev.

7. The hacienda was one of the locations in the film *Que Viva Mexico!*

The real Mexico ten years after I had conjured up its image in my first theatrical work.[8]

People.

Khudyekov[9] — owner of the *St. Petersburg Gazette* — and a story of how, in 1917, I try to sell him caricatures.

Gordon Craig, who writes from Italy to "drop everything" and meet him in Paris so that we can again browse among the bookstalls along the Seine.

George Bernard Shaw, whose radiogram catches up with me on the Atlantic, giving me permission to produce *The Chocolate Soldier* in America if I wish, but on condition that the text remain unchanged.

Stefan Zweig, discussing his work on *The Perfect Scoundrel*, a character in whom he hopes to "fuse" all ignoble personality traits (in a letter from the time when he was writing *Fouché*).

That live Himalaya — the aging Dreiser — looming across the table from me in my home in Moscow on Chistiye Prudy, or in a basement speakeasy in New York during Prohibition, or dressed in a Canadian mackinaw, chopping wood in the wilderness of his country home on the Hudson. Downstairs there was a fireplace, and upstairs a room, decorated with "Pompeian" frescoes, that served as my bedroom. The unusually deep-throated voice of his young wife, who is attempting to prove to me that mixed blood is the best soil for genius.

An entire gallery of American movie bosses.

Sticking in my memory the fleeting profiles of my film colleagues: von Sternberg, von Stroheim, Lubitsch, King Vidor.

Profiles . . . (There is a charming American habit, particularly cultivated by *The New Yorker* magazine, of writing profiles. Later they're published as books, usually by Knopf, with some biographical facts, details of careers, a customary dash of malicious gossip, a little poison, some anecdotes, and items of scandal.) . . . I don't intend to do any profiles here. Let God define the curve of the brow, the corner of the mouth, the screwing up of the eyes, or the way of smoking a cigar.

After all, I'm not a journalist, striving to fit into newspaper columns profiles of an interesting businessman, a popular woman dramatist, a match king, or a musical idol. I'm not writing about them, about what they expended their time and energy on. I'm writing about my times. And they are simply a counterstream of images that time — bearing me away at a gallop — permitted me to meet fleetingly. Sometimes merely with the brush of an elbow, sometimes pausing for days, sometimes years, but falling behind, out of step with the length of the contact, but in step with the brightness of the impression . . .

These are not literary characterizations. All of these are no more than two

8. Eisenstein was referring to his dramatization of Jack London's story "The Mexican," which he produced in the Moscow Proletcult Theater in 1921.

9. Sergei Nikolayevich Khudyekov (1837–1927) was a journalist, a historian of the Russian ballet, and the publisher of the *St. Petersburg Gazette*.

rows of young teeth biting into the ripe peach of life's experience. Much too hurriedly at the moment of actual encounter, but retaining for many years the taste, the flavor, and the uniqueness of the experience.

Mayakovsky, and how we never really became friends.[10]

The ugly mug of the deacon at the christening of my cousin. I had to entertain Father Dionysius through the long hours before the immersion of the infant Boris in the baptismal font. A stroll around the garden with my grandfather — me, a twelve-year-old godfather at the side of a distinguished old man with spectacles on his nose and a compulsive need to give every plant in sight its generic name, so that to this day I remember and puzzle over one name: *olsha*.[11]

Is all this of any use to anyone but me?

That's irrelevant. Above all, it's necessary to me.

Beyond didactics, beyond edification, beyond "the historical background," beyond "man in his epoch," beyond "history reflected in consciousness." Simply and quite possibly as a new loss of time in search of times lost in the past . . .

If needed, it will be published.

If not needed, it will be found in my "literary heritage."[12]

Still, it may be needed.

For these are impressions — flashes of a prehistoric past, those seemingly antediluvian years preceding the birth of the atomic bomb.

And perhaps for yet another reason.

I once asked my students what they would like to hear during the course of my lectures at the GIK.[13]

I was ready for all kinds of requests except the one I heard.

Quite timidly, but not at all obsequiously, someone said: "Don't tell us about montage or films or production. Tell us how one becomes an Eisenstein."

It was terribly flattering, though rather incomprehensible. Who would want to become him?

However, there it was.

And here it is, how one becomes what he is.

And if anyone is interested in the final result — then here are the scattered notes about the progress of the process itself.

---

10. Eisenstein and Mayakovsky first knew each other in Moscow from 1922 to 1925. Both contributed to *LEF* (the journal of the Left Front, or Futurists). Each held the other in high regard. In his lectures, Eisenstein repeatedly cited Mayakovsky's poetry; and the poet, in 1927, called Eisenstein "the pride of our cinematography."

11. *Olsha* is dialect form of *olkha*, meaning elder tree.

12. In the USSR, posthumous works of famous writers are published in a series called *Literaturnoe Nasledstvo (Literary Heritage).*

13. GIK are the initials of Gosudarstvenny Institut Kinematografii, the State Institute of Cinematography.

The Boy from Riga

Not a brat, nor an imp; just a boy of twelve.

Obedient and well brought up. A boy who shuffled his feet. A boy from a good family. A typical boy from Riga. That is what I was like at twelve, and that is the way I have stayed.

The boy from Riga became famous at twenty-seven. Douglas Fairbanks and Mary Pickford came to Moscow "to shake by the hand" the boy from Riga, who had made *Battleship Potemkin*. In 1930, after my lecture at the Sorbonne, the combined strengths of Premier Tardieu and Monsieur Chiappe were unable to chuck the boy from Riga out of France.

As he signed his name to a Hollywood contract for three thousand dollars a week, the boy from Riga trembled for the first time in his life.

When the boy from Riga was threatened with expulsion from Mexico, and was refused a visa to the United States, twelve United States senators sent their protests. And instead of expulsion — he received a ceremonious handshake from the Mexican president at one of the countless festivals in Mexico City.

In 1939 the boy from Riga was showered with clippings from American newspapers about Franklin Delano Roosevelt being shown *Alexander Nevsky*, at his special request, in the White House.

In 1941, as a survey of the cinema's first forty years, the first bulky volume of the American *Film Index* was published. According to the introduction, the quantity written about the boy from Riga put him in fourth place, behind Chaplin, Griffith, and Mary Pickford.

At the height of the war, the boy from Riga published *Film Sense*.[1] The book instantly sold out its American and British editions. The mail brought a

---

1. *Film Sense*, S. M. Eisenstein, was translated and edited by Jay Leyda (New York: Harcourt Brace, 1942; and London, Faber and Faber, 1943).

"pirated" edition in Spanish from Argentina. After the fall of Japan, it was discovered that a translation had been published there during the war. Russia, meanwhile, was not miserly in awarding the boy prizes, degrees, and honors.

It would seem high time for the boy to see himself as an adult.

But the boy from Riga is still twelve years old.

It is not a very original thought that there are few who can see themselves as they really are. But everyone sees himself as somebody and something. Still, this is not what is interesting. What is interesting is that this imagined person is far nearer the exact psychological image of the one imagining than is his objective semblance.

One person sees himself as d'Artagnan, another as Alfred de Musset, another, to a lesser degree, as Byron's Cain; still others modestly satisfy themselves with being the Louis XIV of their district, their region, their studio, or their group of relatives on their mother's side.

When I look at myself face to face, I see myself as David Copperfield. Frail, rather thin, small, defenseless, and very shy.

Now, in the light of what has been enumerated above, this may seem amusing. But what is more amusing is that perhaps because of this very self-awareness, all this biographical baggage (samples of which I have just mentioned) has been collected, so intoxicating for one's vanity.

The figure of Don Juan has many hypothetical interpretations. There are many different examples of practical "Don Juanism," but no doubt one is just as true as another. The semipsychoanalytical interpretation sees in Don Juanism only an anxiety about one's virility, which shows with each fresh conquest only a new proof of that virility. But why allow Don Juanism in love only? It is found, of course, to a much greater degree in all other fields involving "success," "acclaim," and "victory," no less brilliant than the trials of love's arena.

Every young man at some moment or other in his life begins to philosophize, to form his own views on life, to spell out to himself or to his truest confidant of those years, or in a diary, his judgments on general questions. Usually the value of these conclusions to mankind is more than dubious. The more so in that they are original not in their personal invention, but only by virtue of the sources from which they have been taken. But within them, as in a child's early drawings, one sees the inescapable bloom of touching curiosity, often well delineated, in which one is able suddenly to discern, in the light of afteryears, the very first beginnings of what was to come.

In the British Museum there is a showcase of holographs. In one corner is a moralizing letter, answering a complaint about the absence of comfort, from Queen Elizabeth to her "beloved sister" Mary Stuart, who was locked in a dungeon. The masculine style of the Virgin Queen, in a curious way, has something in common with the little sketch (of a slightly later period) pinned in another corner of the showcase. This is no more nor less than the *mise en scène* of the imminent execution of the unfortunate, but far from blameless, Scottish queen, presented by one of the lords for the approval of that "ginger wench Bess," as our Tsar Ivan the Terrible called the English queen. Right alongside this drawing is fastened a small sheet of graph paper, on which, in block capitals, a few words are sprawled out in the childish hand of the future Queen Victoria, at an age when it had not entered her mind that she would wear the crown of the United Kingdom.

But the most moving of all these notes is the fourth. It is written by a young, suntanned French commander-in-chief of Corsican blood.

Not long before, according to heroic legend, he had evoked the many centuries that gazed from the pyramids upon his troops,[2] who were taking a none too willing part in the young commander's brilliant landing operations on the hot sand of Africa. Victory piled up on victory, and the fame of the young military genius proclaimed the name of Bonaparte across several continents.

And what at this same moment did the young Corsican in his field tent write to his brother? "Everything has been experienced. Grief and joy. Success and defeat. One thing only is left — to become an egotist locked in oneself." And this is not from *Eugene Onegin's Diary*,[3] but from the depths of an almost prehistoric stage of the future Napoleon's biography . . .

Napoleon has come to mind here with good reason. The first analogous note by the boy from Riga, striving to find his bearings in reality, refers to him in particular: "Napoleon did all that he did, not because he was talented or a genius. He made himself talented in order that he might do all that he did . . .

If you take it as an axiom that such jottings by fifteen- to twenty-year-olds (I was seventeen) are the embryos of future autobiographical intentions (the words of the Corsican general represent not only Childe Harold–like pessimism, or an anticipation of what Stendhal would so skillfully play on in the future, but also a certain principle, realized with a total shamelessness — egotism!), then the image of this David Copperfield from Riga is, perhaps, not altogether unexpected.

But where does this injured pride come from? In childhood I never knew poverty, deprivation, or the horrors of the struggle for existence. Somewhere a little farther on you will find descriptions of my childhood background. For the time being, take them on trust!

---

2. Eisenstein paraphrased the words of Napoleon, uttered during his Egyptian campaign: "From the heights of these pyramids forty centuries look down on you!"

3. See *Poems, Prose and Plays of Alexander Pushkin*, edited by Avraham Yarmolinsky (New York: Random House, Modern Library, 1936).

Souvenirs
d'enfance

I REMEMBER CERTAIN things that definitely go back to the time I was six.

A summer cottage at the seashore during what had to be 1904, because Uncle Mitya, my father's younger brother, came to pay the family a farewell visit before going off to the front. He was killed at Mukden during the Russo-Japanese War.

Besides my uncle, a dashing officer with a marvelously gleaming curved saber, I remember the blood-red color of the wood chips strewn along the pathway to our cottage and the whitewashed stones that bordered it.

I can also recall our neighbor. Very slim, her black hair parted in the middle. Especially vivid is the memory of her flowing Japanese kimono of delicate blues and pinks (a war trophy? Perhaps, for her husband was also away at war). An impression of a tiny head and the rest of her figure one whirl of flowing cloth. The sleeves are particularly fixed in my memory, because she would carry a little puppy in one of them.

I remember our cottage's garden decorated with lights to celebrate my cousin Olga's saint's day.

Home theatricals. I remember a performance of *The Unreliable Valet.* It was one of our home theatricals and apparently the very first play I ever saw. I recall a sense of immense enjoyment, but also a feeling of fear, caused most probably by the black mustache painted with charcoal on the face of Uncle Lely, my mother's younger brother.

The clearest memory of these early years is of some fantastically delicious pears in a syrup somewhat like zabaglione. Later in life I would eat zabaglione like this with Pirandello, in a tiny Italian restaurant in Charlottenburg, in Berlin. But this would be much, much later . . . twenty-five years later.

And there was a gramophone with an enormous silvery pink horn. I can still hear its hoarse voice singing:

A bug is crawling on the wall.
I'll slap it hard and make it fall!
I adore it all!
I adore it all!

And from the village street I could hear the pleading voice of an old Latvian woman, mispronouncing the Russian words:

Fresh flowers! Forget-do-nots! Forget-do-nots!

Along with the cries of the balloon vendor:

Here they are — balloons, balloons! Luftballons!!!

I can see a Christmas tree all aglitter with candles, stars, golden walnuts, and tinsel cascading down from the crowning star at the top. Festoons of gold paper chains crisscross the threads of tinsel.

These are the only chains known to a child from a bourgeois home, at the tender age when solicitous parents decorate a Christmas tree for him. The only other possible association he might have would be with the safety chain that limits the door opening and makes it possible to scrutinize visitors before they are admitted. Chains to keep out thieves. Thieves are not liked in bourgeois homes, and this aversion is instilled in children from a tender age.

Now we come to the child himself — a curly-headed boy in a little white suit. He is surrounded by gifts. It is hard to recall now whether this is the time he received the tennis racquet or the tricycle, the toy trains or the skis. No matter; the child's eyes are shining. It is not the candlelight but joy that makes his eyes glow. Among the toys he spies the yellow covers of two books; strange as it may seem, it is these which make him most happy. This present is special. It is one of those entered on the List of Requests compiled by bourgeois families for Christmas. For the boy the books are not just a gift, but a dream come true. And now our curly-headed boy has already buried his nose between the yellow covers, while the Christmas lights on the yellow chandeliers and candelabra flicker and die.

The curly-headed boy is I, myself, aged twelve.

The yellow book, Mignet's *History of the French Revolution.*

Thus, on Christmas Eve, by the fir tree decorated with walnuts and cardboard stars, I have my first encounter with the great French Revolution. . .

Why? From what did such total dissonance arise?

It is difficult to re-establish all the links in the chain, to recall with any degree of certainty what had prompted that curly-haired head of mine to ask for, of all things, that particular gift for Christmas. Most likely Dumas's *Ange Pitou* and *Joseph Balsamo* had already captured the imagination of the "impressionable youth."

True, he was already showing troublesome signs of curiosity and inquisitiveness, traits that in later life would spoil many pleasures derived from mere fleeting impressions. Instead of simple satisfaction, his searching curiosity rewarded him with many moments of profound enjoyment. He wanted to know not only the literary versions of great events but also their genuine history. Here his curiosity, quite accidentally, gave him a passion for the French Revolution much earlier than for the historical past of his own country.

From the very outset, French sources seemed to influence me. They found their way into my earliest impressions. It may at first have been an accident, but a logical progression takes place as first impressions are strengthened by second.

By some miracle the impressionable youth found another historical revolutionary document in his father's library. It seemed so out of place in the library of this loyal man, whose faithful service qualified him for high rank and government decorations. And yet, right next to the monographs of Napoleon Bonaparte — the idol of my father and every "self-made man" — was a richly illustrated edition of *1871 and the Paris Commune.*

The French Revolution captured my imagination even at this early age. At first because of its romanticism, colorfulness, and singularity. I devoured book after book. I was fascinated by images of the guillotine, amazed by photographs of the Colonne Vendôme, enthralled by caricatures of André Gill and Honoré Daumier, and disturbed by the figures of Marat and Robespierre. My ears filled with the crackle of the rifle fire at the Versailles executions, and the ringing of the Paris alarm bell, *le tocsin.*

Soon another strand was woven into the texture of impressions of early nineteenth-century revolutions: Victor Hugo's *Les Misérables.* Here the romanticism of the barricade battles acquired an added dimension — the ideas for which people fought on those barricades. For while the social depth of Hugo's outlook was shallow, the exposition of his homily on social injustice contained passion enough to ignite and capture the minds of those who are young and stand at the threshold of the world of ideas.

Interest in the Paris Commune helped to excite my curiosity about 1852 and Napoleon III. At this point, the sagas of Dumas, which roused me from the ages of twelve to fifteen, gave way to Zola's epic work, *Les Rougon-Macquart.* This work not only captured my young mind in its tenacious clutches but profoundly and subconsciously influenced the budding artist.

In 1906 at the age of eight I was carted off to Paris, since things were too unsettled for us to go to our country cottage after the Revolution of 1905. I remember very little of Paris, only typical childlike things. The dark wallpaper and the massive feather pillows of the hotel. The hotel's elevator shaft, no doubt the first I had ever seen. The tomb of Napoleon. The *poilu* in red trousers in the barracks nearby. The vile gustatory sensation from mulled wine, which spoiled my impression of the Bois de Bologne. The gray cloth dresses and white headdresses of the girls in Papa's favorite restaurant. The films of Méliès, the Jardin des Plantes. The black calico sleeves of the pinafores worn by the girls playing with hoops in the Tuileries Gardens. The terrible fact that no one told me we were in Notre Dame, about whose gargoyles I had dreamed after seeing photographs of them. And of course, before everything, more than anything, above everything — Le Musée Grévin[1] — an impression never surpassed.

In the Musée Grévin I remember seeing Papa being carried triumphantly in a sedan chair, under ostrich feather fans held by a dozen wax figures. There was Sado-Yakko[2] — a life-size figure between Japanese fans and numerous little tableaux, spaced along the sides, and, in another scene, Abd-el-Krim[3] surrendering to the French.

There were dark passages in which suddenly, from right and left, an underground arch appeared, through which I saw life in the early Christian catacombs.

In one arch they were praying. In another, one was being baptized, silver water frozen in midair between the hand with a chalice and the head of the convert.

In still another, someone lay behind iron bars, torn to pieces by a lion's claws.

In the distance — the panorama of a circus.

In the foreground — terrifying Roman soldiers seize a group of Christians, huddled in fear around an old preacher.

At the top of some steps you were met by Demosthenes with his lantern; Demosthenes, vainly searching for a human being.[4]

You climb higher and pass by Napoleon being received at Malmaison. Here are Josephine and Bonaparte himself, shining in his armor and medals, amid the brilliant Parisian society.

By the columns, near the barrier cord separating the Napoleonic brilliance from everyday contemporary life, stands a gray-haired, mustachioed Frenchman, tightly holding a tiny black dog. He seems to be unable to tear himself away from the scene.

You pass through once.

You pass through once more.

The old man still watches how, with an elegant gesture, Josephine offers someone a cup of golden tea. The old man doesn't take his eyes off her. But the old man's no fanatic about Napoleon's glorious age. The old man is one of the many wax figures scattered amongst the sightseers to mystify them — standing

---

1. The Musée Grévin was the French equivalent of Madame Tussaud's waxworks.

2. Sado-Yakko was a Japanese actress.

3. Abd-el-Krim was the leader of the Rif tribes in Morocco who fought successfully against French and Spanish colonial troops. But Eisenstein erred here; he probably meant Abd-el-Kadir (1807–1883), the Arab emir known for his struggle against the French in Algiers from 1832 to 1841.

4. Here Eisenstein made another slip. It was Diogenes who was "searching for an honest man." (H.M.)

near the tableaux or sitting on the museum benches. My cousin Modeste, in order to check the "real" wax figures, pulls the nose of a live French lady . . .

But the most powerful impression of the Musée Grévin is made by the Chamber of Horrors, situated just above the catacombs of the early Christians, with the obvious intention of establishing a connection between them . . .

In the Chamber of Horrors there's the little unfortunate (Louis Dix-septième)[5] with a drunken cobbler, there's Marie Antoinette in the Conciergerie, Louis Seize himself in his cell, with the patriots coming for him. And an earlier scene when the "Austrian bitch" (*"L'autrichienne"* for *"L'autre chienne,"* one of the first puns I enjoyed) falls in a faint, seeing through her window a procession carrying the head of the Princesse de Lamballe on a pike.

I pass on from the fate of individual personages of the Revolution, as represented in the Musée Grévin, to the life of the masses in the pages of Mignet.[6] But simultaneously to something greater: my first idea of historical events, conditioned by social lawlessness and injustice.

Luxurious panniers and gigantic white wigs, the figure of Sanson,[7] and the camisoles of the aristocrats, the colorful knitting women, or Théroigne de Méricourt,[8] or even the clicking of the slanting blade of the guillotine as it was raised, the visual impression of what was probably the first "double exposure" that I saw on the screen as well in those immemorial times — Cagliostro showing to Marie Antoinette in a glass of water how she will mount the guillotine — none of these vivid impressions could wipe out Mignet's descriptions of the social hell of prerevolutionary France.

I remember with particular clarity Mignet's scene of the Paris Commune, when in the concentration camps of Versailles French ladies poked out the eyes of the Communards with their parasols.

The image of those parasols gave me no rest, until, despite my common sense, I included them in a scene of the beating-up of a young worker in the July days of 1917 in Leningrad.[9]

Thus I rid myself of this importunate memory, but pointlessly overloaded my "canvas" with this scene, which in tone and essence bore no relationship to the 1917 Revolution.

•

---

5. The reference is to Louis XVII (1785–1795), son of Louis XVI and Marie Antoinette. He died in prison.

6. Françoise Auguste Marie Mignet (1796–1884) was a historian and archivist.

7. Charles Henri Sanson (1740–1795), public executioner in Paris, was in charge of the beheading of Louis XVI. His son Henri executed Marie Antoinette.

8. Théroigne de Méricourt was the pseudonym of Anne Joseph Terwagne (1762–1817). An actress, she became a heroine of the Revolution and was one of the leaders of the assault on the Bastille.

9. Eisenstein had in mind a scene in his epic film *October*.

The word "citadel" nowadays is not very much in use. Now and then one meets the phrase "the Citadel of Capitalism." But hardly anyone writes "the Citadel of Fascism." At its best, *The Citadel* is the film by King Vidor or the novel by A. J. Cronin.

In the days of my childhood the citadel in the city of Riga was a reality, just like the "castle" where the governor lived or the Powder Tower, one of the sights of the old city, with three stone cannonballs alongside.

The garrison of the military administration was concentrated in the citadel. There was a parade ground, a garrison church (where in my preschool years I was escorted for confession to Father Mikhovsky), a striped sentry box, and a flag flying. Under the flag towered a two-story building — the barracks apartment of one of the staff officers of the garrison, General Bertels. We became acquainted with Alyosha Bertels in the citadel before his retirement.

The citadel is memorable to me because I was very rude there to a strange gentleman who was visiting the fortress at the same time as my mother. What form my rudeness took I can't now remember, but no doubt it was something less modest than the joke I played some years before on Madame Reva, a friend of Mother's, when I released a pigeon under her then fashionable long skirt.

Imagine my horror when, a few days later, this gentleman suddenly appeared in our school, during one of the lessons, dressed in a glittering uniform, and turned out to be none other than the trustee of the Educational Department, Mr. Prutchenko.

Horror turned into stupefaction when he not only recognized me, but uttered some flattering remark to the effect that he had had the pleasure of meeting my mother and me while visiting . . .

I remember a similar case in Mexico, when, with the combined authority of us three film-makers we ejected an unauthorized occupant of my Pullman sleeper, a black-eyed, bronzed citizen with blazing eyes.

No sooner had we stepped onto the promised land of Mexico City than we were instantly summoned to the chief of police. Without any apparent pressure, but purely as a formality. Still, it wasn't very pleasant and was not without some tension.

Imagine our astonishment when we beheld, sitting next to the police chief, none other than that same black-eyed fellow, who turned out to be the chief's brother!

He said in Spanish, "We have met the señors," with a half-moon smile of white teeth from a bronze face . . .

Schoolfellows usually find common interests, and many school acquaintances become cemented in friendship on the basis of similar interests and tastes. But it didn't happen with me. In that sense school to me was an empty place of little significance. And that was mainly because I was a terribly exemplary boy, madly diligent in my studies, and none too democratic in my choice of acquaintances. For in the school, the children expressed even more openly than in society the national enmity between the different ethnic groups to which their parents belonged.

I belonged to the colonizing group of Russian bureaucrats, toward whom both the native Latvian population and the descendants of the first of their conquerors, the Germans, felt equally unfriendly. So from my school desk I didn't succeed in making any genuine friendships . . .

It mustn't be forgotten that Riga was once the dwelling place of Bishop Albert,[10] around whom gathered knights of the Livonian and Teutonic orders, whose "shadows of the past" I have been battling on the screen for the last ten years.[11]

At home Papa sat in an armchair with a great register in his hand while Ozols[12] climbed onto the top of a wardrobe on which rested a curious construction resembling a vast rabbit hutch, with numerous square nesting boxes. Each cell of this construction — and there must have been at least twenty-four or thirty-six or even forty-eight — contained a pair of Papa's lacquered black boots.

Papa wore only black blunt-nosed lacquered boots, and recognized no others. And he had a tremendous selection for all occasions. The register was his record of these boots, each of which had special descriptions: "new," "old," "scratched." From time to time he had a review and a checkup. Ozols climbed up and down, opening wide the little doors of this boot garage.

I never had a musical ear. To recall a tune that was even recognizable to others was always very difficult for me. And to recall a tune so that I could hum it to myself was simply impossible.

Still, there were exceptions.

I remember how I lay all night in bed in Riga, after seeing and hearing *The Tales of Hoffmann* for the first time, and hummed incessantly the chorus from "The Barcarolle." And I can still hum to myself, but not aloud, the waltz from *The Dollar Princess*, which I also first heard in Riga, when I must have been about twelve years of age.

I remember my first encounter with the opera *Eugene Onegin*[13] on the stage of an amateur dramatic club in Riga: the usual romantic decoration of the first act — through a colonnade to the house, or through columns into endless fields

---

10. Albert, Bishop of Riga from 1199 to 1229, a bloody fanatic, was the first inspirer of the *Drang nach Osten*. He formed the order of Swordbearers, which merged into the Teutonic Order.

11. Albert was eventually depicted by Eisenstein in *Alexander Nevsky*.

12. Ozols was the courier of Eisenstein's father.

13. Tchaikovsky's opera *Eugene Onegin* is based on the dramatic poem by Pushkin.

(Rabinovich[14] in the Bolshoi Theater!) — was here reduced to a simple green park bench up against the backdrop.

I also remember I was first intrigued by the comedians: Fender, Kurt Busch, and Zachsel in the German Riga Theater of Opera and Drama, where at a very early age I became acquainted with their repertoire, from *Hansel and Gretel* to Goethe's *Götz von Berlichingen*, from Schiller's *Wallenstein's Tod* to Carl von Weber's opera *The Marksman* and Sardou's *Madame Sans-Gêne* (the unforgettable Fender here spoke but three words in the role of a cobbler, and the flowing arabesque with which he pronounced the words *"Wie eine Fee,"* referring to the gait, soon to be seen, of the marshal's wife, I still see before me to this very day!); and then I saw *Around the World in Eighty Days* and the operetta *Feuerzauberei*.

I saw *Feuerzauberei* before the war (before the war, of course, here meaning the *First* World War). I remember Zachsel, in *Madame Sans-Gêne*, playing wonderfully the role of Bonaparte himself, and also playing the part of Napoleon in a cinema film, riding onto the stage on a white horse toward a prop cinema camera (this was the first "film shooting" that I ever saw) . . .

Since my cradle days I have been fond of "gingers"[15] and was always a little embarrassed by this. Papa also liked the circus, but above all he was interested in high-class horsemanship and William Truzzi's group of horse trainers. My weakness for gingers I deliberately concealed and pretended that I was madly interested in chestnut horses!

In 1922 I "recouped myself" to my heart's content, drowning my first independent production (*Enough Simplicity in Every Wise Man*)[16] in all tones of ginger and white clowns.

Madame Glumova — ginger.

Glumov — white.

Krutitsky — white.

Mamayev — white.

All servants — ginger.

Turusina also — ginger.

(Mashinka, who did the strong-arm act, was performed by a maiden of mighty frame, a fellow tribeswoman of the town of Riga, Vera Muzikant.

---

14. Isaac Moseyevich Rabinovich (1894–1961) was an Honored Worker of Art of the RSFSR (Russian Soviet Federated Socialist Republic) and a Soviet theater designer. In 1936 he designed the Bolshoi Theater production of *Eugene Onegin*.

15. Traditionally, the ginger clown was the "fall guy" to the white clowns and always "got it in the neck." (H.M.)

16. *Enough Simplicity in Every Wise Man* by A. N. Ostrovsky (1823–1880) was produced by Eisenstein in the Proletcult Theater.

Kurchayev — the "trio" hussar, in pink tights and lion-taming costumes. Gorodulin was played by Pyrev[17] — that was worth three gingers!) . . .

At a very young age I fell in love with photoillustrations of the nineties. Papa had a whole pile of Paris albums, many dating from the International Paris Exhibition of 1900. I knew the *Exposition Universelle* from cover to cover no less well than the Articles of Faith or Our Father.

In fact, the *Exposition Universelle* was perhaps the first photomontage I held in my hands. The principle of the composition of these illustrations consisted of separately posed figures isolated and photographed and afterward mounted together with a correspondingly suitable background. In some illustrations it was a photographic background; in others, the backgrounds were drawn.

There was, for example, *The Coulisse Café-Chantant,* and the figures represented were popular stars in extremely daring costumes, as Queens of the Night, cats with bushy ears, jockeys, marquises.

And of course the fireman, *le pompier,* with a gigantic handlebar mustache stuck on. Another picture revealed *Le Foyer de l'Opera,* in which gentlemen promenaded in top hats, and high-society ladies were dressed in silk shawls in a sea of circling frills. Yet another depicted the Carnival Ball, with everyone in a mask.

A turn of a page gave you a general view of a fireworks display at the exhibition. The figures were shown watching in wonder, though it was obvious that the light that fell on them did not correspond with the source of light of the fireworks, and their looks were not at all in the direction in which, quite clearly, they were supposed to be looking.

These montages were printed in different tones: pale orange, violet, light chocolate, or mignonette.

Maybe my interest in montage began to form from that day, although this type of "compound picture" is much more ancient.

There are many beautiful examples from the 1820s and 1830s of pictures composed of cut-out engravings. These early montages commonly decorated folding screens or fire screens.

Such screens were still to be seen in 1927 among the nonmuseum relics of the Winter Palace.

Similar screens, with portraits of the best English actors in their leading roles, were once possessed by Lord Byron.

The hobby of composing such compound pictures, together with the art of cutting silhouettes, stretches back to the *dix-huitième siècle* and Moreau le Jeune, Eisen, and Gravelot.

This operation was called *découpage,* and there are many pictures preserved showing ladies engaged in this pastime . . .

---

17. Ivan Pyrev (1901–1968) was a leading Soviet film producer.

The Knot That Binds

A Short Chapter on the Divorce of Mom and Pop

THE BIGGEST stationery shop in Riga was on Kupecheskaya Street, now called Kaufstrasse. The width of this street, paved with close-fitting square slabs, was actually greater than its length. This was particularly obvious because all around were the tiny and narrow streets of the old town. To the left of the stationery shop was the Jonk Polievsky bookshop; catty-corner was Diebner; and opposite, the huge linen draper, Homs. Over the stationery shop was the sign AUGUST LYRA, RIGA.

This store was a paradise of stationery. Pencils of all kinds, crayons of all colors, paper of all sorts; a vast collection of blotting paper, writing pens, corrugated paper for flower vases, erasers, envelopes, penknives, files. And picture postcards!

In those days photopostcards were very fashionable.

Black and white reproductions (printed in high contrast) of famous or fashionable pictures were in abundance.

An angel guarding two little children marching along a precipice.

A Jewish settlement engaged in stoning a young girl for some transgression.

A suicide of two lovers, bound together with rope and ready to throw themselves into an abyss.

A young girl dying of tuberculosis, looking into the rays of the sun breaking through into the room . . .

These picture postcards were collected like postage stamps and just as carefully placed into albums.

(Perhaps in these picture postcards can be found the roots of my hostility to "the plot" and to "stories" that marks the beginning of my film career?)

The shop also sold pictures in a larger format. Most of them foreign.

In those years America captured England and Europe with a particular type of girl. She was tall, with an energetic chin thrust forward. She wore a long skirt and had dreamy eyes under the little waves of her hairdo. This girl, created by Gibson and known only as "the Gibson girl," flooded the journals and the humor magazines, including London's *Punch*, just as, in the period of the Second World War, the whole surface of the globe, wherever the American Army went, was flooded with the so-called Varga girls.

I remember distinctly one of the drawings in the manner of Gibson — so sensational in the years 1908 and '09. It was called *The Knot That Binds*. It represented a big black bow knotted in the middle. On the left wing of the bow was the traditional profile of the young Gibson girl. On the right, the profile of the no less typical young Gibson boy. All Gibson girls had the same face, and the young men seemed like their twins, so alike were they. And in the center of the knot was the little face of a smiling child.

Why is that picture etched in my memory?

No doubt because I saw it at the very moment when I myself was in the role of the knot that binds. A knot that did not succeed in binding and holding together the family that was splitting up, the parents who were divorcing.

Now, it's nobody's business that my parents were divorced in 1909. It was sufficiently commonplace for the times, as somewhat later, for example, it was quite popular to arrange a suicide. But the divorce was very important to me. It poisoned the atmosphere of the family, the cult of family principles, the joy of the family hearth, in my ideas and my feelings.

Speaking in literary-historical jargon — from earliest childhood the "family theme" disappeared from my mental make-up. But the process of the disappearance was painful to me. And it comes back to my memory now, like a film with cuts, missing sequences, unrelated scenes stuck together; like a film with only a thirty-five percent commercial distribution value.

My room was next to my parents' bedroom.

At night the fiercest quarrels flew through their room.

How many nights did I run barefoot into the room of my governess, burying my head in a pillow? And no sooner had I fallen asleep than my parents came running in to wake me and sympathize with me.

There were other moments when each parent would consider it his or her duty to open my eyes to the other. Mother cried out that my father was — a thief. Father cried out that my mother was — a fallen woman. Court Councilor Eisenstein didn't hesitate to call her more precise names. Yulia Ivanovna, daughter of a First Guild Merchant, accused Papa of being still worse.

Then more names poured out — all lions of the Russian settlement then in the Baltic Provinces — and Papa had a duel with somebody.

One day Mama, dressed in a beautiful checkered red and green silk blouse, ran screaming out of her room and threw herself down the stairwell. Papa carried her back up, shaking with hysterics.

Naturally, I was told nothing about the divorce proceedings. Instead, I heard odd bits: that our courier, Ozols, gave evidence as a witness; that testimony was also given by our cook, Salomé.

Then there was a time when I was taken for a series of walks in the city for the entire day. A sobbing Mama bid farewell to me and went away. The porters came and took away the furnishings that had been part of Mama's dowry. At the same time, the piano left, and I was freed from music lessons, which I had just begun to take.

The rooms became completely empty and excessively large.

Somehow, I accepted all this. I began to sleep and really rest, and during the daytime rode round the empty dining room on my bicycle.

I don't smoke.

Papa never smoked.

I always modeled myself on Papa.

From the cradle I grew up in order to become an engineer and architect.

Up to a certain age I kept up with Papa in everything.

Papa rode horseback.

He was very heavy, and only one horse from Riga's Tattersalls could bear him, the giant Pik with a blue walleye.

I was also taught horseback-riding.

I never became an engineer and architect.

I never made it as a cavalryman.

I don't play the piano, only the gramophone and radio.

Yes! I don't smoke simply because at a certain age I didn't let myself get captivated by it.

First, because my ideal was Papa, and second, because I was so insanely humble and obedient.

Herr Eisenstein

"*KINDER, SEID STILL — der Vater schreibt seinen Namen!*"

"Children, be quiet — Father is signing his name!" This expression, inscribed on a postcard with an appropriate scene, was very popular in our home. It was exactly the image of Papa. Our papa was just as important as the papa on the postcard. Our papa was very vain.

The ranks and orders — from court to state, from state to higher state, from the Anna to the Vladimir decoration round the neck — to which he had been promoted were an inexhaustible quarry of excitement, expectation, and joy to him. The appearance of his name in the *Government News*, in fact any mention of his name, tickled Papa's self-esteem.

Papa, for example, never missed one performance of the operetta *Die Fledermaus*. He always sat in the first row of the stalls and blissfully closed his eyes when they sang the famous duet:

"*Herr Eisenstein!*
"*Herr Eisenstein!*
"*Die Fledermaus!*"

Because Papa was an exemplary, hardworking home-lover, he was impressed by the nocturnal adventures of his coincidental namesake, Herr Eisenstein: externally more than respectable, but essentially a débauché and rake.

I have no need to be embarrassed by Papa's vanity. In that respect I have far surpassed him.

Granted, I had a greater diapason of gratification of this trait through burdensome heredity.

The third German line was not current at home.

This was the notorious formula "*Wie sag' ich's meinem Kind?*"

"How can I tell this to my child?"

That is how the parent's problem is expressed when an excessively questioning look appears in children's eyes, and the stories about storks and cabbage heads have lost their conviction.

"Where do babies come from?"

For Mama and Papa, this problem did not exist. Not because, being ahead of their time, they had kept me fully informed of these facts, but because both of them simply avoided this tricky question and continued to evade it. No doubt Mama was, as the Americans say, "oversexed." And Papa, in his turn, was "undersexed."

At any rate, in this probably lies the basis of their divorce and, in me, from early childhood, the fall from prestige of the Lares and Penates, of the family hearth, and the cult of the "old homestead."

Dismantling
a Tyrant

IN THE FOREWORD I wrote that this work would be completely immoral. This is evident not only in the absence of any planned objective, but in the complete absence of any general plan. You must agree that in a planned economy and an ideological system such an approach is, of course, completely immoral!

On beginning a chapter, I never know where it will lead to. Only on finishing it do I, at times, begin to suspect that some kind of theme may have emerged. More often than not this theme is a complete surprise for the author himself. This is what happened with the material I have just written.

I sincerely thought that this was a piece of biography about an offended child whose parents had no time to open his eyes in the proper manner. I even thought to begin it with a heated altercation on this subject, with Papa, in the summer of 1916.

It was in a horse cab, driving out of the delightful Rossi Street, bordered on the right and left by the purest orange and white Empire walls. The architecture of Alexandrinka is so beautiful that it is not content with the theater building alone.[1] It stealthily runs into the lane behind the theater and encompasses it on both sides. And here in the course of centuries the right and left sides have been admiring each other. They grew shy in their mutual admiration. The right and left sides of the lane are completely identical. And identically beautiful. If they had been mirrors, one could have placed a candle in the middle of the street and told fortunes about the bridegroom, who would come out of the rear façade of the theater, which the street leans against. If hands were thrust out of the façade, they would have touched each other, as in a

---

1. The former Alexandrinsky Theater is so called because it stands in Alexandrinka Square. It is now the Pushkin State Academic Theater, Leningrad.

quadrille, and the cabmen would have seemed like bowing couples, running under the raised hands of a couple dancing on the spot . . .

In such a cab I am traveling with Papa, a son taking stern account of his father.

Hands do not stretch out from house to house.

Outstretched hands do not hold round golden rings of agreement.

Nor is there a golden ring or outstretched hand of mutual understanding between the two passengers on this ride.

Such hands and rings never existed in Nikolayev Street Number 6, Apartment 7.

Strange, therefore, is the architectural fantasy, in the wildest *style moderne*, that possessed Papa when he erected similar many-storied figures on the façade of the houses he built behind the corner of Albert Street in Riga.[2]

Eight giant maidens made out of cast-iron drainpipes stand along the façade.

Their hands are stretched out in front of them, perpendicular to the façade.

It looks as if they are engaged in Sokol[3] gymnastics.

Hands stretched out into emptiness.

And in order to conceal these circumstances, sixteen gold rings were placed in their hands.

Emptiness, as it were, was turned on its side and bordered with gold hoops.

The emptiness of the undertaking is more difficult to hide, and the maidens are not eternal. I hardly remember the day of their unveiling, but I do remember that day when, taken apart, like drainpipes, they left in pieces their proud pedestals.

Rain is very conservative. It is utterly indifferent to the fact that the gestures of the drainpipes are given an artistic form and cease to be a means for conducting water.

Rain stubbornly beats on the crowns of the figures but cannot find an opening . . . The maidens on Papa's façade are blocked up, above and below. The rain beating on their crowns, unable to pour into them, floods over their bodies and runs into the drains beneath.

And so the obstinate rain begins to streamline them; to feel with its streams of water — like living hands — the contours of the figures.

The breasts stand out like islands in the flood.

Dark streams pour out from under their stomachs.

The rain surges down. And its fleeting contact leaves behind dark tracks on the imitation alabaster of those athletic figures.[4]

---

2. M. O. Eisenstein, as well as being the chief engineer of the Highways Department of the Lifland District from 1903 to 1917, had a private practice as an architect.

3. Sokol stands for the Czechoslovak sports organization.

4. Eisenstein didn't explain how cast-iron figures became imitation alabaster. (H.M.)

The effect is shocking, and one fine day the maidens, broken into torsos, breasts, hands, waists, and legs, end their strange existence.

However, they were useful to me in one respect . . .

No doubt, remembering them, I broke into pieces, with such delicate excitement, the giant figure of Alexander III in the first episode of *October*.[5]

And if I add that the dismantled and overturned naked figure of the tsar served as a symbol of the February overthrow of tsarism, then it is clear that the beginning of the film, reminding me, through the image of the tsar, of the downfall of Papa's creation, also spoke to me personally of my liberation from Papa's authority.

The image of Papa's hollow maidens arises twice again in my work in parallel variations on the image of armor. Strictly speaking, not so much the armor, as such, as the whole empty accouterment of a man in armor.

In the epilogue to *Do You Hear, Moscow?*,[6] at the unveiling of a memorial to the ruling prince of a tiny German principality, the official court poet reads an ode of greeting on the conquest of semicultured natives by the German men in armor. The poet is in armor and on stilts — just like his stilted poetry. The knightly costume envelops his figure and stilt legs, forming an iron giant. At the critical moment the straps break, and, with a clatter like that of empty pails, the empty armor falls from the poet.

In *Ivan the Terrible* the empty armor of Kurbsky is found by Malyuta Skuratov in the tent of the traitor-prince, pitched under Weisenstein Castle, whence all have fled.[7] The bucket-helmet of the Teutonic knight gives out a hollow sound when it is hit with a wooden shaft by Vaska Buslai.[8]

. . . Papa was a domestic tyrant. But though tyrannical papas were typical of the nineteenth century, mine survived into the twentieth!

And don't these pages cry out against the moral oppression that ruled in our family?

How many times the exemplary boy, Seryozha, like a learned parrot, replied to Papa's question "Aren't my creations wonderful?" with studied formulae of delight — profoundly against his own ideas and convictions!

Let me cry out in protest, at least now, at least here!

In my early years — the rustle of cuffs and starched collar, where instead I should have torn my trousers and got smothered in ink. Ahead — my path is mapped out, straight as an arrow. School, institute, engineering.

From year to year.

---

5. The film re-created an actual event, the dismantling of the statue of tsar Alexander III in Moscow.

6. In November 1923 Eisenstein produced the play *Do You Hear, Moscow?*, by S. M. Tretiakov, in the Proletcult First Worker's Theater, Moscow.

7. *Ivan the Terrible* was filmed in 1944. The filmscript was published in 1961 by Simon and Schuster.

8. The scene with the Teutonic knight is in *Alexander Nevsky*, 1938.

From diapers through the uniform of a realist (that was the only period when I was a realist!) to the student's bronze shoulder straps with the initials of the Tsar Nicholas I . . .

I am astounded that, with my predisposition for outlines, I demolished all that predesigned race along the assembly line.

The seeds of social protest were planted in me not by the misfortunes of social injustice, of material deprivation, not in a zigzag struggle for existence, but directly and wholly from the master symbol of social tyranny, the father's tyranny in the family, the survival of the clan chief's tyranny in primitive society.

And so in a roundabout way we have returned to our initial subject, to our outing with Papa.

Of course, our ride has long since passed along Rossi Street, between the gray granite and heavy chains of Chernyshevsky Bridge, and somewhere in the district of Five Corners we end our argument.

But the path of this ride on paper passed through the cast-iron maidens, the overthrown image of the tsar, to the deposed authority of Papa, like a lullaby of rebellious deeds — not only in the social themes of my life, but in the area of film form, repeating the evolution from protest against enslavement by the head of the family to protest against servitude under a tsar.

And the coronation of the "young" tsar (in the guise of Ivan IV) — is that not the coming to maturity of an heir, freeing himself from the shadow of the prototype father? The scuffle around the throne, the brawling for the tsar's crown and scepter? Does that not represent the reflection in consciousness of the same struggle in the arena of history that passes through generations and whole strata of social formations?

What is now most interesting for me is how this whole host of interrelationships with Papa's authority, in analysis atavistic, merges in me inevitably with evolutionary ideas, as, indeed, does my approach to any question.

Can it really be a mere coincidence that caused this powerful and ultimately enigmatic and sensual moment to become linked for me with the picture of evolution, to merge so inevitably with my craving and need to view each phenomenon from the aspect of its evolutionary becoming?

Surely what we have here, in crystal purity, is the nerve, the principle, of evolution and becoming, so intoxicating in natural phenomena and so little understood in the processes of artistic creation, in the physiology and biology of forms, styles, and works of art.

Anything that resonates with this, in the slightest, is at once included in the orbit of interest.

The construction of the language proper to the cinema, its syntax, alphabet of form, principle of stylistics, which evolve from the system of technical phenomena. The roots of counterpoint and its culmination in the audiovisual cinema. Finally, the outlines of the history of the cinema, beginning with pre-cinematic arts. A history that traces the development of each element within the cinema, like the crowning and culmination of a tendency rooted in the distant past; ecstasy as the striving to the utmost null point both of the individual and of the species.

The most striking thing is that the limitations of the field of research are themselves, as it were, delineated by this very fact. Their limit, the outlining of their boundaries, coincides with that point at which the awareness of the mechanism of human evolution flares up. There, where the white blinding light of revelation burst upon me.

It did not coincide with *man*!

Not only physically did it fail to coincide with the meeting with the object. But even abstractly.

"The knowledge of good and evil" as pure knowledge has surpassed knowledge as spontaneous action.

And so an explosion of questions found response in wonder at the wisdom and coherence of the system of the universe, and not in the frenzied immediacy of embraces!

And so moreover *ratio* surpasses *sex*.

And wonder diverges in circles of research from a point, without touching on the problem: man — not as the highest stage of evolution — but as Martha Petrovna, Peter Kornilovich, Boris, or Lucy!

Hence my field of theoretical investigations, hence the bias of my creative limitations — a symphony and not a drama, the mass as a prestage of the individual, music as the bosom of the birth of tragedy (*Ce M. Nietzsche n'a pas été si bête!*[9]); hence the inhumanity of the system of images in *Ivan the Terrible*; hence my own peculiar path and style.

Scrutinizing more closely this a-human feature of my constructions and investigations, you seem to see at almost every step this same picture of a research interest that abruptly dies away as soon as the threshold of the narrow human stage of evolution is reached, somewhere at the level of the wise spiders!

Interestingly, it is constructive and progressive. For example, in relation to Freud. Years were needed to realize that the primary fund of impulses is broader than is the narrowly sexual, as Freud sees it; that is, the frame of personal biological adventures of the human individual.

The subject of sex is no more than a concentrate, drawn into a knot, which already, through countless spiral turns, re-creates an ordered progression of circles of infinitely greater radius.

That is why I find D. H. Lawrence's ideas agreeable; they forced him to go beyond the bounds of sex to the (unattainable-for-a-limited-individual) cosmic forms of fusion into wholeness.

---

9. "This M. Nietzsche wasn't such a fool!"

That is why I am drawn to my own conception of the zone of the prelogical, of that subconscious which includes, but is not enslaved by, sex.

That is why the subconscious itself is depicted, above all, as the reflection of earlier and undifferentiated stages of social being.

That is why, in analyzing the genesis of the principle of form and its different variations (devices), one goes beyond the limits of one circle to another, as it were, of Dante's Hell.

That is why, for example, the widely known device of synecdoche, including both its use in poetry and in the close-up in cinematography, and the notorious understatement of American practitioners and American anthologists (the bulk of whom stop at the threshold of anthology, avoiding analysis and ensuing generalizations), go beyond the application in reflecting thought on the model of *pars pro toto* (the limit of conception for the year 1935).

That is why, ten years later, this conception breaks through into a still earlier prehuman sphere, and indicates that this very *pars pro toto* is, on a higher emotional-sensual level, a repetition of the purely reflex manifestation of the conditioned reflex, arising wholly through the reproduction of a part of its element, serving as an irritant.

That is why the propagation of the dramatic, and therefore one of its basic themes — that of vengeance — is not exhausted within the framework through which it reflects the inevitable reaction, provoked by action in the connecting of human psychology (tit for tat)!

This very reaction it sees as part of the general law of the equality of action and reaction, dictated by the pendulum of its looming movement. (Both in the waging of, say, a vendetta going back to this cause, and in the interpretation of the corresponding structure of the work of art that reflects this. Almost all of Elizabethan tragedy grew out of the original *Revenger's Tragedy* — remember the tragedies of Shakespeare!)

Cruelty

IN PETERSBURG MAMA lives at Tavricheskaya Street Number 9. Main entrance through the courtyard. A lift. White marble fireplace downstairs. For me, it is always winter here: year after year I come here only at Christmas.

The fireplace is always burning merrily. A soft red carpet runs up the stairs. Mama's boudoir is upholstered in a light cream material. On a light background are scattered tiny pink wreaths. So with the draperies. The carpet — the same tone as the wreaths — is pale rose. The boudoir is also the bedroom. This is divided by two screens, hiding Mama's bedstead. The screens too are in rosebud crowns.

Many years later — already a student, already living permanently with Mama — I catch measles here for the second time. The windows are curtained. The sun beats through the blinds. The room is flooded with a bright pink light . . . Is it a fever?

Not only a fever: the lining of the blinds is also pink. The sun's rays, piercing through the lining, turn pink. The same pink light that shines through your fingers when you hold them up to the lamplight, or when, with closed eyelids, you turn your head toward the sun.

The rosy light merges with the fever and delirium of sickness.

Grandmother's bedroom — I remember being in it when very small — was all blue. Blue velvet on the low chairs and long blue draperies. Did Granny have a blue period? And Mama a pink one?

Now the draperies and furniture from Mama's boudoir spend the rest of their life in my summer home. The pink wreaths can hardly be seen. The upholstery is now gray. The velvet on the armchairs is torn in places, and the bottoms of the seats seem like jaws from which several teeth are missing.

The gray period?

When my mother lived among the furniture, the divans, settees, and sofas were strewn all over with books. More often than not they were the yellow volumes published by Calmann-Lévy. Books from the library of a lady of decisive and independent views.

Holding first place: *Nietzschéenne*, then the invariable *Sur la Branche* by Pierre de Coulevain, and, of course, *Demimondaine* by Bourget, relieving *Demi-Lumière* by Dumas fils.

I never looked inside those yellow covers . . .

In the little divans and sofas I found two other books. I did look into these, and more than once, but with apprehension, with a certain excitement, even with . . . fear.

Those books I assiduously crammed between the back and the seat of the armchairs and divans. I covered them up with cushions, embroidered by Mama in the manner of "Richelieu." (Fretted drawings, parts of which are held together by means of a system of tiny straps. How many of such patterns I traced from journals for Mama! How many I later combined or created independently!)

I hid those books out of embarrassment, out of fear, because of what was in them, and because I wanted to make sure I could get at them when I wanted to. For there were many frightening things in *The Garden of Torture* by Octave Mirbeau and Sacher-Masoch's illustrated *Venus in Furs*.

These were the first examples of "unhealthy desires" that fell into my hands.

And even though Krafft-Ebing came into my hands somewhat later, it is toward the first two books I still retain a feeling of sickly hostility.

Sometimes I wonder why I never play games of chance. I don't think it's from a lack of inclination. Quite the opposite. It is from my fear of being afraid. This fear came to me in childhood when I wasn't frightened of the dark but was afraid that if I awoke in the darkness, I should be frightened.

That is why I make a wide circle to avoid games of chance. I am afraid that if I touch them once, I should never be able to hold myself back.

In my mother's white rosebud boudoir, I feverishly followed the stock exchange reports when Mama decided to gamble on the exchange with a small sum of "free" money.

Not in vain did I manage to evade the attraction of Mirbeau and Masoch. I came in contact with the alarming vein of cruelty much earlier through a living impression, a living impression from the cinema screen.

It was one of the earliest films I ever saw, no doubt produced by Pathé. The story took place during the Napoleonic Wars. In the house of a blacksmith was a military billet. The young wife of the blacksmith commits adultery with a young Empire sergeant. The husband finds out, catches and binds the sergeant. Throws him in the hayloft. He tears off the soldier's uniform, baring his shoulders, and brands him with a red-hot iron.

I remember vividly the naked shoulder, a great iron bar in the muscular hands of the blacksmith, the black smoke and white steam rising from the charred flesh.

The sergeant falls senseless. The blacksmith brings a gendarme. Before them — a man lying unconscious with naked shoulders. On his shoulder — the brand of a convict.

The sergeant is arrested as an escapee and imprisoned in Toulon. The film's end is sentimentally heroic. The smithy is on fire. The former sergeant saves the wife of the blacksmith. As he does so, the "brand of shame" disappears in his new burns.

Why does the smithy burn? Many years later? Does the sergeant save the blacksmith as well as the wife? Who pardons the convict? I have forgotten all that, but the scene of branding remains ineradicably in my memory to this very day.

In childhood it tortured me with nightmares. I imagined it at night. I saw myself either as the sergeant or the blacksmith. I caught hold of the bare shoulders. Sometimes they seemed to be mine, sometimes someone else's. It was never clear who was branding whom. For many years fair hair (the sergeant was blond) or black barrels and Napoleonic uniforms inevitably recalled that scene to my memory. Indeed, I developed a partiality for the Empire style.

To this day no sea of fire has swallowed the branding of the convict; no oceans of cruelty, which permeates my own films, have drowned the early impressions of that ill-starred film and the two novels on which it was undoubtedly based . . .

Let us not forget that my childhood was passed in Riga, during the climax of the 1905 Revolution. And there are still so many more terrible and cruel impressions all around — the rampaging reaction and repression by Meller-Zakomelsky and his kind.[1] Let us not forget this, all the more so because in my films cruelty is inextricably intertwined with the theme of social injustice and rebellion against it.

---

1. In 1906 A. N. Meller-Zakomelsky, already notorious for his punitive expedition in the Transbaikal area in 1905, was appointed governor-general of the Baltic Provinces. He crushed the revolutionary movement in Latvia with great ruthlessness.

Novgorod—
Los Remedios

FROM THE EARTH A column of water spurts four stories high. It is like a geyser in a textbook on geography. The water has a slightly sulphurous odor . . . and that reminds us even more strongly of new textbooks still smelling of printer's ink in those days when they were still interesting, on that first evening when one turns the pages of a newly purchased book, not like someone sampling boring spiritual food, but like a . . . bibliophile.

On such evenings, textbooks, particularly on geography, are cast into life like promissory notes for adventure, which someday must be paid. The picture postcard of a train riding through a gateway bored in a gigantic tree will torment one's memory until one eventually *does* drive through a giant sequoia in the American national forest.

So it was with me.

The columns of water gushing from the earth help one to rid oneself of an *idée fixe* linked with another picture postcard, illustrating a geyser in Yellowstone Park.

Perhaps the fountain was the reason that I didn't go to Yellowstone, but contented myself with Yosemite Park.

By day the fountain refracts the rays of the sun. At night it burns with the rays of a multicolored projector. It spurts upward in front of the *Kursaal* (casino). A horde of confused people is milling around it.

For some reason, during the last summer before finishing secondary school, I don't live with Papa on the Riga seashore but with Mama in Staraya Russa.

A fountain spurts in front of the *Kursaal* of Staraya Russa. And the people are milling hysterically. It is July 1914, and war has just been declared.

Among the galleries of the *Kursaal* the people are sobbing; complete strangers embrace each other. In a wheelchair a colonel, wearing dark glasses and covered with a Scots plaid, sobs aloud and, taking off his peaked cap, reveals a head covered with a pitiful growth . . .

People behaved the same way three years later, when Petrograd suddenly heard the news that Rasputin had been killed. In 1917 he was present invisibly in every home, under every skull, and was the subject of all gossip. Only the *Vechernaya Birzhevka* (the *Evening Stock Exchange*) managed to squeeze in a stop-press paragraph about his murder. The paper was at once confiscated. I am proud to be the owner of one copy, which by some miracle fell into my hands on that memorable day . . .

But in July 1914 there was an even worse panic. The railway station was filled to overflowing with people.

It was impossible to get out of Russia by train, although some smart ones managed to go by ship through Lake Ilmen to Volkhov and from there by train to Tikhvin.

That summer brought me three powerful impressions. Just before the declaration of war, at the height of a July heat wave, I saw an ikon procession during a religious festival for the opening of a new church.

Vivid memories of it were the basis of the religious procession in my film *The Old and the New*. The second important event was my first "literary meeting" with Anna Gregorievna Dostoyevskaya. But the most powerful was — a trip.

White chapels, bunched together like the white-clad saints of ancient ikons, where they almost fused into one. The war forced me to float past the most ancient bits of our country as in a beautiful fairy tale. Otherwise, the war touched me very little in 1914.

During the last school year the students took part in several demonstrations. We shouted till we were hoarse, carried portraits of the tsar and torches whose soot filled our nostrils.

Papa donned his military uniform and general's epaulets . . .

In the spring of the following year I experienced my first evacuation — the exit of civil servants' families from the city of Riga.

This coincided with my removal to Petersburg to enter the institute.

And so, quite naturally and painlessly, I left Papa for Mama, and on state transport, at that.

But that's all a year later. For the moment . . .

The course of the ship from Staraya Russa through Lake Ilmen. A marble sea in the evening. A white belfry far on the distant shore — a white lighthouse. We float slowly past moon-drenched Novgorod on the River Volkhov. Innumerable white churches gleam against the solid darkness. Silently, we glide past.

A magic night!

Where did these cathedrals come from, resting at the edge of this majestic flow? Did they come like white doves to take the waters? Did they come to wet the hem of their white chasubles?

Many years later, preparing for the production of *Alexander Nevsky*, I visited Novgorod. This time not just passing by but staying. My memory still retained a living picture of the bunched-up whiteness of churches along the Volkhov.

It turned out the churches were scattered throughout the city. In the market section. In the Sophia section. On the outskirts of the city. And farther afield.

If I were a poet, I would no doubt have said that the churches of Novgorod on both sides of the Volkhov had descended its banks to look at each other by moonlight, as in ancient times saints journeyed to "see" each other. However, I'm not a poet but a director. Therefore I am no less astonished, in my wanderings around ancient Russia, at the amazing ability of the ancient builders in choosing points of placement for churches and belfries, dispersed over the landscape. *Alexander Nevsky* brings me not only to Novgorod but also to Pereslavl, a charming town made of those same white cubes and onion domes and looking as if the buildings had escaped from a toy workshop. Indeed, along the route from Zagorsk to Pereslavl, where Alexander Nevsky spent his boyhood and where Peter the Great tested his miniature fleet, the white churches seem to be scattered at random. It is as if some gigantic thief had swept them up and then, in haste, let them fall from his sack as he made his escape. (According to legend, the hills and dales were created by the devil, who, running from the bright apparition of the cherubim, on his way dropped clods of earth stolen from the Holy City. In response, the saints dropped monasteries and churches on the hills which were created through the cupidity and cowardly haste of Satan.)

But the churches along the route are not accidentally scattered. They are placed with great calculation by wise hands. And the belfries in the midst of a sea of green Russian valleys — rising like lighthouses for ships at sea — point the way for hosts of pilgrims journeying hundreds of miles to pay homage to their saints. One may travel five, ten, or twenty miles at a single stretch. The path winds up hills and takes you down into dales. Still, wherever you look, the belfries are always to be seen. Along the path you imagine countless multitudes of pilgrims holding their course over the centuries from belfry to belfry, never varying from a route mapped out for them long ago by wise direction.

The last stage of the journey is across the White Sea. This part of the pilgrimage to the Holy Relics of Solovetsky is also carefully crafted to produce a lasting effect on the faithful. Barges carry the pilgrims from the shore to the island. Their holds are packed full, overloaded with pilgrims. The air in the holds quickly bcomes thick and murky. The barges as they set off from the shore begin to pitch and roll. For hours in the night the teeming vessels are hurled on the swell from crest to crest. From the fetid hold come endless groans and cries as pilgrims suffocate and suffer as if they were in Purgatory.

Just before dawn the barges reach the monastery. On shore the roar of a choir enfolds them, and under the resounding of the deacons' bass chants, the hold opens with a rumble. The panic-stricken pilgrims surge up into the fresh air as the dawn wind tears at the sails and the waves surge. A gigantic image of the Savior looms over the pilgrims. The image is illuminated with the light of candles and wreathed in incense from heavy censers swung in the strong hands of the monks on the shore. The deafening singing increases in volume. Around the barges the white towers and domes of the monastery appear to rise right out of the waves.

In that moment it seems as if all the torments of life have come to an end, and ahead lies the promised land. The pilgrims prostrate themselves on the deck and then, as dawn breaks, step in trembling reverence onto the sunlit, holy soil.

The location of Catholic cathedrals in Mexico is no less skillful.

Here for tens of miles one can see the cupola of Santa María Tonantsintl on the approaches to Pueblo, or the shimmering crosses of the Virgin de Los Remedios at the entry to Mexico City.

But here the Catholics do not earn any particular merit. They did not choose these sites. These were the sites of ancient pyramids, at one time crowned with temples by Aztecs and Toltecs.

The wisdom of the Catholics probably lay only in that, having destroyed the temples, they raised churches in exactly the same places, on the peaks of those pyramids, in order not to sidetrack the pilgrims, who for thousands of years had come from all the corners of the land to the foot of these very pyramids.

Mass pilgrimages in our time seem a strange mixture of epochs, helped by the odd apparel of the holy *danzantes*, unceasingly repeating from dawn to dawn their one and only unchangeable rhythmic foot movement — in honor of the Madonna. Who knows? Is it in honor of the Madonna?

Perhaps it is in honor of a far more ancient goddess — the mother of the gods, who, only seeming to yield her place to her alien rival, the mother of the god of Christianity, remains unchanged within the changing generations of the descendants of those who created her cult. Holy Fathers look through their fingers when those fingers are free to receive gifts. Does it matter in whose honor they are brought? The important thing is that, transformed into money, they should flow in an inexhaustible golden flood to Rome.

The dance is intoxicating in its unchanging melody. The cries of the pilgrims' children rend the air. The mothers thrust out their breasts for them. The organ sounds. The candles burn. Heat and intoxication. And the endless flow of human figures, pouring with sweat, crawl on their knees from the base of the pyramid to its holy heights. Knees are wrapped in rags. Sometimes in cushions that get torn to shreds. Often on their heads are fantastic headdresses of feathers (the brotherhood of the *danzantes*).

Eyes blindfolded with rags.

Sweat pours down.

A sufferer is supported by old women pilgrims, each wrapped in a cheap blue shawl — the *reboso*.

Breathing heavily, they reach the last step.

And triumphantly the blindfold is removed.

After the murk and the torment, in front of the sufferer, in the flame of burning candles — the wide open doors of the temple of the Madonna de Guadalupe, de Los Remedios, the Cathedral of Amecameca, with a naked, bare, tattered, gray, leafless trunk before them.

How I Learned to Draw

A Chapter about Dancing Lessons

LET ME START WITH the fact that I never learned to draw.

But this is how I draw and why.

Who in Moscow didn't know Karl Ivanovich Kogan, wizard and sorcerer of stomatology and osteology? Who didn't take to him their worn-out teeth? Who was not fascinated by the superior new jaws that emerged from under his hands?

Let us take Karl Ivanovich. Let us make him very thin. If his nose doesn't stick out enough yet, lengthen it a little. Let us make his figure sharply convex, make what in Riga we called "Madame Sit-Upon" protrude. Dress him in the uniform of a railroad engineer. Let him have on his arm a spouse with the highest chignon in Riga. And before you will be the gray railroad engineer — Afrosimov.

It is to Engineer Afrosimov that I am indebted for instilling in me an irresistible need to draw.

Like every society lady, Mama had her Thursdays at home. Besides which, Mama and Papa organized enormous receptions on the evening of their name days.[1] The usual circular dinner table was extended by all its twelve leaves so that it occupied the whole length of the dining room, and was weighed down with a rich supper.

Alongside the big table stood a buffet table. Guests ate after playing cards and making light music on the piano. The society was very select. The honored guest was the governor himself. His Honor Zvyagintsev. He sat on Mama's right. Papa sat at the opposite end of the table.

Sometimes smaller tables were brought in and formed into three sides of an oblong, a kind of "private" dining room. Where Papa then sat I don't remem-

---

1. In old Russia, the name day was the namesake's saint's day.

ber, but I do remember that I was seated inside the oblong, right opposite Mama. Up till then I had been brought only to visit the table — sleepy and dreamy. Still, earlier, put to sleep before the guests came. So all I saw was the table laid, glittering with silver and crystal. Fussing round the table was our maid Minna and Papa's courier, Ozols, specially dressed up for the occasion.

At first they merely showed me the big table, then allowed me to nibble from the cold buffet table. I loved pickled champignons and fresh caviar, didn't care for salmon, and didn't understand oysters.

After the divorce of Papa and Mama no receptions were held; the household fell apart. At the same time, Papa's business began to falter. And anyway, there was nowhere to receive people. Mama had taken the furniture with her.

My attitude to all this was very lighthearted, even merry.

The unbearable domestic quarrels (mostly at night) ceased.

I amused myself by bicycling up and down the empty dining and reception rooms. There was a kind of triumph in it.

Before the divorce, I was ruled very strictly by a stern papa. I was not permitted into the reception room at all. The dining room was linked with the reception room by an arch blocked by a row of chairs, along which I crawled, peering from the dining room into the promised land of the reception room.

Later I cycled daringly around the room, which looked like no-man's-land now that they had taken away the divans, armchairs, tables, lamps, and mountains of *Nippessachen*, knickknacks — mostly Copenhagen chinaware, which by its milky blue color and gray-wash drawings and its streamlined forms captivated the dilettante of the elegant in those happy years . . .

But now, that future desert swarms with people.

The reception room is full of them. Mama's boudoir. Papa's study.

Any minute now they will pour into the dining room for supper.

Meanwhile, they seat themselves around the card tables.

I am now at the age when I'm allowed to join the guests, but still not allowed to sit at the table.

I wander among the guests. I remember them.

There's the governor. An aristocratic head with an eagle's glance from beneath thick brows. But the rest of him is what we called a *Tischriese*, a giant at the table — a giant only from the waist up. His legs inappropriate — too small. And therefore only a giant when sitting at the table and disappointing when he stood up.

The governor had a magnificent head, magnificently placed, slightly askew, mounted on magnificent broad shoulders. In like manner, slightly askew, the Mexican pelican holds its head when it dives from the skies for fish in the amber bay of Acapulco.

Governor Zvyagintsev should soar over battlefields. Or in any case high over the heads of subordinates and others in his charge.

However, that would be impossible, even if those subordinates and inferiors bowed almost to the ground. For, as I said, the governor was very short.

As to the ladies, I remember only the young ones. The daughter of the vice-governor, Mademoiselle Bogolovskaya. And that no doubt because, though her name was Nadyezhda (hope), she was called by the French, Esperance. (On the fiftieth birthday of Dolores Ibarruri in 1945,[2] my greeting to her was built on that. I expressed a wish that for the next fifty years she would change her name from Dolores (suffering) to such names as Victoria, Gloria, and Felicidad.)

Besides Esperance I clearly remember the Wenzel sisters: Mulya, all in blue, and Tata, all in pink.

Why is it that out of all the flower-bed colors and constellations at these receptions I remember only the painted colors of the Wenzel sisters? In my memory, in accordance with all the rules of "agglutination," the sisters merge with the lampshades. There wasn't much difference in those years between lampshades and evening dresses. Similar puffs, pleatings, flounces, and lace . . .

On another day the sisters Wenzel were no longer the sisters Wenzel, but the sisters Amelang. Two young sisters, dressed in their Sunday best so that it was impossible to distinguish between dresses and lampshades.

Papa's crowded reception room is not Papa's reception room but quite another. Empty. With a blindingly polished, horribly empty parquet floor. Shortly, engulfed in spasms of fear, I must move in a waltz on that parquet desert.

I am still young. And this is our first dancing class. Boys and girls, we sit on those stools and look at that terrible parquet. That great reception room is in the house of another transport engineer — the chief of the Riga-Orlov Railway, Daragan. Here we are to learn to dance.

The carpets are rolled back and the palms moved right up to the windows.

I am benumbed by the parquet floor of the Daragan family's parlor. And I am benumbed mainly by those sisters — the Mademoiselles Amelang. They are much older than I. They are English. And are, I believe, twins, differentiated only by nuances in the color of their dresses. They dance in pairs with some of the older boys. To my lot falls the dreamy Nina and the carnivorous Olya, the younger daughters of the Daragan family. But I am madly in love with the unattainable Amelang sisters. With both at once.

What a blessing they were twins! And that I just couldn't take to dancing lessons.

---

2. Dolores Ibarruri (1895–   ), known as La Pasionaria, for many years was general secretary of the Communist Party of Spain, vice-president of the International Democratic Federation of Women, and, after the end of the Spanish Civil War, an émigrée in the USSR. In 1977, after the death of Franco, she returned to Spain.

However, we left Mama's guests just as they were seating themselves at the card tables.

Let us return to them. All the more so because Mr. Afrosimov sits at one of the card tables. Presently, swishing silk, Maria Vasilyevna Verkhovskaya[3] comes and sits at the table. She has the most *retroussé* nose in Riga and finger-thick painted eyebrows.

I hurry from the other end of the room right away, because, while awaiting the game, Mr. Afrosimov draws on the dark blue cloth of the card table, using a sharply pointed piece of white chalk covered with pale yellow paper — for me.

He draws animals for *me*.

Dogs! Deer! Cats!

I remember most distinctly the height of my rapture — a fat, bandy-legged frog.

The finely drawn white contours stand out sharply on the dark cloth background. This technique permits of no shading and illusory shadows. Only contours. Nor was it only a linear contour. Here, before the very eyes of the delighted onlooker, the line of contour springs up and moves. Moving, it traced the invisible outline of the object, and magically made it appear on the dark blue cloth.

A line is the trail of movement . . .

And no doubt, in the years to come, I shall remember that sharp sense of line as a dynamic movement; line as a process; line as a route. Many years later it impelled me to write in my heart the wise saying of Wang Pi, of the third century B.C.: "What is a line? A line speaks of movement."

How rapturously fond I would become of the seemingly dry matter of Descartes's analytical geometry at the Engineering Institute, for it spoke of the movement of lines expressed in the mysterious formulae of equations.

I would devote many years to *mise en scène* — those lines of the actor's movement "in time."

My constant passion remains the dynamics of lines and dynamics of moving on and not of staying put, both in lines and in the system of phenomena and their transitions from one to the other.

Perhaps here too is the reason for my inclination and sympathy for teachings that proclaim dynamics, movement, and becoming as their basic principles. On the other hand, I shall always love Disney and his heroes, from Mickey Mouse to Willy the Whale. Their agile figures are also animals, also linear, and at their best without shadows or shading, like the early creations of the Chinese and Japanese — made up of real running lines of contours!

---

3. Maria Vasilyevna Verkhovskaya was the wife of A. V. Verkhovsky, an engineer of the Riga-Orlov Railway and a good friend of the Eisenstein family. The Verkhovsky house was one of the most cultured salons in old Riga; people interested in theater, music, and the arts met there, and the young Eisenstein was a frequent visitor.

The fleeting lines of childhood, delineating the contours and forms of animals in their flight, come to life again in the real flight of real lines in the outlines of animated cartoons. And maybe it is because of these childhood impressions that with such relish and gusto I draw incessantly with chalk on the blackboard during my lectures, engrossing and amusing my students by my sketches and striving to instill in them a perception of lines as movement, as a dynamic process.

No doubt it is for this reason that the purely linear drawing remains my particular favorite, and why I use it almost exclusively. Patches of light and shade (in sketches intended for embodiment on the screen) spread over them, almost as a record of desired effects.

Similarly, Van Gogh, in letters to his brother, and on sketches of proposed paintings, wrote the names of the colors in the places he wanted them to be.

But it wasn't Van Gogh who occupied my mind in the beginning.

Though, incidentally, wasn't it the linear graphs of his colored brush strokes and the clearly preserved unsmudged image of their flight that first attracted me to him?

But as yet I hadn't seen or known Van Gogh. The first healthy influence was the sharp naked contour of Olaf Gulbransson's[4] drawings.

And mountains of graphic riffraff and rubbish, like the arid PEM[5] from *Vechernaya Vremya* (the *Evening Times*) and the album *War and PEM* (full of dull Wilhelms), so loudly acclaimed during the First World War, absorbed me so uselessly at the time.

During that period I drew excessively and very badly, soiling the original correct source of inspiration with a myriad of low-quality models and a "genre" predilection for subjects, instead of an ascetic's search for form.

For some reason, I didn't learn draftsmanship. And so when I came across plaster casts, teapots, and the mask of Dante in school, I got nowhere . . .

And now it appears that recollections of my first dancing class, though creeping up here behind the sisters Amelang, are much more relevant than at first they seemed. Or rather, not so much the lessons as my total incapacity to learn from them. To this day I cannot manage to plough through a waltz, although the foxtrot, with its sharply expressive Negro aspect, I have done with great success even in Harlem, and only a short while ago I danced myself into a myocardial infarct, which laid me up for months.

But what's the point here and what's the connection?

Drawing and dance, of course, grow from one and the same source and are but two different embodiments of the same impulse.

---

4. Olaf Gulbransson (1873–1958) was a Norwegian caricaturist who contributed to the famous German satirical journal *Simplicissimus*.

5. PEM was the pseudonym of P. P. Matyunin, a Russian cartoonist.

Considerably later, after my rejection of draftsmanship and a new return to drawing, after a "paradise lost" and once again a "paradise regained" of graphic art (which I found in Mexico), I was honored with my first (and only!) press review as a graphic artist.

I have a similar single review of my acting talent, and I am inordinately proud of it. Just imagine! Not only does it say that all the performers (including myself) "scandalously overacted," but also that "they were transformed into circus acrobats"!

That was at the end of 1919, and referred to an amateur performance of engineers, technicians, and accountants of our Military Engineering Service stationed in Velikie Luki. The review was in the local paper. The review of my drawings was about fifteen years later in *The New York Times*.

In Mexico, as I said, I once more began to draw. And now in the correct linear style. The influence here was not so much Diego Rivera, who drew with thick, broken strokes, but rather the "mathematical" line, so dear to my heart, that is capable, by the varying movement of its unbroken lines, of a whole range of expressiveness.

In my early films I was also attracted by the mathematically pure movement of montage concepts rather than the "thick" strokes of the accentuated shot.

My enthusiasm for the frame, strange though it may seem, came later (incidentally, completely consistently and naturally. Remember Engels: "First attention is drawn to *movement*, and only afterward to *what* moves"[6]).

In Mexico, my drawing went through a stage of inner purification in its striving for a mathematically abstract and pure line. The effect is particularly telling when extremely sensual relationships between human figures, usually in some whimsical and odd situation, are drawn by means of this abstract, "intellectualized" line!

Bardèche and Brasillach[7] consider the basic hallmark of my creative style to be an especially powerful expression of sensualism combined with the most abstract abstractionism. A flattering comment that suits me very much.

I repeat that the influence here is not so much Diego Rivera, although he has to a certain degree synthesized all the different forms of Mexican primitivism — from the *bas-reliefs* of Chichén Itzá through primitive toys and ornamentation of utensils to the inimitable pages of street-song illustrations by José Guadalupe Posada.[8]

---

6. Eisenstein was paraphrasing, from memory, some lines from the introduction to Engels's *Anti-Dühring*.

7. Maurice Bardèche and Robert Brasillach were the authors of *Histoire du Cinéma*, published in 1935.

8. José Guadalupe Posada (1852–1913), a Mexican artist, was known for his woodcuts and illustrated broadsheets.

Here, it is a case of the direct influence of the primitives, which, in the course of fourteen months, I avidly sensed with my hands and eyes.

Or perhaps even more the Mexican landscape's amazingly pure linear structure. The rectangular white clothing of the peons. The circular contour of their straw hats. The felt sombreros of the hacienda guards.

Be that as it may, I did a lot of drawing in Mexico.

On my way through New York I met the owner of the Becker Gallery (I think it was Becker).

He was interested in my drawings and asked me to leave them with him.

Their subjects were bizarre enough; for example, the cycle *Salomé Drinking Through a Straw from the Lips of the Severed Head of John the Baptist.* In two colors with two pencils.

There was also the *Bullfight Suite,* in which this theme merged with the theme of St. Sebastian. Sometimes it was the martyrdom of the matador, sometimes of the bull. There was even a drawing of a bull crucified and pierced with arrows, like St. Sebastian.

But I am not to blame for these particular images. Mexico is to blame. For during one Sunday festival, the Blood of Christ in the cathedral's morning Mass merged with the flood of bull's blood in the afterdinner *corrida* in the city arena. The tickets for the bullfight were adorned with an image of the Madonna of Guadalupe, whose four hundredth anniversary was celebrated not only by many thousands of pilgrims and dozens of South American cardinals in scarlet robes, but also by particularly magnificent *corridas* "to the glory of the Mother of God."

Be that as it may, the drawings aroused the curiosity of Mr. Becker (or was it Mr. Brown?).

And when the ill-fated, emasculated version of the film *Que Viva Mexico!* appeared on the screen, transformed by someone's unclean hands into the pitiful jumble of *Thunder Over Mexico*, the "enterprising Yankee" exhibited these drawings in a tiny side lobby of one of the cinemas. Because of this, a note about my drawings appeared in the newspaper, and one drawing was actually sold. And I received a payment of . . . fifteen dollars.

If I find in the piles of printed cinematographic fame this unique yellowing clipping about me as a graphic artist, I shall certainly pin it to this spot. But I remember what was important in the notice, which was the testimony to the lightness with which my drawings were sketched on the paper "exactly as if they were dancing."

Drawings and dance, growing from a single impulse, here meet each other. The lines of my drawing skim along like the tracks of a dance, and in this is the key to the "mystery" of my inability to learn either dancing or draftsmanship.

The plaster casts that I drew at the entrance examinations of the Institute of Civil Engineers, and in the first course of that institute, are more repulsive than those I scrawled in high school.

B-r-r! I still remember that stuffed eagle, clawing me for months in Mr. Nilendor's[9] drawing class, as bad as the eagle who attacked Prometheus bound. And the theme of Prometheus and the eagle is one that invariably returns to my pen and pencil when I begin to festoon page after page with drawings, particularly hotel notepaper. Incidentally, there are more holes here than in any cheese. Drawings of the most telling and uninhibited frankness were torn to pieces almost immediately, and it's a pity — they were almost automatic writing. But my God! How very indecent.[10] No, those stubborn, stupid, and corpselike plaster casts were not to my taste! Perhaps because a finished drawing was supposed to have volume, shadow, half-shadows, and reflections, but a *tabu* was laid on graphic skeletons and lineal edges. But more so because there was such an inviolable, iron canon for the method of drawing from plaster casts, as in the strictness of *pas* of all those dances of my childhood and youth-hood — *pas de patiner*, when one held hands crosswise, *pas d'Espagnole*, when one had to "feel one was Spanish!" So cried another dance teacher in the Riga School: Mr. Kaulin, a Latvian with a waxed mustache and a beard, in a black frock coat with padded shoulders, short satin trousers, and black stockings and shoes. Yes-yes-yes, can you imagine?

It was in 1914. I remember this precisely, because it was from the windows of his dancing class that I saw my first patriotic torchlight procession, with roars, shouts, and portraits of the tsar.

They were still dancing the Kikapu Hiawatha (in the style of *Hacken-Spitzechen-eins-zwei-drei*, heel and toe, one-two-three) and the inevitable Hungarian czardas.

Now I know exactly what put the brakes on me then — the aridity of indestructible formulae and canons both in relation to the movement of dance and of drawing.

I understood this when, in 1921, I went to study the fox trot under the feeble fading smile of Valentine Parnakh,[11] whom I invited to teach my actors in my Moscow Proletcult Studio.

During my fox trot lessons I learned one basic thing: in contradistinction to the dances of my youth, with their strictly prescribed patterns and rotation of movement, the fox trot was a "free dance," held together only by a strict rhythm, on the framework of which one could embroider any freely improvised movement.

---

9. Nilendor was the drawing teacher in the Riga Municipal High School from 1908 to 1915.

10. This is the only time that Eisenstein admitted to his indecent drawings, which got him into trouble with Upton Sinclair. He was accused of pornography. All this is revealed in the published correspondence of Sinclair and Eisenstein, called *The Making and Unmaking of Que Viva Mexico!*, edited by Ron Gottesman and John Geduld, with Herbert Marshall as a consultant (Bloomington: Indiana University Press, 1970).

11. Valentine Parnakh (1895–   ) is a poet, translator, ballet master, and author of *Introduction to the Dance* (Moscow, 1925).

That's what suited me!

Here once more I found that captivating free running line, subordinated only to the inner law of rhythm through the free run of the hand.

To the devil with inelastic and brittle plaster of Paris, whose main use is to bind together broken limbs!

For the same reason, I could never master the tap dance. I conscientiously and hopelessly learned it by rote under the leadership of the incomparable and charming Leonid Leonidovich Obolensky, when he was still a music hall dancer and not yet the director of the notorious film *Kirpichniki*, and "connected" with Anna Sten,[12] nor yet the immutable assistant of my directorial course in GIK (beginning with GTK[13] in 1928); and never dreaming that he would one day become a monk in Rumania, where he found himself after escaping from a German concentration camp, having fallen off a truck he was trying to board during our retreat from Smolensk in 1941!

My complete inability to grasp the secret of the technique of the tap dance deprives my memoirs of some pages on how I tapped it while standing in a queue of excited males awaiting entry into the bedroom of Madame Bruno in the production of *The Good-Natured Cuckold* . . .[14]

How full of license were our productions in those years!

But, then, didn't I shove into my production of *Enough Simplicity in Every Wise Man* an Aristophanean-Rabelaisian detail? A detail (on a large scale, to say the least!) that surpassed the attributes of the Atellan mimes.[15] In this scene, I made Madame Mamayeva mount a "mast of death" — a "perch" sticking out from under the belt of General Krutitsky and reaching up to the balcony of the dance hall in Morozov's mansion on Vozdvizhenk Street, where we performed the mad spectacles of "my" Moscow Proletcult Theater!

Many years later, in that very hall, a banquet was given in honor of the recently arrived J. B. Priestley, the anniversary jubilee of the *British Ally*,[16] and the departure of the British Military Mission.

My God! I sit at the table with our honored guests, and on the very spot where our little portable platforms once stood, my actors now perform before them on a circular carpet, embroidered with the wide red band of a stylized circus barrier.

---

12. Anna Sten was an actress in early Soviet cinema who, in the 1920s, immigrated to Hollywood.

13. GTK was the Gosudarstvenny Tekhnikum Kinematografii, or State Technical School for Cinematography.

14. *The Good-Natured Cuckold*, a play by F. Crommelynk, was produced by Vsevolod Meyerhold in 1922.

15. The reference is to the *Atellanae Fabulae*, Roman farces of the first century.

16. The *British Ally* was the Russian-language journal published by the British Embassy during World War II.

And I sit on the very spot where, from a hook in the stalls, a steel cable stretched diagonally through the hall to the balcony at the other end.

On the upper wire-rope, balancing an orange parasol, in top hat and frock coat, to the accompaniment of music — moves Grisha Alexandrov.

Without a safety net.

And there was an instance when machine oil was found on the upper part of the cable.

(From a wheel on which hung Mishka Eskin,[17] going up and down the same wire-rope. He died outside our theater during a tour of the Blue Blouse Troupe,[18] when he had an accident on the railway line and his legs were cut off. What a terrible end for an acrobat! And what a wonderful acrobat and clown Mishka was!)

Grisha sweats, puffs, pants. His feet, shod in soft shiny-soled slippers, although he is gripping the wire with his big toes, begin mercilessly to skid backward.

Zyama Kitayev, our pianist, begins to repeat the music.

His feet slip.

Grisha won't make it.

Finally someone, realizing what is happening, holds out a pole to him from the balcony.

And Grisha alights safely on the balcony.

And it all seems only yesterday! . . .

Only yesterday I ran through the cellars of Morozov's mansion, through the blue-tiled kitchen, stopping my ears, striving not to think that any second now Verka Yanukova[19] will climb on the perch and that Sasha Antonov Krutitsky wasn't quite sober that evening.

Dead silence.

Everyone froze up there during the "Flight of Death" number.

Then Verka — Verochka! — finished the number and dashingly cried out, *"Voilà!"*

And, my God, how long ago that was . . .

I try to find under the table a lighter spot in the parquet floor, indicating the place where once a hook for the wire-rope had been attached.

And I realize how long ago that was only when the English general with steel-gray temples sitting beside me (he's the head of the departing British Mission) carries on polite conversation about . . . the education of children.

"I educated my sons," he says (and one of them, a giant in a droll British uniform, dances not far away, on the same parquet floor where once I studied

---

17. Mikhail Matveyevich Eskin (1903–1925) was an acrobat and actor with the Proletcult Theater.

18. The Blue Blouse Troupe was a touring drama group for agitation and propaganda.

19. Vera Dmitriyeva Yanukova (1895–1939), an actress with the Proletcult Theater, played the part of Mamayeva in *Enough Simplicity in Every Wise Man.*

under Parnakh), "to appreciate the fact that when one climbs a mountain, he eats even a dry crust of bread with relish . . ."

My God! Surely I'm not so old that I must listen to such talk, and on the very spot where I once taught — but quite differently — a whole horde of young enthusiasts, on the very spot where we sit now, climbing no mountain with puritanical slogans, but up the slope of a cable to the balcony, turning somersaults on mats, making love to each other at night on rolled-up carpets, under stage flats plastered with dried-up placards, and bringing into this very hall . . . a live camel to participate in one of my productions.

On it rode the now thriving Honored Artist Judith Samoilovna Glizer[20] in one of her roles — and certainly her first grotesque role . . .

But far worse than the tap dance were my dealings with rhythmics.

By "rhythmics," I mean that idle occupation, the teaching aftermath of that vicious system of Dalcroze. At "metric," I quite simply and inevitably fell flat both in the preliminary exams and the finals, in Meyerhold's Directors' Workshops on Novinsky Boulevard of blessed memory![21]

Good job I had other qualities; otherwise, I would have been thrown out onto the street after every exam!

And who will believe this after reading what they wrote in America, that in *Potemkin* I opened the eyes of the world to rhythm in cinematography, and that rhythm actually turns out to be one of the most powerful means used in my productions?

And so I have recorded the discovery in myself of an old-standing conflict between the free unfettered current of *all'improviso* flowing line of drawing, or the free run of the dance, subject only to the laws of the inner pulse of the design's organic rhythm, and the framework and blinkers of canons and rigid formulae.

But to mention formulae here isn't quite fair. A formula has a charm all of its own in that, expressing a fundamental law, it gives room for the free flow through it of a flood of particular interpretations, particular cases and magnitudes. There lies the charm in teaching functions in the theory of limits and differentials.

Here we touch on one of the basic themes that permeate practically all the basic stages of my theoretical researches, invariably repeating this primordial pair and the conflict of relations between its component parts. Only the particular interpretations change according to their problematics, whether it is expressive movement or the principle of the structure of form.

---

20. Judith Samoilovna Glizer (1905–   ) was a People's Artist of the Mayakovsky Theater and the wife of the famous Maxim Shtraukh.

21. The Advanced Stage Directors' Workshop was organized under the direction of V. E. Meyerhold in 1921. Eisenstein studied there until he started to work as an independent director in the Proletcult Theater in 1923.

This is not accidental.

For this contains the permeating conflict of the relationships of opposites, on which, like the ancient Chinese symbol of yin and yang, everything stands and moves.

Thus moves my work.

I create a capricious and arbitrary flood in my films. Then I endeavor to divide this flood with the dry beats of a metronome, according to its conformity with certain principles.

But even here I am always searching for a volatile method and not an inflexible canon. The favorite theme of my research remains the question of the initial "protoplasmic" element in creations and works of art and its role in the structure of perception of the form of phenomena.

It is this flood which inundates my theoretical writings when I give it free run in a myriad of deviations from my main theme, and hopelessly desiccates them when it banishes itself from their pages like those plaster casts in the art classes or the spasms of stupor I suffered on meeting the Amerlang sisters at Daragan's in Kaulin's dancing class.

To gratify that primary flow I began to write these memoirs with the sole purpose of giving myself free rein to drift in the vortices and whirlpools of free association.

And the correcting and editing of that which deserves to be printed lies alongside — shamelessly, culpably, and humiliatingly — like immovable plaster of Paris. I don't want to whitewash that which, in my rough draft, poured like a flood beyond frames and limitations!

There is pleasure also in writing this because here I am free from any categories of space and time. I do not force myself to be consistent either in describing the unfolding events or in the placing of them according to any geographic categories.

I am also free of their synthesizing brother — the strictness of the logical enduring principle of consistency in the area of judgment and disciplined thinking.

And finally, and perhaps what is most fascinating, a completely shameless narcissism, for these pages are like innumerable mirrors, in which one can look and see oneself at every age.

This is a paradise, a picture of that happy stage in our life, more beautiful than our secure childhood; that blessed stage when, lying in the first cradle of our existence and rhythmically rocking ourselves, protected and inaccessible to aggression, we dream in the warm wombs of our mothers!

First Drawings

Aᴿᴷᴬᴰʸ AVERCHENKO[1] himself rejected my drawing, haughtily, contemptuously, barking at me, "Anyone can draw like that!"

His hair was black. His face, a yellow color. A puffy face. He had a flower in his buttonhole.

Was he wearing a monocle, or was it his way of wearing pince-nez as if they were really a monocle?

My drawing really was rather poor. The head of Louis XVI in radiance above the bedstead of Nicholas II. The caption was "Easily got rid of."

Arkady Averchenko, the magazine *Satirikon*, and the theme of the drawing easily locate the episode in time.

A. F. Kerensky[2] was thundering against those who wanted to see a guillotine on Znamensky Square. (A policy that I considered a direct attack against me.) How many times, walking past the memorial to Alexander III, had I mentally measured "the Widow" — the machine of Dr. Guillotin — for its granite base? I wanted dreadfully to be a part of history! And what history could there be without the guillotine? . . .

Still, my drawing really was bad.

It first had been drawn in pencil, then outlined in ink. The ragged contours were lacking the dynamism or expressiveness of a spontaneous flow of thought or feeling.

Rubbish!

I doubt whether I would have admitted it then. To put it down to "politics"

---

1. Arkady Timofeyevich Averchenko (1881–1925), a writer and humorist, was editor of the St. Petersburg journal *Satirikon*.

2. A. F. Kerensky (1881–1970) was the prime minister of the short-lived Provisional Government, which was overthrown by the Bolsheviks in 1917.

(as self-consolation) never struck me. I put it down to "genre" and switched over to "domestic affairs."

Domestic affairs demanded a different approach. So here I was in the waiting room of the *St. Petersburg Gazette*.

After some time I was called into the holy of holies, into the office. To see "him," Khudyekov. He was tall, and he loomed, quite motionless, over the writing desk. A ring of gray hair. Puffy, reddish lids under pale bluish eyes. Narrow shoulders. A gray suit. Apart from that — he had written a big book about the ballet.

My proffered drawing was, in its draftsmanship, more daring than the previous one. Drawn straight off in ink. Without pencil and eraser. Its theme — a scuffle between militia and housewives.

"What's this? Highway robbery?" he said.

"No. The militia preserving law and order," I replied.

The militiamen wore armbands with the letters GM.[3]

I wore such an armband myself during the first days of February. Our institute had been turned into a center for the preservation of law and order as a company in the Izmailovsky Regiment.

Khudyekov nodded his head.

The drawing dropped into the tray on his desk.

Later, it appeared on a page of the *St. Petersburg Gazette*.

I was very proud. Just think of it: I had seen this organ of the press every day since my childhood, when, before giving the paper to Papa, I had greedily scanned the sensational crime columns and the daily tidbits.

Now I myself was on these illustrious pages! More than that, I had ten roubles in my pocket. The first money I had earned . . .

I submitted a second drawing on the theme of how accustomed the inhabitants of Petrograd had become to shooting. (There was shooting in the town at that time. Quite a lot of shooting.) Four small drawings in a *crescendo*. The last of them: "Citizen, it looks as if a shell has hit you!" "What? Really? Are you sure?" And half a shell was sticking out of the man's back.

Profound?

Funny? Hmm . . .

On the other hand — true to life!

I remember coming under street fire myself.

Banners were moving down Nevsky Prospekt.

Demonstrations.

I turned off into Sadovaya Street.

Suddenly, shooting.

People running.

---

3. GM were the initials for Gorodskaya Militsia (Town Militia).

I dived under an arch of Gostiny Dyor.[4]

How quickly streets empty when there is firing!

On the roadway. On the pavement. Beneath the arches of Gostiny it was just as if a jeweler's shop had been thrown out onto the paving stones.

Watches. Watches. Watches.

Pocket watches with chains.

With pendants.

With seals.

Cigar cases. Cigar cases. Cigar cases.

In tortoise shell. In silver.

With monograms and inscribed dates. Plain ones, even.

One could see the hopping run of people unaccustomed to running or unable to run.

Watches with seals flew, jolted out of waistcoat pockets.

Cigar cases out of cigar pockets.

And sticks. Sticks. Sticks.

Straw hats.

This was summer. In July. (The third or fifth of the month.) On the corner of Nevsky and Sadovaya.

Of their own accord legs carried people out of range of the machine gun. Yet there was nothing frightening about it.

We were used to it! It became a habit.

These days became historic.

The history I had so longed for and that I had so wanted to touch physically.

I re-created these days ten years later in the film *October*, when, together with Alexandrov, I stopped the traffic for half an hour at the corner of Nevsky and Sadovaya. But we did not succeed in filming the streets littered with canes and hats from scattered demonstrations (although there were people especially in the crowd to strew them about). Several thrifty old men from the volunteer crowd (I think from the Putilov factory) assiduously collected the property, on the run, in order that it shouldn't get lost! . . .

However, somehow the drawing captured the habit.

Profound or funny?

Not important!

Before me was a miracle. Himself. The boss.

Suddenly he burst out laughing.

That drawing brought me twenty-five roubles.

Not enough! Ten and twenty-five would not make forty roubles no matter how they were added. And I needed just forty because *The History of the Theaters of Antiquity,* by Lukomsky, cost exactly forty roubles. And I would not be

---

4. Gostiny Dyor was an arcade of shops in Leningrad.

able to save this thirty-five anyway. I borrowed forty roubles at home and bought *The History*, planning to widen the field of my activity considerably.

I was advised to go to see Propper.[5]

That day I simply slipped away from the School for Ensigns of the Army Corps of Engineers.

Heaven knows what had been going on in the school for several days.

Studies had ceased or went on only in fits and starts. After a delightfully tense period of training in camps — and, moreover, after romantic night patrols in rain and bad weather on the highway outside Petrograd, during the alarming days of Kornilov's attempts at an offensive — after a tense time of midcourse examinations (mines, pontoons, motors, etc.) — suddenly, for day after day, stagnation and boredom. And now this morning, on top of everything, no one was to be allowed outside the gates.

Well, that was too much! I knew a side passageway out onto Furshtadtskaya Street. And vanished into thin air . . . Better than roaming up and down our corridors . . .

I was at Propper's, and Propper's was something else entirely. I don't remember the waiting room at all. I probably was admitted very quickly. The room was very small. No Empire windows disappearing upward behind heavy curtains. A cigar between his teeth. Small, thin, and not very expensive.

In my hands I had a packet of rather virulent anti-Kerensky drawings. The subject clearly embarrassed Propper. The artist evidently attracted him. The flow of words went on ceaselessly: "You are young . . . You need money, of course . . . Come and see me the day after tomorrow . . . We'll get it all fixed up. I'll give you an advance . . ."

I came out a trifle deafened, having agreed to everything . . . Where that publishing house was, I can't remember either. Nor where I caught the tram. Or how I came to be opposite the Admiralty in the Alexandrovsky Garden.

This was where the Ninth of January had taken place.[6]

It was still quite light. Somewhere in the city there was shooting. But who paid any attention to it?! There was even a cartoon on the subject in the *Petersburg Gazette*, with the signature "Sir Gay."[7]

The tram ran along Nevsky Prospekt.

Remembering how Propper had run his cigar from corner to corner of his mouth, and how Propper himself had run from corner to corner of the small, bright room, I sat down, tired and happy to sort out the notes I had been making recently in the public library.

---

5. Stanislav Maximilianovich Propper was publisher of the *Stock Exchange Gazette* from 1887 to 1917, when the Revolution put an end to its publication.

6. January 9, 1905, a Sunday, was the day that a demonstration, headed by the agent-provocateur Father Gapon, was fired on by the tsarist police.

7. Sergei Eisenstein signed his earliest drawing with an English pseudonym, "Sir Gay."

These were notes on the eighteenth-century engraver Moreau le Jeune. I had picked up his color engraving *La Dame du Palais de la Reine* for ten roubles in a dirty packet from one of the shabbiest booksellers at the Alexandrovsky Market. Soon I had a whole series of others. And notes, painstakingly collected from the catalogues of engravings in our ancient library . . .

I spent an hour or so putting in order my notes on engravers of the eighteenth century, and went to bed.

Somewhere far off in the town there was more than the normal amount of gunfire, but all was quiet near us on Tavricheskaya Street.

As I went to bed, I pedantically recorded the date that the notes had been put in order: October 25, 1917. By the next evening that date was already history.[8]

8. The Bolshevik Revolution, known also as the October Revolution, because it took place on October 25, 1917 (on the Julian calendar), has been commemorated in the Soviet Union on November 7 since the adoption of the Gregorian calendar.

The Bridge Course

A̲T ANOTHER TIME — during the time of the civil war, I was unexpectedly sent off on military construction work as a technician to the town of Kholm in the Pskov Province, although Kholm was ninety-five kilometers from one railway and seventy from the other.

We were building fortifications there: trenches, dugouts, blockhouses . . .

While we were stationed in the environs of Velikie Luki, our unit put on some amateur productions and I acted brilliantly the part of the silent servant with the napkin in a sketch, *The Double*, from the repertoire of a prewar little theater (the Liteiny, I think).

(This was one of my very first essays in the field of amateur direction.)

I must also confess in passing how it came about that I found myself serving as a technician (even, indeed, an assistant junior works superintendent) in military construction.

This has a direct, immediate, and very considerable significance for the study of my *Lehr und Wander*[1] years as a future director.

And therefore — briefly — one more digression.

Up to the civil war I had had an interrupted education as a future ensign of military engineers.

And in a dual capacity — as this and as an incompletely educated civil engineer — I volunteered for military construction as soon as the Red Army was formed, and was put to work on the ring of defenses round Petrograd.

From the period of studying to be an ensign, I recollect marvelous borsch and buckwheat porridge at the Izhorsk camps outside the future Leningrad, wet foggy nights on patrol along the highway during the days of Kornilov's attack on the capital, the first passion for Jacques Callot, Dürer, and Hogarth, who

---

1. The phrase *Lehr und Wander* is from Goethe's *Wanderings of Wilhelm Meister*.

56

spent the night on the boards beneath my pillow, and of the splendor of pontoon-bridge laying.

I have never played in any orchestra, but I think that strange occupation draws people now to involve themselves, now to divorce themselves, from the peculiar tracery of collective action, in which there are ever-different and changing configurations of combinations of separate units — those very same amazing sensations which seize one during the process of laying a pontoon bridge.

It isn't for nothing I say that military experience also played its part and left a deep impression. No, for it determined my passion for one of the subtlest branches of our art.

What is it that fascinates the participant in the lightning-quick action of laying a pontoon bridge?

Not, of course, the carrying of the beams or decking, intended for the mighty shoulders of the amazingly fit sappers but laid on the scraggy shoulders of a student intellectual, pressing him down to the ground, even though his little shoulders are covered with great squares of thick leather with soft padding (a sort of shoulder yoke, as if parodying the not yet abolished epaulets, which now have been resurrected). And not, of course, the merrier rocking back and forth on the splashing pontoons. Nor, of course, the process of erecting delicate metal structures for the rope rails, which seemed, after the heavy carrying, like fine needlework; nor the unwieldy casting of the anchors. What amazes, inspires, takes hold of one, is something else.

The collectivism of the work, almost a collectively measured dance, uniting the movement of dozens of people in a single symphony. The steady flow of the four-sided beams, the sheets of decking laid in pairs and looking, from afar, like notebooks. The blunt nose of the bridge gradually edging out into the cross-current of the river. The pontoon's calculated shifting back and forth. The sun's rays flooding the whole moving picture of people and parts of the uncompleted bridge, merging into a single green-gray stream, cutting across the bluish-black waters at right angles.

And in this picture, the main thing is the sense of measure, the calculation of space and time, weighed to the minute and the second; the streams of people, by their ebb and flow, seem now to have become part of the clockwork of some gigantic common undertaking, then to have left it in order, once again, to take part in the general movement according to a strict program. The sense of measure of time and space, the changing movements of separate streams of people; nature and people united by the swiftly growing connecting link of technique.

The devil take it! Surely this is what lies at the basis of the merging of diverse objects of environment and people, of being and behavior, of movement and time — both in the film as a whole, and in the combination of its fragments, the montage pieces, and also in that special space-time engineering which elevates the most complex crowd *mise en scène* or the gesticulation of a character before the lens: interweaving the actions of collectives one with another, interweaving the individual act with the general action (so many seconds to bend down, so many to pick up, so many paces to walk, so much time to stand), weaving the action with calculated time, the temperament of behavior with apprehended space, gesture with word, music with the scene, the thesis with the sensual image, the ideological conclusion with emotional excitement!

The first school to teach me the art of *mise en scène* was the School for Ensigns on Furshtadtskaya Street. And in this school it was the so-called Bridge Course.

But, as should any school, it did more. And in the first place it gave me a taste for that very special, very engrossing, and quite all-embracing field, which in its initial and simplest stage is the art of *mise en scène*.

So at first the schooling I received led me not to the stages or lots of film studios, where battles were later to be planned . . . but to fortification work in the Kholm defensive region during the civil war.

Amid the motley impressions of that turbulent era there is found a tiny, fleeting impression that has nothing in common with the scale of the period and its events. Something quite accidental, taking place far from the center of the general course of those years' historic events.

Something that is not even really an event, and needs only — a very narrow bench, a village concertina, a pair of wet feet, which forced one "to get warm" by gulping down some sort of home-brewed village liquor, a trip across the river to where maidens were dancing.

I had eaten a hearty snack in a house belonging to a not yet dispossessed family of kulaks who were ready to show any expression of friendship if it would serve to keep their only son employed as foreman at the military construction site. As a student-turned-technician I was one of the chiefs and on a par with the other chiefs . . .

I slept heavily after the unaccustomed and abundant food — the first occasion on which I had eaten from the common round bowl in a peasant house.

On a narrow bench by the outside wall of the hut, I woke to a dreamlike sunset, beset by insidious sunset drowsiness. Meanwhile the maidens danced and the concertina worked itself up into a frenzy. And the other participants of our trip also worked themselves into a frenzy, stamping drunkenly on the beaten earth fronting that spacious log cabin by the silty river — slimy, smelly water, on which tossed a leaky boat, its chain and rowlocks knocking against each other . . .

In my life I have dozed a great deal in highly varied surroundings. Dying from the heat in a flat-bottomed boat, among the sharp-tailed rayfish, in the lagoons of the Campeche bird sanctuaries. Among the vines growing down the treetops, greedily sucking moisture from veinlike waterways, which allowed the tentacles of the Pacific Ocean into the impenetrable palm forests of the Oaxaca massif. In the distance gleamed the eye of a crocodile lying with its upper jaw on the mirrorlike water. I dozed, lulled by the airplane that was taking me from Veracruz to Progreso across the azure waters of the Gulf of Mexico. The even flight of flamingoes glided like pink arrows between us and the emerald surface of the gulf. Drowsiness engulfed me among the sun-scorched bushes near Izamal, bushes growing from the clefts between the countless kilometers of stones, with their peculiar carvings, once the proud cities of the ancient Toltecs, now looking as if they had been overturned and scattered by the hand of some angry giant. I dozed off over the red check tablecloths in the Negro bars of suburban Chicago. Nor could I keep my eyes open at the *bal musettes* of Paris dance halls — Los Javas, Boule, Blanche, Aux Trois Colonnes — where young workers, little older than young Gavroche,[2] waltzed so inimitably, hugging their girls and twirling round without losing contact with the floor. . .

But for some reason it was only much later, after the Pudov family's abundant food, in a chill damp sunset over a nameless river, that I tangibly experienced that strange apparition, a fantastic farandole of an independently existing gigantic nose, now a cap with a life of its own, now whole garlands of dancing figures, now a vastly exaggerated pair of ears, now separate little crosses from the embroidery on someone's Russian shirt, now a distant view of the village almost lost in the darkness, now again the overlarge tassel of blue silk cord round someone's waist, now earrings among locks of hair, now flushed cheeks . . .

Five years later, when I first tackled the peasant collective farm theme, these vivid impressions were still with me. The ear and neckline of the kulak filling the whole screen — the great nose of another, the size of a house — an enormous hand hanging helplessly, sleepily over a pitcher of kvass — a grasshopper, equal in size to a mowing machine — incessantly interweaving in the sarabande of landscapes and village genre scenes in the film *The Old and the New* . . .

---

2. Gavroche was the heroic young Parisian in Victor Hugo's *Les Misérables*.

Dvinsk

ABOUT BEDS.

World literature knows two superlative pronouncements on beds.

One is from Groucho Marx's book called *Beds*.

In this book there is a famous chapter, worthy of *Tristram Shandy*, consisting of a title on an empty white page, and the author's footnote to the heading.

The title is "The Advantages of Sleeping Alone," and the footnote reads, "The author did not wish to say anything on this subject."

The other piece belongs to de Maupassant. It is not a book, but a little essay of the same title: "Beds." In it is the delightful idea that the bed is man's truest field of activity: here he is born, here he loves, and here he dies. It is bed that is man's exclusive principality. This conquest of man's is inaccessible even to God. Gods, the essay reflects, are born in mangers and die on crosses . . .

In Dvinsk I slept on a mirror in a hurriedly evacuated apartment — after the Red Army had taken the town. There were no beds left, and camp beds were not yet available. But a mirrored wardrobe stood proudly in the empty room. This wardrobe was laid on its back, and onto the mirrored surface of its door, which reflected the world, a straw mattress was laid. And onto the mattress — me.

Heavens, how I would like to make some profound metaphor or image of this!

But nothing comes.

So let us leave me lying on a straw mattress placed between myself and the mirrored surface of a wardrobe door . . .

Books en Route

BOOKS AND ROADS. A journey through pages and a journey through mountains, fields, and steppes.

No matter whether I'm traveling to a sanatorium, from city to city, to a spa, with a film expedition on location, or just on a short trip — my primary concern is always:

what book companions will travel with me.

I am indifferent to a clash between ties and socks, between the color of a hat and the texture of a coat (if they are not in my films but on me). But when I am en route, books must harmonize with each other and be arranged as carefully as flowers in a bouquet. The choice is influenced, to a degree, by the expected landscape.

Often not to harmonize, but rather to contrast.

I don't understand poetry; have never really got into it. But the clatter of wheels and the rhythm of prose — for me that's an absolutely indispensable combination, which began very early.

My parents, as I said, separated when I was still a young child. I remained with father in Riga. My mother moved to St. Petersburg, where I would visit her each Christmas.

From a very early age they would pack me away in a train carriage in Riga and I would open my eyes in the morning in Petersburg.

I would always take books with me, to read.

My first companion was *Viy*, by Gogol. My first railroad reading — his stories: "The Old-World Landowners," "Ivan Ivanovich and Ivan Nikiforovich," "The Bewitched Spot," and, of course, "The Terrible Vengeance," in an illustrated edition by Pavlenkov. As a special supplement to the book — a small bag of hard candies either greenish and translucent, like onyx, called Duchess, or tiny multicolored ones known as Malyutka. I would often fall asleep with a book in my hands and a candy in my mouth. In the morning there would be a kind of pinching sensation behind my cheek where the hard candy had slowly melted through the night.

Journeys and books are inseparable.

Already in the civil war I always see myself with a book, no matter where I travel with my military construction unit. Here I am in Novosokolniki with Schopenhauer in the shade, beneath a boxcar of our troop train, waiting for our echelon to be switched to a different track. There is a nice cool breeze under the car, and the paragraphs from a tiny German edition of *Parerga and Paralipomena* settle down neatly in my memory. And there, stowed right alongside, are the *Theater Notes* of Kleist[1] and Immermann.[2]

Kleist's words on true organic movement are packed with feeling right here: "True organic movement can be achieved only by marionettes or demigods." (Organic in the sense of a mechanism answering all the laws of nature and the law of gravitation above all.)

The teaching on "supermarionettes" by Gordon Craig or the first two or three attitudes of biomechanics[3] point in the direction first indicated by Kleist.

On a journey of many days along the River Desna from Dvinsk glide our unit's two barges, heavily laden with military construction materials.

Among the crates, sacks, shovels, and pickaxes, I see myself bent over a tiny book. The author — Bibliophile Jacob[4] — whom we know well by his heavy red and gold-tooled tomes, dedicated to different eras of culture and costume in France.

The engravings and colored lithographs of these volumes are dry, badly executed, and soulless. The inimitable spirit of the epoch, preserved in sculpture, in Gobelin tapestries, in embroidered pictures, in carved ivory, has faded away from the lines of the costumes, from the rhythm of composition of the figures, from their proportions.

Perhaps even worse are the innumerable volumes of *The History of Costume* by Racine, from which also it is impossible to deduce the movement or the character of the people or their manner of wearing the costume or their gait.

One can study costumes only from reproductions of original paintings, sculptures, sarcophagi, and miniatures, and not by these castrated illustrations.

Yet Jacob's text is good, and his explanations intriguing. As literature the books are also dry, angular, and do not convey the vivacity and living spirit of the past. But as information about the past they are fascinating . . .

---

1. Heinrich von Kleist (1777–1811) was a German dramatist and novelist.
2. Karl Leberecht Immermann (1796–1840), a writer, was founder of the Düsseldorf Theater and was its director from 1835 to 1838.
3. Biomechanics was Meyerhold's system of body training for actors.
4. Bibliophile Jacob was the pen name of Paul Lacroix (1806–1884), an author of historical novels and histories of French costume.

Our barge moves. Ahead is the point where we will have to build a bridge and fortify its approaches. I am lost in the story of *le pont ancien* that falls into the Seine, taking with it the tiny houses and shops that had nestled on it, as on most bridges of the past (for example, the Ponte Vecchio in Florence). A new bridge has appeared in its place, the romantic and dazzling Pont Neuf.

My God! How many romantic impressions are connected with it! Here Dumas's musketeers fought with drawn rapiers. Somewhere on this bridge the cry of Tabarin[5] was heard: "Why does a dog lift its leg?" Here quacks pulled teeth and "witch doctors" sold their elixirs.

Obliquely opposite from it — the Bouridan Tower. I fell in love with it not long ago in an etching by Jacques Callot. In the center, an equestrian statue of Henry IV. How many mysterious, cape-clad figures, in wide-brimmed hats, meet here in the moonlight on the pages of novels! Here flitted Arsène Lupin.[6] Here with firm steps passed Javert.[7] And here stands the shadow of Fantomas.[8] Here, too, the heroes of Paul Féval.[9] Here are Rocambole and Captain Fracasse.[10] Here passed the inhabitants of Cour des Miracles to their haven.[11]

Still preoccupied by this replacement of old bridges by new . . .

I find myself dashing along the river bank, leveling the approach to our new bridge, which is being built from opposite banks of the Desna. The construction chief races back and forth across the river in his launch. From midstream the mighty voice that issues from this stooped figure in high boots and engineer's cap hits both banks at once with a thunderous fusillade of curses:

"Hey, you! Engineer! Rat-a-tat-tat! Why in hell aren't the slopes ready?"

Engineer — that's me. A very poor one indeed! A much too romantic engineer, with a head full of fifteenth-century Paris — a rather untimely preoccupation, under the circumstances.

Several years later this same engineer will climb the supports of the Palace Bridge in Leningrad and discuss with the bridge operators the possibilities of raising it several times within the alloted half-hour when the bridge is scheduled to be up, from six o'clock to six-thirty in the morning.

It is six-ten before the sun reaches the right position. At six-thirty sharp the bridge must be down. Otherwise, the arrival of streetcars at the Finlandsky

---

5. Tabarin was the name used by Jean Salomon (1564–1633), a charlatan who, in addition to selling quack medicines, performed street farces.

6. Lupin was the name of the Gentleman Thief in the novels of Maurice Leblanc.

7. Javert was the detective in Victor Hugo's *Les Misérables*.

8. Fantomas was a character in the adventure stories of Marcel Allain.

9. Paul Féval (1817–1887) was a novelist and playwright.

10. Rocambole appeared in the novels of Pierre Alexis Ponson du Terrail (1829–1871). Captain Fracasse was the eponymous hero of a novel by Théophile Gautier (1811–1872).

11. The Cour des Miracles, the quarter of Paris that served as a sanctuary for beggars and cripples, is in Hugo's *The Hunchback of Notre Dame.*

Railroad station will be delayed and the commuters from the suburbs will be late for their factories. We know that only too well.

On the last day of shooting we take advantage of the slackened vigilance of the operators, who, so absorbed in what was going on above, keep the jaws of the bridge open for ten extra minutes. And oh, what a scandal it causes! Disruption of work, lateness. The arguments, the troubles!

But honestly, who can blame us? After all, twenty minutes a day is nothing when, during that time, we had to: kill a white horse galloping wildly and pulling a buggy; let a young, golden-haired girl fall down into the river; let the bridge start separating; let the golden strands of her hair stretch across the widening gap; let the dead horse and carriage dangle from the edge of the raised bridge before the carriage plunged downward . . .

On the screen, all of it will flash past in less than twelve minutes. But to film it takes hours!

Day after day, in "spoonful doses" of twenty minutes, we hammer out, link by link, the montage fragments for the scene, which climaxes the July 3–5 massacre sequence on the corner of Sadovaya and Nevsky Prospekt.

It must have been God's will that prompted me one early dawn, after an all-night session of shooting interiors of Tsar Nicholas's library, to look out the window and see the gigantic jaws of the Palace Bridge raised to the sky like the arms of a drowning man. And all at once, there on the blades of the bridge appeared the vision of the battered buggy and the wounded horse, and the golden sunbeams playing on it became the strands of a dying girl's golden hair.

That is why the ex-engineer was crawling inside the mechanical bowels of the Palace Bridge and calculating with its operators how to maintain a certain rhythm and tempo in raising the bridge, resulting in one of the most powerful scenes in *October*.

Later, the bridge grew into a symbol. The symbol of separation between the center of the city and its working-class suburbs. Both in a direct tactical sense and in the sense that, in July 1917, the working masses were not yet firmly grouped around the organizing nucleus of the Bolsheviks.

This in turn brings to mind, for the start of the October uprising, the picture of another bridge, a neighbor of the Palace Bridge — the Nikolayevsky. The historic battleship *Aurora* was anchored alongside, especially dispatched to us from Kronstadt to take part in the reconstruction of the historical events.

The Nikolayevsky Bridge swivels horizontally.

The idea is that the sharp switch that closes the gap between the two ends of the bridge, and so connects the suburbs with the city (despite orders from the Provisional Government to keep all bridges open), starts the avalanche of events that change the course of history forever.

According to the plan, even the small Bankovsky Bridge over the Krukov

Canal, with its gilded griffins, had a part to play. It would repeat, but as a parody, the idea of unity and solidarity. In the center of this bridge the giant figure of a sailor would suddenly appear — a brother of those who closed the Nikolayevsky Bridge and the Baltic descendant of the Black Sea sailors who brought *Potemkin* through the Admiralty blockade. He would merely raise his powerful fist, and the procession of elderly citizens, the last stronghold of reaction, with Mayor Schreider at their head, would turn to flight.

Noisy and brash, they march to the Winter Palace in support of their ideological representatives — the "ten capitalist ministers," forsaken by Kerensky, who flew the coop. But in their flight they resemble wet chickens, as they scurry in panic, past the indifferent griffins, across the narrow bridge between Kazan Cathedral and the state bank. They are as pitifully insignificant as the size of this tiny bridge in comparison with the sweep of the Troitsky or Liteiny, the Palace or Nikolayevsky Bridge, across which pours, from beyond the Neva working-class districts, a never-ending stream of the victorious pro-letariat.

Thus, an accidental early-dawn impression of a raised bridge became an image, grew into a system of images, developed into a symbol of two out-stretched arms locked in a firm handshake, and finally evolved as a pivotal structure in the total conception of the film.

Unfortunately, overloaded with details and lacking time, we were prevented from giving final form to the film by editing; and it hides this structure so much that it escapes the analysis of even those who consider *October* more important than *Potemkin*.

That eternal curse of film-making — the mad rush — simply ruined another one of my bridges — the Novgorod Bridge in *Alexander Nevsky*, which was the locale for the famous fistfight between two districts of the ancient city, the Sofiasky and the Torgovy.

The scene was important for the romantic line of the plot, for it records the first meeting between Vasilisa and Vaska Buslai. At the peak of the fight, Vaska suddenly shouts, "What a beauty!" to which Vasilisa replies with a resounding slap in his face.

I regret the loss of the romantic encounter of my two heroes. I also feel very sad about those plucky young fellows, who, in the chilly month of October, repeatedly had to plunge off that bridge into the cold water of the Moscow film studio pond, where the bridge "across the Volkhov" had been constructed.

But what saddens me most is that the entire scene had to be chucked into the waste-film bin. In the rush to meet our deadline we were unable to take the time to realize fully, through montage and sound-editing, all the potentialities of the scene.

Will the importance of time in film-making ever be understood? Not just the seconds or minutes of screening time, but the hours of creative work at the cutting table, the days of sound-recording, the weeks of polishing? A finished film is born in the complex process of an audiovisual counterpoint, and it is precisely during this stage that the weaving of the most delicate living and organic tissue of the film takes place . . .

Curiously enough, my interest in the principle of counterpoint, as a combination of limitless, independent, separate actions woven into a strict structure of time, was first prompted by certain structural problems I had to solve in building bridges.

Many years ago during my training at the Ensigns' School at Izhorsk we were constructing pontoon bridges across the Neva.

Shortly after the summer camp, our entire school stood guard on a dark misty street in Petrograd, with rifles ready, to defend one of the approaches to the city against an imminent attack from the Kornilov hordes and the "Savage Division." And even then, there was a book in my army coat pocket, on the side opposite my holster. I remember it was Dürer's *Journals*, brought along, just in case. Near our position was a concealed shack to which we would run from time to time to warm up a bit.

While building sets for *Alexander Nevsky*, in order to get a bridge of adequate length we built it across the studio pond on a diagonal. Oddly enough, it wasn't logic that suggested this solution, but a memory!

A bridge that, contrary to logic and nature, spans a river at an angle, does exist; a covered bridge I saw in the city of Lucerne. Any traveler through Switzerland cannot help being charmed and amazed by this bridge, which is not only oblique but also features rows of oil paintings suspended from the roof on either side!

No one was able to explain its curious position. I teased my Swiss friends by suggesting that the bridge that had been built was evidently too long, and when it was laid across the river, this was the only way it would fit. Then I forgot all about it until it came to me when I was already working on *Alexander Nevsky* . . .

However, let us return to our temporary bridge across the Desna, which is perfectly straight, though a bit wavy in profile. This happens because the river bottom is not uniform and the supports sink down unevenly in different places.

And there is reason for this subsidence, as we young soldiers were to discover.

During the night we are awakened by a tremendous din.

The clanking of gun carriages rolling down the slope. A rattle of ammunition boxes and the clatter of cannon on the bridge. A crashing noise! Voices shouting in the darkness. Confusion!

One span of the bridge collapsed. It seems that it wasn't built for retreat, but for orderly advance, and suddenly a panicked army attempts to rush over it at night.

Fortunately, this time we don't have to depend on inexperienced local hands; we have skilled sappers to do the work. In total darkness they rebuild the section. Glimpses of backs, axes, logs. And the black stream of the retreating army once again pours across the river, the surface of which is paling under the light of an early dawn, while against a fallen tree I leaf through the pages of Maeterlinck's play *La Princesse Maleine*.

It has been decided to reinforce our present position with another circle of trenches and barbed wire. Now the local citizens diligently dig in the sand, anxiously waiting for the return of the troops, who had retreated through here during the night.

La Princesse Maleine in no way interferes with my role as supervisor. I argue, explain, yell, give orders, and swear vulgarly.

Nevertheless, my subordinates and I are on the best of terms. Aside from a few refusals to work, there have been no labor troubles between us, but one of those who does complain is a puny young brunet in smoked pince-nez who wears a white pinstripe suit and an old-fashioned straw hat with a striped ribbon. He is terribly thin and there is an odd jerkiness to his movements. Probably a malingerer. Still, I assign him to light duties, counting planks or something else of that nature.

It never entered my head to make fun of his white suit. But my colleagues told me laughingly that it was considered usual to give people in white dirty work, like unloading coal or mucking around with axle grease. If they wore black suits, then they had to unload chalk or flour.

Among those sent to help us we even get the local village idiot. A bearded man with uncommonly short legs and a very tall hat. True to the literary cliché, he is followed by a gang of taunting boys.

Without understanding their dialect, I suspect they are egging him on to jump into the river.

Sure enough! He jumps in and begins to imitate a duck flapping its wings. He is a smash hit!

Overall, however, the population proves to be peace-loving, frightened, and confused.

Elsewhere it was worse.

Near Dvinsk, they mobilized all the prostitutes. In the trenches these ladies lifted their skirts and cried out that they also had days off, when they did not "work." During a lull they came forward and propositioned, lounging along the parapets, and afterward took away the whole of the eligible but small male contingent into the bushes. . .

My own contingent swarms diligently around the roots of the pine trees and even expresses some interest in how to shore up with the planks the seeping sandy walls . . . Surely, neither the Princesse Maleine nor little Tintagiles[12] ever expected to find herself in such surroundings. But then, could Maeterlinck ever

---

12. Tintagiles is in Maeterlinck's play *La Mort de Tintagiles*.

have dreamed that in his venerable old age he would have to abandon all his possessions and flee from the Nazis in a tiny rowboat, with only a cage and two little bluebirds? He did, and the poor refugee from Belgium and his bluebirds later found asylum in Hollywood . . .

A few weeks later. Again, a barge. A changeover, and then the town of Polotsk . . .

This time — *The Memoirs of Saint-Simon*. Not Saint-Simon the Utopian, but Saint-Simon the charming stylist and chronicler of the eighteenth century.

Interestingly, the portraits of Louis XIV's family and courtiers, drawn with such poetic sensitivity, irony, and sharp insight, did not harmonize with the incongruous surroundings of the grimy, shabby houses and crooked streets of the town of Polotsk.

The only thing that has anything in common with it is the Baroque architecture of the Roman Catholic Church.

My new construction foreman also turns out to be a lover of literature. But his taste runs more toward Boussenar,[13] Stevenson, and Xavier de Montépin.[14] With terrifying energy, his shovel, for hours on end, tears apart the cave beneath the ancient church. It is a narrow, moldy corridor with walls that drip water. Slippery stones are under foot. A slushy, sucking sound comes from the shovel when it by-passes the stones and finds itself deep in the liquid muck. This scene, illuminated by the flickering light of a kerosene lantern, is like an illustration for Nat Pinkerton or a "Leichtweis Cavern" book jacket. Not counting the flood of sweat and the torn shirts, all the ingredients are here, except for the treasure hidden in the bowels of the church, which my assistant has learned of from some frightened citizen's whispered rumor. But no Polish Cortéz or Captain Kidd ever buried his treasure here. No, there is no evidence of any florins or doubloons, or goblets or golden candelabra. Besides, there is no time for further digging. Our equipment has already been loaded and we are moving on . . .

The dynamiting of some old German trenches, abandoned during the absurd Kerensky offensive in July of 1917 — I direct in the company of Henrik Ibsen.

But I never have enough time. So many dramatists I don't know. *Rosmersholm* and Cardinal Niklas from *The Pretenders*, Solness in *The Master Builder* and Dr. Stockman are still among my liabilities.

---

13. Louis Boussenar (1847–1910) was a writer of popular novels.

14. Xavier de Montépin (1823–1902) wrote many novels and melodramas of low literary standard.

Sergei Mikhailovich Eisenstein, 1926

The Early Years

Eisenstein as "a well-behaved boy" in Riga

Eisenstein with his mother, Yulia Ivanovna, and his father, Mikhail Osipovich

An exemplary report card on the young Eisenstein in 1909-1910. A "5" represents the highest possible score.

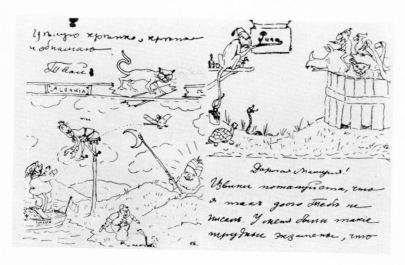

Relieved to be out of school for the summer, the young Eisenstein sent this fancifully embellished letter to his mother.

Automobile, 1908

Roller skater, 1908

SOUVENIR D'ENFANCE

*Eisenstein's drawing
of one of the clowns
so dear to him in his
childhood*

*A sequence of drawings by
Eisenstein on "The War
of 1914"*

Eisenstein's design for a Proletcult theater production of "Heartbreak House," 1922

Costume design for Boss Mangan, "Heartbreak House," 1922

Design for "Macbeth," 1921

The great director Meyerhold, Eisenstein's mentor
and teacher

A self-caricature in Moscow in 1920

Eisenstein during the Proletcult theater period

Sketches of Russian life and characters

With his first major film, "Strike," Eisenstein's innovative cinematic genius is already evident in these stills.

Stills from "Strike"

Eisenstein editing his first masterpiece, "Battleship Potemkin"

Eisenstein making-up for his role as a priest in "Potemkin"

One of the numerous posters for "Battleship Potemkin"

The critical moment in history and art. A sequence of stills from "Battleship Potemkin."

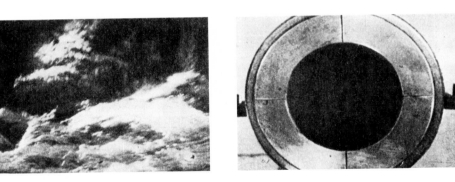

Eisenstein (seated, center) with the cast and crew of "Ten Days That Shook the World"

With Douglas Fairbanks (center) and his cameraman, Tisse (left), in Moscow in 1926

On Bones

WHAT IS BEFORE US looks like one of the dead cities of Rider Haggard. But what lies at the approaches to its walls has not yet been celebrated in any epic tale.

No human foot has trodden here for three years.

The Germans have left.

The population has not returned.

The ramparts were burned or completely destroyed by the German artillery.

We have been ordered to blow up the abandoned positions on which Kerensky's attack of July 1917 foundered, for a new invasion by the Poles is expected, and the positions must be destroyed.

Suddenly, there they are before us — those strange installations! At one moment they seem a dead and deserted Bruges,[1] from which the waters had receded many kilometers, killing the life of the rich seaside town. A dead Bruges, buried waist-deep in earth . . .

At another moment, they look like the underground dead city of Karakhoto,[2] which the Russian traveler Kozlov discovered; a Karakhoto half-emerging from those Mongolian caverns and letting its galleries run free.

They seemed like narrow Asiatic streets running and intersecting Gothic lanes. Their complex structures lifted high by a chain of mounds, but their open spaces biting deep into the body of the mounds.

---

1. In the thirteenth century Bruges was a center of world trade. It flourished until the late fifteenth century, when the Zwyn, which connected it to the North Sea, silted up, stranding the former port.

2. The Russian explorer of Central Asia, Peter Kuzmich Kozlov (1863–1935), during an expedition in 1909 discovered in the Gobi Desert the remains of the ancient city of Karakhoto. In 1923 he published a book on his archaeological excavations and discoveries.

Thin wire, like chain mail, winds across the slopes of the German trenches. Like curved breastplates, the semicircular, corrugated iron arches over the underground roads.

Rusty rails and small railroad wagons.

Concrete blockhouses shut in by the creaking visor of shutters.

Tiny windows closed in by bluish glass with wire veins.

Throw a stone at it. Cracks run in a star across the glass.

The steel nerves hold on tenaciously to the fragments of safety glass. And the stone drops back helplessly before them.

Like white bones, a pile of prefabricated concrete posts lies in the grass, and a broad, rusty, barbed belt in three layers curls along the sinister hillocks. The farthest, the outermost one, is scarcely off the ground; the middle one, chest-high, is aimed at the heart; and the most dreadful is the nearest.

In immense coils it forms loops of toothed barbed wire. And there is no escape, no way out for anyone who, having tripped over the first, tearing his chest open on the second, falls into the clutches of this third deadly belt.

The rusty snake twangs its coils in the wind.

And all around — not a soul.

If only a bird would fly past.

If only a field mouse would run by.

Nothing!

We climb carefully down through the descending belts of wire. What is that, gleaming white at the foot of the wire web? They are not concrete posts. They are not metaphors.

— Bones . . .

Vesuvius sent streams of lava and clouds of ash down on Herculaneum and Pompeii. And in the layers of that sediment all the diversity of life, caught unawares, was petrified. Freed layer by layer from the solidified streams, there unfolds a picture of life, stopped in its tracks . . .

And so it is here, under the open (too open) sky in this field near Dvinsk: a frozen picture of a senseless attack; men launched by the wave of the hand of a hysterical maniac to a certain death.

For three years no foot has trodden here.

For three years no bird has flown here.

For three years rain has poured here, frosts have come and gone.

The bones lie.

"Washed by the rains . . ."

Covered by snow.

Then spring comes again. And they bleach like canvas under the rays of the burning summer sun.

Skin and cloth have rotted away. Flesh and muscles have rotted away. Eyes and hair have vanished. Ribs laid bare. Only bones are left . . .

The skeletons lie in an immense fresco of a frozen *danse macabre*. Belt buckles have remained whole. Epaulets. Individual packets of pink bandages. Little tin ikons. The smaller sapper spades. Here and there the peaks of caps . . .

Go to Death Valley in California and you will see endless phalanxes of bones of fallen horses, oxen, and buffalo. They lie in shapeless heaps only their general outlines echoing the tracks lost among the cracks in the dry ground.

Here the spectacle is different. A soft green sward covers the earth, so that the frozen bones lie, as if on velvet, just as the bodies fell in the attack.

Each skeleton is an individual drama within the sweep of the overall tragedy. These two, bent double, are trying to dig in; beside their hands are spades. But they succeeded only in cutting the first turf before dropping on the spot. You can even see, by the way his spine is bent, that one was hit in the stomach.

Here is a skeleton lying on his back, arms outstretched in a St. Andrew's Cross. Here is one entangled in the wire. And here is another, bent to one side. He is especially ghastly, for he has no head. We find the head thirty or forty feet away.

Out of a boggy pit sticks half a torso, and nearby . . . the legs. A bluish-gray mist like cigarette smoke creeps in a watercolor erosion between them, eternally frozen . . .

Few have seen such a battlefield. Like a special preserve, untouched. Like a graveyard, inviolable. Like the memory of a great drama, imperishable. But tomorrow these strongholds of the German military will disappear forever in the thunder of explosions . . . And then that which opposed it is revealed still more horribly.

What are these, carelessly uncovered graves? No — our trenches, littered with rotten leaves.

Thus died at Dvinsk, Mukden, on the approaches to Kars and Erzerum, our supremely heroic Russian soldiers — robbed, betrayed, deceived. Thus they fell in the criminally absurd offensive of 1917.

But I myself suffer a defeat on Dvinsk's field of death. Do the fuses misfire? Are the charges of gun-wadding insufficiently strong? Does the stubbornness of the concrete emplacements exceed calculations? Nothing of that sort!

The earth bursts into the air as it should, solicitously filling up the trenches and machine-gun nests, leaving behind an inarticulate jumble of concrete, rails, net, and wire. No, my defeat is not on the battlefield. It is on a sheet of paper, where I try to set down these skeletons in terrible and indelibly foreshortened delineations.

One of the inducements in writing these notes is the minimum of stylistic adjustments and corrections I force myself to make.

I shuffle and reshuffle the rows of bones, skeletons, and ribs as if they were cards, but they will not settle into a frightening or terrifying design.

I shuffle and reshuffle . . .

The field remains engraved on the memory by virtue of its frozen horror.

But no matter how much they are shuffled, those bones will not settle into horror on paper. It won't work. It doesn't come off . . .

It doesn't work either when I cart a truckload of real bones and skulls to the shore of Pereslavl Lake and spend hours shifting them about, carrying them back and forth, scattering them across the pock-marked green slope.

"Oh, field, field, who has littered you . . ."

Having conceived the prologue to *Alexander Nevsky* as a panorama of fields littered with the "dead bones" of those who had fallen in the battle with the Tartars for Russian soil, I could not help remembering that field near Dvinsk. I ordered a pile of human and horse skeletons and from their elements carefully tried to lay out on the grass a horizontal fresco of the frozen battle. I remembered the skeleton with arms and legs outstretched in a St. Andrew's Cross. One I skewered with a lance, by the side of a shield. One skull lay in a helmet. Another stuck out from a collar of chain mail. Not a damn thing looked right!

It looked revoltingly "posed" to the eye, and completely unconvincing on the screen. The skeletons on the screen looked like white monkeys, parodying live people. I threw them out in the wastebasket. I left only those which protruded at an angle, spontaneously, from the grass. And I spared the two initial skulls. I am sorry that I spared them. Their whiteness didn't look "washed by the rains," but more like a china pot. (The late Alexei Tolstoy taunted me, saying that these were not skulls, but ostrich eggs!) What was the reason?

Part of the failure lies, of course, in the fact that these accurately separated bones had come from an anatomical museum. But . . . though there are all the bones you want on these pages, they will not settle into a frightening combination, no matter what!!

I have been attracted by bones and skeletons since childhood. An attraction amounting to a sort of malady.

Any one of our actions is always determined, of course, by a whole bundle of motives.

But among the cluster of motives there is always one, usually the wildest, most impractical, illogical, often ridiculous, and very often quite irrational secret, which, however, decides everything.

"Wie Sag' Ich's Meinem Kind?"

AND SO. THERE YOU HAVE IT. My passion to teach is very curious. I've devoted many years to work in the GIK. It was partial compensation during the years, following the Mexican trauma, when I could not make films. My most intensive "teaching period" was from 1932 to 1935.

It was then that Volume I on film direction was blocked out. But I have been teaching since 1920, when I was just beginning to grope for knowledge myself. And by 1930 I was already well known even abroad. Colleagues in America asked me in bewilderment: "How can one teach others? They'll grow up and you'll soon be out of a job! We can't try to teach others. If we should even start to think about what we're doing and how to do it, we try not to think about it when someone else is around. But you keep teaching, writing, and publishing!"

I am not going to examine here the social peculiarities of the approach to this problem from the point of view of a Soviet citizen. Nor the fact that we have enough work for very, very many film directors and that there are not enough of them. But I shall give you the basic slogan that has always guided my pedagogic work.

Whether in live contact with students, in published essays on principles I've come across, or in the exposition of methods and the peculiarities of the method of our art and of art in general, my slogan has been, is, and presumably always will be: "Tell all. Hide nothing. Make no secrets of anything."

A question immediately arises: Is not this very slogan, this position, this now long-established practice the sharpest of rebuffs to Papa? To Papa, who hid "secrets" from me; to Papa, who didn't initiate me in them, allowing me to drift with the current and in one way or another drift onto a discovery of the facts of life.

Of course, throwing someone into the water is one way to teach swimming, even if it is a method more suitable for a puppy than for a boy.

The fact that pups have been a family joke of the Eisensteins since before my birth, right up to my professorship, can't serve as a complete justification for applying this method to me!

Sasha Fantalov, a distant cousin of my mother's, said to her, after my parents' marriage, "Well, Yulenka, now you're married. And you'll be having Eisen-pups."

I usually recall Sasha Fantalov (I got to know him a little later, and loved him very much) when I begin my course every year. In my interpretation it sounds more academic and a trifle unctuous.

After the usual "one cannot be taught — one can only teach oneself" I usually tell my students that I'm interested in arming them with the objective facts of our experience so that each will be able to go his own way.

I have no wish for followers of my stylistic manner. "It is no part of my task to bring forth . . . Eisen-pups." This always goes down well. And no pups have been brought forth, incidentally.

Another academic expression that has always met with approval, particularly during the years of persecution against formalism, runs: "It's a mistake to call a man a formalist because he's interested in problems of form. There's as much justification for this as there is in calling a man a syphilitic because he's studying syphilis."

Childish resentments lie deep. And a reply to them takes various forms. However, I think this fact alone, concerning Papa and his puppy method of bringing me up, would still have been insufficient for shaping my attitude toward educating the young.

A foundation had been laid here. But I had to encounter almost the same situation again, in a new aspect, before I could base a principle and method on this foundation. In other words, this would not have happened if I had not met "the seal of secrecy" for a second time, and concerning a problem no less passionately demanding than that hidden by Papa.

Apart from one's physical father, one always finds on the highways and byways a spiritual father. This statement by itself is the most banal truism, but a fact remains a fact. Sometimes they coincide — and this is not too good; more often they are different. God's will determined that in regard to "secrets," my spiritual father should be the same as my physical father and, when questioned about art, be just as silent.

Mikhail Osipovich [Eisenstein] was eternally evasive when it came to questions about the secrets of biology. Vsevolod Emilievich [Meyerhold] was still more evasive about questions dealing with the secrets of the art of play direction. Possibly because of the biblical injunction, I'm ashamed to admit I didn't feel any special love toward Mikhail Osipovich. However, the Bible demands basically that one should honor one's parents: "Honor thy father and thy mother that thy days may be long upon the land." A dubious reward, incidentally. And anyway, what are parents to be honored for? . . . We shall go no further. This may all be printed someday. And such thoughts could prejudice . . . an American edition!

However that may be, it was natural for me to lavish my adoration on my second father. And I must say, of course, that I never loved, idolized, worshipped anyone as much as I did my teacher.

Will one of my lads say that about me one day? No. And the matter lies not in my pupils and me, but in me and my teacher. For I am unworthy to undo the straps of his sandals (even though he wore felt boots in the unheated theater workshop on Novinsky Boulevard). Until I reach extreme old age I shall consider myself unworthy to kiss the dust from his feet, although his errors as a person have evidently swept away forever from the pages of our theatrical history the footprints of the greatest master of our theater.

It is impossible to live without loving, worshipping, being carried away by someone — and he was an astounding person, a living contradiction of the statement that genius and villainy cannot coexist in one person. Fortunate was he who came into contact with him as a magician and wizard of the theater; unfortunate was he who depended on him as a person. Fortunate was he who could learn by watching him; unfortunate he who went to him trustingly with a question.

Once I myself went naïvely to him with a series of questions about concealed difficulties. It was extraordinary to see how, on Vsevolod Emilievich's aquiline face, with its piercing gaze, astoundingly molded lips under the rapaciously curved nose, Mikhail Osipovich's expression suddenly recurred. A glassy look, which shifted right and left, then became infinitely withdrawn, then officially polite, just a trifle mocking in its sympathy, then hanging over the question ironically as if at a loss: "Well, now, how strange! Mm . . . yes."

I can say with certainty how the expression "spit in his eye" came to be born, but this did not affect my love and worship. (Buddhists spit chewed prayer-paper at the graven images of their idols!) It was just that a very great sadness filled my soul.

I was unlucky with my fathers . . . Meyerhold's lectures were like insidious songs: "He who these songs hears, will everything forget . . ."[1] It seemed as though Sirin was on his right, Alkonost on his left.[2] He waved his arms. His eyes flashed. In his hands was a Javanese marionette. The master's golden hands moved the little gilded arms of the puppet. The little white face with its slanting

---

1. The words are from the song of the Sirens in the *Odyssey*.

2. Sirin and Alkonost, fairy-tale birds with human faces, are often depicted in Russian folk art.

eyes twisted to right and left. And now a puppet had brought to life Ida Rubinstein,[3] whose profile we remembered from Serov's portrait. And in Meyerhold's hands it was not a marionette, but Ida Rubinstein in *Pisanella*.

Throwing his hands up sharply, Meyerhold conjures up cascades of sparkling cloth in the seaside market scene on the boards of the Opéra in Paris. The hands freeze in the air . . . And the imagination conjures up the final "Waxworks" scene from *The Inspector-General*. There stand the waxwork dolls, and those who sparkled the whole evening in their images on the stage whirl past them in a wild dance. The inimitable master stands there like Gogol in silhouette. Now his hands have dropped . . . And we sense the very faintest applause from kid-gloved hands, signifying the approval of the guests after Nina's song in *Masquerade*,[4] on the Alexandrinsky stage on the eve of the February Revolution in 1917.

Suddenly the sorcerer breaks the thread of enchantment! In his hands are sticks of gilded wood and a piece of colored cloth. The king of the elves has vanished, and at the desk sits the lifeless archivist Lindhorst.

His lectures were mirages and dreams. The listener would jot down something feverishly. But on waking up, he would find "the devil knows what" in the notebooks. One can recall in the finest detail how brilliantly Aksyonov[5] analyzed *The Merchant of Venice*, what he said about *Bartholomew Fair* and the triple plots of the Elizabethan dramatists. But one cannot remember what Meyerhold *said*. Aromas, colors, sounds. A golden haze over everything. Elusiveness, intangibility, secret upon secret, veil behind veil — not seven of them, but eight, twelve, thirty, fifty!

With their various nuances, they flutter around the secrets in the magician's hands, but strangely. It still seems as if the wizard has been filmed in reverse motion. The romantic "I" listens, enchanted, absorbed. The rational "I" grumbles to itself. (It had not yet been to America and therefore does not taunt by calling this dance of interminable veils a "strip-tease" that has gone on too long. "Strip-tease" is an American variation on the dance of the seven veils: an auction in which the public is sold the hat and cloak, dress and underslip, unmentionables and brassière from off the live girl. And then a bow, a second and third, ribbons, strings of pearls, hiding the last isle of modesty. The audience yells, shouts, storms. But beneath the bow is a bow, beneath the ribbon, another ribbon, beneath the string of pearls . . . Darkness cuts the spectacle short . . .) The third "I" is the most patient of all.

The subconscious "I." The same third "I" from Evreinov's play *The Theater*

3. Ida Rubinstein (1895–1960) was the Russian-born actress for whom Gabriele d'Annunzio wrote *Pisanella*. It was produced by Meyerhold, with décor by Léon Bakst, at the Théâtre Châtelet in Paris in 1913.

4. *Masquerade* is a play by Lermontov.

5. Ivan Alexandrovich Aksyonov (1884–1934) was a writer, translator, and theater historian.

of the Soul,[6] from which I have borrowed the first two characters: the emotional "I" and the rational "I." In Evreinov, the subconscious "I" waits. Waits until the emotional "I," having played on the nerves, plucks the strings in the depths of the stage fringed with drapes for lungs and a regularly beating red bag of a heart near the flies, smothers its rational opponent — and the rational "I" rings up the brain on a little telephone:

"On the right, in the desk drawer . . ."

The sound of a shot.

Strips of crimson silk hang down as theatrical blood from the burst heart. It becomes dark on stage.

A tram conductor comes up to the sleeping, subconscious "I." He has a lamp in his hand.

"Citizen, all change here! . . ."

Similarly, the subconscious waits, languishing somewhere, while the romantic "I" gets drunk on the lectures, and the rational "I" grumbles acidly — the one educated at the Institute of Civil Engineers in differential calculus and the integration of differential equations.

"When are the secrets going to be revealed? When shall we get on to the methods? And when will this strip-tease *à l'envers* cease?"

Winter passes in a sweet trance, but nothing of practical value . . . Then Nezlobin's theater is poured into the First Theater of the RSFSR.[7]

Nelidov,[8] of the young idealists. Nelidov participated in the production of *The Fairground Booth.*[9] And *The Fairground Booth* was to us as the Church of Spas Neriditsa was to ancient Russia.

In the evenings Nelidov would talk about the wonderful evenings of *The Fairground Booth,* about the conference of mystics who look at us now from Sapunov's[10] sketches in the Tretiakov Gallery, about the première, and about how Meyerhold, as the white Pierrot, stood like a stork with one leg behind the other and played on a thin reed pipe.

But one can't get fat on memories . . .

Sometimes I ask myself: Was it perhaps simply impossible for Meyerhold to speak out and reveal? For there was no opportunity to see and formulate for

6. Nicholas Evreinov (1879–1934) was a dramatist, director, and theater historian.

7. The First Theater of the RSFSR was organized in Moscow in 1920 under the artistic direction of Meyerhold. In 1922, K. N. Nezlobin's theater merged with it, and it became known as the Meyerhold Theater.

8. Anatoly P. Nelidov, an actor in Vera Kommissarzhevskaya's theater, later became a director of the Leningrad Pushkin Theater (formerly the Alexandrinsky).

9. *The Fairground Booth*, a lyrical play by Alexander Blok, was produced by Meyerhold for Vera Kommissarzhevskaya's theater in St. Petersburg in 1906.

10. Nicholas N. Sapunov (1880–1912), a painter, was the scene designer for Meyerhold's productions of Blok's *The Fairground Booth* and Ibsen's *Hedda Gabler* at the Vera Kommissarzhevskaya Theater in 1906, and the pantomime *The Scarf of Columbine* at Intermedia House.

himself. However that may be, what fluttered about Novinsky Boulevard as an elusive secret in the autumn and winter gave itself away in the spring. It is impossible not to reveal oneself fully at work. At work you can't be crafty. At work is no time to weave the invisible golden web of fantasy, stealing away into dreams. At work one has to *do*. And what had been carefully and playfully hidden from us for two semesters was triumphantly revealed during the three days of rehearsals.

I have seen quite a few people in my time:

Yvette Guilbert showed me her skill all one *après-midi* at her place. I have been present when Chaplin was shooting. I have seen Chaliapin and Stanislavsky, the Ziegfeld Follies and the Admiral's Palast in Berlin, Mistinguett in the Casino de Paris, Katherine Cornell and Lynn Fontanne with Lunt, Alla Nazimova in plays by O'Neill, and Mayakovsky rehearsing *Mystery Bouffe;* I have talked with Bernard Shaw about the sound film and with Pirandello about the conception of plays; I have seen the Montagues[11] in a tiny theater in Paris, the very same Montagues whom Vladimir Ilyich Lenin crossed the whole city to see; I have seen Rachel Meller[12] and Reinhardt's productions, rehearsals of *The Cuckold*,[13] dress rehearsals of *The Dybbuk* and *Erik XIV*, Mikhail Chekhov as Fraser and Vakhtangov as Fraser,[14] Fokine's *Aragon Jota* and Karsavina in *Chopiniana*, Al Jolson, and Gershwin playing *The Rhapsody in Blue*, the three rings of the Barnum & Bailey Circus, and flea circuses at fairs, Primo Carnera knocked out of the ring by Schmeling in the presence of the Prince of Wales, Utochkin's flights[15] and a carnival in New Orleans; I have worked at Paramount with Jackie Coogan, heard Yehudi Menuhin in the Tchaikovsky Hall, lunched with Douglas Fairbanks in New York and breakfasted with Rin-Tin-Tin in Boston, heard Plevitskaya[16] in the Red Army and Navy Club and have seen General Sukhomlinov[17] in the same hall in the dock; seen General Brusilov[18] as a witness at this trial, and General Kuropatkin[19] as a neighbor in the same apart-

---

11. The Montagues were a French music hall act.

12. Rachel Meller, a Spanish music hall singer and actress, in 1926 played the lead in Jacques Feyder's film *Carmen* in Paris.

13. Crommelynk's *The Good-Natured Cuckold* is the play Eisenstein refers to.

14. Fraser was the hero of the play *The Flood*, by G. Berger, produced in 1916 by Vakhtangov, who played the leading role. Mikhail Chekhov acted Fraser in a later production.

15. Sergei Isayevich Utochkin (1874–1916) was one of the first Russian aviators.

16. Nadyezhda Vasilyevna Plevitskaya was a popular singer of Russian songs.

17. General Vladimir A. Sukhomlinov (1853–1926) was minister of war under Tsar Nicholas II. In 1917, he was tried in Petrograd for treason. He later emigrated.

18. General Alexei A. Brusilov (1853–1926), commander-in-chief of the Southwestern Front during World War I, was inspector of the Red Army cavalry after the Revolution.

19. General Alexei N. Kuropatkin (1848–1925) was commander-in-chief of the Russian Army during the Russo-Japanese War.

ment house at his morning exercises; I have observed Lloyd George speaking in Parliament in favor of recognizing Soviet Russia, and Tsar Nicholas II at the unveiling of the monument to Peter I in Riga; I have filmed a Mexican archbishop and adjusted the tiara on the head of the papal nuncio Rossas-y-Flores before the camera; I have gone for a car ride with Greta Garbo, gone to bullfights and been photographed with Marlene (Legs) Dietrich.

But not a single one of these impressions will ever erase from my memory the impressions left on me by those three days of rehearsals for *The Doll's House* in the gymnasium on Novinsky Boulevard. I remember shivering continuously. It was not cold; it was excitement, it was nerves stretched to their limit. The gymnasium was bordered, as if to emphasize it, by wooden wall-bars. This was our workbench. And for a day we assiduously wrenched our leg joints to the abrupt commands of Lyudmila Getye.

Lost in thought, between the uprights and the wall, back toward the window, holding my breath, I look before me. And perhaps it is from this that my second tendency stems. To dig, dig, dig. To dig down into every crevice of the problem myself, to penetrate into it, trying to understand it ever more deeply, to get ever nearer to the core. Expecting help from nowhere. But not to hide what I find: to drag it out into the light of day, in lectures, in the press, in articles, in books.

But . . . do you know, that the very surest means of concealment is complete revelation?

Nooneh

WHEN READING biographies I am always overcome with excitement as I reach the description of that unique, never-to-be-repeated moment contained in the magic words "and that morning he woke up famous." It used to be from envy and desire. Now . . . it's a nice thing to remember.

Take, for instance, Zola's biography. The morning after the publication of his first novel, he rushes out for the morning paper, still in his bedroom slippers, and is terribly upset, on looking at the proper page, not to find any notice. Later, he discovers that there is a notice! Yes, there is indeed, and in the most improper place — the first page! "That morning I woke up famous."

Similarly, in the biography of George Antheil,[1] in the account of his first concert. "That morning he woke up famous" goes the familiar refrain.

The same thing happened with the première of *Potemkin* in Berlin. The film was shown in a small theater on the Friedrichstrasse. All sorts of news of *Bombenenfolg* reach Moscow. At that time the Germans are much less preoccupied with real bombs. Telegrams arrive from Berlin. I am to go there at once. Reinhardt[2] is ecstatic. And Asta Nielsen.[3] A special gala night is in preparation.

The film is moved from the Friedrichstrasse to the very center of the city — to the Kurfürstendamm. Crowds. Long lines. It's a sellout! Now they show us not in one theater. But in twelve. And the newspapers trumpet, "That morning he woke up . . ."

1. George Antheil (1900–1959), American composer and pianist, was an exponent of Futurism. He lived and studied in Germany and France and composed music for films. In his *Ballet Méchanique*, he used propellors and other machines as instruments.

2. Max Reinhardt (1872–1943), the Austrian theater director, specialized in Impressionistic effects. He moved to Berlin, where he produced Shakespeare, Molière, Gorky, Strindberg, Shaw, and others.

3. Asta Nielsen was a famous Swedish actress of silent films.

I cannot get to Berlin. The train would bring me too late for the gala performance. Going by plane is out, too. Because the Kovna Airport is washed out. (In 1926 the spring floods are still a hazard, even to air travel.)

Telegrams. Telegrams. Telegrams. Then comes success in America. And again: "That morning he woke up famous." What a thrill to wake up famous!

And then to reap the fruits of your fame: To be invited to Buenos Aires for a series of lectures. To be suddenly recognized in the remote silver mines of the Sierra Madre, where the film was shown to the Mexican workers. To be embraced by unknown, wonderful people in the workers' district of Liège, where they screened the film in secret. To hear Alvarez delVayo's[4] account of how, back in the time of the monarchy, he himself had sneaked a print of *Potemkin* into Spain for a showing in Madrid. Suddenly to learn in some Parisian café, where you happen to share a little marble table with two dark-skinned Sorbonne students from the East, that "your name is very well known to us in . . . Java"! Or, on leaving some little garish roadhouse, to receive a warm handshake from a Negro waiter in recognition of what you have done in films.

When you arrive at the tennis court, Chaplin welcomes you with: "Just saw *Potemkin* again. You know, in five years it hasn't aged a bit; still the same!" And all of it as a result of . . . three months' (!) work on the film. (Including two weeks of editing!)

But now, twenty years later, it is easy for me to shuffle through these dry laurel leaves, to shrug my shoulders at the three-month schedule of my record achievement. It is far more important to remember the springboard for the jump itself. That plunge from which our young team came out a record winner . . . And here, first and foremost, we think of dear Nooneh.

Nooneh is the Armenian equivalent for the Russian name Nina. Nooneh herself is Nina Ferdinandovna Agadzhanova. *Strike*[5] has just been released. Awkward. Angular. Surprising. Bold. It contains the seeds of nearly all the elements that, in more mature form, appear in my works of later years. It is a typical "first work," bristly and pugnacious, as was I in those years.

These qualities spill over beyond the limits of the film. There are battles with the leadership of the Proletcult (the picture was made under the joint auspices of Goskino[6] and Proletcult). These arguments continue during the writing of the script, all through the period of shooting, and after the release of the film. Finally — after five years of work at the Proletcult Theater, and now on my entry into the film arena — a complete break with the Proletcult leadership. Controversy. The unequal struggle of the individual and the organization (not

---

4. Julio Alvarez delVayo (1891–1975) later became an ambassador of the short-lived Spanish People's Republic.

5. *Strike* was Eisenstein's first film.

6. Goskino is the short form of Gosudarstvenny Kinematografii, the Soviet state film organization.

yet exposed for its pretensions to a monopoly in proletarian culture). Any minute the controversy threatens to turn into a witch hunt.

On my part there is a great deal of the passion and ferocity of the young tiger who, raised on the milk of the theater, suddenly tastes the blood of cinematic freedom! A ridiculous situation, risky and disruptive in terms of further development and creative work.

At moments like this you need a friend,

a friend's counsel,

a word of advice to help you tame unruly passions and prevent you from persisting in foolish acts that can only do you harm. That is why I want to write of Nooneh.

Nina Ferdinandovna Agadzhanova — small, blue-eyed, bashful, and unbelievably modest — who stretched out her helping hand to me at this very critical moment in my creative life. Given an assignment to do a script for a 1905 anniversary film, she secured my participation in the project. With a resolute hand she led me away from further controversy, in which, because of my pugnacious nature, I persisted, despite possible troubles from Proletcult — and she placed me upon the firm soil of productive work.

Nooneh had the uncanny ability to collect around her small samovar a great number of hurt egos and lives abused by fate, and put them on the path of reason and a return to the calm of creativity. She did it with much sensitivity and no self-consciousness, like a child who collects, in matchboxes or in artificial nests of cotton wadding, grasshoppers with torn legs, baby birds that fall out of nests, or grown-up birds with broken wings. How many such disabled and injured rebels, mostly "leftists" and "extremists" of art, have I met around her homely tea table?

The illusion of a moral Noah's ark, temporarily protecting its passengers from the overzealous and grim gusts of wind and storm, was played out to the end by the fierce terrier Beauty, inevitably jumping between us, and . . . a living "dove of peace," which, following some quarrel with Nooneh, I brought as a peace offering, together with a palm-leaf branch from the undertaker occupying the corner of Malaya Dmitrovka, by the not yet demolished Strastnoy Monastery.

(Incidentally, that dove — during its two-hour sojourn in that apartment on Strastnoy Boulevard, in its panic-stricken flights from the sideboard to the partition, from the chandelier to the telephone, from the cornice of the Dutch oven to the shelf with Byron's *Collected Works* — so soiled her two rooms that it was ignominiously ejected.)

At times it seemed as though you were in the waiting room of Dr. Aibolit's[7] animal hospital, slightly expanded to include not only little rabbits with bandaged paws or a hippo with a toothache, but also suffering egos injured by life,

---

7. Dr. Aibolit is a character in famous Soviet children's tales by K. Chukovsky.

blind defenders of stubborn misconceptions, victims of temporary creative misfortunes, or chronic cases who seemed destined to carry the stamp of failure.

However, the inoffensiveness of these little rabbits with their bandaged paws was, of course, not all that it seemed. It is enough to remember that it was here, at Nooneh's (alongside the silver-gray actor Gabrielle in the black velvet shirt, who never made it, or the grim inventor Vasia), that I first met (and grew very fond of) such an indefatigable, stubborn man of principle as Kasimir Malevich,[8] during the time of his fierce battles over the direction of the institute that he headed rather aggressively. And it is difficult to overestimate the full moral significance of the atmosphere of those evenings for seekers, particularly "extremists," who were in very frequent and inevitable dissension with the everyday order of things, with the usually accepted standards of art, with its legalized traditions.

The most important thing that happened to us at Nooneh's was that each one gained renewed confidence in himself by realizing that everyone was needed to do the work of the Revolution. Each one, moreover, was needed in his own, special, unique, clumsy, individual way.

We found that it wasn't at all necessary to take up a plane and smooth away individualistic facets of personality (as the RAPP[9] gang proclaimed so vehemently at the time); that in the common work of the Revolution each one must and can find the proper application for his own uniqueness. We began to see how, frequently, you bring on yourself failure and trouble by undertaking something for which you have no inclination. How sometimes you break the spine of your own individuality because you have not searched sufficiently for that one area of activity where your special abilities and talents are, at the same time, the very ones needed for the job at hand.

At Nooneh's we gained understanding and insight. There, each one of us always found moral support and help. Not only in words, but in deeds. That certainly was the case with me. Nooneh did more than involve me in important work. She involved me in an experience that provided me with an authentic feeling for the history of the revolutionary past.

Despite her youth she was an active and important participant in the underground movement before the October Revolution. When you talked to her about the historic struggle, any episode became a living reality — no longer a dry sentence from an official history, nor a juicy bit fit for a detective thriller. For her, the events of the Revolution were domestic affairs, everyday work. But at the same time the highest ideal, the goal of an entire young life dedicated to the very end to the welfare of the working class.

---

8. Kasimir Malevich (1878–1935) founded the school of abstract painting known as Suprematism.

9. RAPP is the Russian acronym for the Revolutionary Association of Proletarian Writers, a sectarian and extreme left-wing movement in the twenties.

First Screening
of <u>Potemkin</u>

APPLAUSE LIKE THE CRACKLE of rifle shots echoes through the semi-circular corridors of the Bolshoi Theater. I am in the corridor, nervous not only about the fate of *Potemkin*, but about its . . . spittle. For, indeed, its last reel revolved around spittle.

Climbing higher and higher, from the orchestra to the dress circle, from the mezzanine to the balcony, driven upward by the growth of excitement, I hungrily and anxiously drink in every sound of the applause.

Then, like a thunderclap, it bursts from the entire audience. One — that is the scene with the red flag. Two — that's the one of the guns of the *Potemkin* firing at the generals' headquarters in reply to the Odessa massacre.

I continue to wander through the empty concentric halls.

Not a soul. Even the ushers have gone inside, a most unusual event: here, in the State Academic Bolshoi Theater, for the first time in its history — the showing of a film.

Now it will come — the third burst of applause as the *Potemkin* passes through the admiral's squadron "flying the victorious flag of freedom."

I am suddenly in a cold sweat.

All other sensations are shocked out of existence.

Spittle!

My God! Spittle!

Spittle!

In the last-minute rush in the cutting room we had forgotten to splice the final reel.

The sequence of the meeting of the squadron was made up of extremely short cuts. To make sure they would not be lost or get mixed up, I stuck them together by licking them with my tongue, and gave the reel to the assistant to splice. Then I took a look at the first version. Tore it apart. Looked at the second. Tore and changed that one, too.

Suddenly I remember that my assistant did not have the time to splice up the final version. And by now it is out of the can and being threaded for projection.

Film cement has not been substituted for spittle.

Yes — I can tell by the music — the last reel has already started!

How can I prevent disaster?

In utter confusion I race through the semicircular hallways and spiral down the corkscrew stairs, possessed by a single desire, to bury myself in the cellar, in the earth, in oblivion.

The break will come at any moment now!

Bits of film will come flying out of the projector.

The finale of the picture will be choked off, murdered.

But then . . . unbelievable . . . a miracle!!

The spittle holds! The film races through to the very end!

Back in the cutting room we couldn't believe our own eyes — in our hands the short cuts came apart without the slightest effort, and yet they had been held together by some magic force as they ran, in one whole piece, through the projector . . .

Without being conceited, I can say that many millions of people have seen *Potemkin*. The most varied nationalities, races, and parts of the world. Many, no doubt, have felt a catch in their throat during the scene of mourning over Vakulinchuk's body. But probably not one of these millions has noticed or remembered a tiny montage piece a few frames long in this same scene. Actually, it's not in this scene, but in the one where mourning turns to anger, and the fury of the people breaks out as a protest meeting around the tents.

An explosion in art, especially a passionate explosion of feelings, is constructed according to the same formula as an explosion in the field of explosive substances. At one time I studied land mines at the School for Ensigns. In that case, as in this, at first an increasing force compresses (though, of course, the actual means and overall set-up are quite different!). Then the containing frame bursts. And the shock scatters myriads of fragments.

It is interesting that the effect is not obtained unless an indispensable "accent" piece, flying asunder and "tracing out" the explosion, is inserted between the compression and the picture itself. In a real explosion the detonator capsule plays this role, as indispensable in the rear part of a rifle cartridge as in a packet of gun cotton slung under a bridge girder.

There are pieces like this everywhere in *Potemkin*.

At the beginning of the "Odessa Steps" it is the large cut-in title with the word *SUDDENLY!* immediately followed by the shaking of a single head in three sizes, "shock edited" from three short, linked pieces. This gives a further impression that the silence has been broken by a rifle volley. (The film is silent, and this is one of the silent means of achieving an effect, as a substitution for the first volley, which is, as it were, "heard outside the frame"!)

The explosion of the final *pathos* of the "Odessa Steps" takes place during the flight of a shell from the muzzle, the first explosion acting as a "detonator" for the perception, before smashing the bars and pillars of the gates of the deserted country house on Malaya Fontanka, which embodies the second and final explosion itself. (Between the two, the lions leap to their feet . . .)

There is a similar accent in the switch from the mourning on the shore to the fury of the sailors running across the battleship's deck to a meeting.

A tiny piece, perceptible no doubt not even as an object, but only as a purely dynamic accent, a simple flourish of a shot, which does not allow one to see what is, in fact, happening there. But this is what is happening there. In this piece a young chap in a paroxysm of rage rips open his shirt. This piece, as a culminating accent, is placed in the necessary spot between the enraged student and the raised fists already shaking in the air. The anger of the people on the shore "explodes" into the anger of the sailors' meeting on the deck and . . . the red flag is now raised over the *Potemkin*!

Reverse Music

WHEN I WAS STILL VERY young, before I went to school, I would howl for hours at being made to go against my will (and how against my will it was!) to gymnastic lessons at the Riga *Turnhalle*. Our teacher there, as later in the college itself (the gymnasium and college shared a common yard), was a bald, spectacled German, Herr Engels, who limped on one leg.

The only nice thing I can remember about Herr Engels is that it was from him I learned my first two examples of German palindromes when I was becoming interested in play on words. As far as I can now remember, these were the Christian name and surname Relief Pfeiler and the phrase *Ein Neger mit Gazelle zagt im Regen nie* (each of which reads identically forward and backward).

Sergei Sergeyevich Prokofiev had a great passion for this sort of play on words, and I am indebted to his extraordinary memory for a whole collection of French examples.

As regards the case of "reverse music," dissimilar forward and backward, I had an instance of this with the composer Edmund Meisel,[1] whose music for *Potemkin* was excellent but for *October* was only relatively so. At the time he was writing the *Potemkin* score (he had come to Moscow for this when the film was being edited), the central heating was being repaired in the viewing room and an unbelievable banging was going on throughout the whole building at Malaya Gnyezdnikovskaya Number 7. I later teased Edmund that he had written into the score not only his visual impressions from the screen, but also the banging of the plumbers. The music justified such remarks. And it included a trick with reverse music.

Potemkin begins with semisymbolic shots of the overthrowing of autocracy,

---

1. Edmund Meisel (1874–1930), an Austrian composer, wrote music for films as well as other forms.

represented in the form of the toppling of the statue of Alexander III, which stood beside the Cathedral of Christ the Savior. For this, a papier-mâché life-size statue was re-created in 1927; it toppled over and fell to bits most amusingly. The falling of the statue was also shot in reverse motion: the armchair with the armless and legless torso flew back onto the pedestal. Arms and legs flew together onto it, as did the orb and scepter. Once again the indestructible figure of Alexander III reposed there, gazing vacantly into space. This was shot for the scene of Kornilov's attack on Petrograd in the autumn of 1917, and these shots embodied the dream of all the reactionaries who linked the general's possible success with the restoration of the monarchy. That was the way the scene was put into the film. And it was for this scene that Edmund Meisel composed in reverse order the same music that had been written normally for the beginning.

Visually, the scene was a great success. But it is doubtful whether the musical trick got over at all. Reverse motion is always very entertaining, and I have recalled somewhere how often and how richly this device was used in the first old comic films.

Later, my relations with Meisel deteriorated . . . He ruined a public showing of *Potemkin* in London, in the autumn of 1929, by having the film projected slightly slower than normal, without my agreement, for the sake of the music. This destroyed all the dynamics of the rhythmic relationships to such a degree that for the only time in *Potemkin*'s whole existence the effect of the "lions jumping up" caused laughter. Thus had been destroyed the unified continuity in which a fusion of the three lions into one manages to take place without allowing the trick by which it has been achieved to be consciously perceived . . .

Prologue
The Sorbonne

LATE AUTUMN 1929. Almost winter, Berlin, on the Martin Luther Strasse, in the furnished rooms of the Pension Marie Louise: two enormous double beds; vast German eiderdowns.

Under one is Friedrich Markovich Ermler.[1] Under the other — is me. Friedrich has arrived today from Moscow and doesn't like Berlin. He is uneasy here.

"What is there for me to do here?" he asks. He already wants to go home.

I've been abroad for some months. I've managed to do a lecture tour of Switzerland. I've given a talk in Hamburg, and I know what's what in Berlin. Tomorrow I shall start showing Berlin to Friedrich. But today he tells me how things are in Moscow: "In Moscow nothing's been heard about you. In Moscow they think that you're not being sufficiently colorful in your travels . . ."

In Moscow, of course, they don't understand that to go to Hollywood (and that is the aim of my trip) is not quite so simple and that negotiations take a considerable amount of time. Nevertheless, in Moscow cinema circles, they think that I am not being sufficiently . . . how had he put it? . . . colorful?

"Now, if I were you," continues Ermler dreamily, "I should cause a political sensation somewhere . . ."

I am very compliant. "Cause a sensation? Not colorful enough?" I grunt and turn over on my side. Just wait! Give me the chance. Give me the time. Moscow will be satisfied. What will happen? Nobody knows yet. The light is turned off. We both go to sleep . . .

A few months pass . . . 1930. Paris. The middle of February. I have managed a trip to lecture in London and I have visited Belgium, where I talked to workers

---

1. Friedrich Markovich Ermler (1898–1967), the Soviet director, was a People's Artist of the republic.

in a famous Liège suburb, whose name, Serin-le-Rouge (Red!), speaks for itself and, escaping the excessive curiosity of the police, I leave a little sooner than I had intended. Still, this prevents my visiting Ostend in answer to old James Ensor's[2] courteous invitation. Regrettably, because I love his grotesque etchings, where skeletons and people intertwine in the most fantastic designs, continuing, on the threshold of the twentieth century, the traditions of his fanciful and strange Flemish ancestors, like Hieronymus Bosch.

I give a talk in Holland. (Not without some minor sensations.) Since childhood, I have associated Holland with Van Houten's cocoa, sharp-pointed caps, and of course gigantic wooden clogs. The first thing I ask on getting off the train in Rotterdam (my first lecture is here) is: "Where are the clogs?" Next day all the newspapers come out with a big headline: " 'Where are the clogs?' asks Eisenstein."

On the way to the Van Gogh Museum in the Hague our taxi almost runs over Queen Wilhelmina. In those idyllic years the queen, who was already quite old, used to walk the streets of her capital like any mortal woman. The taxi managed to avoid her at the last second.

We got drunk on the coloring of the best collection of Van Gogh canvases in the world. Here, beside the astounding drawing of *The Harvester*, hangs the famous portrait of the postman with the orange beard. It hangs in the place of honor, its colors sparkling. Streams of chrome yellow, ocher, and brownish gold snake unrestrainedly down to the points of his forked beard, as streams of blue-black and dark green soar up in the twisting spirals of the cypresses.

Part of the very friendly reception given to me by the newspapers in Amsterdam was an article by a certain Catholic priest. The Father wrote most warmly of the great propagation of humanitarian ideas carried out by Soviet cinematography. The next day an absurd newspaper storm burst over the poor Father. The general tone was expressed especially succinctly by one paper: "That the Bolsheviks are able to enter into league with the devil we haven't the slightest doubt. But to see them protected by the cassock is too much!"

And now Paris again. Paris full to overflowing with impressions. But not a single sensation yet. The negotiations with America drag on. "New Babylon's" diversions pass stormily. I zealously go the round of the obligatory tourist routes. Chemin des Dames and the battlefield at Verdun. The Musée Cluny, which one visits solely to see the metal chastity belt on display. The Musée Carnaval, dedicated to Paris's history. Then, finally, in answer to insistent requests, I agree to give a lecture in the Sorbonne.

Nothing special!

A short talk on Soviet cinema.

---

2. James Ensor (1860–1949) was a Belgian painter and etcher.

A showing of the film *The Old and the New*.

Under the aegis of the department *des recherches sociales*. In the Richelieu Hall to a thousand people.

The Old and the New has still not been passed by the censor. But a show within the Sorbonne is extraterritorial. Such a viewing does not require the censor's permission, and somewhere under the seated figure of Cardinal Richelieu a portable film projector has been set up for the film.

It is good that the showing can take place without the permission of the censor's committee. The censor, of course, would never pass it in the anti-Soviet atmosphere prevailing here. Only recently one of our newsreels showing an ordinary physical culture parade was banned. The reason was that those in the parade were smiling. Did this mean, then, that things in the Soviet Union were not so bad? Soviet propaganda! *Ban it!*

The French censor is clearly extravigilant. How different from the English Board of Censors in London! I've just returned from there. One of the censors is blind; perhaps he looks after the silent films? Another is deaf; perhaps he looks after the sound films? While I was there a third just upped and died! It is true, though, that this in no way prevented our films from not being shown anywhere in London, even though the censor is not a government organization.[3]

A good thing that in Paris, at least, there are unassailable citadels of freedom for the visual arts! Thus, little blue tickets, invitations, fly around Paris. It turns out that the evening is awaited with great impatience. But someone's despicable and treacherous hand tosses a blue ticket onto a writing desk belonging to Monsieur Chiappe, the notorious prefect of the Paris police.

Well, what of it? We don't mind if Monsieur Chiappe is in the public. "We shall be like the sun."[4] We shall shine on both the good and the evil. However, the incident is not as innocent as it appears.

I arrive at the Sorbonne half an hour before the start of the lecture, and I meet Léon Moussinac[5] and Dr. Allandi[6] (our chairman for the evening) in a long corridor. On one side the sound of many voices reaches us from the hall. There is a crush at the entrance doors; the entrance to the building is a babel. It is not, of course, so much my person as the fact that the voice of a visiting Muscovite is to be heard in Paris — a Paris so unfriendly toward Moscow in those years.

---

3. I do not understand why, in 1946, Eisenstein should write this obvious untruth, for only a few pages earlier he had written of a showing of *Potemkin* in London in 1929. In fact, Soviet films were shown even when *not* passed by the Board of Censors, which was, as he acknowledged, a private trade organization and not a governmental body. (H.M.)

4. *We Shall Be Like the Sun* was the title of a book by the Russian poet K. D. Balmont (1867–1943). It was published in 1903 and became one of the literary manifestoes of the Russian Symbolists.

5. Léon Moussinac was a leading French Communist writer and film critic.

6. Dr. Allandi, a French politican, died during the German occupation.

Allandi and Moussinac look awful. It seems that the innocent blue ticket on the prefect's desk was not an invitation to the prefect to attend a viewing at all. Because a ticket was sent to the prefect of the police, the private meeting has turned into a . . . public meeting; and a public meeting at which a film is shown requires the permission of the censor's committee. *The Old and the New* does not have this permission. Naturally, an order had just arrived from the police forbidding the film to be shown.

The side door into the hall is opened slightly for me, and through the crack I can see that the audience is assembling. Many are already in their places. The seated figure of Richelieu towers above them. At its feet is the projector, and beside the projector, in full-dress uniform with traditional cape and white gloves, is a policeman, his hand firmly clamped on one of the projector's legs.

"*Quel outrage!* This is the first *flic* who has been within the walls of the Sorbonne since the time of Napoleon III!"

"He arrived together with the ban. It's his job to see that the film is not shown."

"*Merde!*" I am already so used to French that I can swear without resorting to translating. Well, what was to be done? Go home? How could I, when both sponsors begged me to stay. I had prepared a twenty-minute introductory talk. Could I not entertain the audience for the whole evening?

Suddenly there was a bang from the other side of the wall, like the sound of a very large cork flying out of a very large champagne bottle. It is the crowd, which has burst through the entrance doors. Brushing aside those checking the tickets, streams of people flood into the hall.

The organizers look at me pleadingly. How can the evening be postponed? We quickly confer on what is to be done. Should we try to show the film in defiance of the ban? That is presumably just what the police are waiting for.

They would try to stop the showing. One of the more demonstrative in the audience would then probably have a go at the policeman near the projector. And as if from nowhere there would be more policemen . . .

One of the younger organizers runs up, pale as a sheet: "The police are forming detachments outside the Sorbonne!"

"*Quel outrage! Quel outrage!*"

"Just wait and see, a brawl will start."

"There's going to be a skirmish with the police."

Among the audience are quite a few comrades — French Communists. The police would be very glad to catch those they wanted in the general mêlée.

A new explosion. Once again the crowd has broken through the checkers at the entrance, who had just managed to regain control. The gangways are packed. People are sitting on the steps and looking at the policeman in amazement. The place is humming like a gigantic beehive. What should we do? There are already three thousand people for the one thousand seats.

Another of the young organizers arrives with still more troubling news:

"There is a large percentage of Camelots du Roi[7] in the hall. Everything is prepared for a great scandal."

We make a quick decision. I cannot make my talk last longer than forty minutes.

And then — all being well — we would play with the public at "questions and answers." And may God help me!

The hall bursts into a storm of impatience. I plunge head first into the raging ocean. The roar that goes up from the audience would drown the roar of any ocean, such is the hurricane of indignation when Dr. Allandi tells them of the prefect's ban on the film. The poor gendarme's face changes color twenty times, from crimson to white. Of course, it would be difficult to imagine a more favorable atmosphere.

There is no need to go into the details of the talk. In addition to describing the general ideological bases and qualities of Soviet cinema, I expounded the idea, dear to my heart, of "intellectual cinematography," cinematography of concepts, which I was especially interested in at that time. All this is discussed very thoroughly and in great detail in special articles. This theory of emotional and intellectual overtones, and the scheme "from the thesis to the image; from the image to the concept" and so on, formed fertile ground for development, arguments, polemics, and the working out of methods for many years. But I repeat: all this is material for specialists and can be found in any number of articles.

During the course of the talk at the Sorbonne I touched slightly on Surrealism, still fashionable then even in Paris itself; "slightly," that is, inasmuch as I stated that what they were doing was the direct opposite of what should be done . . . But what is most interesting to set down here, of course, is the dramatic side of the evening, the more so as that side has never found its way into the theoretical articles. To begin with, I hate appearing before the public. I go numb. But on this occasion, so heated was the auditorium with electrified anger that all numbness and constraint melted like wax.

And I did not attack my enemy, the Goliath of French reaction, with peals of thunder — but with bursts of laughter. Especially in that part which I call playing at "questions and answers" with the auditorium, and which began after the lecture. The choice of weapons proved to be absolutely right.

The next day *Le Matin* (or some other similar organ) wrote: "Be frightened not of Bolsheviks with a dagger in their teeth, but of those with laughter on their lips!"

There was no possible excuse for police intervention. What, for heaven's sake, could they intervene in? An audience of thousands who are delightedly and peaceably amusing themselves? But, my God, was there anything they

---

7. The Camelots du Roi were members of a Royalist youth organization.

didn't laugh at! I can't remember now what answers I gave to the most innocent and inoffensive questions. I think this is the only time in my life that I have held a conference and had to rattle off answers without thinking.

A theoretical explanation.

Boutade!

A factual answer.

And bang! A hoof at the censor's committee.

Another *boutade*.

Another factual answer.

And again, bang! — this time for the Ministry of Foreign Affairs.

And bang! bang! bang! at the prefecture.

The auditorium is beside itself with laughter. It is already captivated and flabbergasted by the fact that a visiting foreigner — from a country that for some reason is considered madly strict and completely devoid of humor (I have already said that the censor banned our newsreel because of smiles!) — suddenly starts talking to an audience quite gaily, and, what is more, using not the literary and academic translation style of French, but the most devil-may-care expressions of the streets, and in places plain argot. They didn't expect to hear this from the lecturer or within the walls where he was lecturing.

I think it was Mrs. Constance Rourke, in the book *American Humor*, who first dwelled in detail on the theme that laughter is the strongest factor in uniting a large number of human beings. Those hours spent in the Sorbonne are a very illuminating example of this . . . However, it is of course difficult to restrain oneself when an official lecturer, on the respected rostrum of the Sorbonne, cuts short a provocative question from the floor by using in his answer a street-slang word, *dépucelage* (loss of virginity). This was in answer to someone's question: "Is it really true, as the lecturer states, that workers' criticism is so valuable for film-makers?" The answer was that only two types of criticism are valuable: the spontaneous, class-based reaction and criticism from the workers' audience for which we work, and the criticism of the professional experts. The least interesting for us is the "in-between" criticism of those who haven't grown to a full knowledge and understanding of film-making, and yet have "lost their purity" of spontaneous appreciation!

On the printed page this may not, perhaps, seem witty. But in the hall filled with laughter, with the figure of Richelieu soaring overhead, with the sweating *flic* at the projector, and the police surrounding the building, the answer exploded like a rocket. As did the answer to the last question: "Is it true that laughter has died forever in the Soviet Union?"

I answered by . . . bursting into laughter. At that time I still had fine, strong, white teeth, and, incidentally, my absolutely sincere laughter in answer to the absurdity of this assumption was completely convincing.

We leave the battlefield. We cross the almost dark courtyard of the Sorbonne. The policemen, who had been called out for nothing, look on gloomily.

We were told later that the figure of Monsieur Préfet himself had been seen among them for a time. Evidently it was true.

We pass through the narrow streets around the Sorbonne. No dead and wounded are to be seen, although it appears that many, many people had been removed by brute force from the entrance. We pass by open courtyards. We cannot believe our eyes! In all the streets, in every courtyard are . . . truckloads of police!

Apparently a real bloodbath had been expected.

We finish the evening in Drunken Boat Bar, named in honor of Arthur Rimbaud's work *Le Bateau Ivre*. The bar is decorated like the interior of a normal boat. The touch of "drunkenness" is given to it by the visitors themselves. Then we go peacefully to our beds in the little Hôtel des Etats-Unis.

Nine o'clock the next morning. A powerful blow of a fist against the door of my tiny room. This *should* have taken place three hours earlier, as the police had called unexpectedly at six o'clock. However, the owner of the hotel, standing astride the staircase, had defended my sleep with his chest.

"Monsieur Eisenstein returned late yesterday.

"Monsieur Eisenstein is asleep . . .

"I cannot allow Monsieur Eisenstein to be disturbed before nine in the morning."

That nice proprietor of the Hôtel des Etats-Unis!

I cannot forgive myself that I cannot remember his name . . .

Rue de Grenelle

A<small>N</small> OLD-FASHIONED, stone-built *"hôtel entre cour et jardin"*; that is, a residence with a stone-paved driveway at the front, separated from the street by railings, with French windows opening from the salon onto a garden at the rear.

At this time, "Rue de Grenelle" (our embassy building in Paris is on the Rue de Grenelle) is like a fortress under siege. You are admitted through a heavy porte-cochère on the left, after having first been examined through a peephole and then having your papers checked while the gate is on a chain. Everyone speaks in whispers. Walks on tiptoe. The embassy staff, girded with firearms, maintains a tense guard, day and night.

The Rue de Grenelle is ordinarily a fairly quiet street. If you take into consideration the added fact that now, with the renewed anti-Soviet campaign, the majority of taxis refuse to go down the street (most taxis have White Guard officers as drivers), then it is not surprising that the Rue de Grenelle is absolutely silent for hours at a time. These days, it is a sinister silence, a deceptive silence. The anti-Soviet leaflets, carried by the wind, silently scream in testimony to this. The flagrant posters and slogans pasted on the walls right up to the very gates of the embassy mutely shout in testimony to this. "Throw the Soviets out of Paris!" "Smash them!"

The newspapers are full of anti-Soviet howling . . . "It would be difficult, of course, to pick a worse moment for this whole affair of yours," Dovgalyevsky, our ambassador, tells me.[1]

He had just recently concluded the complex matter of finally establishing diplomatic relations with England. Now he is possibly on the brink of being witness to a break of relations with France . . .

---

1. In connection with the Sorbonne affair, the French government decided to expel Eisenstein from France.

Dovgalyevsky has the black whiskers of a Kipling or Nietzsche. He graduated from Toulouse University and looks like a Frenchman from the south.

Dovgalyevsky has my sympathies . . . He had been attacked over "the secret affair" of General Kutyepov's disappearance.[2] The whole of the reactionary and gutter press was blaring out accusations that the "Soviets" had kidnapped him.

"Useless to send a note to Tardieu about you. I'm sure you understand that . . ." Dovgalyevsky twitches his black whiskers. From a packet of sensational newspaper stories of the Kutyepov affair, he takes out a clipping about three mysterious Soviet cinematographers who, for some reason or other, recently traveled to Saint-Cloud in a blue Hispano-Suiza.

Yes, that was us, all right.

Gaumont's flamboyant representative, a former member of the Yellow Hussars, had accompanied us from London to conclude an agreement with his firm, and indeed, among other entertainments, had driven us in a gigantic Hispano-Suiza belonging to his friend, a record-holding racing driver. It all had nothing to do with the general, though.

The voice of one of Dovgalyevsky's colleagues breaks in: "Why don't you leave? To be expelled from France! What could be more honorable than such a stamp in one's passport?" . . .

Of course it is honorable to be expelled from France. There is, however, a considerable "but."

The world's intelligence services have an inflexible rule: the dossier of an undesirable alien who has been expelled from one or another of the large states is immediately sent to the intelligence services of all other countries. This is called *communication du dossier* and automatically carries with it all manner of difficulties for the subject when entering any country; and my planned tour is still far from completed. Ahead lies America, Hollywood.

I ask Dovgalyevsky not to take any steps at all. This affords him visible relief. "We'll do everything through the French!" His colleague shrugs his shoulders skeptically, and on this we part.

And this is exactly where the phantasmagoria and kaleidoscope begin. To paraphrase a famous Frenchman:[3] "If my expulsion had not happened, it would have been necessary to provoke it." In my whole life I have never seen such an atmosphere as that in Paris, such an abundance of people, of unimaginable types, and surely will never see such again.

---

2. General A. P. Kutyepov, head of the French White Guard organizations, disappeared in 1930. The Soviet Union was accused of kidnapping and murdering him.

3. Voltaire wrote, "If God had not existed, it would have been necessary to invent him."

Friends, For
and Against

TRUE FRIENDS ARE FOUND in time of trouble. False friends also. I return from the Rue de Grenelle to my tiny Hôtel des Etats-Unis. After the talk with Dovgalyevsky, the sign outside seems even more symbolic, signifying what is, in the present instance, still farther removed from reality. In the lower foyer of this little hotel is a cramped little telephone booth.

Parisian telephones are frightful. It's almost impossible to get a connection and, having got it, it's almost impossible to hear anything. That's when you're trying to get other *Paris* numbers. Long-distance calls can be heard perfectly. The longer the distance, the better the reception. I am calling St. Moritz in Switzerland. Naturally, the first thing to do is to get in touch with someone who might show a financial interest in our staying in Paris.

Just such a person is Monsieur Leonard Rosenthal, the millionaire Pearl King. He has the Légion d'Honneur for having brought the center of the world pearl trade from London to Paris. In his extraordinary book, with its significant title *Let's Be Rich!*, he describes the simple method that enabled him to do this. An undoubted expert in human psychology, Monsieur Leonard thought up the idea of paying the pearl fishers of the Hindu oceanside villages in small silver coins rather than checks. The caravans of camels, loaded with sacks of small silver, were so impressive that step by step Monsieur Leonard was able to draw still more pearl fishery areas of India into his sphere of influence.

In 1930 his brother stays uninterruptedly in India for three quarters of the year, directing operations on the spot. Then he spends three months drinking and making merry in Paris. Monsieur Leonard himself spends the whole year in Paris, selling and exporting pearls to every corner of the world. What has Monsieur Rosenthal to do with us? This is where Marie Gris comes in. Madame Marie is not Madame Rosenthal. She is much more. She is Monsieur Rosenthal's mistress, and little Rachel, who was born recently, ensures the bonds of this union, which cannot, however, be legalized, as the real Madame Rosenthal refuses to give the necessary divorce.

In addition to little Rachel, Marie Gris had another daughter, already grown up. With this daughter in her arms (the child was then still quite small) Madame Marie had collapsed from hunger on the steps of a luxurious residence that faced, on its other side, the Parc Monceau. Before doing so she had just managed to ring the gilded bronze bell at the splendid entrance.

Thus, the poverty-stricken wanderings of this young woman, who had fled from the Crimea in the tracks of Wrangel[1] and starved first in Constantinople, then in Paris, came to an end. But for Madame Marie the moment she fell on the steps a pearl dream began, sprinkled with diamonds (and what diamonds! I saw those "Rivieras," cascades, and streams of diamonds at some première). And all because, for some reason, the legendary Rosenthal himself came out on the steps in all the glory of his red, spade-shaped beard! He wore this red beard provocatively, and in conjunction with white tie and tails it didn't make a bad color combination. Monsieur Rosenthal was captivated by the beauty of the young lady lying senseless at his door. And the young lady was provided for, for many years.

So *Cinderella* and *Sleeping Beauty* are not just ballets. But what has Cinderella to do with us? *Cinderella* is our potboiler. One has to live! Grisha Alexandrov met Goldilocks and her patron during the time I was lecturing in London. Madame Marie sings a little and dreams of being in films, and a little musical film[2] is being made in which Madame Marie, now Marie Gris, sings at a blindingly white piano . . .

At the other end of the wire in St. Moritz Monsieur Rosenthal is more than evasive. Quite obviously, he doesn't want to be involved in this whole affair. In my opinion, he wouldn't even mind if I left France in a hurry.

Anyway, it is Alexandrov and Tisse who are making the film. The police are not bothering them, and they travel inoffensively around France, filming landscapes for the little film. They get permission for their travels very easily. We are all kept under surveillance, of course. But the police can't afford a sleuth to travel from Paris to Finisterre and from Normandy to Nice, what with his daily expenses, hotels, and sustenance . . . "Now if Messieurs would agree to cover these expenses themselves . . ." The messieurs, with Rosenthal's approval, agree. And Tisse and Alexandrov travel untroubled around France, accompanied by a certain ever-present Monsieur Kurochkin, kindly appointed to them by the prefecture.

---

1. Baron P. N. Wrangel (1878–1928), who had served as a general in both the Russo-Japanese War and World War I, fought against the Bolsheviks. He took command of the Crimea, but was eventually defeated and fled first to Yugoslavia and then to Belgium.

2. This short film, *Sentimental Romance*, was actually made by G. V. Alexandrov and E. K. Tisse, but it is attributed to Eisenstein.

Monsieur Kurochkin is a full member of the film group, and during leisure hours confides his innermost dreams to the other two participants. Monsieur Kurochkin has his eye on a middle-aged widow. She has not only a little bit of money (not a great deal, but quite enough), but also a motorboat. And Monsieur Kurochkin is as attracted to motorboats as Jeeter Lester's dissolute and inimitable son is to cars in Erskine Caldwell's *Tobacco Road* . . .

You find your false friends in time of trouble. Your true friends, too. I am scarcely out of the telephone booth before a ruddy, curly-haired young man with gay, darting eyes (which would suddenly become still and thoughtful) rises from a chair to greet me.

He wears a black hat, black shirt, and black tie. Everything except black gloves. But the clerical black is no more than a protective coloration in his case. It would be difficult to find a more radically inclined young man. Or a more bitter anticleric. It is my friend Jean Painlevé.[3] "Papa has already written a protest to the prefecture," he says. "The news has sped around Paris."

Papa. For someone, of course he is Papa. For the rest, though, he is the former minister of war, a famous mathematician, and now holds high rank in the Order of the Légion d'Honneur.

Hmm . . . Hmm . . . I can imagine Monsieur Oudar's face when he sees a protest from a person of such position. Painlevé and I go to have lunch. He is still very young, but he makes remarkable scientific films. At the recent Congress of the Independent Film I was very interested to see a film of his, beautifully shot, about the underwater life of the hermit crab.

There is also his microfilming of the life of water fleas and the fantastically beautiful film of sea horses, some shots of which are worthy of the intricate compositions of Méliès. On the basis of his warm regard for the Soviet Union — friendship.

Tucking into what looks like crab or something similar, which in its live state would have been food for his screen work, he laughingly tells about his encounters with the police. He recalls how, when still a young boy, at the climax of some political disorder, he led a group of armed people to storm . . . the Ministry of War. He knew all the exits and entrances: the minister of war was his father. On this occasion the affair of Painlevé blew over somewhere between the nursery (his future film laboratory) and Papa's office.

But there was more.

The enterprising and indefatigable Jean Painlevé contrived to take part in everything that had the slightest whiff of social protest and disorder. He especially enjoyed getting himself arrested, thereby helping other more involved

---

3. Jean Painlevé (1902–   ) was a French producer of scientific films. His father, Paul Painlevé, was all that Eisenstein said, and was premier of France, as well.

comrades to get away. But getting arrested was a special diversion for him. He adored the confusion of the police inspectors when he told them the name and occupation of his parent. The gendarmes who had arrested him got a fearful dressing down and, begging his pardon for having troubled him, would take him by the arm and ask him to go home quietly.

He would have none of it! Jean would demand that he be treated in the same way as the other prisoners. He would kick up a fuss and, talking eighteen to the dozen, demand to be led off to a cell. So to a cell he would go, and thus cause untold trouble for the poor police inspector, who would be trembling at the name of his peculiar prisoner's omnipotent papa.

Once, however, he came up against a certain inspector with a ginger mustache. After having argued with Jean for a long time, he growled his consent to locking Jean up in a cell. First, though, he handed Jean two forms to sign. Jean, excited by the argument, signed with a flourish — without looking at them. Immediately an agent took him by the scruff of the neck and ejected him into the street. The whole station collapsed with laughter: one of the two forms that had been palmed off on him said he was a prisoner; the other said that he had been freed.

There's no room here to dwell on Jean's escapades with priests, as by this time we've finished our lunch and I return thoughtfuly to my room in Montparnasse, where a small, blue racing Bugatti is parked near the hotel.

Renaud de Jouvenel, another friend of mine, jumps up nervously from a chair in the hotel's little lobby.

"I know all about it! Papa has already sent his protest to the prefecture!"

Things are getting more difficult by the hour for Monsieur Oudar. First Painlevé, now Senator Henry de Jouvenel. There is no hint of liberal sympathies in this. Senator de Jouvenel is sent to Rome. The result of his mission is a friendly agreement with Mussolini. I have never met the senator. But his son is a fanatical car enthusiast, and even the little magazine on aesthetics that he publishes is called *Grande Route*. I often go racing with Renaud in the car, and he got an article out of me for his magazine . . .

I am called to the telephone. "We're going immediately to de Monzie!"[4]

It is Toille's voice; he is another *cinéaste*, but not yet a professional.

"I've arranged everything. We'll meet there. Set off at once!"

At that time de Monzie was still wholly in sympathy with the Soviet Union and just recently had made his political mark by advocating a rapprochement with the Soviet Union.

Another old hotel. With driveway and garden. I think somewhere off the Luxembourg. The recently appointed minister is turning silvery gray. Horn-

---

4. Anatole de Monzie was a French senator who was, at the time, sympathetic to the Soviet Union.

rimmed spectacles. A check bowtie. A Basque beret at an angle. A blinding background of large red copper sheets, forming a screen.

He has just finished seeing the endless queue of daily visitors: provincial curés, bewhiskered military pensioners, retired businessmen, ladies in mourning veils.

"You're being expelled? Strange! Why? Maybe it's connected with the vice squad? No! It doesn't look like that . . . We'll look into it. We'll see. Your twenty-four hours expire tomorrow? First we'll get you a week's extension. A telephone call to a certain place."

The next day, without calling on Monsieur Oudar, I automatically receive a seven-day extension, during which time we must mobilize all our forces.

De Monzie tactfully avoids any further involvement, passing me on to his former assistant in the ministry, Monsieur Robert.

"*C'est le pape!*" shouts this expansive peasantlike man in one of the tiny offices in the labyrinth of corridors of, believe it or not, the Tuileries Palace. What his job is there, I never found out. "*Le pape*" in this instance is not a father, but the Pope. "That's what it is! You've got on the wrong side of the Catholics! This is the hand of the Vatican!"

I feel Rodin's bony fingers closing on my throat — not the Rodin whose sculptures I managed to admire in his museum, but Rodin, the sinister hero of Eugène Sue's *The Wandering Jew*, the greedy and pitiless agent of Rome.

"Try to remember!"

Where, when, in what way could I have encroached on the omnipotence of the Vatican and the Pope?! I try swiftly to envisage my comings and goings from the point of view of the spiritual police. *Mon Dieu!!* He is right. Behind me lie countless trips to all the well-known cathedrals of France. I haven't yet lost my passion for architecture. There is the excursion to Rheims. There are the two trips to Chartres. There is Amiens. There are the frequent visits to Catholic bookshops. I am interested in the problem of religious ecstasy as a particular problem of pathos. In my hotel, in the wardrobe, among the books on primitive thought by Lévy-Bruhl, are works by St. John of the Cross, the works of St. Theresa, and the *Spiritual Exercises* of St. Ignatius Loyola.

As it happens, I was surprised recently to find these books lying in an unusual order. And our floor porter — Jacques of the striped waistcoat — had been guiltily avoiding my gaze.

Heavens, and I had only recently gone with Toille to Lisieux to see this shrine of bad taste to the recently canonized "little saint," St. Thérèse de Lisieux.

However, Lisieux is not enough for me.

I am dying to see Lourdes.

I am very interested in the display of mass ecstasy during "miraculous cures" as a crowd psychosis.

Also in the behavior of the audience at boxing and football matches.

I was very disappointed with the Longchamps races: the French go to horse-racing as if to a job. They place a bet: if it wins, it wins; if it doesn't, it doesn't. No mass effect at all. Not even a sporting one.

I don't manage a trip to Lourdes: my visit to France is at the wrong time of the year for the pilgrimage.

However, I am more than compensated by the arena's behavior during bullfights and by the religious frenzy of the Mexican holy dancers.

But that lies in the future.

It is true, I do see the miraculous grotto of Lourdes with its figure of the Madonna and even with a tiny figure of little Bernadette Soubirous, but a full-scale copy I see in . . . Marseille.

This structure, painted in bright color, is, as it happens, just around the corner from those little streets on which are Marseille's countless houses of ill repute . . .

Such a close association of holy virgins and priestesses of love should shock no one.

I'm not the first to make the association.

Near the churches and cathedrals they always sell, in addition to the amulets and *ex voto* objects, pictures of the saints.

With the growth of modern techniques, painted pictures are more and more often being squeezed out by photographs.

Pretty girls pose in the vestments of St. Thérèse de Lisieux, holding roses, or as the regal or kindly Madonna.

In Toulon they also sell to sailors postcards with pictures of girls. The subjects here, though, are rather more frivolous, without (as they are on open sale) being actually offensive.

Still . . .

Well, it is delightful to see that both sorts of photographs are put out by one and the same firm.

And as the firm is intelligently economical, it uses the same girls for both lines.

It is touching to see the postcards side by side — the little girl, in very scanty clothing, being embraced by a sailor, and there she is again, in the heavy vestments of a saint.

The firm is not, of course, guilty in any way.

Which of its owners could suppose there'd be such a queer fish collecting samples of sailors' folklore in the form of postcards from the cigarette kiosks of Toulon, and then, around Notre Dame de Lorette, collecting, just as assiduously, photographs depicting the saints?

However, the "Lorettes"[5] themselves are frivolous girlfriends of students and artists.

---

5. The Lorettes were girls of light virtue who frequented the district of Notre Dame de Lorette in Paris.

And, as we have seen, they even have their own "Notre Dame" — the Madonna!

All this is very diverting . . .

Heavens! Suppose for a moment that even for ten percent of my "spiritual wanderings" I had been trailed by a *flic* or that some of these trips have appeared in an agent's reports . . .

"Well, now do you see?" crows Monsieur Robert. *"C'est le pape!"*

"Come on, let's go!"

Strange though it seems, Monsieur Robert is to a considerable extent right. As it turns out later, my dossier contains, among other things, the note that I "made trips to collect material for antireligious propaganda"! For the time being though this is only wild supposition.

"Come on, let's go!"

I hurry off in another direction, to the Café des Deux Magots, the headquarters of the "left" wing of the Surrealists, who had broken away from Breton's[6] group. I am friendly with them and I find instant advice on how to proceed with my affairs.

Georges Henri Rivière, a curator of the Trocadéro Museum, who is sympathetic to but not quite one of the group, takes me off to see the museum's director, who can pull strings in the Ministry of Foreign Affairs.

Toille goes to talk with Deputy Gernoud, who runs the League of Human Rights, an organization of former Dreyfusards, defenders of Dreyfus and Zola.

Maître Philippe Lamour gets in touch with the young writer André Malraux[7] in the publishing house Nouvelle Revue Française (NFR). Malraux will set in motion the professoriate (Langevin[8] and the Sorbonne, for when all is said and done the Sorbonne has suffered an outrage; the Sorbonne had not seen a gendarme within its walls since the time of Napoleon III!).

I was introduced to Maître Lamour, a very young advocate, by Germaine Kroll, a delightful photographer of the "objectivist" and "documentalist" wing, whose members are especially eager to be nice to the creator of *Potemkin* and *The Old and the New*. She specializes in documentary "photonovels," and together with her and Joris Ivens,[9] we even film some bars in outlying bistros.

Maître Lamour goes to see Malraux. Toille sets off to see Gernoud. Rivière and I go to the Trocadéro.

---

6. André Breton (1896–1966), poet, essayist, and critic, was a Dadaist and a founder of the Surrealist movement.

7. André Malraux (1901–1976), the writer and critic, was once sympathetic to the Communists. He later became minister of culture in De Gaulle's administration.

8. Paul Langevin (1872–1946) was a French physicist who worked on the theory of magnetism, the theory of relativity, and the movement of gases.

9. Joris Ivens (1898–   ) is a Dutch documentary film director who works now mainly in Communist countries. His last film was made in Cuba.

Here, for the first time, I saw what was then most sought after by collectors, more valuable than carved Chinese jade or Ming and Tang horses; namely, flat, greenish, bronze plaques of a now quite undatable, ancient Chinese origin. Their value is purely archaeological, and with the best will in the world I can find no aesthetic response at all toward them . . . Rivière is, it seems, upset by this. But now we make our way through a forest of African sculptures, masks, shields, and to the little office of the chief curator of the museum, who can pull some strings in the Quai d'Orsay.

But while he writes his letter, I have time to admire the carved African monsters that have been temporarily removed from exhibition . . . I've seen better examples only at Tristan Tzara's, one of the founders of the famous Dada movement, who always wore a monocle and had a rich collection of masks and early Picassos. At his place I meet the cropped Gertrude Stein.

But there's no time to pause here to analyze Gertrude Stein's innovations, or to go into her advice to me about my trip to America. Nor is there time to stop for Dadaism, the last stage in disintegration of the conception of art and a regression not so much to childhood as to infantilism. Only Tactilism, perhaps, goes further — Marinetti's[10] fireworks of the twenties, an art to be touched instead of seen.

But all this had long since passed away, even at the time I am writing about, when the very newest thing in Paris was Surrealism, with Max Ernst in painting and Luis Buñuel in the cinema (*Un Chien Andalou* had just been completed, and shooting just begun on *L'Age d'Or*).

Also forgotten is the once popular hypothesis that in Negro art (in its proportions or, to be more exact, in its disproportions) is preserved the appearance of pygmies, as if they were forebears of all later Negro tribes . . .

But my letter has been written, I bid the treasures and their kind curator farewell, and off I go to the Quai d'Orsay.

Monsieur Marx (sic!) is also very nice, but completely at a loss. There is absolutely nothing he can do. And his kind, distressed face, with its protuberant eyes beneath bristling, gray hair, is somehow very like the Negro idols in the Trocadéro Museum.

Maître Philippe Lamour's mission is more successful. I meet Malraux in a tiny room with a sloping ceiling in the editorial block of the NRF. He is still quite young, but even at this time a lock of hair falls across his face, just as it did many years later when we walked the streets of Moscow together . . .

Somewhere near the "National" he was to boast of his truly phenomenal memory.

He knows by heart the whole of . . . Dostoevsky.

---

10. Emilio Filippo T. Marinetti (1876–1944), Italian writer and founder of literary Futurism, became a Fascist in 1919.

"Do you want to try me? I can quote you from memory any passage from any novel!"

He stops opposite a baker's and launches into the beginning of a chapter of the sad story of Prince Myshkin, then an extract from *The Brothers Karamazov*, and to the words of Raskolnikov I take him by the arm and lead him to the hotel.

But he stops again.

"If you wish I can recall exactly what we said as we left the NRF building?"

As we left to go where? A café, of course.

All the meetings during these feverish days start in cafés, are held in cafés, or are concluded in cafés, if not in suburban restaurants or bistros . . .

André Malraux will do all that is necessary: *la Sorbonne marchera*, the Sorbonne will be set in motion. In a day, the protest of the professors headed by Langevin is ready. With Toille at the League of Human Rights we are most successful. I am very glad, more for his sake than mine. He had been so sincerely depressed when he didn't manage to make Millerand act.[11]

This attempt had been limited to a very nice lunch with Madame Millerand, but didn't lead to anything at all. The most interesting thing turned out to be the elevator in their house, one of the first to have been installed in Paris. And therefore now one of the capital's most old-fashioned.

Luxuriating in the decorative splendor of the absurd *art nouveau* (vying in this with our sleeping cars or Maxim's restaurant, famous from *The Merry Widow*,[12] which has preserved its décor unchanged), this attraction took us up to the first floor, equivalent to two flights of stairs, in ten to fifteen minutes.

Toille's mission turns out to be the most successful of all. I meet not only Gernoud but also Victor Basch. A charming old man in a soft collar and a black tie done in an old-fashioned knot, he is one of the few active Dreyfusards remaining, now that Anatole France and Clemenceau are dead.

How difficult it is to associate the distinctive figure of the ancient "imperialist tiger," Clemenceau, with his ardent participation in the affair of Colonel Dreyfus and later that of Zola. And yet I remember that the windows of Parisian bookshops were crammed with pictures and books about him.

"The Tiger" was buried, I believe, at his birthplace in Vendée.

And buried, I believe, according to the local custom — standing up. Of course, this angry and aggressive little ape, who caused our young country so much harm, could find peace only standing up. Quite recently (recent in this

---

11. Alexandre Millerand (1859–1943) was the eleventh president of the republic and an editor of Socialist journals.

12. *The Merry Widow* is a famous operetta by Franz Lehár; it was made into a film in 1934 by Ernst Lubitsch.

case to 1946) we saw him brought back to life on the screen in Henry King's film *Wilson*, in the scene of the meeting of the Big Four of Versailles.[13]

I am generally lucky with the eminent departed. I had been in Berlin, about six months before this time in Paris, when Stresemann died.[14] And I remember the Reichstag with its funereal draperies and Stresemann's body being carried out. There was a lot of newspaper ballyhoo at the time, about Stresemann's death, caused by the graphologist Raphael Sherman. It seems that Stresemann had been ill, and someone who worked in the Ministry of Foreign Affairs brought Raphael Sherman a line of anonymous handwriting. Sherman jumped up from his chair and shouted hysterically: "This man is on the brink of death! Don't allow him to become excited! He will die of a heart attack!"

A few days later Stresemann, against doctor's orders, went to the Reich-stag. He had a skirmish with someone in some committee or other. And fell to the floor. A heart attack.

The anonymous handwriting belonged to Stresemann. The man from the ministry, who had paid no attention to Sherman, the Cassandra, was in despair. He poured it out all over the pages of the newspapers. An interview with Sherman followed, and then the whole story at great length.

I hadn't met Stresemann, but did get very friendly with Raphael Sherman. He explained to me that his system of graphology was based on cryptograms, and that he read the images and outlines that a person unconsciously puts into his handwriting, revealing an obsessive thought or the illness that is troubling him. Those contemplating suicide inevitably have the outline of a pistol some-where. Stresemann was worried about the condition of his heart, and the infa-mous anonymous line was full of drawings of "broken hearts" (incomplete contours of a special sort in the letters *a* and *o, v* and *w*) . . .

Sherman had one trick that always worked. When you entered his office, this bundle of exposed nerves jumped up and transfixed you with his eyes, then, his hand jerking across the paper, he began to write . . . your own hand-writing! The exact character of your writing. He did this with me, and I saw the same thing done with a number of other people. But I won't go into the far from miraculous solution of this phenomenon (in no way the trick of a charlatan!) . . .

I do not even ask any questions of Victor Basch. It is pleasant just to see him there alive before me and to touch a real, live participant in one of my favorite and most exciting *épopées*. I mean the case of Zola. But from Dreyfus, I dissociate myself in much the same way, and with as much distaste, as did the

---

13. The Big Four at the Versailles Conference in 1919 were Georges Clemenceau of France, Wood-row Wilson of the United States, Lloyd George of Great Britain, and Vittorio Orlando of Italy.

14. Gustav Stresemann (1878–1929) was German minister of foreign affairs from 1923 to 1929. He was awarded the Nobel Peace Prize in 1926.

most ardent Dreyfusards after his final rehabilitation. The central figure in one of the world's greatest campaigns and battles of contradictions — this insignificant little officer, completely ignoring the battle of principles being waged by the progressive section of the French intelligentsia against the reactionary French military establishment — dreamed only of removing the stain of undeserved dishonor from his tunic. One is involuntarily reminded of Lao-tse,[15] who said that the wheel turns, but at the center of the wheel there is emptiness, nothing, the hole for the axle. So, its spokes playing, the wheel turns around its own emptiness; so paltry a personality was he who could have gone down in history as a high-principled heroic martyr of Devil's Island, the equal of Silvio Pellico,[16] Vera Figner,[17] or Sacco and Vanzetti.

It is interesting that the most damning feature of his biography is revealed by an episode from the Dreyfus family chronicles.

When my Parisian adventure was already over and I had signed a contract with Paramount to go to Hollywood, the firm's representative and I examined some possible subjects. Among them was *The Trial of Zola* (the play was causing a sensation at the time in Berlin).

There was a time when I longed to do this subject. For me, my analysis of the subject was clear: with the vivid impression of my own experiences still fresh, I wanted to settle my score with reactionary France, to cut a longitudinal section through the many-layered cake of French reaction, merging the prototypes of the characters in Zola's novels with my own live impressions, and to wage a titanic mass struggle around the trial of my favorite novelist. And, by the way, to settle one or two personal accounts . . .

The framework within which the film was envisioned and later realized through the efforts of William Dieterle didn't interest or engage me in the least. I wanted to end the gigantic, international commotion around "the martyr of Devil's Island," and his defender Zola, with a tiny epilogue, what the Americans call an anticlimax (in this case an anti-apotheosis).

The material for this would come from a little story about the aging Dreyfus, imprudently divulged to me by a Monsieur Lévi, one of his distant relatives. Monsieur Lévi was a small, sharp-nosed man in pince-nez, who ran a small publishing business specializing in luxury editions. An album of photoreproductions of the treasures of the Hôtel Rambouillet[18] (hôtel in the sense of a

---

15. Lao-tse was a Chinese philosopher of the sixth century B.C.

16. Silvio Pellico (1789–1854), a writer associated with the Italian national revolutionary movement, was sentenced to fifteen years of hard labor for his political activities. Freed early, in 1830, he worked for prison reform.

17. Vera Nikolayevna Figner (1852–1942), the Russian revolutionary (Narodnik), was imprisoned in Shlisselburg fortress from 1884 to 1904. When she was released, she was exiled, and did not return to the USSR until the 1917 Revolution.

18. The Rambouillet was a museum in Paris.

palace) was typical of such an edition, and during the thirties Léon Moussinac worked on such editions for him. From this stemmed our acquaintance and trips together to the outskirts of Paris, together with Monsieur Lévi and his little girlfriend.

The fuss surrounding the trials has long since died away, goes the tale. The ocean of wrought-up public opinion has long calmed down. Dreyfus is now a very old man. He no longer leaves his chair or gets out of his dressing gown.

A family council. The patriarch attends but sits to one side, as if such everyday trivialities do not concern him.

A heated debate breaks out around the table. It seems some suspect that the cook has been stealing. In time, all sides are heard; some for, some against. The defense makes its case. The prosecution launches its attack.

But finally, the outcome is that the charge is not proved.

The matter is ready to be consigned to oblivion when, suddenly, in the silence comes the voice of the patriarch, Dreyfus, who has been forgotten in the heat of debate. His voice says: "Still, there's no smoke without fire . . ." And THE END comes up on the screen.

Devil's Island! The three trials! Anatole France and Clemenceau! The high command and the secret *bordereau*! Zola's flight! *J'Accuse* and the oceans of the press! . . .[19] If I sometimes regret not making that film, it is only because of this ending! . . .

By evening my legs can scarcely support me. But in the hotel (this time really meaning hotel!) I am met by a tubby little man in pince-nez and a bowler hat, with an umbrella between his knees.

It is amazing how we are loved by those who lose money on us! Sometimes their love is thereby paradoxically much greater, like the love of Monsieur Perrichon[20] not for the young man who had saved him, but the one he himself saved. Do you remember Labiche? The monsieur in the bowler hat has lost a lot of money on us. Not on me personally, but on Soviet cinema as a whole. He published a very respectable film magazine and suddenly got the idea of bringing out a special issue dedicated to the Soviet cinema. As of the next number, all the firms that had been advertising in his magazine stopped doing so. The nice monsieur went ignominiously bust, losing the magazine and his money.

---

19. Some facts about the Dreyfus case: After the first trial, Dreyfus was sent to Devil's Island. The military court in the second trial acquitted Esterhazy, the true culprit. The third trial brought a reduction of Dreyfus's sentence, and he was then "pardoned" by the French president. Among those who defended Dreyfus and brought about the third trial were Anatole France, Emile Zola, and Clemenceau. Zola published a series of articles called *J'Accuse!*, for which he was tried on charges of libeling the court-martial. He spent some time in exile in England. The "secret *bordereau*" was the forged document that had been used to convict Dreyfus.

20. The reference is to the eponymous hero of *The Travels of Perrichon*, a comedy by Eugène Marin Labiche (1815–1888).

Yet this does not prevent him from being the most ardent supporter of Soviet cinema, or from being one of the first to greet me warmly on my arrival in Paris, bringing as a present a copy of that ill-fated issue of his magazine.

I've met such enthusiasm and ardor on two other occasions. From Eugene Klopfer, who had lost a great deal of money when he thought of "capitalizing on the fuss over *Potemkin*" by distributing .`. . *Strike*, my first film, which naturally didn't get distributed. Then there was the owner of a cinema in San Antonio, Texas, who proved still more devoted to us. He had managed, by some means, to lose money on *Potemkin*. (But then, if you show *Potemkin* in Texas, a reactionary farming state, what else could you really expect?) Be that as it may, this puny, graying man, having found out that we are stuck in Nuevo Laredo, on the Mexican border with the United States, drives specially down to see us. And tells us delightedly how he had lost money on *Potemkin*. Nonetheless, his re-peated visits are not entirely disinterested. On his second visit he starts inquir-ing whether we don't find Laredo very boring? Then he begins asking if we wouldn't like an interesting way of passing the time? And finally he comes straight out and asks whether we would think about making a picture on the subject of the struggle of Texas.

He has in mind, of course, the battles of Palo Alto and Resaca de la Palma, north of the Rio Grande, in 1846. "My friends," he says, "owners of the biggest ranches around here, will get you all the horses you want . . ."

We explain tactfully that, for one thing, just horses are not quite enough to make a picture with, and, for another, showing films is not the only way of losing money.

You can lose a great deal more by making them.

The old man gives a grunt and rubs his stubbly chin, but the next day he is back with us again, with a new plan. Señora Montoya is the idol of Mexico and South America. "Señora Montoya!" The old man says the name in a chant, clicking his tongue. "Señora Montoya!" She is the Sarah Bernhardt of South America. He has not heard of Eleonora Duse, or he would have called her the Duse. "Señora Montoya . . ."

Señora Montoya is on tour. Señora Montoya will perform in a few days' time in Monterrey, the first large town below Nuevo Laredo in Mexico.

"Imagine a film with Señora Montoya! It doesn't matter what film. Any of the plays she does. Can you imagine the magic of that name for distribution in South America, 'Señora Montoya?' "

I ask, "But have you seen her?"

"Who, Montoya? Never! Still . . . Señora Montoya . . ." He rolls his tongue around the name as if it were a lollipop.

It is decided that we should take a look at this wonder, but I cannot be bothered with going to Monterrey.

Eduard Tisse does not mind where he is going, does not mind why he is going, as long as he *is* going. He goes to see Señora Montoya with the enterprising Texan.

Late at night, after the performance, my theater fans return. Tisse is doubled up with laughter. The señor from San Antonio spits furiously, and suddenly reverting to the tongue of his forefathers, growls angrily between his teeth, *"Alte Hure!"*[21]

It seems that Señora Montoya's theater is far from being on the same level as that of *The Plays of Clara Gazul.*[22] According to the sufferers, it was a sort of provincial puppet show, with a touch of *danse macabre.* Before me, I see vividly the image of a certain sixteenth-century Italian play, in which the enterprising spiritual fathers, staging the Second Coming at the town's cemetery, employed real corpses from the mortuary. The show was evidently something like that.

"Montoya!" our acquaintance snorts disgustedly as he vanishes in his Ford into the darkness, in the direction of San Antonio. And we see no more of him.

The next morning the local head of the Immigration Service runs joyfully across to us from the American side. He often comes to see us and help while away the time.

"The visas are through!"

Within an hour or so we are speeding across the promised land of the United States, through the state of Texas . . .

But back to the little Frenchman in the bowler who has come to help me. And he does!

"Don't be fussy! Come round to my place. I live just a stone's throw from here."

It is an extraordinarily dirty, middle-class bourgeois flat. That special sort of dirt which the French expressively call *crasse.* This word always conjures up in me a feeling of oily soot, and there's as much oily soot here as you could want! In the "salon" is an oval table, covered for some reason in green baize. The salon also serves as our host's study. And also, probably, as the editorial office of the now defunct magazine. On the green baize is a white and gold inkpot. Extremely dirty. And here also are little cups of hot, slopped coffee. Almost lost in the darkness are some broken, gilt Louis Seize chairs. On the chairs are two sinister fat characters in dark suits. There is also a slovenly-looking lady, the wife. But she doesn't sit still, and I can't get her in focus. In its way, this is another council of war.

My tubby friend turns out to be neither more nor less than the secretary of the Des Anciens Combattants, some kind of veterans' organization. It is a most reliable organization — or, in plain language, completely reactionary. What is

---

21. "Old whore!"

22. These plays by Prosper Merimée (1830–1870), imitating Spanish drama, were published in 1825.

more, the Première Arrondisement (the central market district) is a nest of reaction. This doesn't prevent him from being a warm and, as his business affairs show, a disinterested and sincere friend of our cinema. He decides to risk his good name and reputation and to use one or another of his connections in the prefecture.

And then, as if out of the ground, appears the Vicomte Etienne de Beaumont (France has more than just the Vicomte de Bragelonne!).[23] At one time he and his wife had been to Moscow. He was interested in films and he visited me in the studio, watched the editing, saw the rushes. I had paid him a visit here in Paris. But I hadn't met this tall, well-built, graying, and slightly stooping version of Monsieur Charlus[24] again since the time he was too frightened to organize a showing of *The Old and the New* for a select circle in his little Winter Garden. But at the moment when a colleague is overtaken by adversity, the dear vicomte, something of a film-maker himself, cannot but appear with his characteristic springy walk to come to the assistance *de son cher ami*.

He himself can do nothing, of course, but his other *très cher ami*, Jean Hugo, will of course be happy to.

Hugo?

But yes! The grandson of Victor Hugo!

Jean Hugo belongs to our caste; he works with Carl Dreyer (the maker of *Jeanne d'Arc*, one of the most beautiful pictures in the history of the cinema).

The grandson of Hugo! What more is necessary? It should be enough. But they keep telling me insistently it won't stop there . . .

---

23. The allusion is to the Vicomte de Bragelonne in a novel of the same name by Alexandre Dumas père.
24. Monsieur Charlus is a character in Proust's *A La Recherche du Temps Perdu*.

Gance and
Colette

THEY KEEP ADVISING ME to get in touch with Abel Gance.[1] He "has" a couple of ministers, not with very influential portfolios, but still! I have met Gance before, and I telephone him myself.

He charmingly asks me to call on him at the studio. He is in the middle of shooting *The End of the World*, or some such title; I don't remember exactly what this latest grandiose venture of his is called. This venture by the maker of *Napoléon* has consumed a mountain of money, but hasn't yet been completed. He is shooting, I think, in Joinville, though it may be some other studio, but it is, in any case, quite a long way from town, and, if I am not mistaken, near the Bois de Vincennes.

On the way, of course, it is impossible to dismiss the literary reminiscences connected with the forest and castle. Here the heroes of Paul Féval were once shot, and the heroes of Ponson du Terrail languished in the castle. Of course, no one at that time imagined that Marshal Pétain would while away his dishonorable old age in this same castle. But everyone remembers that Mata Hari was shot in the courtyard of Vincennes castle. Marlene Dietrich will play this role, powdering herself and looking at her own reflection in the sword blade of the young officer who is in command of her execution (a splendid *trouvaille* of von Sternberg,[2] so convincing in films of low life, yet so pathetic in his vain attempts at aesthetics!). Meanwhile, we tear along and swing around on the wide studio courtyard. There is the usual commotion in the studio. Chaos. Only there's a

---

1. Abel Gance (1889–1981), the famous French pioneering film director, was the first to use a triple-screen projection; it was for his epic film *Napoléon*. That film was shown in the United States in 1982.

2. Joseph von Sternberg (1894–1969), Austrian director and screenwriter, came to the United States in 1925. *The Blue Angel*, his best-known film, was made in Germany in 1930.

little more than usual because of the recent arrival of "unmotivated" sound in cinematography and because of the absurd idea that you can shoot a film in three languages simultaneously.

That is what Gance is doing. He is making three versions at once: French, English, and Spanish. Almost all the figures in *The End of the World* are semisymbolic. There is a virgin. There is Satan. The part of Satan is taken by two actors. One knows Spanish and French; the other, only English. There are three virgins, one for each language. Another participant in this same scene knows French and English, and there is another actor for the Spanish version. Try to imagine shooting three times consecutively, in three languages, with half the cast changed, plus all the numerous takes!

I think Gance is glad of my arrival, so willingly does he tear himself from this babel of languages and versions, dialects and accents. He is extremely sympathetic, and in a little room somewhere in the depths of the studio makes detailed notes for conversations with ministers. He can't promise anything, of course . . . But meanwhile tells me all about his own role in the film.

He acts in the prologue. In *Napoléon* he played Saint-Juste.[3] Here he portrays the carpenter who plays the role of Christ in a mystery play of the Oberammergau type.[4] During the course of the action he is crucified, and Gance assures me that he experiences ecstasy to such a degree that he has begun to prophesy in ancient Hebrew.

Is this possible? *"C'est à prendre ou à laisser,"* take it or leave it, as the French say. Perhaps when a director takes to acting, it is possible, but no self-respecting actor, of course, would ever spend himself in that way.

I had occasion to remember quite recently how Pudovkin auditioned for me at Alma-Ata for the role of Archbishop Pimen in *Ivan the Terrible*. He was so imbued with the feeling of being eighty-three years old that, although he was himself in perfect health, he suddenly "swooned" in front of the cameras from . . . a heart attack.

In any case, the photograph of Gance in a crown of thorns, big curls, and a beard, with drops of blood running down his cheeks, and a touching inscription in the corner, I shall keep as a happy memento of a very nice person, since the film brought him no laurels — only thorns.

I remember my first meeting with Gance a few months earlier. I was astounded by the surroundings — pseudo-Gothic and spurious Gothic, uncomfortable chairs with straight backs, and for some reason, in the center of the room, a life-size plaster copy of a statue of an androgynous figure. Little dummy arches had been built into the apartment for decoration, arches that were early

---

3. Louis Antoine Saint-Juste (1767–1796) was a revolutionary journalist and a collaborator of Robespierre's. They were executed together.

4. Oberammergau, in Germany, is famous for its passion play.

Renaissance rather than Gothic, and were cream in color and rough in texture. Between the arches were dark velvet curtains. Behind the curtains was a light blue background. And concealed lighting, evidently of various shades, played on the columns and walls.

Beside Gance, on one of the pseudo-Gothic chairs, sat his financial director (a White Guard émigré, I think; a Monsieur Ivanov) with the expression of a greedy chimera. It was clear from his greedy expression when he looked at me that his claws were trying to feel a way to shift the financial backing.

I think Gance was going through the third phase of overexpenditure and was searching for new capital investment.

This was not long before Chaliapin,[5] by devious means and through the agency of some jeweler on the Rue de la Paix, sent his "matchmakers" to see me.

Chaliapin was thinking of acting Don Quixote on the screen, and was very nervous about his first venture in talking films.

I was suspicious of Monsieur Ivanov's operations in this matter, although his rationale was that Chaliapin was "afraid" and wanted to start with "his own people."

His use of the word "own" after 1920, when he forsook our common homeland, is relative, to say the least, and the proposition was left hanging in the air.

Many years later I saw Pabst's *Don Quixote* on the screen, and though it grieves me to say it . . . I could not sit it out.

I remembered Chaliapin from the one occasion when I, a student on the balcony of the Marinsky Theater, heard him in *Boris Godunov* perform the unforgettable final aria "Hush, My Child" and saw him, in the ghost scene, sweep the cover from the table with a convulsive gesture of his left arm.

I also saw him on the screen as Ivan the Terrible in the film *Woman of Pskov*,[6] produced by either Khanzhonkov or Drankov, and here, even through the clumsy, galloping tempo of sixteen-frames-per-second shooting shown at twenty-four-frames-per-second speed, the nobility, the sculptural and dramatic qualities of the acting were not lost. But what was shown in *Don Quixote* was so endlessly sad and so clearly a talent in decline.

But there is no time to grieve about talents perishing far from their native soil. The tempo of recounting our further misadventures urges us on . . .

About further meetings.

From now on there twirls a kaleidoscope of characters involved in the *épopée* of my expulsion from Paris.

Colette. Colette! Paris is unthinkable without Colette, without Colette, the

---

5. Feodor Chaliapin (1873–1938) was the internationally known operatic basso. He left Russia in 1927 to live in Paris, and became a French citizen.

6. *The Woman of Pskov* was directed by Ivanov-Gai in 1915.

colorful author of *En Ménage*, Colette the wife of Willy, Colette the writer of those wonderful notes about how she worked the music hall. *L'Envers du Music Hall.*

Quite recently Colette was the "wife" of my friend Renaud's father. However, she exchanged him for her elder stepson, Renaud's brother Bertrand. And now it is awkward for Renaud to have any dealings with her. It is enough that he takes me like the wind in his little racing Bugatti from one end of Paris to the other, to all the meetings that my adventure involves; and when I get tired, when I can scarcely stand, or when I get bored by this game, he whisks me off in a flash by road to Versailles, where the unique rhythms of the parks and the palace staircases, the motionless surface of the lakes, give us new reserves for new adventures the next day.

Another friend of many years' standing, Léon Moussinac, puts me in touch with Colette. "Madame Colette will, of course, be only too pleased . . ."

She lives in a surprising place: on the mezzanine floor of the Palais Royale[7] galleries. On the side where the Palais Royale is, as it were, squeezed into a labyrinth of old, tiny streets, all corners, full of ups and downs, and in the dusk seemingly peopled by the characters from Balzac's *La Comédie Humaine.* Here one feels one might see the ghost of Gérard de Nerval,[8] who hanged himself on the very spot now occupied by the prompt box of the Théâtre de Châtelet.

Colette lives in a few tiny rooms above the arcade of windows that face inward onto the gardens of the Palais Royale. Beneath the lofty apartments of the upper floors. What these little windows must have seen in their time from beneath the half-arches of these mezzanines! The elegant, strolling crowds, in the manner of Debucourt[9] on the eve of the great events at the end of the eighteenth century. Once could be seen promenading in line her priestesses of love. Lists of their names have survived, exact inventories of their customs, information on their prices. And here the inflammatory speeches of Camille Desmoulins[10] were heard, and from here the revolutionary townsfolk swept in a flood to storm the Bastille.

How different these arcades and gardens seem from the backdrop we once painted at far-off Velikie Luki, in the days of the civil war, for a production of Romain Rolland's *The Storming of the Bastille!*[11]

---

7. The Palais Royale was built in 1629–1636 for Cardinal Richelieu.

8. Gérard de Nerval was the pen name of Gérard Labrunie (1808–1855), a poet and eccentric. He translated Goethe's *Faust* into French.

9. Philibert Louis Debucourt (1755–1832) was an engraver and painter, especially of genre scenes.

10. Camille Desmoulins (1760–1794) was a politician and journalist who supported Danton and was executed with him.

11. The Rolland play was produced and designed by Eisenstein in April 1920, in the Garrison Club at Velikie Luki.

Later, the hero of Balzac's *The Fatal Skin* would glide beneath these very Palais Royale arcades to a gaming house. The window embrasures are the same ones. They have seen the Commune, the first siege of Paris by the Germans, and the city's liberation. The second siege. And its second liberation.

Colette's flat is filled with a collection of glass. She arrives a little late, so I have time to take a look at the quaint glass with flowers, fruit, and little birds set into it and oblong cabinets with glass figurines of saints, monks, and angels soaring inside them.

Colette arrives, with tousled fringe and in a jacket of masculine cut, sporting dark eyeshadow.

She will do everything for me. She is dining tomorrow at a certain house, and Philippe will be at the dinner. She will talk to him about me.

Philippe is Philippe Berthelot. Berthelot is the all-powerful head of the Ministry of Foreign Affairs, the notorious Quai d'Orsay, as the ministry is called in the press.

There is something of the Regency period in my bow and kiss of her hand. At the very least, I feel like *un roué*. Her surroundings have got the better of me already. The finishing touch is the white wallpaper with wide, pink *fraise écrasée* stripes.

Epopée
Cocteau
"Forgive France"

W HEN EVENTS ARE AT their most hectic I suddenly receive a quite
unexpected letter from Cocteau[1] with a distorted pentagram in the corner of the
page. The letters are like pictures or like lace, and the lines crawl across the
paper, like caterpillars, in different directions.

In this letter, the words fail to transform themselves into the verbal but-
terflies of Cocteau's whimsical turn of phrase. It is a purely business letter. Poor
Cocteau, *ce pauvre Cocteau*, is in despair. He has only just found out about
my troubles. He begs me to call on him. He wants to help me. He is waiting
for me.

Cocteau lives in the very heart of Paris. In a street behind the Madeleine.
Though it is in the city center, the district behind this hulking mass of Greek
pediments and columns enjoys ill repute. "Magdalene" in the biblical sense has
a precise meaning, and the district teems with such Magdalenes.

Cocteau likes the district. He feels fully at home. And why not? It is the true
tradition of French aesthetes . . .

Cocteau greets me with his usual collection of affectations. He agitatedly
extends to me his enormous hands, the famous hands of Cocteau, with their
thick veins; hands that look as if they have been detached from some quite
different person — *The Hands of Orlac* (remember the film with Conrad Veidt?)[2]
— and then affixed to the frail figure of Cocteau. He begs me . . . "to forgive
France" for her rudeness, for the unbearable insult to me. He wants to help me.

---

1. Jean Cocteau (1889–1963), the novelist, playwright, poet, artist, and scriptwriter, wrote *Les
Enfants Terribles*, *Antigone*, and many other works.

2. *The Hands of Orlac* was a German Expressionist film directed in 1925 by Robert Wiene, with
Conrad Veidt playing the lead.

He is in despair. He cannot, at the moment, use his connections with the police. "That brigand," his valet, a young Annamite,[3] has just been caught with opium again. Or was it hashish? Or cocaine? At any rate, it was not marijuana, the miracle-working smoke with which the Mexican soldiers stupefy themselves.

There is a theory that the astounding ornamental disintegration of the forms of nature in Aztec, Toltec, and Mayan architecture was either created in a marijuana trance or depict memories of one. A normal conscious condition would hardly be capable of such extravagance. Cocteau's sketches and jottings are done in just the same way, while he sobers up from the effects of opium fumes. So the young Annamite, "that brigand," has most probably been caught actually buying the opium . . .

But never mind.

"In France everything must be done through the ladies," Cocteau declares. "Will you permit me to do that?"

Marie Marquet is an actress of the Comédie Française as well as the mistress of Monsieur Tardieu, the prime minister. Cocteau at present has his one-act play *La Voix Humaine* at the Comédie. He has included *The Carriage of Holy Communion* by Clara Gazul in the same program, and Marie Marquet plays in *The Carriage.* "She is earning a lot of money through me. She won't refuse to have a talk with Tardieu in bed . . ."

Hurrah! The final touch. My case has reached the prime minister's bed! The picture of France as exposed in the light of my visit is complete.

"And now you must forgive me. I must just finish earning enough for our lunch. They're bringing the money in fifteen minutes. The order will have to be completed by then . . ." This order is for some verse in couplets to advertise silk stockings for one of the largest Paris firms. Cocteau sits down, and couplets flow as if from a cornucopia . . .

This is not my first meeting with Jean Cocteau. We had seen each other before, soon after my arrival.

Once, long ago, I had, pinned to my wall, a little round portrait of him, which had been cut out of, I think, the magazine *Je Sais Tout*. Drawn on the thoughtful face, made out of a gigantic globe, was a little figure in a black frock coat supporting the globe with its hand. This little portrait hung in honor of his scandalous new play *Les Mariés de la Tour Eiffel*. It had caused a scandal in that it had broken all the conventions of a play, as well as of the theater. It was this play which had the "radio town criers," dressed in Cubist costumes by Picasso, standing right and left. And it was these which I had parodied, albeit in unrealized sketches in an unrealized production in Foregger's theater, in the

---

3. Annam was part of Indochina, now Vietnam.

characters of "mother, the automatic restaurant" and "father, the water closet" for a new transcription of *Columbine's Scarf*,[4] alias *Pierette's Veil* . . .

I had been warned that Cocteau had two ways of receiving guests. He either poses as the *Maître* and is condescending, or he plays the imaginary invalid and receives the guest lying down, grumbling about his health in a complaining voice, his vast hands limp on the blanket. I was received in the second variation. And even accorded the highest degree of recognition: in the middle of our talk there came a quite unexpected expressive pause. Then he said to me, "You suddenly seem to me to be bathed in blood . . ."

Our second meeting was less sanguine. It was the private première of his play at the Comédie Française. That same *Voix Humaine* that has ensured for him Mademoiselle Marquet's friendship. This première in the respectable and decorous Comédie Française also erupted in a scandal. The scandal, it is true, was not in response to any "leftist" slant; on the contrary, it was because of his unconditional retreat from pranks and his return to traditional theater at its most boring. The actual cause of the scandal, when you come right down to it, was . . . me.

In his letter, Cocteau had written that he wasn't at all upset with me. Indeed, we shall see that he even had cause to be grateful to me.

I had four invitation tickets to the première. I dined with some friends, four antiquarians with a charming little antique shop, which had carved gilt Madonnas and a whole cellar of Peruvian pitchers, most of them made in the form of a dog. The fashion for them and hence the demand had begun to decline, and they no longer served as bait in the shop windows.

Lunching with us was Aragon,[5] now a well-known and much loved comrade of ours, though then still wholly in the Bengal lights and fireworks of the Breton wing of the Surrealists; and also Paul Eluard, another poet and another pillar of the group at that time. I am on rather cool terms with this group of Surrealists, grouped around their central leader, André Breton. I think Breton, who poses rather unsuccessfully as a "Marxist"(!), is somewhat hurt by the fact that, on arriving in Paris, I did not consider it necessary to visit him and present my compliments. Any sort of contact with the "Marxist" salon snobs is generally unpleasant, but now there occurred something even worse.

The crippled Prampolini, an Italian artist whom I had met at the Congress of Independent Cinematographers in Switzerland, dragged me along to some soirée of young Italian Futurist painters and poets. The paintings were bad. The

---

4. In 1922, Eisenstein worked with S. Yutkevich on a script of the pantomime *Columbine's Scarf* for N. Foregger's theater. It was never produced, but the director's sketches are preserved in Eisenstein's archives.

5. Louis Aragon (1897–1982), novelist, poet, and essayist, was a leading Dadaist. He was a member of the Central Committee of the French Communist Party. His sister-in-law, Lily Brik, was loved by Mayakovsky; her sister, Aragon's wife, was the writer Elsa Triolet.

poetry worse. But I was introduced there quite unexpectedly to . . . Marinetti! There could not be the slightest cordiality on my part, of course, at this meeting.

As one newspaper wrote in its report on the opening of this exhibition, "It was piquant to see under one and the same roof one of the soothsayers of Fascism beside an out-and-out adherent of Communism."

Breton could not get over the fact that this meeting took place before my meeting with him, although I consider both Futurism and Surrealism equally far removed, both in ideology and form, from what we have done and are doing.

It was very intriguing, of course, to have a look at the live Marinetti. I had never imagined him to be as he was: fat, a black mustache; like a policeman or fireman of fairly large proportions, dressed in plain clothes, with a "beery" paunch sticking out through the cutaway of his morning coat, and with coarse, greasy hands. This, then, in 1930 was the reigning philosopher of Futurism, Urbanism, Tactilism, and, above all, aggressive militarism.

He was just as "colorful" in the French poem of his that he read with so much "greasy" relish. I can still hear today his greasy "*je flair*,"[6] which he pronounced "*fle-e-er*." What was this aroma inhaled by the author of the poem? The poem was written as if by the author's dog!

Yesenin merely addressed himself to Kachalov's dog. Not so Marinetti. He writes directly in the "person" of his dog. And the greasy "*fleeer*" concerns the moment when, near the end of the poem, the dog chances on human excrement and trembles before the instant when he will ingest "the inner substance," the true secret of his master's nature — of Man. Um-m-m. *Parlez pour vous*, my dear *maître*!

I am not exaggerating here in the least. It can be checked. "It" is printed in the collection entitled *I nuovi Poetti futuristi* (1930), with a pompous dedication to me — to my "*grand talent futuriste*" — and signed with a flourish by the author. The book is preserved somewhere among the particularly paradoxical rarities of my chamber of horrors.

But what annoys Breton even more is that I have become friendly with a group of the more democratic youths that have broken away from him. They have their headquarters in a café with the figures of two Chinese idols over the door — hence its name, Café des Deux Magots — and are without the arrogance, the posing, and snobbism of their elders, whose blunders they bitterly attack. And as it happens, one of the group has just put out a delightful pamphlet, *Un Cadavre*, aimed directly at Breton! . . .

After lunch Aragon dashed off quickly somewhere. So I offered Eluard the remaining fourth ticket.

Paul Eluard . . .

---

6. "I catch the smell."

The *Larousse Dictionary* has a table comparing the heights of the world's tallest structures. Here are cathedrals, here the Eiffel Tower (I once saw Eiffel himself when he was an old man, sitting outside the gates of his little villa while on an excursion from Paris), and here are the pyramids. Eluard, in his bearing, the way he held himself, in his shoulders, jaw, and his challenging face, resembled Mayakovsky to some extent. But in a comparative table of figures (not to mention creative power!) he might occupy a position somewhere about level with Notre Dame Cathedral, if the late Vladimir Vladimirovich Mayakovsky was allotted the Cheops Pyramid or the New York Empire State Building, not yet included in the *Larousse* of those years.

"But I warn you," says Eluard, "I'll raise a scandal!" (The Surrealists loathed Cocteau.)

Either disbelief in his protestations, or curiosity concerning a possible scandal (I had just let slip the chance to be at a night club scandal, where some group had organized a nocturnal cocktail party in pyjamas. Oh! the gay twenties!), causes me to pay no attention to what he says. And here we are in the Grand Circle at the Comédie Française. Starched shirts. Cuffs. Gold pince-nez. Well-groomed beards. Ladies in formal attire. A nauseatingly respectable gathering.

"The tabs are up," as the old-timers say backstage. A correct drowsiness starts to percolate into the decorum. There is only one actress in the play. With an imagined partner . . . at the other end of the telephone. It is an interminable monologue. The interminability slowly swallows up the grains of possible drama in the scene. And suddenly there rises between me and my view of the stage the tall, square figure of Eluard.

His sharp voice: "Whom are you phoning?" An instantaneous hush. The actress falls silent. The audience, unable to believe its ears, turns toward Eluard.

But Eluard gives the public no time to collect itself. Like the blows of a hammer he rhythmically intones the classic *"Merde! Merde! Merde!"*

The hush passes, and a sort of hoarse screech answers him from the black depths of the stalls. The screech becomes a roar. The roar, a trampling of dozens of feet on the staircases leading up to the circle.

Gold pince-nez go flying, torn from their ribbons. Cuffs fly from raised fists. Hairy arms protrude from sleeves. There is the sound of starched shirt fronts bursting on overfat men, infuriated Tartarins[7] running up the staircases. Eyes are inflamed. Bald, perspiring heads are flushed. Ladies scream from the darkness below.

The actress jumps up, runs to the footlights, and, in the best traditions of one playing Racine and Corneille, mimes her anguish with an immensely broad

---

7. Tartarin was the fat character in Alphonse Daudet's *Tartarin de Tarascon.*

gesture (she has exceptionally long arms), alternating it at correctly judged intervals with an entreaty, then another mimed anguish, then again the crossed arms of the entreaty.

In vain! Short fat thighs have already run up the staircase, and short fat little arms have seized hold of Eluard. Eluard stands still, with the expression of a St. Sebastian and the self-consciousness of a Gulliver in Lilliput. But the Lilliputians, spluttering with rage, bring him to the floor.

His jacket rips. Dinner jackets rip in return. The pale face of the poet, jaw tightly clenched, emerges once more, like a sinking frigate, from the crowd, before Eluard rolls with a heap of other bodies down the monumental staircase of the Grand Circle.

Stormy applause directed toward the stage demands that the play continue, and, having expressed her "deepest gratitude," the actress returns to the interrupted text. And continues unhindered to the end of the play, of which, thank heavens, there is not much left! The public has not had time to cool off, and gives vent to its pent-up emotion, which has been only partially spent, by thunderous applause. Thus, Cocteau's work is assured of success.

"The fire lent her much enchantment," he remarks later.

Would there have been such an ardent ovation without an incident? When all is said and done, perhaps Cocteau doesn't have much cause to be annoyed with me? Perhaps he should even thank me? . . .

However that may be, I try to slip out of the theater without meeting him, but find it quite difficult. By a crafty maneuver, all the side doors have been closed, so that, whether you like it or not, you are forced to go through the little foyer, where the author, leaning "nonchalantly" against the base of someone (it might be Molière, it might be Coquelin Aîné[8]) with regal condescension, is thanking the public, as it files past, for its kind attention.

At last I find some sort of emergency exit, and in a few minutes I am in the fresh air, in a sort of cleft between La Maison de Molière and the outer wall of the Palais Royale.

Whew! . . .

"Whew!" exclaims Cocteau, straightening up. The couplets are ready, and we spend some time laughing at them until the bell rings. Cocteau brings in five hundred francs and we can go to lunch.

It seems there are any number of ways to make money. Cocteau sells the titles of his books as names for restaurants — books that always cause a stir, and that, in the 1930s, were very often artificially inflated. Such a place is the notorious bistro Boef sur le Toit (in memory of one of Debureau's[9] pantomimes).

---

8. Benoît Constant Coquelin (1841–1909), known as Coquelin Aîné, was a star of the Comédie Française and father of the actor Jean Coquelin.

9. Jean Gaspar Debureau (1786–1846) was a great pantomimist, famous for his creation of Pierrot in the Parisian Théâtre des Funambules.

In its cellar I meet the incomparable Kiki,[10] the model for all the greatest artists of Montparnasse. Kiki, doing a belly dance in Spanish shawls on top of a grand piano, which is being played by Georges Henri Rivière of the Musée du Trocadéro.

Kiki, who has given me a book of her memoirs with the inscriptions *"Car moi aussi j'aime les gros bateaux et les matelots."*[11] Finally Kiki, having herself begun to paint, draws my portrait. Grisha comes in unexpectedly toward the end of the second sitting. She screws up her enormous almond-shaped eyes, the eyes of an unfailingly good-natured mare, as she looks at Alexandrov, and my portrait turns out to have the lips of the future director of *The Merry Lads*.[12]

The title of Cocteau's latest novel, *Les Enfants Terribles*, also lands on the signboard of a restaurant. My copy of *Les Enfants* has the inscription, written in the same mannered, caterpillar writing and with the same pentagram, *"A celui qui m'a bouleversé en me montrant ce que je touchais avec les doigts d'aveugle. A Eisenstein, son ami Jean Cocteau. Paris, 9.1. 1930."*[13]

Nevertheless, we do not go to eat at a restaurant with one of these signs. We climb up out of the cauldron of unceasing traffic, out of its hubbub and roar, out of all that the French call so colorfully *brouhaha*, to one of the heights drawn like a belt around Paris. (Those who know Paris will pick me up on this and say that the hills do not form a complete ring; however, I shall stick to "drawn like a belt," for a city like Paris could be encircled only by a broken . . . unfastened belt!) This time it is not the height of Sacré Coeur, smothered in what they call the *bon Dieu séries*,[14] little medals with the burning heart of Christ, ex voto with healing properties, flowers, little ikons, ribbons, postcards with swallows whose beaks have real medals sewn on, bearing witness to the fact that the faithful pilgrim has genuflected at the foot of this hideous structure of Napoleon III's time, in its own way skillfully disfiguring the image of Paris. Nor is it the height of Montmartre, with its windmills, Place du Tertre so dreadfully familiar from paintings, with the bistro Au Lapin Agile,[15] where the incomparable Aristide Bruant once sang his songs. This time it is a special treat. The heights of La Villette. Where the slaughterhouses operate and the butchers do their work. Where there are the best little restaurants for underdone steaks, just as down

---

10. Kiki was the professional name of an artist's model, Alice Irene, famous in the 1920s.

11. "Because I too love big ships and sailors."

12. *The Merry Lads*, a popular slapstick comedy by G. V. Alexandrov, was his first independent film. He made it after his return from Mexico.

13. "To him who astounded me by showing me what I had merely touched with the fingers of a blind man. To Eisenstein, his friend Jean Cocteau. Paris, 9.1.1930."

14. *Bon Dieu séries* is an idomatic expression for various religious souvenirs sold in Roman Catholic churches.

15. Au Lapin Agile was a café once famous as a gathering place for artists and writers.

below, in "the belly of Paris," you can get incomparable onion soup with cheese that is drawn up from the plate by the spoon like golden seaweed; or where the best types of snails are found in other restaurants, which scare you at night with the long horns of gilt snails over their entrances. (Oh, you must not fail to dedicate one predawn matins to looking at this heathen temple of gluttony, whither caravans of victuals converge through the night.)

Over underdone steaks, Cocteau and I agree on everything. In addition to Marie Marquet, he will also have a talk with Philippe, as soon as Philippe returns from Geneva. This is the same Philippe to whom Colette has promised to talk. And within a few days, tiny sheets of paper start coming in regularly, covered with the microscopic handwriting of the head of the Ministry of Foreign Affairs. They tell Cocteau how my case is going. Cocteau sends them to me. And I keep them as souvenirs . . .

An unusually tall, lean, athletic-looking man appeared among us. The head of publicity for the Swiss firm Nestlé and its main specialty, condensed milk. The evening before, he had seen *The Old and the New,* and said that he had never before seen on the screen such a stirring sensation of milk as a natural element. The proposition: an advertising film for his firm. The subject: a trip around the world. The story: any or none. The essential conditions: to show that the children of Africa, India, Japan, Australia, Greenland, etc., etc., drink Nestlé's condensed milk.

We differed, I think, on the size of personal expenses, but the "difference," of course, went much deeper: the Soviet state hadn't educated me as a cinematographer for this!

On the Rue d'Astor in Paris is our trade mission. In 1929, the trade mission did not have a film department. There is, however, a department for the sale and dissemination of diamonds and precious stones from the Urals. It is run by a gloomy and deadly boring comrade. He has been given the extra function of selling our films. He flounders quite helplessly in deciding the commercial fate of our films . . . One fine day this diamond-trading comrade passes an official propostion on to me, for I am considered a specialist in historical "canvases."

Belgium is celebrating one hundred years of independence. And the Belgian government would like to see a commemorative film for the anniversary made by me. After this, of course, it is much less surprising to receive an invitation to go to Venezuela and shoot another commemorative film, to the glorious memory of Bolívar, the fighter for South American independence. It is interesting that in London, the Crown's agents for the colonies make me a proposition through Grierson.[16] To make a film on Africa. The only requirement

---

16. In 1929, John Grierson had set up the Empire Marketing Board Film Unit, which pioneered the English modern documentary film movement. He engaged Basil Wright and Herbert Marshall as his first editors.

is to show how England's colonial dominion has benefited the cultural growth and well-being of the Negroes!

Grierson has enough tact not to pass this proposition on to me! I learn of it later and regret that Grierson had more tact than sense of humor; God forgive me for the answer I might have burst out with on hearing such a proposition as this!

When, much later, I sit on the border of Mexico and the United States at Nuevo Laredo, between two stools, as it were, I receive the proposition to film the history of the state of Texas and the assurance that the local ranch owners will let me have as many horses as I want . . .

The first story suggested to me in Hollywood was "The Martyrdom of the Jesuit Missionary Fathers at the Hands of the Redskins in North America"; the last stories, Feuchtwanger's *Jud Süss* and *The Road Back* by Remarque.

We got no further than talks.

It was just the same with *Grand Hotel* and *The Life of Zola*, which Paramount tried to talk me into at the time the contract was signed in Paris.

It was in Paris that Chaliapin sent me a secret invitation to join him in making *Don Quixote* . . .

In Yucatán, at Mérida during the height of shooting *Que Viva Mexico!* a proposition arrives from my former supervisor at Paramount to film Kipling's *Kim* with him in India!

The Lady in the Black Gloves

THERE ARE NICE apparitions in childhood; vague visions, usually feminine. Very often they are memories of an early separation from one's mother, or sometimes a vague premonition of the way the future object of one's affections will look. Poems are written about them, as the young Goethe *an eine unbekannte Geliebte,* to an as yet unknown sweetheart. But this is by no means always the case.

A similar romantic image can become implanted in young dreams from a quite accidental impression, especially if this impression has something of the natural inclinations or predisposition of the perceiver. It is most interesting that this romantic vision need not be lyrical-romantic, like the ghostly bluish vision of the good fairy with the glass beads above the cradle. It can belong to another kind of romanticism, to its most fascinating aspect — irony.

The vision of an ironic fairy has hovered over me since I was very small. She wears black gloves to her elbow and has an actual address in Paris. She holds contracts for the café concerts of France, and, with an unforgettable sharpness of outline and contour, lives on the posters and in the etchings of one of France's greatest artists, caught forever by his eagle eye.

What was it about her image that first enslaved me? Was it the black gloves, the stories of my father, who had seen and heard the immortal *diseuse*[1] during his trips to Paris? Was it the texts of her songs, which, for some reason, fell into my hands very early? Was it Toulouse-Lautrec's drawings or the memoirs, *La Chanson de Ma Vie* and *L'Art de Chanter une Chanson?* Was it the elusiveness?

In 1926 Guilbert was appearing in concerts in Berlin while simultaneously

---

1. Eisenstein meant Yvette Guilbert (1865?–1944).

playing Martha Schwertlein in Murnau's *Faust*.[2] She had left for France only a few days before my arrival. In 1929, I missed her Paris concert by exactly three days.

Fatalité. Princesse Greuze[3] in black gloves is most elusive. Nevertheless, we did meet. I was extremely bored, then, even though I was in Paris and was being expelled from that wonderful city on suspicion of being engaged in Communist propaganda.

Later, Berthelot showed me Chiappe's secret report on me. The most fascinating item about my subversive activity (along with the fact that all Soviet pictures were made by me!) was the line stating that M. Eisenstein, *par son charme personnel,* was winning friends for the Soviet Union.

It was deadly boring that afternoon in the hotel. Someone was doing something to get my stay extended, and I had to wait for telephone messages.

Boulevard Montparnasse had not yet turned lilac in the dusk, the Jockey Club across the way had not yet turned on its lights, the Coupole and the Rotonde had not yet become a magical, nighttime fairy scene, and I was bored. Bored in the Paris of Daumier and Lautrec, Mallarmé and Robida,[4] *The Three Musketeers* and Yvette Guilbert.

Tiens! Why not phone my fairy in black gloves? Just like that, with no introductions, no friends in common. Her telephone number is not unlisted, and Madame answers the telephone herself.

"Well, but of course! How could you have thought that? Of course I know you. After all, I'm not an American!"

I visit her the next day.

"Money, money! You should take a lot of money from them. You go to America. Take as much as you can from them!"

Dame Yvette does not love America, and Dame Yvette loves money. Her memoirs are full of fights over contracts, over increases. Dame Yvette loves solid investments. Her salon is almost like a store, a shop, a warehouse of solid, lasting things. Little marble tables and lamps. Little gilt chairs and china. Bronze vases. A little old-fashioned but durable, intended for a space eight times larger, everything stands there looking like the Egyptian section of the British Museum, where the exhibits are six rows deep, mummy hiding mummy.

The walls are completely covered with pictures (portraits in black gloves) like the famous restaurant in New York, where you eat "tenderloin" steaks

---

2. *Faust*, a German film, was produced in 1926 by F. Murnau.

3. Princesse Greuze is the name of the title character in *La Princesse Lointaine*, a play by Edmond Rostand (1868–1918), written in 1895.

4. Albert Robida (1848–1926), an artist, illustrated an edition of Rabelais and contributed to *Le Caricature*.

while looking at the countless photos of racing accidents that cover the walls and ceiling.

Perhaps not. Dame Yvette's drawing room ceiling, unlike that of the restaurant, is bare. If you don't count several chandeliers, distributed in accordance with the variously arranged corners of the room. Or maybe some chandeliers were not hanging in the drawing room then. Maybe it's an impression given by the shaggy lampshades of the nineties on the table lamps, and the long-legged standard lamps rising from the floor to the very ceiling. But the impression that remains is of clusters of chandeliers.

Madame is in despair. She has a head cold. Otherwise she would have sung her repertoire for me, and *Dieu sait* how I adore her repertoire! My visit is to be, if not a matinée of song, then most certainly one of drama. Her reddish wig and trumpetlike nose. The too-expansive gestures and the exaggerated walk. All merging with the trumpeting declamation, too much for normal conversation, so that the *après-midi* is a continuous performance.

Just before I leave, I am bashfully slipped a little book . . . Sacher-Masoch. "Read it on your journey."

The book is dedicated to Catherine the Great. "If you think of doing it . . . then here is a Catherine."

Now I understand the performance. Madame was showing off her wares. And that was why Catherine, in all her aspects, passed before me during that memorable *après-midi*.

Madame likes Bernard Shaw's one-act play on the subject. *"Elle est vieille!"*[5] snarls Madame, and, cleaving the air powerfully with her arm, she shows how the empress extracts from a rank of strapping guardsmen the most strapping and most handsome.

The exaggerated gesture is eloquent. You see the rank before you. Her heavy step measures its length. You see the happy recipient of the empress's benevolence. A tenacious hand beckons the lucky one to her. Or the doomed one.

"Mais pas trop vieille,"[6] weakly protests her husband, Dr. Schiller, from the depths of a not very deep chair. He is so frail and small. Like a field mouse, gopher, or gerbil, he is lost in any chair, even in a miniature gray and gold Louis Quinze (stylish, of high quality, correctly evaluated).

In this sigh is a whole drama. The doctor's dying romanticism, and the sober, feminine sagacity of the realist Yvette.

"Sarcey m'a dit."[7]

(Heavens, Sarcey! The siege of Paris. The seventies! Perhaps the next to be mentioned will be Rabelais or Saint-Simon?)

---

5. "She's an old woman!"

6. "But not too old."

7. "Sarcey told me." Francisque Sarcey (1827–1899) was theater critic for *Le Temps*.

"Tu est folle, Yvette! On te sifflera!"[8]

She tells how, playing something about the guillotine (probably Ksanrof[9]), she came out in a working cap (these *casquettes* of the workers immortalized by Steinlen[10]) and a red scarf. A piece of lead was hidden in the cap, and when, in the song, the head fell off the guillotine, she let this *casquette* fall with a thud.

"And what do you think? The public broke the benches with delight!"

Then Dame Yvette begins to cover the upper part of her face with white semimasks. They are all different. Comic masks and character masks. Before me pass *avant la lettre* the inventions of a great *artiste*. She prepares a sketch in half-masks, and the acting and movements bring the masks to life. It seems as though it is not Yvette but they who are making faces, now sinister, now comic.

Once Miklashevsky[11] (I think he later became a string puppet manipulator in Italy) read a lecture on the play of masks on the stage of the Troitsky Theater and, snatching masks out of the desk and putting them on, made their expression change by acting. The chairman's table was in the depths of the stage, dignified, like the mystics at the start of *The Fairground Booth*, but I remember and see only one of those seated at it. The others have vanished into the slits of their own cardboard busts, disappeared in memory, as those in *The Fairground Booth* disappeared.

The only one — you have guessed it — the divine! The incomparable! Meyer-hold.

It was the first time I had seen him. And I was to worship him all my life.

---

8. "You're mad, Yvette. They'll give you the bird!"

9. L. Ksanrof, a leading French humorist, wrote many of Yvette Guilbert's songs.

10. Théophile Steinlen (1859–1923), a French artist of Swiss birth, was known for his posters, lithographs, and book illustrations. Many of his subjects were working-class people.

11. Constantine M. Miklashevsky, a Petrograd actor, became a puppeteer and was the author of a book on the Italian comedy of masks.

The Crimson
Ticket

Everything is at a standstill . . .

Days pass and there is no progress at all. My crimson ticket's[1] validity is running out, and I shall be in Berlin in a few days. Is the game lost, then, and all the effort in vain? A great pity!

But before leaving France, I want to see Vézelay.

The most astounding examples of Romanesque architecture are there, the most intricate figured capitals. The most severe and yet the most fantastic portal tympanum.

On returning, I cannot resist sending to Dr. Erwin Honig, in Berlin, a postcard showing one of the capitals of the Vézelay cathedral: an angel, leading the devil by the horns, is expelling him from the divine palm-encircled gardens. (As a reporter, Dr. Honig had once visited me in Leningrad during the shooting of *October*, and is now one of the editors in the gigantic Ulstein concern, which has just published with enormous success Remarque's *All Quiet on the Western Front*, in an edition of many thousands.) I inform Dr. Honig that I shall no doubt soon be in Berlin, as the Paris authorities are like that dock-tailed Romanesque angel.

The *Berliner Zeitung am Mittag* arrives in Paris a couple of days later. There, in the center page, is my devil being chucked out by an angel and a facsimile of the reverse side of the card, together with some gloating German taunts at the French. My *épopée* has assumed an international character!

Painstaking hands carefully enter another copy of this same paper in my ever-growing dossier. It does me no good, of course.

But I make matters even worse.

A certain little Socialist paper is out to do its best for me.

---

1. The crimson ticket was the police permit one needed for remaining in France.

One favor deserves another: they ask for an interview.

I am very irritated. Moreover, I have nothing to lose now — it seems.

I let myself go in my interview.

"What is the aim of your visit to Paris?"

"I want to meet the abbé who took Huysmans[2] to the bosom of the Catholic Church."

"What have you to say regarding the incident in which you were involved?"

"I made a mistake in coming to Paris without donating the necessary sum to the Hospital for Old and Infirm Gendarmes, of which Madame Chiappe is the patron . . ."

(This is one of the best known of the devious ways of bribing Monsieur Chiappe!)

And so on, riposte after riposte.

Next day there is great merriment in Montparnasse.

That evening I sit at one of the outer tables beneath the awning of the Coupole. My acquaintance, the Hungarian photographer, emerges from the dusk. A few days before, he had emerged from the shadows in just the same way, and, facing in another direction, had informed me confidentially under his breath: "I have seen your dossier . . . Everything's OK, I think . . ." Today he is furious. He shouts at me quite openly.

"You're out of your senses! . . . Your interview . . . Everything was fixed and now it's all ruined! Finished!"

To hell with it!

Tomorrow my permit expires . . .

---

2. J. K. Huysmans, author of *A Rebours* and other novels, converted to Catholicism and lived in a Benedictine monastery.

The Middle Years

Eisenstein in 1929

Shots from the milk separator sequence in "The Old and the New"

Eisenstein's wife, Pera Attasheva, in 1934

Eisenstein in fancy dress at the 1929 International Congress of Filmmakers at La Sarraz, Switzerland (Courtesy of the Swiss National Tourist Agency)

Eisenstein in Paris in 1929 with Hans Richter (left) and Man Ray (right)
(Courtesy of Philippe Sers Editeur à Paris)

A Russian cartoon showing Eisenstein besieged by the French police at the Sorbonne. The Russian legend at top reads: "The great victory of democratic France."

*Kiki de Montparnasse as
photographed by Man Ray (Courtesy
of Philippe Sers Editeur à Paris)*

*Eisenstein with Léon Mousinnac at
La Sarraz, 1929*

Eisenstein in England, en route to Hollywood, in 1930.
Left to right: Tisse, unknown, Alexandrov, Eisenstein,
Jacques Lipschitz, and Lionel Britton

Eisenstein at work in Hollywood, 1930

Eisenstein with Charlie Chaplin at Chaplin's home in 1930

Eisenstein pursuing the ill-fated project "Sutter's Gold" in northern California (By permission of Sovfoto)

TRAILS OF '49
HOCK FARM—HOME OF
GENERAL JOHN A. SUTTER
FROM 1842 TO 1868

THEODORE DREISER

200 West 57th Street,
New York City,
September 1, 1931.

Dear Eisenstein:

I am very much interested by your letter
and obliged to you for picturing the difficulties from your
point of view. Nothing grieved me more than their refusal
to let you make the picture. I was satisfied Paramount
had no one who could do it as well as you could have done
it, and the absolutely practical and material way in which
they side-tracked this original plan infuriated me.

As you saw, I did my best to prevent
production, but the decision enclosed will make clear
to you what happened. Also the judicial attitude in regard
to the moving picture in America as such. We now have a
legal interpretation of what its approach should be!

What are you doing in Mexico? Are you making
a film, and if so, what kind of a film are you making, and
how are you managing to live and be comfortable down there?

Have you any idea that "AN AMERICAN TRAGEDY"
could ever be filmed in Russia? I wish it might be. At any
rate, I want you to know that I hold you and your very distinguished work in the greatest admiration, and that I hope
the time will come when there may be something of mine that
will fall not only into your hands but your power to produce.

Did you ever read my tragedy entitled THE HAND
OF THE POTTER? If not, I should like to send you a copy.

My best wishes as always.

Theodore Dreiser

*A letter from Theodore Dreiser to Eisenstein
after the plan to film "An American Tragedy"
collapsed*

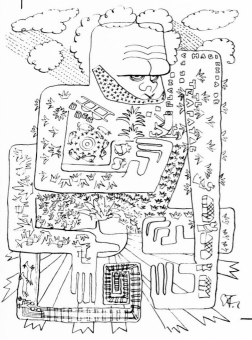

*Eisenstein's caricature of himself as a
Mexican rain god*

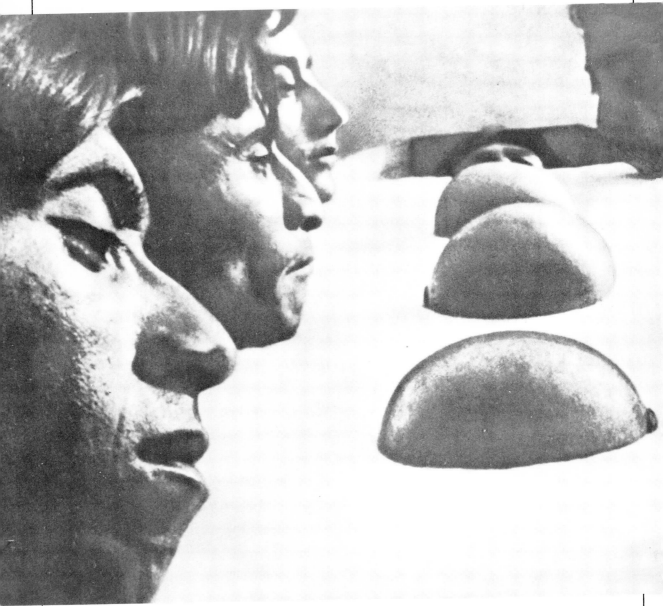

A striking shot from the never-finished "Que Viva Mexico"

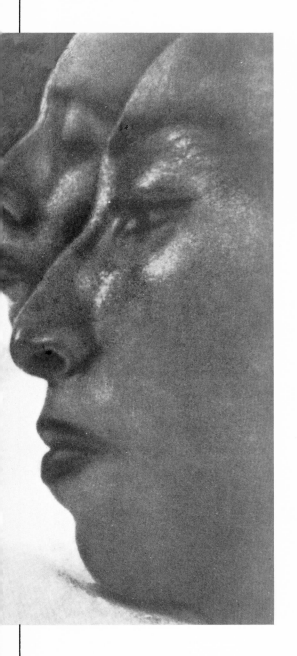

A shot from "Que Viva Mexico" and (below)
a pre-production sketch and notes

Eisenstein in Mexico with a candy skull

Mexican "types" from Eisenstein's sketchbooks

A series of sketches by Eisenstein on the relationship of bullfighting and Christianity in Mexican culture

From "Que Viva Mexico"

*A finished drawing by Eisenstein of
Mexican youths*

From "Que Viva Mexico"

A mystical drawing of Mexico by Eisenstein

The Mexican Christ by Eisenstein

Comrade Léon

WHICH OF US IN HIS youth has not enjoyed *The Three Musketeers*? Which of us has not loved the team of Athos, Porthos, Aramis, and d'Artagnan; has not chosen as his ideal one of these desperate and unfailingly united youngsters, always ready to lend their swords to a noble cause?

Some prefer the more sedate Athos, but the athletic will incline more to Porthos. Still other youths, whom God has endowed with good looks, lustrous black mustaches and elegant manners, will prefer Aramis.

But d'Artagnan, the selfless, ardent, and loyal comrade, friend and indestructible enthusiast, unfailingly wins the heart of everyone.

We remember Athos for his ghastly family relations with the dreadful Milady; Porthos for his titanic death beneath the pile of boulders; Aramis for those pages in one of the novel's sequels where, with unforgettable slowness, he climbs the deck of the frigate that is carrying him off to captivity and, with a wave of the hand, becomes the undisputed master of the ship: on that hand gleams the amethyst ring of one of the generals of a most powerful secret organization, to which the captain of the ship also belongs. But we remember d'Artagnan primarily for the whole range of his moral qualities.

For his marvelous readiness to serve an ideal, to fulfill the tasks entrusted to him, and to fight for them, unsparing in his efforts, energy, bravery, and selflessness.

And this is why d'Artagnan remains the favorite of the young.

Richelieux and Mazarins, Buckinghams and Annes of Austria[1] may come

---

1. The names, given here in plural form, are those of characters in Dumas's *The Three Musketeers* and *Twenty Years After*. All are based on historical people.

and go. Come and go, as aims and tasks, aspirations and ideals replace each other in history. But what is always alive and unchanging is the striving for the ideals. What is always necessary is selfless service to them. And their attainment is possible only through utter fidelity, selflessness, and ardor.

Who can remember d'Artagnan's first name, naturally assuming that d'Artagnan is the surname? Is it even mentioned in the novel? I'm too lazy to search through the pages to find out.

And that is why, if I were called on to invent a name for him, I should christen him Léon.

Léon, in honor of my dear friend Léon Moussinac.

I remember an ancient medieval castle.

In the distance: a mountain chain. Nearby: impassable moats and loopholes in the walls. On the towers are catapults for projecting cannonballs. Stone floors. And all around, green carpets of lawns.

With the aid of three different-colored ostrich feathers, a crumpled straw hat, and my own striped bathrobe, I try to turn a mustachioed, laughing Frenchman, with a gleaming set of teeth, into Alexander Dumas père's immortal Gascon, d'Artagnan.

The Frenchman who is suffering at my hands is Léon Moussinac. I mold him plastically as d'Artagnan long before I find the moral affinity of these two fine sons of France.

The action takes place in Switzerland at the castle of La Sarraz in 1929.

The circumstances: the Congress of Independent Cinematographers, held in the Castle of La Sarraz, kindly made available for the purpose by its owner, Madame Hélène de Mandreau.

The congress is not in session at this particular moment.

It is having fun.

The castle, crammed with relics of the Middle Ages (halberds, pikes, helmets, and breastplates), is, of course, a marvelous background for the screen, on which, between sessions, are projected the achievements of the newest and most advanced of the arts, the cinema.

The latest innovations of the time succeed one another on this screen, spread between the ancient arches: the first film on the subject of building up the collective farms (our own *The Old and the New*), telling of the rising Socialist state system of one sixth of the world; shown here with a film absolutely and definitively revealing the extent of the distintegration of bourgeois consciousness in Surrealism — Buñuel's *Un Chien Andalou*.[2]

On the same screen is shown the tragic image of Carl Dreyer's *Jeanne d'Arc*,

---

2. Salvador Dali worked with Buñuel on *Un Chien Andalou*.

Cavalcanti's and Man Ray's[3] abstract trifles, the experiments of Richter, Ruttman, Eggeling,[4] the latest film by Joris Ivens.[5]

The aims of the congress are not very clear.

The Soviet delegates spend a long time expressing the thought that in the capitalist system "independent cinematography" is as much a fiction as the "independent press." They speak of another basic and leading task of the West's creative intelligentsia: the necessity for an ideological rapprochement with the radical-revolutionary movement in Western countries.

Aesthetes and paladins of pure art begin to bristle, but it is fairly easy to rout them.

There is an even more pernicious group. The congress is international. And among the apolitical, aesthetic-minded rank-and-file delegates from France, Germany, and England hovers the slightly limping little figure of the Italian Prampolini, tiny but hostile, representing the camp of militant followers and minions of Marinetti, still quite active and considered authoritative by Italians. During those years, Italian Fascism galvanized the town crier of long-outlived militant Futurism, now become shameless propaganda for militarism. The representatives of two or three film magazines, far from radically inclined, naturally adhere to Prampolini.

And strange though it seems, there is something that unites them all with the immeasurably polite, silent, and forever bowing delegates from Japan.

When the moment approaches to submit resolutions (resolutions that are, incidentally, pretty abstract), passions are bared. We experience a practical lesson in the fact that there is no such thing as apolitical art . . .

Indeed, the idea of the whole congress, apart from entertaining Madame de Mandreau, who had kindly taken on herself all the expenses of its organization, surely didn't go further than exposing that among the avant-garde cinematographers of the West (unconnected with large firms) there was the same irreconcilable split of social and political contradictions as among the intelligentsia in

---

3. Alberto Cavalcanti's avant-garde films were *Time Only* (1926), *La Petite Lili*, and *The Eyeless Train* (1927). They were mainly a subjective editing of documentary material. Man Ray's films *Emac Bacchia* (1926) and *Star of the Sea* (1927) were an editing of visual images, mainly abstractions.

4. Hans Richter, Walter Ruttman (Germany), and Viking Eggeling (Sweden) into the early twenties created the first abstract animated-cartoon films. Richter and Ruttman went on to make films based on documentary material: *Inflation* and *Berlin — A Day in the Life of a City*. Later, in London, during Eisenstein's lectures, Richter made a short film in which Eisenstein played a London "bobby." The material was sent to Richter in Switzerland to edit, but nothing more was heard of it for many years. It is now, I believe, in the British National Film Archives. (H.M.)

5. The films of Joris Ivens, purely documentary, were *Rain* (1929) and *Phillips*. In 1931 Ivens went to Moscow, and together with me and another student of Eisenstein's, made a film of the New Iron and Steel Center at Magnitogorsk, with music by Hans Eisler and lyrics by Sergei Tretiakov. It was called *A Song of Heroes*. (H.M.)

literature, painting, or music. The aesthetes, shocked by politics, retired to the background. The reactionary wing showed its shamelessly Fascist tendencies, and the left-wing members, known to each other by articles and films, founded or strengthened personal contacts, setting up bonds of friendship for many years to come, in place of what had previously been just hearsay about each other.

By a "united front" of revolutionary and even of radically inclined groupings we were able to switch the totally apolitical character of the congress's "conclusions" and, more than that, to eradicate completely the anti-Soviet tinge of several proposals that the lame Prampolini and someone from the group of French organizers of the congress tried to impart.

Here for the first time we meet up with that potential of the intelligentsia which would in time put on the lackey's livery of Fascism and assist it in its vile and bloody work. We stand shoulder to shoulder against them in real action with two friends who are very dear to me: Ivor Montagu, from England, and Léon Moussinac, from France.

I meet Ivor for the first time.

He would become one of the organizers of the London countertrial[6] to the trial of Dimitrov in Leipzig.

Léon I have met before — back in Moscow.

In the future his path would shine with crystal purity in his days as a most active member of the French Communist Party, in the complex zigzags of the prewar class struggle in France, and in terrible ordeals in concentration camps during the German occupation, which were unable to break the spirit of this revolutionary and patriot . . .

Tisse and Alexandrov have come to the congress with our ever-present film camera. After all, how could one resist capturing on film a congress of cinematographers? Especially with the subject already at hand: the struggle of the "independents" against the "firms."

So here we have the French journalist Mademoiselle Bouisinouse, dressed in white vestments, with rusty chains found in the castle cellars, wearing an independent-cinema paper sash, chained to the monumental chimneys on the roof of the ancient structure, while fat, red-haired Mr. Isaacs from London,[7] in pince-nez, looking like Bluebeard, sweats in a suit of armor, portraying "the boss" of a film company.

---

6. The London countertrial was organized by the Comintern in response to the Nazis' trial in 1933 of the Bulgarian Communist Georgi Dimitrov, who was accused of planning the fire at the Reichstag. During the Stalinist purges, Dimitrov became general secretary of the Comintern, and later was prime minister of the Bulgarian People's Republic. He died in 1949.

7. John Isaacs, who taught English at the University of London, was one of the organizers of the London Film Society, where the early Soviet films were shown despite the disapproval of the Board of Censors.

Moussinac, turned by me into d'Artagnan, rushes to the roof in order to cut short the sufferings of poor Mademoiselle Bouisinouse, from beneath whose feet the ancient tiles slip uncontrollably, threatening to plunge both her and Tisse's tripod into the depths.

Jean Georges Auriol, beneath the waving standards made out of the numbers of the *Revue du Cinéma*, which he edits, fires the machine guns that the congress's typewriters have turned into.

He keeps up the pressure of attack from the "villains," who with lances and halberds and with Béla Balász[8] as cuirassier at the head, are trying to foil Moussinac's knightly gallantries.

The final shot of the *épopée* is performed by one of the more likable Japanese representatives, who kindly agrees to perform before the camera, in the mask of the "commercial cinema," the full ritual of the traditional hara-kiri (the result desired by the congress!).

Old Madame de Mandreau, "eternally young in spirit," minute by minute grows more horrified at the way her family relics are being treated, at the appearance of her trampled lawns, at the suffering geraniums and wild vines, the mutilated halberds. But finally this nice lady can hold back no longer: she herself brings from her ancient trousseau the sheets we need for some episode or other with ghosts, and gives wonderful cooling drinks to the cuirassiers, who are dying from the heat, as the Crusaders must once have been.

The previous year Madame de Mandreau had a congress of "left" architecture. Next, a conference of "left" musicians is expected. Madame de Mandreau's patriarchal castle has never suffered such a cataclysm since the time of militant feudalism.

However, for all this, our *belle châtelaine*, as we constantly call her, is far from indifferent to the Soviet delegation. She sighs tragically when saying good-by to us: "Oh! the Bolsheviks, the Bolsheviks . . . They're the only gentlemen!"

The little film we made vanished at one of the countless customs posts that divide the motley and varied face of Europe into a system of separate states . . .

In dressing Moussinac as d'Artagnan, I thought least of all about the fact that the hero's most captivating features are those of the no less enchanting Léon. But it is not simply his boldness nor the overflowing gaiety and *joie de vivre*. It is much more. Service to the great cause of revolution permeates his whole life. A life that is far from easy, full of thorns. The life of a practicing revolutionary. A

---

8. Béla Balász (1884–1948) was a Hungarian Communist scriptwriter and cinema theoretician. He lived in Moscow during the twenties and early thirties, and wrote various articles for the Soviet press. He was the author of *Theory of the Film*, edited and with an introduction by Herbert Marshall (London: Dobson, 1952). Eisenstein wrote articles in which he debated with Balász. (H.M.)

connoisseur with a refined taste in poetry and himself a poet, a fine connoisseur of books. The talented worker in a publishing house, specializing in albums dedicated to the artistic treasures of France. A gourmet, even. This is how I remember him in Paris.

I knew him and his employer, the owner of the firm, "Little Lévi," as he was called, who was some sort of distant relative of the notorious Dreyfus.

Often with Little Lévi and his lady love, but always with Moussinac and his nice wife, Jeanne, we would go for all manner of trips round the outskirts of Paris, admiring Versailles, Fontainebleu, Compiègne, looking at the châteaux along the Loire.

We visited Amboise, where Leonardo da Vinci died, and once took a trip by car from Paris to Brussels. Another time from the capital to Marseille and Nice, via Corrèze, with a stop at Toulon and one at Cannes to visit Henri Barbusse.[9]

Everywhere Léon showed himself to be an expert on and fine judge of the culture of the past and present, an expert on and judge of folklore, not by handbooks, but from the living voice. I listened with delight to the songs (especially the sailors' songs) he sang together with the late Vaillant-Couturier[10] after a traditional bottle of "good red wine."

Moussinac is also the author of a vast, monumental volume illustrating the main stage-décor experience of the most turbulent period in left-wing theater history. In the years leading up to the war, he directed the French Communist Party's publishing house and was one of the first, long ago, to write about the Soviet cinema.

He wrote as if with d'Artagnan's sword, blazing a trail to acquaint the West with what was coming from the young land of the Soviets and to ensure that the West saw our films.

The chain of Communist film clubs, using their right of "private meetings" to stay free of the censor, was one of those channels, one of those measures by which their organizer and inspirer, Moussinac, realized his dream on a wide scale.

A book of Moussinac's militant articles lies before me now as I write.[11]

Was it so long ago that they surged, piled with events "as exciting as an ocean sea"?[12] The polemics that surrounded them have now died down, as have the censor's bans, the police raids, the reactionary attacks, the fight for the living versus the dead. And only we, the older generation of Soviet cinematographers, still remember what fearless pioneer work ("work" is the right word)

---

9. Henri Barbusse (1873–1935) was an editor, poet, novelist, and essayist. *La Feu*, a novel about the trenches in World War I, won the Goncourt Prize. In 1932, he published a critical study of Zola.

10. Paul Vaillant-Couturier (1892–1937) was the editor of the Communist newspaper *L'Humanité*.

11. The title of Moussinac's book, published in Paris in 1928, is *La Cinéma Sovietique*.

12. The quotation is from Pushkin's *Boris Godunov*.

was Moussinac's untiring fight in the first few years after our cinema was set up, in the first years of its general recognition in Europe, before recognition was accorded to it throughout the world.

Thus Moussinac fought year after year — for culture, for art, for progressive ideas, for the revolution, for France during the war years. Thus he is fighting now[13] for a bright future for his country, an exemplary son of progressive Western thought, one of those who have, once and for all, chosen as their life's path that path on which the Soviet Union stands as a beacon.

---

13. Eisenstein wrote these words in 1948. Moussinac died in 1966.

Otto H. and
the Artichokes

"FIERY ANGEL — Pir-andello."

The old man is enjoying a play on his name while I cannot tear my gaze from his waistcoat. It is a combination of a waistcoat and a soft collar that normally sticks up from under the waistcoat. And a soft tie.

Pirandello takes me out to one of the tiny Italian restaurants on some inconspicuous Berlin side street.

He has had an invitation from Paramount, but I am still waiting for one. And that is the reason, really, for our meeting with a comrade from the Trade Mission and with one other person. But although this "other person" was the most important one at this meeting, I can't remember his name or even, strange to say, what he looked like — a bifurcated beard, I think, and pince-nez. Maybe not.

This other person is a good friend of the mysterious and all-powerful Otto H.[1] Otto H. means an opportunity to fix up a contract to go to America. The comrade from the Soviet Trade Mission is trying to get us together.

He is a strange comrade, with curly hair and soft hat, who puts an *H* before names when there is no need. And drops it when the name actually begins with this letter. So Heine becomes Eine, and so on. What's more, he is married to the daughter of the greatest modern mathematician. The business worries of a business meeting don't concern me much. I am more interested in the Fiery Angel before me, although the angel is here more for the business discussion.

I am not one of his admirers. And if "in search of an author," I would hardly apply to him.

---

1. Otto H. Kahn (1867–1934), the banker, was a patron of the arts, especially of opera.

He is somehow *par trop fin du siècle*,[2] as they were *par trop Régence*[3] at the beginning of the nineteenth century. There is something of the strange waist-coat in its owner.

Pirandello hasn't gone to Paramount, although, in his own words, his idea is entertaining. He would have the screen argue with the projection booth. The people on the screen don't want to submit to the will that sends them out of the booth as a ray of light. How boring! How old! How self-imitative!

The lined face. The soft waistcoat. The soft tie. The fiery angel of life-giving thought has flown from here long ago, and soon the Fiery Angel himself, Pirandello, will leave our sad world.

Our zabaglione is getting cold, but our zabaglione will wait. Zabaglione will be still served when Pirandello, the once Fiery Angel, is no more.

Today even the mysterious, all-powerful Otto H. has departed *ins Jenseits*.[4]

The intended business ties with the "great" man are not made, but I meet him *post factum* when I have entered Paramount.

An Italian palazzo on Fifth Avenue. A millionaire. A banker. And the financial director of Paramount. Four Gainsboroughs on the walls of his country house on Long Island. The head of a bearded man above the fireplace in the palazzo.

"Do you recognize the brush?" asks Otto H.

I do not.

"Only a Jew could paint a face so subtly!" he exclaims proudly. And, as if in passing, remarks, "Rembrandt."

Rembrandt is not a god in my pantheon. However, I make a show, as if I were looking at El Greco . . .

Artichokes, artichokes! Artichokes are what stick in my memory most. Though this at another luncheon meeting, where for the first time I experience what a colossal inconvenience it is to have a footman behind the high back of your chair. Hands appear from beyond the range of vision and simply paralyze your digestion.

Moreover, these endless, countless sets of forks and little forks, spoons and little spoons, knives, little knives, and littler knives!

And on top of everything there are artichokes!

The company includes the gray-haired Horace Liveright, the publisher of intentionally scandalous books.

It makes no difference whether his books are political, social, morally risqué, or simply amoral. They are always sensational. A court case. A ban. The subsequent permission. The public campaign against the court's decision. Everything works for the sensation. Apart from ancient erotica and the extreme

---

2. Too, too end of the century.

3. Too, too Regency.

4. To the other world.

theoreticians of psychology, Horace publishes with much fuss and publicity the earlier Dreiser. *An American Tragedy* finds a place on the shield of his publishing victories, too.

Some six months later, Horace Liveright would turn out to be my supervisor on the very *American Tragedy,* which Paramount offers me. Only considerably later do I find out that this clearly unrealizable (on moral grounds) film project is always offered to foreigners by Paramount. However, offering it to me caused such a fuss that after my break with Paramount it finally had to be produced. Von Sternberg made it. After having broken off all the thorns, tediously and badly . . .

Meanwhile, the artichokes. Artichokes . . . according to *Webster's Dictionary* . . . To hell with what family it belongs to! They serve me this noxious fruit of the earth at the very instant that I am called to the phone!

Alexandrov is on the line.

He is calling from "The Island of Tears"[5] and has only today caught up with me in New York, after having been stuck for a month in Paris.

Grisha is having trouble with the visas, and he is not being allowed onto the mainland. Together with a group of Soviet engineers, he is looking through a barred window at the distant silhouette of New York, bisected vertically by the Statue of Liberty, situated so suspiciously close to the Island of Tears.

I make arrangements to fetch this new Prisoner of Chillon as soon as I finish lunch . . .

And in the meantime the company has finished its artichokes.

I sit down. Behind me is a footman. Beside me, the white mustache of Otto H.; on the other side, his daughter's welcoming smile.

The shimmering silver services, the exotic flowers (orchids? camellias?), the diners' dinner jackets, run together into blurred concentric circles. The buttons on the footman's green livery glint insipidly. And there it is, against the blinding white of the tablecloth, before me.

Just one ar-ti-choke.

Everyone is silent.

And I fancy (but perhaps it is not my fancy!) that everyone is looking, just as attentively, at the little gray-green cupola, sitting there before me on the plate.

Life's spontaneous impressions on those of us with so-called creative natures have a habit of being stored as recollections.

And the live impressions emerge quite unexpectedly, but at the exact moment when they, and they only, suddenly seem essential in their emotional experience.

Why does the artichoke on Otto H.'s white tablecloth keep coming to mind?

---

5. "The Island of Tears" referred to Ellis Island, the point of disembarkation for many immigrants, some of whom were refused entry into the United States.

Perhaps because I shot the episode with the notorious candle in the scene of the capture of Kazan.[6]

One candle burns underground, right next to the powder charge in the famous tunnel; another burns up above. All the different versions of the song about Ivan the Terrible's capture of Kazan agree on this. The upper candle is watched because it will tell when the approaching explosion is to come. It is assumed that both candles will burn out together. The upper one, in the wind, burns out quicker, of course.

No explosion.

Ivan begins to fume: "Bring the gunners!"

And here are the gunners, with nooses already around their necks . . .

Just as an invisible noose strangles me when I contemplate the still uneaten fruit of the earth.

Looks. The looks of those around me . . .

Evidently I remember the scene with the artichoke as an association with the scene of the Kazan candle.

For the candle is even stuck onto the spike of a helmet whose very shape is reminiscent of the ill-fated artichoke, which in its turn seemingly copies the characteristic outline of a church's cupola.

And the eyes of the tsar and Malyuta, the gunners and the Tartars, of Kurbsky and the clergy, are riveted to the candle for an unbearably long time in close-up.

And the question is automatically posed in reverse.

Perhaps the tense strucure of close-ups, frozen in expectation, the rhythm of the tension, and, finally, the very fact that the candle is stuck onto such a cupola-shaped helmet top have as their "emotional springboard" that very far-off but, as we have seen, insistently memorable, rhythmic sensation of confusion with the artichoke at Otto H.'s table!

For even the name of the first half of the scene (up to the successful explosion) could be covered by the word "confusion"!

Thus is the present fed by the store of rhythmic recollections of sensations in the past.

Recollections of the past also lead me out of the difficulty with the artichoke . . .

But I have forgotten to mention the main thing.

Namely, that the difficulty lay in how to swallow this strange fruit of the earth, whose petals forming the cupola are each crowned with a small sharp spike maliciously pointing upward.

More precisely, how this is accomplished at millionaires' tables.

For one remembers from childhood that tsars eat only chocolate, and every

---

6. The scene with the candle appears in *Ivan the Terrible* (Part I).

other dish must be sweetened with sugar. How, then, do millionaires eat artichokes?

Only the soft, fleshy, tender base?

Or do they, like other mortals, have to suck out the fleshy bottoms of the separately torn-off leaves?

I go hot and cold at the thought that I shall have to execute this operation, even more delicate than the sucking out of lobster claws, before the whole gathering which has long finished this operation and is watching with folded arms to see how the Russian barbarian will get out of this tricky situation . . .

The Road to
Buenos Aires

PLACE THE TIP OF A BARED sword at my breast or the muzzle of a pistol at my temple. And make me declare which of two of my favorite books has the title *The Road to Buenos Aires*. Is it the sequel to Brousson's[1] *Anatole France in His Dressing Gown*, or Albert Londres's[2] collection of essays on the white-slave traffic? I would have to reach out a hand to the right shelf to make sure.

But I can't be bothered. The shelves are in town, and I am at the *dacha*.

So run me through with your blade, pull the trigger, or hear me out!

Each book has its place in my life's wanderings.

To be absolutely honest, Brousson's book psychologically determined my trip abroad.

I have already bemoaned my incurable indecisiveness regarding everything that lies beyond what I need at any given moment for my work in art.

I have also mentioned that many acts have been determined only by the stimulus *"y yo tambien"* — "and I also" (I can, I want, I shall).

It seems that I have never suffered from petty envy.

But to this day I experience, to an unbearable degree, great, stimulating, yet often ardent and misplaced envy.

Once, long ago, I was entranced by someone at one of the meetings of the Comintern (I don't remember which session) reading his speech in three different languages consecutively.[3]

---

1. Jean Brousson was secretary to Anatole France from 1902 to 1909. In his memoirs, published after France's death, Brousson wrote scathing comments on his employer's private life.

2. Albert Londres, a French journalist, exposed the white-slave traffic between Europe and Buenos Aires.

3. Karl Radek (1885–1937?) was famous for giving speeches in three languages. I remember him doing so in his lectures in the early thirties. Radek was tried during the purges and probably died in

I was consumed with a desire to give lectures at some future time in various countries and various languages. I desperately wanted to be invited somewhere, sometime, to give lectures . . .

This, of course, was not as foolish and impudent as the passion, which had only just passed, for imitating . . . Balzac.

In my bathrobe, similar to his white monastic vestments, I took to writing all night long, no less passionately than he, putting pen to paper and swallowing cup after cup of black coffee, although I could have done this in quite normal clothes, during the day, and with the usual glass of tea.

However, this "playing at Balzac" didn't turn out to be fruitless.

I was sufficiently prudent not to undertake the writing of novels, of which I am not capable, but began with no less fervor to delve into a theoretical examination of my own experience in the cinema, which had accumulated to some extent by 1929.

"The stimulus of France" was evidently very great.

It is sufficient to tell you that then, as now, public speaking was absolute torture for me and demanded an unbelievable effort if I was to overcome certain restraints. Of the many things I am no good at (and which I therefore hate doing), speaking in public is one of the most hated.

And yet, regardless of this, I gabble addresses and lectures in three languages in Zürich, Berlin, Hamburg, London, Cambridge, Paris (the Sorbonne), Brussels, Antwerp, Liège, Amsterdam, Rotterdam, The Hague, New York (Columbia University), Boston (Harvard), New Haven (Yale), at the universities of Chicago and California, before Negroes in New Orleans and Dorchester, at countless meetings and lunches, and in Mexico City, where I even opened an exhibition of the works of Sequeiros in the Spanish Royal Club, which had just become the center of Republican Spain and had covered up portraits of the Spanish kings with the first canvases by a Communist artist.

And finally — finally — the cherished telegram lies before me: an invitation to go from the U.S. to Argentina and give two lectures in . . . Buenos Aires!

At last!

And I do not even go and give them.

The curious thing is I'm not a bad speaker . . .

One grows numb on the eve of an address, hardly noticing almost a full day's travel across Switzerland — not because of preparations for the lecture, but trembling in fear of it!

Which occasion was the worst?

There were two, I suppose.

---

prison. It must have been because he had become a "nonperson" that Eisenstein avoided mentioning his name. (H.M.)

And both in America.

One at the convention for Paramount's distributors, held in Atlantic City; the second in Hollywood.

The gigantic express liner *Europa*, sister ship of the *Bremen* and *Columbus*, was carrying us across the hospitably smooth Atlantic Ocean, as if we were on a magic carpet.

The contract had been signed in Paris. And I was crossing the ocean with my boss, Mr. Lasky, vice-president of Paramount.

Mr. Lasky began his career in the cinema as an orchestra player. He played, I think, the cornet or trumpet.

He was one of the original pioneers of the film business. One of the first to tread golden California's well-endowed soil, and one of the first to think of inviting the luminaries of the stage to play in films.

It was for him that Sarah Bernhardt made her first film, I think.

Mr. Lasky gives me a fatherly talking-to.

Al Kaufman, his assistant and a one-time bouncer for a nickelodeon, backs him up.

"Now, we're going to arrive in the States on the eve of the annual distribution convention . . ."

The convention will be in Atlantic City (a special train from New York, a vast hotel engaged for the congress, a gigantic hall with the flags of Australia, Africa, France, England, and the various states: Buffalo [*sic*], Kentucky, Virginia, Maryland, and so on, endlessly).

"You'll have to make an appearance before those who'll be selling your future pictures . . ."

Both Mr. Lasky and I seem firmly to believe that this time we shall really come to an agreement on a suitable subject, though back in Paris we had failed to come to any understanding on the treatment of *Zola* and Vicki Baum's *Grand Hotel*.

"A lot depends on personal impression . . ."

"But don't be too serious . . ."

"Point out your shock of hair . . ."

"But at the same time, don't frighten them off by being too trivial . . ."

"Though in general, Americans like speeches to have jokes . . ."

"In New York you'll have to stay at the Savoy Plaza . . ."

"That's in your contract . . ."

"You've got to keep up both your prestige and ours . . ."

"Now, when the press meet you in the hotel lobby . . ."

It feels as if the waves are making us roll, but the ocean is quiet and peaceful. It is simply that my head is slowly beginning to spin.

And now here we are at the convention.

Honest to God, I cannot remember a single word I said!

All I remember is that a woman spoke before I did, and that she and her husband had made the first big film about elephants, *Chang*.[4]

I dimly remember that I stumbled after I had spoken, and nearly fell down from the rostrum.

As if in a dream, I recall the dreadful slap on the back (the sign of utmost affection in those parts) from Sam Katz, a lanky giant of a man, then head of world distribution for Paramount.

"I don't know what sort of director you are" — quite typical for the "trading sector" of large firms! — "but I'd sure snap you up to sell pictur_s!"

One could expect no greater compliment . . .

The second occasion was more frightful.

It was in Hollywood at a lunch with all the press representatives of the film mecca.

This is where a slip of the tongue, a mistake, a nervous tone, and you have four hundred of the sharpest-tipped fountain pens not for but against you, forever!

Almost from the moment of my arrival in the United States, the reactionary press, in particular Major Pease's newly formed Fascist black-shirt organization, had raised an insane howl of fury about my invitation and had demanded the expulsion from American soil of men whose presence in America was "more dreadful than an invasion by a thousand commandoes."

My bosses kept up a brave front and did not give way to panic, although they prudently refrained from making any extraordinary fuss about our arrival. Still, the press was burning with curiosity.

One has to remember that we three[5] were just about the first Soviet people in California. And that the America of the thirties was an anti-Soviet America, a Prohibition America, Hoover's imperialist America, before becoming (two years later) Roosevelt's America and the America of the New Deal, of democratic tendencies that, with Roosevelt's repeated presidency, were crowned by the military pact with us. And Paramount, looking nervously over its shoulder at the Hays Office[6] and hearing the first rumors of the Fish Committee,[7] gathered the press together for a lunch at the Hotel Ambassador, in the Bird Room, I think.

---

4. *Chang*, an American documentary, was made in 1927 by M. Cooper and M. Shedzak.

5. Eisenstein was traveling with G. V. Alexandrov and E. K. Tisse.

6. Will H. Hays, president of the Motion Picture Producers and Distributors from 1922 to 1945, administered what was called "the Hays Code," a standard of moral censorship promulgated in 1934.

7. The Fish Committee (named after its chairman, Representative Hamilton Fish) was a congressional committee set up to investigate anything considered a breach of morals in films.

At any rate, I remember the walls being painted with colorful humming-birds.

Or perhaps it was only the twittering of the large percentage of women reporters who had flown in for this lunch!

I remember how we walked to this hall. The way they walk to the scaffold. Beside me, smoking his ever-present cigar, strides Paramount's California boss, Mr. "B.P." Schulberg.

On the way, he cannot resist going into the hotel's stock market office to check on the blackboard how the price of his shares had changed.

They are all gamblers.

They gamble on everything.

On pictures. On stars. On contracts. On scenarios. On races. On the sup-posed number of knots the liner will do in a day. And, even more, on elections — state and national (this gives every election campaign an added thrill).

They lose fortunes, win them back again, and squander them again.

The other Grand Old Man of the old Californians, Papa Carl Laemmle of Universal Pictures, said to me that he had lost enough at roulette in Tijuana,[8] the Californians' Monte Carlo, to buy the whole establishment three times over.

When we were not allowed back into the States from Mexico for six weeks, Hollywood gambled on us!

We were also being gambled on at the time of this meeting with the press, although we didn't suspect how the different interests of the New York and Hollywood branches of the firm were playing around us.

I was the protégé of the old "risk-takers," who sought what was new and adventurous, and who were represented in the firm by Jesse Lasky.

In opposition to him were the "bankers," representatives of the banking interests, in particular "B.P.," who would bet only on dead certainties, without risk or adventure, more often than not repeating again and again the type of film that had enjoyed success.

The bankers were in the ascendency and were making agreement with us more difficult, thus getting at the "romantics" of the film-making side, who had imported us.

In the unequal struggle of these two tendencies within the firm, Paramount lost pride of place in these years to M-G-M, which developed brilliantly under the inspired "neo-adventurism" of Irving Thalberg, who led his firm not along

---

8. The following note is by Eisenstein: "Tijuana is on the Californian border, in Mexico. During Prohibition, when gambling and drinking establishments were banned from the territory of the U.S.A., drinking and gambling moved beyond the bounds of legal jurisdiction. To gambling ships beyond territorial waters. And over the borders. And out of sight in the fantastic "speakeasy" in the center of New York, for example, behind a secret door among the coats in the cloakroom, or in Brooklyn behind the rear wall of a seemingly tumbledown little shop."

the line of boring certainties, but by producing an unexpected phalanx of film successes.

The feudal dissension within the firm helped only to increase the natural difficulties of our agreements with the firm regarding scenarios. I had the right in my contract to veto its proposals, and it avoided agreeing with mine.

Finally, after six months, nothing had been done.

We parted.

And at the parting, B. P. Schulberg, taking the cigar out of his mouth, described what was ending as "a noble experiment."[9]

However, both "feudal lords" were soon to find themselves out of the firm.

---

9. This note, too, is by Eisenstein: " 'A noble experiment' was the way the Soviet state system was described in America at that time."

Hospitals·
Grosz·
Sternberg·
Jannings·
Supervisors

THE GOOD GRAY POET Walt Whitman used to visit the wounded and dying. He brought them comfort and tobacco. He kissed them on the lips. Occasionally several times. He wrote letters for them. He kept a strict account and record of all this: the letters, tobacco, the kisses, and the small change that he distributed to them.

I went to entertain the wounded when I was sixteen, in 1914. I also took cigarettes to them. I didn't kiss anyone on the lips, but I entertained them with drawings.

On my right and left are luxuriantly mustachioed noncommissioned officers. Chests covered with crosses and medals. I sketch at a table between their beds. A caricature of some sort on patriotic subjects. Wilhelms. Franz Josefs. Everything but Krylov's fables[1] in pictures.

The noncommissioned officers politely stick it out for a day. And for another. On the third day, they ask me to draw "girls," and order subjects from the ever-popular themes of "water-closet folklore." This is what George Grosz[2] calls the graffiti on urinal walls, which, by his own testimony, he took as stylistic models for his drawings.

I would get to know Grosz in Berlin in 1929. I was not any sort of Vargas predecessor.

I can't do "pinup Varga girls."

At home they find out about these subjects, and my visits to the hospital cease.

---

1. Ivan Andreyevich Krylov (1768–1844) translated La Fontaine's fables into Russian and wrote many of his own. He was also chief librarian of the Imperial Public Library.

2. George Grosz (1893–1959), a leader of German Expressionism, was condemned by the Nazis for painting "degenerate" pictures. He immigrated to the United States.

The wounded lie in the halls of the Riga Shooting Society, beside the rifle range, which faces the windows of our apartment across the street.

Amateur shooting competitions are held there.

Skating in the winter.

And a military band on the bandstand in the summer.

Visiting the wounded ceases for exactly thirty years.

Only in 1944 do I once more find myself going to a hospital to entertain the wounded, when some particularly idle woman worker in the Alma-Ata Party Committee Mass Propaganda Department highhandedly lands me with this job. This time I tell the wounded about the wonders of cinematography.

And in the front row there is a living copy of my friends the noncommissioned officers — the same great mustaches, the same medals.

I go there with a feeling of great dread: the hospital is a special one — for those who have lost limbs. I expect to see much that will be depressing. And I am completely mistaken. The hospital is full of those "who have done their bit," and, though they have suffered loss of limbs, are still alive.

It is marvelous to see how a soldier, having tucked up his dressing gown, hops around on one leg, skillfully using his crutch as a cue to strike the ball in table billiards . . .

Mary Pickford has told how she prepared to play a blind girl and for some time lived in a home for the blind to learn their ways.

No depression! On the contrary.

Full of high spirits. No cautious moving around.

They move quite freely.

They bump into objects and obstacles like anything.

And find this madly entertaining.

However, it was not Mary herself who told me this, but von Sternberg, who was to have made this film with her. We talked about other things with Mary.

Sternberg, of course, perhaps more than anyone else, suffers from an inferiority complex. He had the misfortune in the past to be a film editor (joining bits of film together), and no matter what decadent oddities he thinks up, throwing dust in the eyes of Hollywood (for example, with *The Scarlet Empress*), the Hollywood aristocracy will not accept him, however much he poses . . .

I drop into the studio during the filming of *Morocco*, with Marlene Dietrich and Gary Cooper. A deathly silence. A crowd scene: a Moroccan *café-chantant* is crammed to overflowing, yet there is not a sound. In the center of the studio is a platform. On the platform, in a black velvet jacket, is the man himself. His head propped on his arm. He is thinking. Everyone holds his breath. Ten minutes, fifteen.

It doesn't help.

Von Sternberg is not accepted by Hollywood's high society. He tries to humble this Hollywood by Europeanism. He collects leftist art, but not quite that which is required. Not the right names.

If the names are right, then the pictures are of the wrong periods.

He commissions a portrait bust from, of course, Tom Belling.[3] It is in metal, chrome-plated steel.

This is the favorite material of the time used for making lamp fittings for nightclubs and shaker sets for cocktail bars. As if that were not enough, the sculpture itself is a combination of extreme overstatement with unfinished statement — to be more exact, with the totally unstated. A gleaming, bulging forehead sticks out (even chrome steel lends itself to flattering a client!) under the metal shavings of curls.

From the forehead a metal strip of nose extends down, with the hint of a mustache beneath.

From the arches above the eyes downward there is nothing whatever.

And through the absent eyes, cheeks, and cheekbones one can see, sunk in deep shadow, the inner side of what, from the other side, is the curve of the back of the skull and the upper neck. All in all, there is a marked resemblance to the original.

The real subject of Tom Belling's sculpture is short, graying, with a slightly arty haircut. He has a graying mustache with pointed ends, drooping down unsymmetrically. He has a liking for short coats and jackets that are square in cut. He is unrestrainedly and, it seems, quite hopelessly in love with Marlene Dietrich.

Three times he has slid back to zero, swamped with dud pictures.

Once more he climbs out again. He is now one of the very highest-paid film directors. (Only Lubitsch is more expensive.) And even so, nothing helps.

He began his career this way.

He was working as some sort of assistant on a picture.

The picture was finished.

Everyone was released.

The director left.

Unexpectedly it became necessary to shoot an additional episode.

An operation.

They didn't want to invite the director again. So they decided to do it using their own resources.

Von Sternberg offered to shoot the episode.

He shot it, and it turned out to be the best in the picture.

He tells me about it himself. He says he shot the operation "in the manner of Daumier."

I don't really believe him.

In my opinion, the reason he mentions Daumier is that he has found out that I admire him.

However, there is something else that is puzzling.

---

3. Tom Belling was a contemporary American sculptor.

How is this "start" compatible with the other start of his career, which he himself has told me about?

For a few pence and at his own expense he shoots a little film in the slums of Los Angeles (all on location): *The Salvation Hunters*.

With the remains of the money, he bribes Chaplin's projectionist, a Japanese.

Let him "by accident" put the reel on one evening when Chaplin is watching some picture.

If it doesn't work, too bad.

But it just might.

The boss might not bawl him out.

He might even watch it through to the end.

The boss doesn't bawl him out.

He watches it through.

What is more, full of enthusiasm, he wants to meet the maker.

He takes him by the arm and goes off with him to the best of restaurants. Von Sternberg is "made."

That is not all.

Chaplin takes him into his own studio, but Sternberg doesn't stay long.

Charlie himself, spluttering with rage, tells me about him: "I've never met such a no-good loafer in the whole of my life."

Snobbism cannot conceal Sternberg's trauma about his own inferiority. This, no doubt, is the reason for his liking actors of high caliber, first Bancroft,[4] then Jannings.[5] Fatty Hussar.[6] Sternberg calls me to Neubabelsberg[7] to meet Jannings and Bancroft, as if it were some elephant hunt.

Both mastodons are madly jealous of each other. One acts "by nature" (Bancroft), the other "by acting" (Jannings).

They are filming some beer advertisement, and raise their mugs to each other in affectionate greeting. But their eyes gleam with quite unconcealed hate.

Sternberg and I have a quiet laugh about it together . . .

He is shooting *The Blue Angel* and later shows me his rushes, about twenty takes to each scene.

Sternberg's liking for hefty chaps seemingly brings him some compensa-

---

4. George Bancroft (1882–1956) was a leading American character actor.

5. Emil Jannings (1887–1950), of Swiss birth and German-American parentage, became an actor in German theater and cinema. He was famous for his roles in the last classic silent films, among them *Variety* and *The Last Laugh*. In 1930, he starred with Marlene Dietrich in von Sternberg's *Blue Angel*.

6. Fatty Hussar was an Austrian comic actor who came to the United States in the twenties. He was not, as Eisenstein suggests, an actor of "high caliber." (H.M.)

7. Neubabelsberg was the location of the Berlin film studios.

tion. In Berlin he even lives in the Hercules Hotel, near Hercules Bridge, opposite the Hercules Fountain, with its great, gray stone statue of Hercules . . .

Yet *The Docks of New York* is a fine picture!

The peeling and wind-torn sets of the docks still stood in the Paramount lot in 1930. One could tell, by the sets, how cleverly the screen effects had been achieved by light and composition.

Now kids are running through them, led by the *Wunderkind*, an overgrown youth, my fellow employee Jackie Coogan.

Jackie is already a long way from the unique charm of *The Kid*,[8] has not yet reached the stage of the repulsive, balding lanky fellow that he is now, in 1946, who, having returned from the front, works as an entertainer in a Los Angeles nightclub.

But in 1930 he takes the part — quite inappropriately, in my opinion — of Tom Sawyer, and, at the head of the other small boys, runs to his studio film set.

I cannot picture Tom as being round-faced, brown-eyed, plump, and well fed.

The first screen Tom, a silent one, was Mary Pickford's brother Jack, who had the necessary angularity of movement and a sort of suitable hollowness of the cheeks.

Filed away somewhere I have a letter that Fairbanks wrote to me at the time I was working on the scenario of *An American Tragedy*. Doug strongly recommended Jackie for the role of Clyde Griffiths.

But he doesn't play Clyde Griffiths for me.

And not only because I don't go on to make *An American Tragedy* . . .

Clyde was eventually played, and very badly, by an actor called Holmes in von Sternberg's production, which was very bad too. So bad that I was unable to see it through to the end. (And Theodore Dreiser took Paramount to court.)

However, this isn't the first time I see Jannings.

I saw him three years earlier during the shooting of *Faust* at Tempelhof, when I was in Berlin as just a plain mortal.

Egon Erwin Kisch's[9] visiting card (he had seen *Battleship Potemkin* in Moscow), warmly recommending me to Jannings, is sent up onto the rock, where he is posing majestically in the gray robe of the Prince of the Underworld.

With a truly royal nod of the head, he gives me to understand that I have had the honor to come within his field of vision.

In 1929, Jannings tries hard to persuade me to make a second *Potemkin*. This time: the favorite of Catherine.[10] With him in the title role, of course!

---

8. *The Kid* was the Charlie Chaplin film that brought fame to the kid — Jackie Coogan.

9. Egon Erwin Kisch (1885–1948) was a German journalist and author and a Communist.

10. Catherine the Great's favorite was her prime minister, Potemkin, after whom the battleship was named.

"Potemkin had only one eye. If the film is to be made by you, I'll pluck out one of my eyes."

My first supervisor in Hollywood was Bachman, a nice man who was a specialist in "Europeans" and had taken all Jannings's films through Paramount; he had "broken his neck" over *Petit Café*, starring Maurice Chevalier and directed by another Berliner, Ludwig Berger.

"While a picture is being shot the supervisor breaks his head, and when it's finished he breaks his neck, if the picture earns less than it should."

This is what happened with *Petit Café*.

Berger wisely went back to Europe.

And Bachman got fired from Paramount.

I saw him again about three months after this.

He hadn't yet found any work.

And I got a quite noteworthy personality as a supervisor: Horace Liveright. And *An American Tragedy*. Paramount's bosses dreamed of making the "sensational" novel into "just another" (though dramatic) story of "boy meets girl," without going into any "side issues."

With me the issues went much farther.

What interested me here was depicting the society and the morals that impelled Clyde to do everything he did, and then, in the hullabaloo of the pre-election fever, in the interests of getting the prosecutor re-elected, Clyde is broken.

Freed from Dreiser's Niagara flow of words and descriptions, the novel is very concise, very savage and accusatory.

It's surprising that I've preserved no recollection of Liveright himself.

Neither from our first meeting, at Otto H. Kahn's lunch.

Nor from our last meeting, the conference at my place in Beverly Hills.

I remember the latter only because it made me miss (my fault!) a meeting with Greta Garbo (the third time!).

To meet Garbo (and on the set!) was something almost totally impossible. And for the special privilege I was obliged to our common acquaintance, Zalka Viertel, the wife of director Berthold Viertel and one-time manager of the Scandinavian star.

I called her Garbel (Beau-bel, Gar-beau, Gar-bel). In return she called me Eisenbahn.

However, this was later, after we did meet.

This was during the period of mutual admiration between herself and the director Murnau. I remember them both sprawled in a lively tête-à-tête on the wide green expanse of Ludwig Berger's billiard table.

Garbo never allowed anyone into the studio during the shooting, as she played (and how amazingly!) purely by inspiration, being almost completely without "academic technique."

As is well known, instinct cannot always be summoned up on order.

And then work turns into hysterics and tears.

For Garbo, work as an actress was a hard way of earning a living.

It is extremely surprising, but Chaplin also acts, rehearses, and shoots in much the same way (*all'improviso*) and from rehearsal to rehearsal does not perfect a certain chosen variation, but displays ever-new variations.

From a hundred variations an artist of genius cannot fail to find several variations of genius! (And it is from these that he chooses, sitting in his famous little black oilskin chair in the viewing room.)

If there are not enough, he shoots more.

And if he is not in the mood for shooting, he goes off on his yacht across the wide expanse of the Pacific Ocean and returns to film, camera, sets, and his fellow workers, who wait for him unquestioningly, when the inner drive again draws him to the studio . . .

Zweig·
Babel·
Toller·
Meyerhold·
Freud

ODAY I CAME ACROSS IN the *Gazette Littéraire* a facsimile of the notes Stefan Zweig made when he was dying.

Stefan Zweig . . .

I think it was Spencer[1] who refused to be presented to Alexander II.

His reason was that personal acquaintance often destroys the far more favorable impression created by a literary reputation. It is often so. Though sometimes only slightly. Following Dreiser and Dos Passos, it is Stefan Zweig's turn to be at the table, covered in oilcloth, in my book-filled room on Chistiye Prudy.

Dreiser will note in a book that I have the largest bed in Russia. Dos Passos will nibble at a gooseberry tart and talk about the smell of prisons in all countries being exactly the same. And a little later, having returned to Austria, Zweig will describe this room in a newspaper under the headline "The Heroism of the Intelligentsia." And include in the description . . . a wash basin, which it didn't contain.

Still, I loved his *Dostoyevsky, Nietzsche, Stendhal, and Dickens.*

Zweig had come to a meeting in memory of Tolstoy. We had met at one of those "international teas," where one finds oneself talking all evening to someone who looks typically German. For some reason in French. And suddenly just before you leave you hear him addressing his wife, in Russian, "Marusya, let's go to bed!"

Zweig is much in demand. We drink tea with a certain Frenchman. Toward the end of the evening he, of course, turns out to be a Russian, Professor Ivanov. What is more, Ivan Ivanovich Ivanov!

A few days later, Zweig visits me.

I meet him with a bomb, an eruption of Vesuvius, at any rate an unexpected question: "Did you write *Conflicts* about yourself?"

---

1. Eisenstein is referring to Herbert Spencer (1820–1903), the English philosopher and sociologist.

"Oh no! No, that was about a friend of my youth . . ." But it doesn't sound very convincing, and I take pity and hastily help him out of the difficulty. I know that he is friendly with Freud (otherwise I would not, of course, have dumbfounded him with such a possibly tactless question!) and I turn the conversation to questions about the great Viennese.

His *Freud, Mesmer,* and *Mary Baker Eddy*[2] have not yet been written. And he tells me much that will later go into the book, as well as much that will not go into the book.

He imparts very vividly that special patriarchal atmosphere which reigns on Thursdays, around the oval table, between Freud and his ardent disciples. The indescribable atmosphere of the first steps of the discoveries, taken as revelations. The unrestrained fermentation of thoughts through interaction with each other. The furious creative growth and elation. But in no less measure, the shady side of the fresco of this new School of Athens, where a new Plato and Aristotle merge in the overwhelming personality of the man with the Wagnerian name.[3] The jealousy and suspicion between the disciples. Among them, Steckel, Adler, Jung. Freud's still greater suspicion toward them. The suspicion and jealousy of a tyrant. The ruthlessness toward those not steadfast in the doctrine. Especially those who try to go their own way, in the light of their own ideas, if these do not correspond in every way with the teacher's ideas.

Zweig describes the growth of revolt against the patriarch. The counteraccusations of desertion, of desecrating of teachings. Excommunication, anathema . . . The Oedipus complex, standing out from Freud's teaching so disproportionately and exaggeratedly — in the play of passions within the school itself: the sons encroaching on the father. In reaction to the father's tyrannical régime, a father more like Saturn devouring his children than like Oedipus' father, the unoffending spouse of Jocasta.[4]

Soon Adler and Jung break away, Steckel departs . . . Zweig's picture of the inner life of a small group of talented fanatics, grouped around the bearer of the doctrine, is drawn with great vividness.

And isn't the biblical legend right, materializing in the image of Judas, the inevitable phantom of these suspicions, who rose before the eyes of the creator of the doctrine?

Is this image no less eternal and immortal than the image of the skeptical proselyte with outstretched hands, wanting to know everything by touch — the figure of Doubting Thomas?

---

2. The three titles were the parts of Stefan Zweig's trilogy *Mental Healers.*

3. The reference is to Sigmund, from Wagner's *Die Walküre.*

4. The note by Eisenstein reads: "However, other more detailed and evil tongues of antiquity tell us quite unexpected and curious details of the reasons and motives behind Oedipus' struggle with his father, which we usually know only in Sophocles' version."

And the very circumstances? Isn't it from this that arises the image of the tribe eating its eldest, the inescapable image in Freud's teaching?

And maybe the very circumstances of his surroundings: the "rebirth" of the forms of behavior, when existence is set in an atmosphere analogous to that of a closed clan and an almost tribal structure? . . .

However, why am I so heated, touching on the inner atmosphere of a group of scientists long dispersed and who, in many respects, long since left any sphere of reality? Quite apart from the fact that Father Saturn himself retired from the fight sufficiently long ago.

Of course, for the reason that from the very first descriptive lines I had already ceased describing the circumstances within Freud's circle and that I've been depicting under these foreign names a similar situation, the one by which I found my own road.

Just the same sort of grand old man at the center. As endlessly charming as a master and as insidiously crafty as a person. The same distinctive stamp of genius, and the same tragic discord and breakup of initial harmony, as with the deeply tragic figure of Freud. There was the same group of fanatics among the pupils surrounding him. The same furious growth of personalities. The same impatience toward any sign of independence. The same methods of "spiritual inquisition." The same pitiless annihilation, alienation, and the excommunication of those who were guilty only of allowing their own inner voice to speak . . .

Of course, I long ago stopped describing Freud's court and am now writing about the atmosphere in the school and theater of the idol of my youth, my theatrical mentor, my teacher.

Meyerhold! A combination of genius as a creator and craftiness as a person.

Innumerable are the pangs of torment of those who, like me, loved him utterly. Innumerable the moments of delight spent observing the magical creations of this unique wizard of the theater.

How many times Ilyinsky[5] walked out!

How Babanova[6] suffered!

What hell — short-lived, thank God! — I endured before being expelled beyond the gates of Paradise, from the ranks of his theater, when I dared to set up my own collective "on the side" — in the Proletcult.

Meyerhold worshipped Ibsen's *Ghosts*, producing it repeatedly and playing Oswald countless times. For the theme of repetition attracted Meyerhold, the theme that so surprisingly permeates the story of Mrs. Alving and her son.

Meyerhold repeatedly re-created the pages of his own creative youth — the

5. Igor V. Ilyinsky (1901–   ) is a People's Artist. He was the star of the Maly Theater and worked with Meyerhold from 1920 until the dissolution of Meyerhold's theater, in 1937. His relations with the producer are described in his memoirs, *Sam o Sebye* (*About Myself*), published in Moscow in 1958–1959.

6. Maria I. Babanova (1900–   ) is also a People's Artist. She acted in Meyerhold's theater until 1927, when she left to join the Theater of the Revolution (later called the Mayakovsky Theater).

break with Stanislavsky[7] — with his pupils and close friends, craftily and directorially provoking the necessary conditions and situations.

His love and respect for Constantine Sergeyevich (Stanislavsky) was amazing . . . even in the very fiercest years of his struggle against the Moscow Art Theater. How many times he spoke with love of Constantine Sergeyevich, how highly he valued his talent and ability!

In what poem, in what legend, was it that I read how Lucifer, the first among the angels, having raised a revolt against God, and "having been cast down," continues to love Him and "sheds tears," not for his fall, not for having been cast out, but because he is no longer to be allowed the opportunity to look upon Him?

Or was this from the legend about Ahasuerus?[8]

Something of Lucifer or Ahasuerus was in the rebellious figure of my teacher, a far greater genius than Stanislavsky, who was acclaimed and canonized by all, though he was absolutely without that patriarchal equilibrium — taken for harmony, but rather bordering on philistinism — which Goethe demanded in a certain measure from a creative personality.

And who better than a dignitary of the Weimar court (Goethe) has shown, by his own biography, that this measure of philistinism ensures calm, stability, a deep-rootedness, and the pleasure of recognition there, where the absence of it condemns a too-romantic nature to the eternal doubts, the searchings, the vicissitudes of fate, and often to the fate of Icarus, to the final way of the Flying Dutchman . . .

In his longing for Constantine Sergeyevich, for this patriarch warmed in the rays of adulation of numerous second- and third-generation admirers and zealots, there was something of Lucifer's tears, of the unutterable longing of Vrubel's *Demon*.[9]

And I remember him toward the end, in the period of the coming rapprochement with Constantine Sergeyevich.

It was touching and pathetic to observe this reconciliation of two old men.

I do not know the feelings of Constantine Sergeyevich, dedicating the last years of his life to the creative direction of his own theater, yet turning away from it toward that eternally vivifying source of creation — the rising generation — and bringing to it the new thoughts of his own ever-young talent.

But I do remember the prodigal son's radiant eyes when he spoke of their coming together once more, avoiding those overgrown paths which had no place in true theater, which one had foreseen and fled from at the start of our

7. Meyerhold acted with Constantine Sergeyevich Stanislavsky's Moscow Art Theater from 1898 to 1902, the year he went to the provinces and began his experiments with stylized theater.

8. Ahasuerus was one of the names for the Wandering Jew of medieval legend.

9. Mikhail Vrubel (1856–1910) was an artist and illustrator. Eisenstein refers to his illustrations for Lermontov's *Tamara and the Demon*.

century and of his career, and the other had abjured decades later, when the tall weeds of these alien tendencies (fostered by the solicitous hand of Nemirovich-Danchenko) began to suffocate the founder of the Moscow Art Theater himself.[10]

They were not to remain together for long. But no inner rift or dissension led to their break this time. Growing out of those very features of an unbalanced disposition, one was carried by the tragic consequences of his own inner rifts to a fatal end; the other, to death . . .

But in those long years, when I had got over my own trauma and had come to terms with him and we were again friends, it seemed to me that in his relations with his pupils and followers he repeatedly played out the break with his own teacher . . . and in those who were rejected, he experienced again his own gnawing grief; in rejection becoming the tragic father Rustum who struck down Sohrab,[11] seeking, as it were, justification for what had happened in his own youth, when there was no evil intent on the part of the "father," but only the creative independence of spirit of the "overproud son."

That is the way I saw this drama.

Perhaps with insufficient objectivity.

Perhaps without being sufficiently historical.

But for me this affair was too close, too much of a family chronicle.

For in a line of "descending blessings," from the laying on of hands by the elder, I am in some degree the son and grandson of these passing generations of the theater . . .

I do not, of course, think about all this during my meeting with Zweig, but listen to him attentively.

Then I entertain him, showing him photographs from the film *October*. He is overjoyed, and praises them quite unreservedly in a sort of strange, slightly whining, singsong voice. He would like just one as a keepsake.

"Oh, how fine they are! Oh, how wonderful!"

I suggest one, my own choice.

"Oh, how wonderful! How fine!" (And without changing the singsong rhythm!) "I would like one of the others." (And again.) "How fine . . . How wonderful . . . If you don't mind?" I like him very much. Although *Amok* disappointed me.

And not surprisingly. Before reading it I had heard it in Babel's[12] most detailed retelling.

---

10. Behind the scenes at the "monolithic" Moscow Art Theater, there was a continuing conflict between Stanislavsky and Vladimir Ivanovich Nemirovich-Danchenko (1858–1943), his coproducer.

11. The story of the father who kills his son in battle is told in *Shah Namah (The Book of Kings)*, an epic poem by the Persian poet Firdausi (940?–1020).

12. Isaac Emmanuelovich Babel (1894–1941), the Russian-Jewish writer from Odessa, was the author of *Red Cavalry*, many short stories, and *Benya Krik the Gangster*, which Eisenstein wanted to make into a film. He was arrested during the Stalinist terror and disappeared. During Khrushchev's rule, he was rehabilitated.

And heavens, what a weak reflection the real *Amok* seemed of that amazing tale!

I heard the story in the evening, at sunset, on the upper verandah of that *dacha* in Nemchinov, where, on the upper floor, I was working with Agadzhanova on the scenario of *1905*, and on the lower with Babel, writing the scenario of *Benya Krik* . . .

During breaks I dined on spiced apples, which carried their aroma and chill from the little cold storeroom right out here to the garden.

Why *Benya Krik*?

Kapchinsky,[13] my enterprising director of production, thought that while working in Odessa on the southern episodes of *1905*, I'd be able to shoot *Benya Krik* in between!

And in a corner arbor we drank Zubrovka with Kasimir Malevich, who had driven out from town.

Propping himself up with his fist on the ground, he talked delightfully about the monumental potential of donkeys.

But, of course, the most amazing were the stories of Babel.

And heavens, how the ball comes to the player!

Who else but Babel, on his way from the Nemchinov Station to the *dacha*, would come across a bonfire? . . . Beside the fire, a Jew . . . a Jew with a violoncello . . . a solitary Jew playing a violoncello beside the bonfire . . . in a copse near the Nemchinov Station . . .

Then Babel went on to tell *Amok* in his own words, and one could see it all vividly: the blindingly tropical moonlit night on deck, the extraordinary woman, the abortion in the black hole on the outskirts of Calcutta, the gangway, falling into the sea together with the coffin, the dreadful sadness of the disqualified doctor, exiled to India.

While I am there, I scribble *The Market of Lust*[14] between jobs and "bung it in" to Proletkino under the pseudonym Taras Nemchinov.

Nemchinov is clear enough.

But Taras is a sort of protest against Grisha's calling his newborn son Douglas (he is now, during the Second World War, a lanky lieutenant), and I insist on Taras!

The affair of Babel's *Maria*.[15] We never uttered a word to each other about it. But this was considerably later.

But here, at the *dacha* in Nemchinov, I first heard of Stefan Zweig from him.

---

13. Mikhail Kapchinsky was the director of the Moscow film studios from 1924 to 1925.

14. *The Market of Lust* was a scenario written by Eisenstein and Alexandrov, who used one pseudonym, Taras Nemchinov.

15. *Maria* was the title of a play by Babel, but what the "affair" was is not known. Perhaps Eisenstein wanted to produce it, as a play or film. (H.M.)

Later I met him.

Still later received a letter from him about his work on Fouché.[16]

Then an invitation to meet in Vienna and go with him to visit Sigmund Freud.

I did not manage to go, and we did not meet again. We lost sight of each other, and in 1942 he committed suicide in Brazil, together with his wife, having turned on a gas tap.

Ernst Toller[17] hanged himself in 1939.

I first met Toller in 1929 in Berlin.

I never thought much of *Masses and Man*. Whereas *Eugene the Unlucky* I consider a great work.

I also embarrassed Toller, as I did Zweig.

He received me in his little, tidy, sweet, and somewhat feminine rooms.

An expansive gesture: "Take anything as a keepsake."

What should I take? If I took nothing I would offend him . . .

There were two early Daumier lithographs on the wall (not very good ones) in narrow gilt frames.

A cup?

A vase or something?

I look for something that has a duplicate in the rooms . . .

There is!

A Mexican horseman — a braided Mexican toy, similar in the way it is made to our Russian bast sandals.

I take it.

Some time later a dreadful confusion becomes apparent.

The horseman belongs to Elizabeth Bergner.[18]

Surprisingly, I shall spend fourteen months in Mexico in the future!

And I bring back only a Toller horseman out of all the braided toys . . .

No, also a crocodile, which I give to Kapitsa.[19]

He collects crocodiles of all types, echoing Rutherford in this.

Pulgas vestidas.[20] Cheap prints of José Guadalupe Posada and much more besides. But of all the braided toys, only a Toller-Bergner horseman!

---

16. Zweig wrote a biography of Joseph Fouché, Duc d'Otrante, a politician and founder of a secret-spy network. Zweig's biography was published in Leipzig in 1929.

17. Ernst Toller (1893–1939) was a German poet, playwright, and anti-Nazi propaganda writer. He was banished by the Germans in 1933, and six years later committed suicide in New York.

18. Elizabeth Bergner (1900–   ), the Austrian-born actress, performed on both the stage and the screen. She came to the United States in 1935 and acted in many films.

19. Peter L. Kapitsa (1894–   ), a leading Soviet scientist and a physicist of international reputation, studied and worked at Cambridge with Lord Rutherford in the twenties.

20. *Pulgas vestidas* (costumed fleas) are a traditional Mexican toy, consisting of a nutshell painted with a miniature landscape and containing the fleas.

Kapitsa and Cambridge

P ETER LEONIDOVICH KAPITSA and I first met in Cambridge. He was then a member of Trinity College, wore a black gown, and showed me his laboratory, where, of course, I understood nothing, except that there was an electric machine there capable of lighting almost half of London, and that all this energy was directed to a field of action a few millimeters in size.

This machine had, I think, some connection with the early experiments on splitting particles of matter.

But the machine and matter are not the point.

The point lies in an idea about the role of time, which was explained to me by Peter Leonidovich.

Specifically, about the shortness of time — as a means of protecting oneself against the action of the incredible temperature that inevitably accompanies such a colossal output of energy.

This energy is expended during such a short time that it can realize its "basic" action, that which the experimenter is interested in, only if the concomitant phenomena (such as, for example, the enormously high temperature) do not get out of control.

I'm not sure I'm accurately describing the principle, but this is the way I grasped it, and it was not erased from my memory even by the subsequent solemnity of lunch at High Table, together with the dons and the master, beneath the high arches soaring into the gloom of Gothic naves in the hall; nor by the Latin grace read antiphonally; nor all the other quaint and charming details of my three days in the surroundings of Cambridge University . . .

Film-Frame
Composition

Rockwell Kent interests me.

I find out about him (apart from the occasional illustrations of his journeys in Alaska) mainly from a strange little book, almost cubic in format, black, with a gold title, that had his wonderful head- and tailpiece ornaments as well as complete illustrations.

It is all about whales: *Moby Dick.*

Moby Dick is a very bad film with John Barrymore in the role of the one-legged captain. I saw it once. Kent's drawings are wonderful and interest me in two ways. First in the collection of graphic examples for film-frame compositions. (Illustrations for a manual I have been planning for a very long time.) In addition to Dobuzhinsky's *White Nights*[1] and Benois's *Versailles*[2] (for examples of the composition of vast horizontal *parterres*), I met with this same problem in filming the pyramids and ruined temples in San Juan Teotihuacán, Degas's canvases (foreground composition), Caravaggio (amazing angles and placing of figures not in the field of the frame; that is, in the outline of the frame, but in relation to the plane of the frame), and so on.

The story is repeated with Aubrey Beardsley: I bought a play by someone called "Johnson" because of Beardsley's illustrations. The play turned out to be Ben Jonson's *Volpone.* I read it in passing and was forever taken with admiration for the great Ben.

And this is how it is here.

---

1. Mstislav V. Dobuzhinsky (1875–1957), painter, member of the World of Art group in St. Petersburg, later an émigré in Paris, was famous for his illustrations for Dostoyevsky's *White Nights*, Pushkin's *Eugene Onegin*, and other works.

2. Alexander N. Benois (1870–1960), a Russian painter, was a leader of the World of Art group. In addition to his book illustrations and scene designs, he depicted the aristocratic court life of the seventeenth and eighteenth centuries, especially Versailles.

Daguerre's Creation

MEMORY RETAINS numerous impressions of first encounters.

The first meeting with Bernard Shaw.

The first skyscraper.

First meetings with Mack Sennett and Gordon Craig.

First time in the Métro in Paris, 1906.

My first meeting with the queen of platinum blondes, Jean Harlow, against a background of peacocks on a marble parapet that bordered the blue-tinted water of the swimming pool at the Ambassador Hotel in Hollywood . . .

Anna Grigorievna Dostoyevskaya, the first widow of the great writer. For this meeting, while still a youth, I first read *The Brothers Karamazov* so as to have something to talk about with the great widow. However, the conversation didn't take place; the meeting remained only a meeting. I swapped the conversation for a gigantic piece of bilberry tart, stolen from the table of refreshments, and for a game of tennis . . .

The first film star I met on American soil was . . . Rin-Tin-Tin, who was the first film star I was photographed with. That was in Boston, where both he and I were appearing in neighboring cinemas, before our respective pictures . . .

My first, live writer was my uncle, the retired General Butovsky, who had written stories for *The Russian Invalid*. In daily life, he was extraordinarily stingy. So stingy that he died of a heart attack on the day War Loans were nationalized in 1917. And he was no less stingy in his literary craft. He wasted no time, for example, in describing nature. "It was one of those dawns that Turgenev describes so inimitably," one could read among the other pearls of the general's pen. When free from writing, this belligerent general with his mighty fist would smash to pulp his batmen's jaws . . .

I even remember my first film fairly distinctly.

That was also in Paris. In 1906.

At the age of eight I was seeing the cinema for the first time! and for the first time too, the creation of Georges Méliès.[1] It was one of his typically half-trick films, from which to this day I remember the curious convolutions of the skeleton of a cab horse . . .

Each of these meetings is marked, in its own way, by its vividness.

And one of the most vivid of impressions was in America, when I first encountered Daguerre's creations.

I don't know if I had never chanced on them before, or had paid them no attention, or if, completely carried away by "left photography," I'd simply never noticed them.

Among other unrealized film projects in Hollywood, I was to have made the story of Captain Sutter,[2] on whose land gold was first found in California.

Like many others, this film was not made either . . .

However, I traveled a good deal around California for its own sake.

I saw Fort Sutter in the capital of California, Sacramento.

In some large firm in San Francisco, manufacturing I can't remember what, I was shown a relic preserved there — the saw from Sutter's sawmill, where the first gold dust was found.

In some out-of-the-way little spots in California, I visited several half-blind old women, who remembered how "the Captain" sat them, then tiny girls, on his mighty rider's knees and made them ride up and down.

Gradually, from partial impressions and lingering traditions (in Sacramento, for example, there is still a beard-growing competition. The competitors are shaved on the same day and at the same time; after a certain interval the growths on their chins are compared), and from the appearance and customs of the people, one can feel the atmosphere of the old America of 1849, the America of the first Gold Rush, the America of the period before the Civil War, but at the same time the America that was inundated with problems, some of which Lincoln's era was to solve, only to be confronted with new ones.

These highways and byways take us from the porches of quiet little provincial houses, with their traditional rocking chairs occupied by old ladies lost in memories, to stern landscapes where dredges have scooped out waste into gray mounds and hills, burying beneath them the green of the fields and meadows. And this landscape seems to tell how the hunger for gold devours the organic joy of nature. . .

---

1. Eisenstein's note is as follows: "And now, forty years later, a cutting comes from that same Paris, from the newspaper *Franc-Tireur* (May 6, 1946) in connection with the showing of *Ivan the Terrible*. It starts: 'For film journalists of my generation, there are a certain number of milestones marking what is now already quite a long road. For Tom Thumbs who have grown up from that age group, such landmarks are the names Méliès, Charlie Chaplin, Eisenstein. There are other names, but that of Eisenstein is always among the first . . .'"

2. The full script based on *Sutter's Gold* is contained in *With Eisenstein in Hollywood* by Ivor Montagu (East Berlin: Seven Seas Books, 1968).

My American bosses were justifiably worried when I chose *Sutter's Gold*, Blaise Cendrars's novel about Captain Sutter, as a subject for a scenario.

"Shall we let the Bolsheviks get onto the subject of gold?" They shook their heads, and finally the whole project was shelved.

Maybe not without reason.

For the California landscape around the mines cried agonizingly of all the stupidity of the hunger for gold, that same fierce accusation which arises naturally from Sutter's own adventurous life and from the pages of the novel about him . . .

However, wandering in the colorful captain's tracks brought us to yet another porch.

The porch of a local museum.

I can no longer recall the name of the little town.

The museum is a modest one.

And two or three real relics from Sutter's time — some buttons, the brim of a felt hat, and, I think, some spurs — are lovingly surrounded here by other objects that have come down to us from the years.

Beaded bags, candlesticks, cracked cups, embroidered pictures, fire tongs, and sugar tongs. And two or three showcases in which lay a revelation: the first daguerreotypes I saw and appreciated.

They are small, in parts almost black, belonging to the zinc period, or with a cunning mirrorlike surface blinking at you and letting you see the image only when the glass surface is turned a certain way; they are enclosed in little folding cases, within which they are surrounded by a fine crimped frame, made from copper sheets as thin as foil.

Bouquets are stamped on the outer lid, and inside is a bit of the living image, a living piece of the times, an example of the living national character.

No doubt all that I had read about the past of California, the numerous stories, and above all my complete preoccupation with this past epoch, was the magic key that suddenly allowed these forerunners of our present-day photographs to reach out to me with such intense vividness from under the dusty glass of the little showcases, though the epithet "dusty" is no more than a literary cliché here: if you have a showcase, it must be "dusty," just as an orphan is always "poor but honest"! The showcase is not in the least dusty. On the contrary, it is polished and even shining, exactly like the linoleum on the floor, the furniture, and the exhibits themselves, which, notwithstanding their antiquity, sparkle like new. "The patina of time" is not the fashion here.

And the little museum rivals the neighboring snack bar and drug store, the filling station and the Western Union telegraph office, in antisepsis and cleanliness.

And at the same time, the past — if not antiquity, another world, another century — looks at us bright-eyed from these tiny open folders, where one half has a slightly worn and shiny velvet cushion, orange, cherry, or chocolate in color, while from the other side looking out at you are the eyes, caps, and "Uncle Sam" beards of the countless once-famous and prominent citizens, now mostly anonymous, but then the lively, busy, and businesslike Americans of the little towns of the forties, fifties, and sixties.

Here they are.

Their wives.

Children.

Young people who have come from the backs of beyond to the first American towns.

Here they are at the start of their careers.

A watch chain being worn for the first time across a bright waistcoat.

The pose a little forced.

The neck sticking out a little too straight from the very low-cut collar.

The vast intricate knot in the tie that seems to be competing with the vast knotty hands.

It is as if you can see, in the way the fingers are bent, where the handles of the plough have been; the fingers that will soon get used not to a pen, but a goose-feather quill for office ledgers, for bank passbooks, for lawyers' court records, legal documents.

Here they are at the height of prosperity.

The lines of watch chains echo the horizontal folds of the dazzling waistcoats. They are damask, silk brocade, velvet, embroidered. The bulge of the tummies wrinkles and stretches their even surfaces.

And security seems to pass over into the calm gaze, which has lost the wide-eyed surprise of youth, confronted with life for the first time.

They sit comfortably.

And there is something servile in the way that a prim, plush armchair tries to make its arms, awkward by nature, fit comfortably under the elbows of Mr. So-and-So, who has achieved prosperity, recognition, general respect.

The surface of another, earlier daguerreotype plays like a laryngologist's mirror. Between the flashes of its surface you can catch the fleeting outlines of faint squares.

These in a splendid variety of checkered silks, in which the wives and mothers of the prosperous gentlemen are arrayed.

Dainty, white, ruffled bonnets envelop like helmets the no less fancifully ruffled curls.

Ribbons and shawls complete the setting of the endless variety of faces.

The poses in the daguerreotypes are also almost traditional. But heavens, what a variety of faces, what thrilling traces life has left in the faces' folds, double chins, lines around the eyes, the victoriously upturned noses of people who have achieved success, or the sad young faces beneath their Confederate caps, seeming to expect a quick end in a field hospital, so pitilessly and touchingly described in the notes and diaries of the good gray poet Whitman.

Some say (and perhaps not without foundation) that the seeds of all vices are present in the most law-abiding people. The inclination to steal, for example. I do not know how matters stand with people of unimpeachable morals, of whom I cannot consider myself one, but I personally know that I do have these sharp urges to appropriate illegally other people's property. I remember how my hands reached out involuntarily toward a penknife to cut out the title page, engraved with the author's portrait, from an old folio of Hans Sachs's[3] farces . . .

Just such a dreadful urge ran like an electric current down my spine in the quiet room of that tiny American town's little museum.

Smash the glass of the showcase! . . .

The impractical lunacy of such an enterprise enters the consciousness almost simultaneously with the desire itself. The trace of the desire remains only in the cheeks, slightly flushed with emotion, and in a special sort of boyish gleam in the eyes. After all, boys steal apples, pears, and nuts, not from greediness, but at least three-quarters from the sense of sporting excitement!

The showcase remained intact . . . But from that day I begin an avid nosing-out among the junkmen's shops, those which sell odds and ends, and the curio shops, of which there are so many beneath intricately bent metal signs on the way from Los Angeles to Santa Monica or Pasadena.

And I find, to my great confusion, that the photographic images of the past that so captivated me are not quoted as collectors' items here at all. Yet, at the same time, those examples which are any good at all, many times better than the chance collection in the little museum, are extremely expensive. It happens that enthusiasts collect not the images and pictures, but the cases in which they were carried, in which they accompanied the owners of those early photo images, just as today every good American under a certain age is accompanied by a photo wallet with pictures of "Pop and Mom," and after that certain age by a similar wallet with the "Wife and Kids."

Among these folding wallet cases there are indeed some very interesting ones, not only in stamped leather, but also in mastic, looking like carved stone . . . However, what the hell do I want with wallet cases? What fascinates me is a little bit of the living spirit of the America of the past, caught alive in these folders like the fabulous djinn.

I lovingly keep a few such early American djinns in the depths of my bookcase. Sometimes I dig them out, wipe the dust off them.

And then, for a time, pictures that seem to come from these cases, pictures of events from America's past, flow in free images through my imagination.

Long before Gladys Mitchell's monumental work or before I knew *Anthony*

---

3. Hans Sachs (1494–1576), a German *Meistersinger*, is the central figure in Wagner's *Die Meistersinger von Nürnberg*.

Adverse,[4] these miraculous glass and zinc plates re-created in my imagination America's amazingly colorful past, the past of its towns, which arose on the sites of buffalo stamping grounds or where nomadic Indians had set up their wig-wams around little mission churches out in the wastes of virgin forests, or the prairies, or on top of ships, which moored inshore by the little mission of St. Francis, dropped anchor forever in the hospitable bay, and, sprinkling sand between each ship and its neighbor, and building stories on the decks, became the first houses of the future city of San Francisco!

The lid of the case closes. The fastening snaps to. The desk drawer, where it is kept, closes. And once again are hidden away for many months memories of those visions which I once glimpsed, and which transported me in thought and feeling to the life of Captain Sutter and the America of his era.

---

4. Eisenstein wrote "Gladys," but he meant Margaret Mitchell (1900–1949), author of *Gone With the Wind. Anthony Adverse* was a famous best seller by Hervey Allen (1889–1949).

Museums at Night

IN GENERAL, MUSEUMS should be seen at night.

Only at night, and especially in solitude, is it possible to merge with what one sees, and not simply to survey it.

Especially when in our Tretiakov Gallery, for example, everything, even the ikons, is vulgarized by the trite set-speeches of the professional guides.

Maybe the groups of visitors trooping around in a throng are not in the least blind, but become so . . . from the presence of the guides. They become blind not because a guide is an integral part of the blind, but because these unattractive misses, with dried-up hearts behind flat bosoms covered with jumpers, divert the visitor from a spontaneous awareness and perception toward their boring discourses and superficial deductions. The brain is not enlightened by these, and the vision is blurred. It is even worse in daytime at the international museum bazaars.

I cannot remember the Louvre without a shudder. Alterations were carried out there in the years just before the war. But I still remember it in all the varicolored, bathhouse glitter of its hall's décor and in the noisiness of its highly indifferent crowds, looking like a cross between a post office and an opera house foyer.

The walls were hung so thickly with masterpieces that it looked as if postage stamps had been stuck on them. The women in the canvases seemed to be warming themselves in the sweaty animal heat of the herd of corpulent visitors. Their rounded (or, in the case of the primitives, ascetic) bodies shone with the texture of the canvas. And it seemed, in this corrupting atmosphere of a bazaar, that these Venuses, Dianas, and Europas were about to climb out of their frames, as Degas's mercilessly flabby women in his caustic watercolors climb out of their baths, in order to take the nosy visitor by the arm and lead him back with them behind the olive, crimson, or cherry-colored curtains in the foregrounds of the canvases they have left.

If . . . if these ladies of the past were not fenced off by locks and bars from the greedy hand of the visitors.

Such was the fate of *La Gioconda*[1] after the famous adventure of the great unknown one in the hands of an international crook.

The bars and the lock are like a chastity belt, fitted on her to prevent new escapades.

Although the chastity belt is an exhibit of another museum, the Cluny Museum.

This museum has fine examples of French Renaissance and Gothic.

Wood sculpture.

Weapons.

Objects of everyday life.

But the herds of visitors here surge in one direction only, with only one aim.

There it lies,

on its little velvet cushion,

under glass.

Toothy and impenetrable.

The chastity belt.

It is a peculiar metal saddle, an iron "wait for me," which preserved the inviolability of wives during the long years their lords were carrying on the military campaigns across the burning sands of the Holy Land.

Mischievous tales of the past tell of duplicate keys . . .

While strolling through the halls, I approached an old attendant.

"Over there, over there!" he shouted at me in a hoarse voice.

I had not managed yet to put my question, but he was already waving his arms, stretching out his index finger toward the corner of the packed hall.

"Over there!"

Poor old man! I was not looking for that at all.

It was not the chastity belt that I was heading toward. (I had already looked at it all I wanted!) His habitual response sticks in his throat: this strange visitor is not looking for the notorious belt. All that he wanted to know was where the toilet was . . .

Museums by day incite one to a frivolous turn of mind.

We go over the Tower of London museum and its amazing collection of armor.

On the staircase at the main entrance stands Henry VIII's steel casing, its legs spread wide. The vast forged globe of the belly is stuck arrogantly forward. The elbows are clasped. The legs wide apart. It seems as if the inhabitant of this armor has only just left it for a moment, his imprint remaining in the curves of the iron sheets, as the traces of the curves of figures are preserved in folds of

---

1. Da Vinci's *Mona Lisa* (also known as *La Gioconda*) was stolen from the Louvre in 1911 and recovered in 1913. It has since been stolen and recovered a second time.

material. The armor is like a steel jacket, preserving forever the character and manner of its carnivorous wearer.

Armor. Armor. And armor.

I walk among it all with a wonderful professor of English literature at King's College, University of London, the ginger Mr. Isaacs. Kind, bright, short-sighted eyes, an ironic intelligence — inevitable in an expert on the past, especially if his specialty is the age of Shakespearean theater — the manner of a Dickensian character, black gloves and an ever-present black umbrella and galoshes, no matter what the time of day or year.

With him I also roam the old streets of Oxford, where each house has a special history and its date.

And this tireless fountain of knowledge, hiding the chinks of his eyes behind thick rimless glasses, knows the date and history of every house.

However . . . I am sure of his looks. I am not sure of the spectacles.

Perhaps he didn't wear them.

But they ask so much to be included with the umbrella and galoshes that I cannot resist wishing them on him. Even if they be in the form of pince-nez on a chain . . .

Our soldiers of the First Cavalry Army during the civil war found that spectacles and pince-nez had a similar irresistible attraction for them. A soldier considered spectacles or pince-nez the highest achievement in elegance. A dashing young warrior would wear two or three pairs at once, seeing in them perhaps an emblem of reliability. Perhaps a symbol of learning, but at any rate something to make him stand out from the crowd . . .

It was Isaacs who took me through Hampton Court and Windsor Castle.

There we admired the heroic compositions of Mantegna and Rubens's strange *Abduction of Ganymede*. Ganymede here is a small, fat boy of six or seven. His mortal fright bursts into a stream, which the little boy cannot restrain.

This stream has found a place in Russian literature.

It was this which made Pushkin recall, in describing the mountains in *A Journey to Erzerum*, a similarity between these mountains and the landscape in the background of this picture, because there too there are precipitous streams seen through the mists, the streams of mountain waterfalls . . .

We are unlucky at Windsor. Only the castle is open. The museum is closed. This deprives me of the opportunity of seeing Holbein's pencil drawings. A pity! An even greater pity is that I shall not see the collection of Leonardo da Vinci's manuscripts. I have to be satisfied with an adoring contemplation of his blackened notebooks in the cases of another museum-cum-bazaar, the Victoria and Albert Museum in London.

Eton is partial compensation.

This is a cold stone pile, where a young gentleman is entered as a pupil ten years in advance, at the very moment of his birth. This is the first step in the education of the future English gentleman in all the indestructibility of British traditions. One can understand nothing about a Briton, especially a British statesman, unless one visits the consecutive scenes of his formation: Eton, Cambridge or Oxford, London with its Tower, Westminster, private clubs, and Whitehall.

Eton. More Tudor arches. Lawns. A "Daumier effect" created by Eton top hats in the sunset.[2] A classroom without windows, as in the days of the Virgin Queen. Huge oak beams running along the center of the premises are unable to compensate for the absence of warmth.

But these oak beams are relics from the victory over the defeated Great Armada. The Great Armada had been familiar to me from the pages of history since I was small, but had always seemed a legend, something like *The Flying Dutchman* or Coleridge's *Ancient Mariner*.

Here, in these ships' timbers, acting as post supports and massive school desks used by descendants of the victors, here the Armada becomes a reality.

With small boys it makes no difference whether they have been born lords or belong to the best families or to the riffraff: they always have an unconquerable desire — to carve the school desk with a knife.

But the desks at Eton are relics. There are traces of knife cuts on the thick boards. But these cuts are so ancient that they too have become relics. No modern cuts are to be seen.

The natural urge of boys to mark their surroundings with the inscription of their own names has been rationalized at Eton and diverted into a kind of cult form. A floor higher, next to the room where the birches (still used to this day) are kept, there is a special room. If the lower floor is remarkable for the complete nakedness of its cold stone walls, this small room is completely paneled in wood. In this it reminds one of the room in Windsor Castle somehow, I do not remember how, connected with the memory of Cardinal Wolsey. This room, by no means all that small, is set aside for the satisfaction of the natural instinct of the growing gentleman. Here with impunity he can give rein to his impulse to cut the crude inscription of his name into the soft parts of the wood.

This is how he will act throughout his life. Not overcoming an avid, instinctive urge, but systematizing the conditions and field of its application, rationalizing the forms his impulses assume. But even more inexorably, having preserved outer impassivity, to plunge the pitilessness of his volitional impulse into the body of the aim and task once set before him.

In Eton this is no more than just a name, together with dates and initials, cut into the wood paneling of the wall. It is not yet a brand seared onto a newly acquired object. It is not yet a sign of possession and power. The names are just names, arranged in columns. The same surnames may be repeated in the column several times in succession.

---

2. At Eton College, the student wore a uniform that included a top hat.

Brothers?
Compare dates.
No!
Great-grandfather.
Grandfather.
Father.
Son.
Grandson.
Great-grandson.
Several generations of Shelleys.
Several of Byrons.
Countless lords.

The most respected names in Great Britain dulled to varying degree, according to the number of years they have been collecting the dust of the passing centuries, and looking like the vertebrae of the single, unbending spine of the prim and proper figure of a British gentleman, as he is seen and imagined by other nations . . .

But let us return to the Tower.

Prior to our visit I had been listening to a lecture by Jack Isaacs.

Clad in his flowing doctor's robes, which made the fiery fringe around his bald crown blaze even more brightly, he had chosen, in honor of a rare visitor, the energy of Elizabethan language as his theme.

For two hours there flowed a steady stream of quotations and examples of this full-blooded language, with its sensual imagery, whose word formations and succulent metaphors could, it seems, be kneaded in one's hands like a wench in the crush of the groundlings in the *parterre* of the Globe, Swan, Blackfriars, or other theaters of that great period.

No doubt the Elizabethan spirit of irrepressible gaiety was conjured back to life by the magician in the doctor's gown, who accompanies me on this trip to the Tower.

My learned friend and I permit ourselves a boyish prank.

Right up the hierarchical structure, from the attendant in the hall to the attendant in charge of the section, from the attendant in charge of the section to the section curator, from the section curator to the department curator, from the department curator to the chief curator, a bewilderment spreads when two visitors, one English, the other a foreigner, protest that the public is being deceived.

The public is being deceived "by the armor being displayed in an incomplete state." One vital detail is missing from the armor. From all the suits of armor — every man Jack of them. (If that expression fits the circumstances.)

Both visitors refer to the Hermitage, in Leningrad, where armor is shown complete. This is indeed the case. It is well known that a knight wore each iron legging separately and that attached between them usually was one more separate little steel guard, sticking out brazenly from beneath the steel covering of the lower part of the knight's belly. The fine examples of knightly armor in the Hermitage's collection stand silent and complete in the halls of the Winter Palace set aside for them. The Tower's puritanical curators have deprived their steel knights of this essential attribute of manly aggression.

The Rabelaisian subtext of protest regarding the "defectiveness" of the armor is first caught on to by the chief curator, after the chief curator by the department curator, by the section curator, by the section attendant, by the hall attendant, and even by Henry VIII's pot-bellied armor. They seem to shake with a good, rich, Falstaffian laughter, which rolls from the chief curator's office down the whole hierarchy through the arches of the Tower, occasioned by the subject of the protest by the two fault-finding visitors: one, an English professor of literature; the other, a foreign traveler . . .

Museums at night, especially museums of sculpture, are amazing! I shall never forget walking during a white night through the halls of ancient sculpture in the Hermitage.

I was shooting the scenes of *October* in the Winter Palace at the time, and, during some resettling of the lights, walked through the connecting passage from the Winter Palace to the Hermitage.

A dim, milky-bluish light filtered in through the windows from the embankment, and in the bluish gloom the Greek statues' white bodies cast white shadows that seemed to be alive and hovering . . .

In Chichén Itzá, when the curator of the Museum of Ancient Mayan Culture decided to take me through the museum's halls at night, it happened differently.

The nights there are pitch black and tropical. Even the Southern Cross, which shamefacedly pokes only its little end above the Mexican horizon, does not light them up.

But in the museum the electricity went off at the very moment we crossed the threshold of the treasured "secret department" of the museum, where the revelry of the ancient Mayas' sensual imagination is carved in stone.

The statues also gained in weirdness, absurdity, disproportion, and scale, because they were suddenly snatched out of the darkness by matches struck now here, now there.

Tolstoy, in *Childhood* — or is it in *Adolescence*? — describes the effect of lightning flashes illuminating galloping horses.

So instantaneous were the flashes that each succeeded in capturing only one phase of the horses' movement.

The horses seemed motionless . . .

The unexpected striking of the matches in the different parts of this hall, filled with motionless stone monsters, made these monsters, on the contrary, seem as though they had come to life.

From the change of direction of the light in the intervals before the matches burned out, it seemed as if, during the periods of darkness, the monsters had managed to change position and place in order to gape with their wide, round, bulging, dead, granite eyes from a new viewpoint at those who were disturbing their age-old peace.

However, for obvious reasons the majority of these stone monsters, rearing out of the dark, had no eyes at all.

But two barrel-shaped roundish gods, in particular, had eyes. I was led to them through the stone reefs of the others (which were in the main ellipsoidal) by the hospitable match of the curator of these precious remains of antiquity.

Light and dark interrupted each other.

Interwove.

Followed each other in turn.

But the speech of my Virgil, who was conducting me through this dark circled Purgatory of mankind's early notions, came pouring out, uninterrupted. Facts and more facts about the history of the belief in gods endowed with "double strength" eddied unceasingly through this interplay of light and dark. The interplay of light and dark itself began to seem an intertwining of the light of reason with the dark depths of man's psyche.

Two globe-shaped granite gods who had this absolute strength faced me with a welcoming smile.

Why two of them?

Each of them was built so that he (or she) had no need at all of his (or her) partner.

One could be sure of this only by touching.

And not just because it was dark in the hall.

But because the object of the investigation was secreted deep under the globes of their bellies.

"Don't be afraid to touch," my guide told me. "Touching it was and still is considered to have curative value and to give the toucher great strength. Feel how much the granite has been worn away . . ."

And I recalled the famous statue of Peter in the cathedral named after him in Rome.

The leg half kissed away by those who fervently pressed their lips to it.

Here the matter was simpler and clearer.

To touch these statues of gods, though a symbolic action, is to join them. By touching their "double strength," you yourself acquire a part of that superhuman strength.

The miraculous strength proves itself.

Suddenly the electricity comes on, and we spend the last part of our pilgrimage to the gods, with their internal contradictions, in the yellowish electric light.

The mystery vanished along with the shadows.

It was frightened away by the shameless indifference of the low-powered electric bulbs.

Lit by the orangy light, the round, goggling, granite eyes of my mysterious acquaintances seemed senseless and stupid.

And this is why everything else connected with them, in the blinding and false electric light of common sense, seemed nonsensical.

But the lamp had only to burn out, or the dynamo at the power station had only to catch its breath, and you would be wholly in the power of dark, latent forces and forms of thought.

The intertwining of illumination and darkness also provides the imagination with just such fairy wanderings down the mysterious paths of art, like that which we trod at the beginning down that hall when the play of light and shade on the bodies of the vertical monsters, lacking the beards, gay eyes, fine hats, or scarves of the Flemish guardians of the law, seemed to move toward us in a way that reminded one of Rembrandt's *Night Watch* . . .

The proper way to visit museums is going alone and at night . . .

Mexico

DURING MY ENCOUNTER with Mexico, it seemed to me to be, in all the variety of its contradictions, a sort of outward projection of all those individual lines and features which I carried and carry within me like a tangle of complexes.

Monumental simplicity and unrestrained Baroque (in each of its aspects, Spanish and Aztec) . . . The duality of these attractions finds expression again in my enthusiasm both for the severity of the peon's white costume (a costume that, in both its color and rectilinear silhouette, seems to be the tabula rasa of costumes in general) and for the sculpturesque sequence of gold and silver *bas-reliefs*, overloaded with gold embroidery, burning on blue, green, orange, and puce satin, that appear under the black hats of the heroic participants of the *corridas*.

This superabundance was combined with the wealth of capes and black and white lace mantillas of their lady admirers, of tall, Spanish combs, of fans playing and gleaming under the scorching Sunday sun on the stepped tiers around the *Blood and Sand*[1] arenas.

One was as dear to me as the other. I felt as much in harmony with one as with the other. And I delved into the mass of both by means of Eduard Tisse's incomparable camera.

The tropics responded to dreamy sensuality. The intertwining bronze bodies seemed to incarnate the latent rovings of sensuality; here in the over-saturated, overgrown grasping of the lianas, male and female bodies wreathed and intertwined like lianas; they looked in the mirror and saw how the girls of Tehuantepec looked at themselves with black, almond-shaped eyes in the sur-

---

1. The novel about bullfighting, *Blood and Sand*, by Vicente Blasco-Ibáñez (1867–1928), was the basis for a film of the same name.

face of the dreamy tropical creeks, and admired their flowered arrays, reflecting on the golden surface of their bodies. It seemed that embodied in me, and flooded with moonlight, was the rhythmically breathing abundance of the bodies of *esposas de soldados* clasped in the embraces of their husband-soldiers; bodies spread across the whole area of the little eight-sided courtyard of the small fortress guarding the Pacific Ocean port of Acapulco. (Guarding from whom? Unless it be the flights of pelicans, their heads tucked away on one side, plunging like arrows into the amber-colored water of the Gulf.)

The bodies breathe rhythmically and in unison. The very earth itself seems to be breathing, whitened here and there by a veil drawn modestly over a pair among the other bodies, gleaming black in the moonlight, that are not covered by anything. Bodies knowing no shame, bodies to whom what is natural for them is natural, and needs no concealment.

The sergeant and I slowly walk round the narrow parapet, with its narrow loopholes, looking down what appears, from above, to be a battlefield after the bugles have finished sounding the attack, a field of death cast in silver, but is, in fact, a vast cornfield where the seed of countless generations of bronzed children is being sown.

Mexico — lyrical and tender, but also brutal.

It knows the merciless lashes of the whips, lacerating the golden surface of bare skin. The sharp cactus spikes to which, at the height of the civil wars, they tied those already shot half to death, to die in the heat of the desert sands. The sharp spikes that still penetrate the bodies of those who, having made crosses from the cacti's vertical trunks, tie them with rope to their own shoulders, and crawl for hours up to the tops of the pyramids, to glorify the Catholic Madonnas — de Guadalupe, de los Remedios, the Santa Maria Tonantsintl; Catholic Madonnas since Cortez's time, triumphantly occupying the places and positions of the cult of the former pagan gods and goddesses.

In order not to change the age-old routes of the pilgrimages, the crafty monks raised statues and temples to the gods on the very same spots (heights, deserts, pyramids) where the overthrown ancient, heathen gods of the Aztecs, Toltecs, or Mayas had once reigned. To this day streams of pilgrims on religious holidays crawl for hours through the dry dust, tearing skin from their knees, in order to press their parched lips to the heavenly Queen's golden hem or to the fragmented remains of the bones of Her most loyal past disciples (which were obtained for us, from under the altar of the church of San Juan de los Remedios, by the cynical and slightly soiled dean of this church on a pyramid, Father Figueroa, a keen photographer, who went off on his motorcycle every Thursday, without fail, to Mexico City's brothels, situated, for some reason, especially densely around the street bearing the most heroic name from Mexico's past, Guatemotzin).

It is impossible not to recall this name when touching on brutality and sadism (and which of us is without them?), and who will cast the first stone at us for this when the Fascist-inclined American magazines met our entry into the United States with the protest "Why let in this red dog and sadist Eisenstein?" (Thus wrote the notorious Major Pease, well known at the time, later unmasked as a German agent, the unsuccessful organizer of Fascist detachments in the shadow of the Statue of Liberty.)

He it was, Guatemotzin, the royal leader with the hawklike, Indian profile, who uttered the famous words "I'm not lying on a bed of roses, either" when the conquering Spaniards, torturing him over fierce braziers, were trying to find out where the wealth and treasure of the land they had enslaved was hidden.

The proud Indian's words were addressed to one of his comrades, who was suffering his share of torture alongside and had dared to utter a groan through clenched teeth.

A *bas-relief* depicting their heroic sufferings now decorates the pedestal of the monument of Guatemotzin with his head thrown proudly back.

Physical brutality, whether in the "asceticism" of monks' self-flagellation or in the torturing of others, in the blood of the bull or the blood of man, pouring over the sands of countless Sunday *corridas* every week, after Mass, in a sensual sacrament; the history of unparalleled brutality in crushing the countless uprisings of the peons, who had been driven to a frenzy by the exploitation of the landowners; the retaliatory brutality of the leader of the uprising, Pancho Villa, who ordered prisoners to be hanged naked in order that he and his soldiers might be entertained by the sight of the last physiological reactions of the hanged.

This cruelty of the Mexican does not lie only in bodily mutilation and blood, not only in former slave-owners' favorite treatment of prisoners — top hat on their heads, clothes off, made to perform a frenzied, naked dance in answer to indiscriminate and continuous shooting — but also in that wicked humor, irony, and that special sort of Mexican wit (the features of which are already borne by this ominous tarantella), the so-called vacilada.

This cruel humor of the Mexican is nowhere exhibited more clearly than in his attitude toward death.

The Mexican despises death. Like every heroic nation, the Mexicans despise both it and those who do not despise it. But this is not enough: the Mexican does more; he laughs at death.

"The day of death," November 2, is a day of wild revelry in mocking death and its bony emblem with the scythe.

Books (1)

BIRDS FLY DOWN TO SOME saints (Assisi).

Beasts run up to some legendary characters (Orpheus).

Pigeons cling to the old men in St. Mark's Square in Venice.

A lion attached itself to Androcles.

Books cling to me.

They fly down to me, run up to me, attach themselves to me. I have loved them for so many years: large and small ones, thick and thin ones, rare editions and cheap little booklets, in blaring dust jackets or thoughtfully enveloped in solid leather, as if in soft shoes.

They should not be too neat, like suits straight from the tailor's, as cold as starched dickies. But they certainly should not be in greasy tatters. A book should lie in the hand like a well-adjusted tool.

I have loved them so much that they have finally begun to love me back. Books burst open like ripe fruit in my hands, and fold back their petals like magic flowers, bearing a fertilizing line of thought, a stimulating word, a corroborating quotation, a convincing illustration.

I am capricious in selecting them. And they willingly come my way. They have me in their grasp in a fateful fashion.

At one time it was intended that just one room in my home should be encircled with books. But step by step, room after room began to clothe itself in books. And so after the library, the study falls victim; after the study, the walls of my bedroom . . .

G. K. Chesterton was once invited to read a paper. "What shall I talk on?" he asked on arrival. "On whatever you like, even umbrellas." And Chesterton composed a paper on the expanding picture of hair covering thoughts, hats covering hair, umbrellas covering all . . .

My rooms sometimes appear to be like that.

Currents flow from the cells of the brain's gray matter through the skull into the bookcase doors, and through the bookcase doors into the very hearts of the books.

But it's not true! The bookcases have no doors; I keep the books on open shelves, and in response to a current of thought they rush into my head.

Sometimes the greed that radiates toward them is stronger. Sometimes the infectious strength that surges from their spines is stronger. One seems a new St. Sebastian, pierced by arrows from the shelves. And one's skull no longer seems a small, bony sphere, containing the fragments of reflections, like Leibnitz's monad, but appears like the outer walls of the room itself, and the layers of books that are spread over their surface are only expanding strata within one's own head.

And for all that, the books are not in the least unusual — unexpected more in their combination than in their bibliographic, antiquarian, or decorative oddness. And perhaps in the unorthodox nature of the collection and the complete absence of what one "should" have!

Often I prize them not so much for what they are, for the complex of ideas in which they are clad for me, but as a result of an occasionally accidental page submerged in the indifference of uninteresting chapters, of a single line lost among pages concerned with quite different problems.

And the tenacity of this aura, this radiation (or mistiness?) encircling the culprits (and for which I prize them more than for the works themselves), almost materializes in the form of a web, over which one skims, fearing to brush against or tear it, like fine and quivering threads of associations. And one seems to be like the wise men of Laputa,[1] trembling for the safety of their webs.

Sometimes halfhearted well-wishers assiduously prove to me that it is not a web at all, but a barbed-wire entanglement, cutting me off with book-learning from living reality.

These well-wishers are halfhearted, and the sincerity of their assertions is only half true.

As are captious objections concerning the wealth of quotations.

Quotations! Quotations! Quotations!

Long ago, Prince Kurbsky, that elegant author of a treatise on punctuation, though in all other respects a traitor to his country, upbraided Tsar Ivan the Terrible for quotations. I quote: "How many holy words you have seized and with what frenzy and ferocity, not just a few lines, not just a few verses, as is the wont of adept scholars (if one needs to write of something, one does so in short words, containing much meaning), but too much, more than good mea-

---

1. Laputa, one of the lands in Part Three of Swift's *Gulliver's Travels*, is the home of fools, not wise men, though they think themselves so. The name itself is a pun on "the prostitute."

sure, excessively and tiresomely, whole books, whole parables and epistles!"[2]

But there are quotations and quotations.

A quotation can be a cover for the uncritical, hiding his ignorance or self-satisfaction behind the words of an authority.

Quotations can be a lifeless complication.

I understand quotations as outrunners to the right and left of the galloping shaft horse. Sometimes they diverge, but help to speed the imagination by their broadening, reinforcing parallel run.

As long as one does not let go of the reins!

But for heaven's sake, not when quotation follows quotation like a tedious procession of coach-and-fours!

---

2. Prince A. M. Kurbsky (1528?–1583), a general and writer, was the author of *The History of the Grand Duke of Moscow*. He is best known for his correspondence with Ivan the Terrible, in which he attacks Ivan for his despotism, his many errors of statecraft, and even for his poor knowledge of the Russian language. The quotation is from that correspondence, in the edition published in St. Petersburg in 1902.

Books (2)

I KNOW A MARVELOUS bookshop that I don't visit very often. Perhaps that is why it preserves its magical attraction.

Though I live in Moscow, I go to it in Leningrad. It lies somewhere between Pesky, where I once lived, and Znamensky Square, where, I remember, a steam tram ran, bright yellow with clouds of black smoke, worthy of a steamboat on the Mississippi. It ran from the Alexander Nevsky Abbey (Old Nevsky) to the railroad station and back.

Somewhere about halfway between Pesky and the square you turn off down a twisty Paris-like side street that leads you to the typically old London-façade kind of shop (the kind of shop window I remember from Berlin). In it are valuable Daumier lithographs, an amazing collection of French prints from Epinale, and many rare books I've long been seeking.

The shop is often shut. But they always let me in. I don't have to hurry to get there when the shop opens in the morning in order not to lose some book I had spotted in the window on the evening before. Somehow the question of money doesn't arise, either. No matter what I choose in the shop, there's always enough money.

The first room is lined with books from floor to ceiling.

Whitman's amazing autobiography. Rochefort,[1] together with the magazine *L'Eclipse*. A complete set of *L'Assiette au Beurre*.[2]

The second room has sloping counters, covered in glass. Here there are some marvelous editions of Rabelais. A thick Ben Jonson. The books are

1. Henri Rochefort (1830–1913), journalist and politician, was editor of *Le Figaro* and publisher of *La Lanterne, La Patrie,* and other magazines.
2. *L'Assiette au Beurre* was a humorous journal.

wrapped up. Taken under my arm. Strange; their edges don't cut into me. They don't weigh me down. They seem somehow weightless.

Not like Kuno Fischer,[3] whose history of philosophy I had to lug by tram in the thirties from the tiny bookshop on Arbat to Chistiye Prudy. A fight. I had jabbed someone in the side with eight volumes. "Citizen! Get your box out of here!" And my threatening reply: "It's not a box; it's Hegel!" The magic of unfamiliar words! The militant milkmaid who had been ready to tear me to pieces suddenly quailed before the unfamiliar word and dissolved into the crowd.

But this parcel of books, bought in my favorite shop, really does dissolve in my hands. Just as the severe English façade of the shop fades, just as the twisty Paris-like side street straightens out, to become the Suvorovsky Prospekt from Znamensky Square to Pesky. Then like an arrow down the railway line from Nikolayevsky Station in Leningrad to Nikolayevsky Station in Moscow. Then both stations become the October stations.

What is it all about?

The cock has thrice crowed its morning greeting to Aurora, not the cruiser, which I had brought up the Neva (as in 1917) for the shooting of *October* in 1927, nor the *Sleeping Beauty*,[4] but Aurora, the goddess of the dawn . . .

And I wake up.

My marvelous bookshop is a dream.

A dream that visits me rarely but unfailingly, year after year.

In this dream is removed my bitterness at not having enough money, and my hesitation at acquiring a book; in this dream I find an *oeuvre* I overlooked, a book I lost (long, long ago), which was snapped up by someone else.

Here, smiling welcomingly down at you from the shelves, is a fantastically complete set of translated Italian scenarios in French, in the form of a whole library of the eighteenth century. As a poor student, I couldn't afford to buy it during a foray from the front to Petrograd in 1918, although I was already raving *ad nauseam* about Harlequins, Capitans, Brigellas.[5] Here, too, Bakst[6] is always at my service, always at a price exceeding my means.

And how many times I've held a full set of Piranesi's *Prisons*[7] in my hands here, only three sheets of which huddle together at home!

Here I have in my hands the marvelous sheets of old Petersburg, at which I

---

3. Kuno Fischer (1824–1907) was a German philosopher and author of the multivolume *History of the New Philosophy*.

4. The leading character of Tchaikovsky's ballet *The Sleeping Beauty* is named Aurora.

5. The scenarios were the scripts of the *commedia dell'arte*, and the characters were stock parts in these plays.

6. Lev Nikolayevich Bakst (1866–1924), known as Léon Bakst, was a portrait painter, an illustrator, and a designer for Diaghilev's Ballet Russe.

7. Piranesi, the eighteenth-century engraver and architect, also designed theater décor.

can only lick my lips, not daring even to approach close to the showcase of the rare-book shop on Liteiny.

Splendeur et décadence of these shops!

Mahogany and bronze. Green carpets. The corners of the cherished folders. Only from a distance. Only through the door. Nervously, enviously.

I hadn't the experience and effrontery to go in and have a look. To refuse what was unsuitable. To demand something else. And not take that, either. And leave, at least having enjoyed myself.

Many years later, in Paris, Darius Milhaud and I, completely muffled up in our overcoats, went to the Galerie Rosenberg.

A house trading only in Picasso and Braque. We walked critically round the lower halls, thus drawing the attention of the elegant salesmen. We mumbled before the canvases, shrugging our shoulders, not like sophisticated bourgeoisie, but like Americans, estimating the size of a picture for an area of wall, no more; for we didn't look much like millionaires able to erect walls or to build a house around a few selected pictures. (Such as Leonard Rosenthal did in his Paris residence overlooking the Parc Monceau, with windows that shot automatically as soon as anyone dared to touch the shutters; here he had decorated one room in rare woods and velvet like a jewel box. A pale light softly illuminated the outlines of a truly divine wooden Bodhissatva,[8] brought from far-off India, whose pearl oyster farms were the basis of Monsieur Rosenthal's wealth. Or Otto H. Kahn, who built the dining room in his Long Island house as a frame for his six Romneys, rhythmically separated by the bays of french windows.)

We are elegantly asked, by those looking after us, whether we would like to see something more perfect. We are led to the small halls of the upper floor and, finally, to a tiny salon, where we see canvas after canvas of all of Picasso's periods, with the exception of the famous ones that are in museums and private collections.

The buyers are hard to please. This merely renders the salesmen more attentive. Soon, however, we "Americans" leave, with barely a nod of the head, saying to each other that the Rembrandt and Géricault they had seen the day before would suit the study's furnishings better . . . Thus I receive a practical course on Pablo Picasso from originals. Darius enriches my education by taking me to one of the foremost dentists. His waiting room has one of the best collections of Cézannes.

But we are now talking of books; paintings we shall leave for another section.

---

8. A Bodhissatva is a statue of Buddha, or one who is able to reach Nirvana.

Streets

I HAVE SEEN STREETS that are unlike streets, such as the Rue de Lappe in Paris. It is so narrow, so dark, and so hemmed in by small, but more than questionable, bistros that it seems more like a gulley. Here now, watch out or you'll be swept away by the flood of dirty, cloudy water that will surely come sweeping down these slippery stones. We'd better dive in through the door of Bal aux Trois Colonnes and hide ourselves in it, beneath the sound of its three accordions.

The little streets of Whitechapel[1] seem like one great counter, and once you have entered their vortex, you begin to feel not so much a customer as an obedient commodity, something like a tie done up in a bow, or a celluloid collar that the salesmen toss to each other.

The Rue de l'Odéon on a spring evening is also unlike a street. Too narrow for a normal street, it is like a wide corridor in a family *pension*, and the doors of the shops are like the doors of the individual furnished rooms. One end of the street should lead into the sitting room, the other into the kitchen. This illusion is created by the silence. The complete absence of taxis and carriages. Even of pedestrians. But more than anything else, perhaps, by the figures of two women. Each stands in the rectangle of her doorway, diagonally across from each other. And they talk, almost without raising their voices, in the manner of people who, for a moment, have just looked out of their rooms into a common corridor.

One of them is gray-haired, in a light blue suit of masculine cut with a short skirt. Above her is a sign that, strange as it may seem, does not destroy the illusion of the interior. Perhaps because what the sign says is itself so unexpected:

---

1. Whitechapel was the Jewish quarter of London.

SHAKESPEARE AND CO.

The other woman is dressed in soft gray. A skirt to her ankles. This is Adrienne Monnier. The first woman is Sylvia Beach. Mademoiselle Monnier sells French books. The poet Jean Paul Fargue autographs a book of his verse for me on the diminutive counter. I have never heard of him before. He, of course, has never heard of me. That does not prevent him, for perhaps the hundredth time, from writing swiftly and impassionately on the title page of the little volume of his poems, *A Eisenstein poète, Jean Paul Fargue poète. Paris, 1930.*

Fifteen years later, in the English edition of the magazine *Verve* (No. 56), I find some lines by Adrienne Monnier about Jean Paul Fargue: *"Fargue . . . Each of his defenseless hands forms little marionettes."* But for the time being these hands do not form little marionettes. For the time being they flutter over the counter, picking out a volume of their own verse.

Sylvia Beach sells English books. More than that, she publishes them. Above all, it was she who published James Joyce's *Ulysses.*

The publishing firm of Shakespeare and Co. is the same sort of treasurehouse for Joyce's works that a tiny shop on the embankment is for editions of Verlaine. There is Verlainiana and everything that Verlaine wrote, even the banned *Hombres* (which is sold under the counter quite openly). Here there is Joyciana. And Joyce's works . . .

I loved this quiet street. I loved this quiet modest bookshop and gray-haired Sylvia Beach. I often dropped in at her place to sit in her little back room and gaze at the walls, hung with countless photographs.

An extraordinary literary pantheon! Was there a single writer Sylvia had not known? Apart from the mustachioed Frank Harris, Oscar Wilde is especially well represented in numerous views, especially in that outrageous costume in which he astonished America: a velvet jacket, soft beret, knee-length trousers, and stockings:

Who's coming?
He's coming!
Oscar Wilde!
The great Aesthete!

Thus the Barnum-style posters announced the great aesthete's arrival in New York.

I remember this advertising formula well . . . I had used it in 1920 for my first theatrical production, *The Mexican* (in collaboration with the late Valentin Smyshlayev). These same lines, the name of Oscar Wilde replaced by that of Denny Ward, and "the great Aesthete" by "the great boxer," were shouted out during intermissions by the "sandwich men" advertising the great boxer, Denny Ward . . .

In Miss Beach's shop I struck up an acquaintance with a young man with a fringe and slightly powdered cheeks; this was George Antheil. Until recently, he had been living in a little room over Miss Sylvia's shop, and had only just become famous . . .

Wherever I have stayed for more than a month, I invariably found such a bookshop. Such a back room. Such a charming book enthusiast.

In Mexico City it is a Greek, Mizrachi. Many of the books on my bookshelves have his shop's labels: they are on a history of the Chinese theater, on the biography of Agrippa von Nettesheim,[2] on a work about Paracelsus . . . It is at his shop that I get to know Carleton Beals, the author of a rather good book entitled *Mexican Maze* and a still better one about the political hell on the island of Cuba during the dictatorship, *The Crime of Cuba*.

Carleton Beals is the son of a very curious figure. His mother is Carrie A. Nation. She is one of those strange and unbalanced women to whom the "dry law" in America owes its existence. She would break into drinking establishments in the Bowery and Brooklyn with a hammer or ax (photographs of her survive, for her picture was often published), and proceed to smash bottles and mirrors, windowpanes and glasses, in the name of the Lord, morals, and purity. She saw in her name the mark of the Lord's finger — Carrie A. Nation (Carry a nation!), and the fanatical old woman in eyeglasses, long veil, and with a hammer in her hand frenziedly carried out what she considered to be her mission.

Her son neatly autographs his book; one after another, readers who have just bought *Mexican Maze* come up to him. To the rear stands the happy Señor Mizrachi. A long queue; the book is selling well . . .

In Hollywood, the little Hollywood Book Store was one more such haven of books. It belonged to another nice and quiet person; Odo Stadé was his name. He was either a Swiss from Hungary or a Czech from the Tyrol. His books were sophisticated. And all the banned editions were available there. It was from his shop that I carried away a paperback dollar reprint of Vandercook's *Black Majesty*, a story about the Haitian king Henri Christophe, which has attracted me for so many years with its possibilities for film production.

I wanted to make this film with Paul Robeson.

Stadé, the quiet bookseller lost deep in the quiet of his life among books (the bright covers of the latest thing, the rare editions, the collectors' items), had had a rather stormy past. He himself was writing a book [*Viva Villa*]. The hero of which was no other than Pancho Villa.

It happens that the quiet Stadé had been a participant in the legendary and fantastic campaigns of that *hombre malo* (bad man), as his Mexican admirers delight in calling him.

At one time John Reed marched with his detachments across Mexico, and Ambrose Bierce followed him as well. The figure of the journalist in the film

---

2. Cornelius Heinrich Agrippa (1468?–1535), called Agrippa von Nettesheim, was a German theologian and physician and a practitioner of the occult sciences.

Viva Villa combines the two men, just as the screen Villa, contrary to reason, combines two quite separate real, historical figures: the historical Pancho and the historical Emiliano Zapata. The first, a general, maker of a *Putsch*, an adventurer; the second, the leader of the peasant uprising, a hero, a martyr. The positive side of the Rabelaisian monster created on the screen by Wallace Beery comes from Zapata's life. The rest from the *hombre malo*, Pancho Villa.

At the height of the Mexican revolution's success, Villa and Zapata, having taken Mexico City by storm from two sides, joined forces for a short time. Then followed the inevitable split, the treacherous murder of Zapata by a group of reactionary officers, and other zigzags in the story of Mexico's liberation movement.

There are photographs showing both leaders sitting solemnly side by side, in gilt armchairs in the Palacio Nacional, the Mexican capital's "Winter Palace." Pancho wears a normal military uniform. Zapata is in typical partisan rig: a vast straw hat and belts of machine-gun bullets. This fact alone is not, of course, enough to justify merging them into one figure!

The character of the journalist, combining memories of both John Reed and Ambrose Bierce, is another discrepancy.

Johnny remained alive and survived Pancho. That was John Reed's destiny.

The scene of the wounded Pancho's death near the meat stall is a very good invention. Johnny improvises an obituary notice for the dying man, poeticizing his passing as a heroic death.

In fact, it happened rather differently.

It was Bierce who wrote about Pancho's brutality for his newspaper. The dispatches fell into Pancho's hands and did not reach their destination, and Bierce . . . disappeared forever from the ken of his readers.

There is a theory that Bierce's bones lie somewhere on the trail of Pancho's campaigns.

I like Bierce and Rochefort very much.

Rochefort's *La Lanterne* (its first twenty numbers) was the first book that I started looking for in the basement bookshops of Paris. And on the famous *quais* along the banks of the Seine. ("Drop everything. Come to Paris for a month. It's spring now. We'll rummage through the books along the Seine . . ." So Gordon Craig, another book and bookshop fanatic, wrote to me from Italy many years later.)

The second book was the classic, and now quite rare, work by Péricaud on the Théâtre Funambule and the incomparable Debureau.

Sometimes I am lucky with books! And I have to admit that I had exactly the right money for these two. I never thought that there was anything that could join them both, Bierce and Rochefort.

However . . . it is not so much a joining as a sharp contradistinction.

What joins them is the title *La Lanterne*.

What separates them is what was printed at different times beneath this title.

Reaction triumphs.

After the fall of the Paris Commune, Rochefort was sent into exile.

The Empress Eugénie was similarly driven from the arena of history and the fairy-decked Tuileries Palace. But the vindictive lady is not satisfied with Rochefort's exile, which was not of her doing. She longed to add her sovereign hand to the business of revenge. Empress Eugénie, herself an exile from France, bought the title *La Lanterne*. From that time on *La Lanterne*, which had lashed her and Napoléon le Petit so mercilessly (and splendidly), was to mock the ill-starred fate of its founder, publisher, editor, and only contributor: Henri de Rochefort.

She entrusted this evil business to one of the most jaundiced of young American journalists. The enterprise lasted for one number. The name of the journalist: Ambrose Bierce . . .

Stadé told me a lot about Mexico. And the seeds of interest in that country, once sown in me by photographs of "The Day of Death" (in an issue of the *Kölnische Illustrierte*, which I happened to pick up) and nourished by the stories of Diego Rivera, when he visited the Soviet Union as a friend, grew into a burning desire to travel there. A few months later the desire became reality.

On the way to the train that was to take me to the country of Pancho Villa and Zapata for fourteen months, I stopped off to say good-by to Stadé. When I left his little shop for the last time, my wallet was lighter by fifty dollars, and my baggage twenty pounds heavier. To it was added a multivolume set of Frazer's *The Golden Bough*, which for many months I had fruitlessly hunted for, high and low, in the various cities of Europe I'd passed through. Apart from this notable work, which has helped me so greatly in the understanding of primitive thought, another slim volume lay in the parcel. And, in fact, it is from this book that the true theme of the present epistle derives.

The booklet's title — *21 Delightful Ways of Committing Suicide.*

The book is absolutely in line with those nonsense books at which Lear and Carroll were so outstanding in England, and nowadays Perelman, Thurber, Steig, and Saul Steinberg in America. The brightly colored pictures present, in a most attractive form, the most astounding ways of taking your own life.

Here is a man burying himself alive in his own back yard; here is another lighting a cigar made from a stick of dynamite; a third, like St. Francis, is kissing a ghastly monster, green and leprous. The book ends with the most unexpected and reliable means: suicide by means of longevity.

The suicide, extremely old, quietly passes away in his armchair from an abundance of so many lived-through years . . . Of course, it would be difficult "to go one better" than this in enumerating and listing sophisticated ways of doing away with oneself.

But perhaps even more impressive is the method by which George Arliss[3] dies on the screen in a film I saw about a year before I got to know Hollywood, Stadé, and the gay little book on a somber subject. The film was a screen version of Galsworthy's play *Old English*. And Arliss plays the hero of *Old English*, who is nicknamed "Old English" (and who is the personification of Old England to the marrow of his bones).

Old English is the head of a Liverpool steamship company, a speculator and swindler, a half-paralyzed old man "with one foot in bankruptcy and the other in the grave." In carrying out the only swindle in his life that has had a good purpose (to provide for his illegitimate son's children), he falls into the clutches of another, no less tenacious, swindler, who has the advantage of being young.

The old man has amazing will power, is despotic and completely devoid of moral scruples. One sees this in the way he manipulates the meeting of his creditors and the way he forces the shareholders to agree to entrust the steamship to him, in what is clearly an unprofitable enterprise for them! More than anything he prizes his independence. "Death is better than having someone else's foot on your neck!" But there is no way out for the old man. Tomorrow he faces exposure, bankruptcy, failure. And now there is a marvelous scene on the screen. There is nothing here of the cinema, of course. The picture was made at the dawn of sound cinema (I saw it in 1929), and basically it's no more than the screening of Arliss's magnificent acting in the role of this old man, which he played countless times on the stage . . .

In September 1941, foreigners instinctively begin to quit Moscow in the wake of the evacuees, like rats leaving a sinking ship. The pulse of their hurried departure beats feverishly in the little bookshop on Kuznetsky. In the prewar years all buying and selling of foreign books was concentrated in this shop. In September 1941, the little back room was bursting with books sold by the departing foreigners. Packet by packet they migrated to my bookshelves. Many books about Argentina and Peru, which could not fail to find a soft spot in my "Mexican" heart. Mr. Laurence Steinhardt, the American ambassador, was getting rid of them. Books by Paul de Kruif.[4] Detective novels in blaring covers. And, on the other hand, the very modest bindings of Sinclair Lewis's novels. A slim volume of Galsworthy's plays. And among the plays was *Old English*. Remembering Arliss's acting, I reread this play year after year.

The old man is on a very strict diet. His daughter, an insufferable bigot,

---

3. George Arliss (1868–1946) was an English stage and film actor. He acted in New York with Mrs. Patrick Campbell and began his U.S. film-acting career in the twenties.

4. Paul de Kruif (1890–1971), an American bacteriologist, was the author of several popular books on science, most of which were translated into many languages, including Russian. Among them were *Microbe Hunters* and *Hunger Fighters*.

keeps strict watch over it. ("What's that whining?" asks the old man. "It's Miss Hawthorn praying," replies the footman.) But on this occasion, unknown to his daughter, who has gone to a temperance ball, the old man orders himself a Lucullan late supper. As the luxurious meal comes to an end, Old English gives free rein to his gluttony. Wine after wine passes through his hands. The footman is in a panic. The angry daughter, when she comes to wish her father good night, moves a bottle of whiskey out of the old man's reach. As soon as she has left, the old man contrives to rise and get the bottle.

He drinks. Memories pass before him: the names of racehorses he had had bets on, the names of actresses he had had affairs with, drinking parties, debauchery, the past . . .

Meanwhile, Old English has got well and truly drunk.

And how incomparably Arliss plays the scene in which the old man gradually loses the use of his hands and feet as he gets drunk!

His arms, from the elbows down, are already motionless. Now he tries to see whether he can still move his fingers. He lets his lower arm fall onto the table. The fingers are motionless. And they knock against the even surface of the table like dice. It is the sound of the knuckles of dead hands.

I would like to see them on stage!

Surely the mastery of Arliss cannot be so perfect that a spasm runs through the end of his fingers? For without this the knocking could not be produced! Or is the knocking added separately? And produces by this means the astounding effect, as if a hand were knocking on the lid of a coffin.

I let my hand fall on the table top. A hollow knock. But there is nothing of that sensation of a numb blow on wood.

Another fade-out. And another fade-in.

Old English is motionless in his armchair. His granddaughter returns from the theater with her admirer. She wants to show her grandfather her new dress. She cannot bring herself to wake him. She tiptoes out. The anxious footman wants to wake his master. "Time for bed." Mr. Hawthorn cannot be awakened.

And Molly the maid, throwing her arms high, cries out over the unusual suicide: "Mother o' Jesus! The grand old fightin' gentleman! The great old sinner he was!" (The curtain falls.)

We are discussing here questions regarding suicides.

I once performed a rather complex means of roundabout suicide myself, and it is interesting to note that the outcome of the attempt is still not clear. Although the affair is very much like a fiasco.

Which may be why one of the first books I read in the Kremlin hospital after my heart attack was *The Idiot*. Not because of the title . . . But because of the scene of Hippolyte's unsuccessful suicide . . .

I decided to do it not by hanging, not by smoking dynamite, not by stuffing myself with a forbidden diet, not by means of a pistol or poison.

I decided to work myself to death . . .

The Later Years

Cherkassov as Alexander Nevsky

*Eisenstein setting up a shot for
"Alexander Nevsky," with cameraman
Tisse at right*

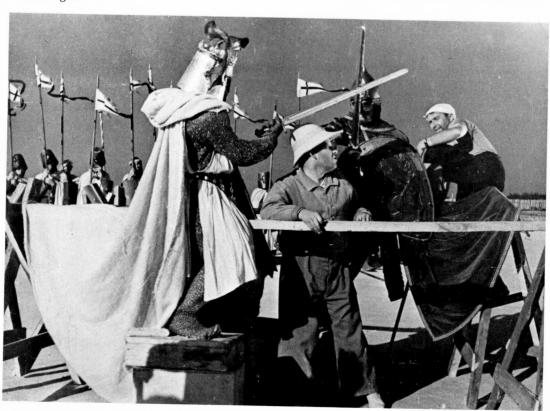

Eisenstein's pre-production costume sketches for "Nevsky," and (bottom) the actors in the finished costumes

Eisenstein's pre-production sketches for a scene from "Nevsky," with the scene as filmed shown below

24. ᵥ 38.

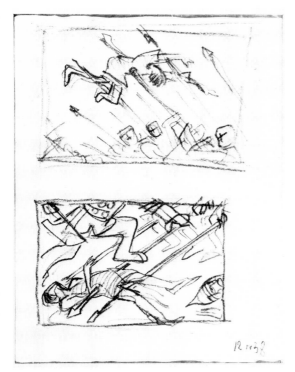

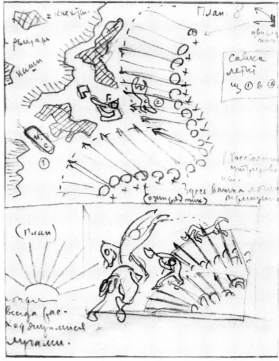

Sketches showing single shots and overall scene dynamics for the climactic battle scene in "Nevsky." (Right) One of the many well-cast characters of "Nevsky"

Sketches showing the opening of the
ice in the final battle scene of
"Nevsky"

Nevsky triumphant

Eisenstein teaching the art of the cinema. Herbert Marshall is seated at center.

Sculpture portrait of Eisenstein by Fredda Brilliant (Acquired by the Ministry of Culture of the USSR for the Eisenstein Museum)

Eisenstein and Paul Robeson meeting in Moscow

A caricature of Eisenstein by his former student
Issac Schmidt

Eisenstein's "Apollo"

"Shadowing" by Eisenstein

During the brief alliance between
Nazi Germany and Stalinist Russia
Eisenstein was persuaded to
produce Wagner's "Die Walküre" at
the Bolshoi Theater in 1940.

Scenes from "Bezhin Meadow"

Cherkassov as Ivan the Terrible

Pre-production sketch for "Ivan the Terrible"

Прием послов.
(Роспись потолка).

Eisenstein filming "Ivan the Terrible"

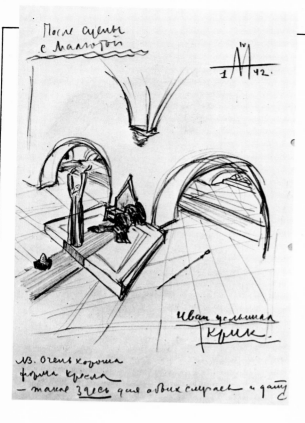

Иван услышал
КРИК.

Mise-en-scène Ивана
после сцены с Малютой.

From "Ivan the Terrible"

*Scene sketch and blocking
diagram for "Ivan the Terrible"*

Mikhail Zharov as Skurator in
"Ivan the Terrible"

Eisenstein directing Padovkin
in "Ivan the Terrible"

The young Ivan determined
to rule

*Pre-production
sketch for "Ivan the
Terrible"*

*The murder of
Vladimir in "Ivan
the Terrible"*

Eisenstein in 1943

I was fascinated by the play of fate in Dreiser's *American Tragedy*, and in my treatment for Paramount[5] I emphasized this line by all possible means.

Clyde arranges Roberta's murder perfectly.

Then the notorious "change of heart" occurs, a change of intention in the boat.

Following this, the real accident, in which Roberta dies.

And once the implacable wheels of evil intent have been set in motion, they later turn against Clyde everything that he had undertaken in his plan to commit murder.

Once set into motion, the fatal machine of crime automatically pursues its course, whether the criminal intention that set it in motion wishes it or not, opposes or eludes it.

A sort of djinn with a skull and crossbones on the bottle, from which it burst out.

At the basis of this obliging image is a living impression. For this is not the first time that I have used this image of an implacable, automatic, machinelike progression. Prior to this, the impersonal, faceless (without close-ups!) rank of soldiers had moved down the Odessa steps with this same blind implacable march.

Just boots!

And later, again an impersonal, soulless machine, the precursor of Guderian's herds of tanks,[6] the rush of the iron "swine" of Teutonic knights in *Nevsky*.

Again faceless. This time physically enclosed by helmets, whose eyeslits echo the slits in the future Tigers and Panthers.

And further, Vladimir Andreyevich's fatal walk to the frenzied roar of the *oprichniki*,[7] implacably black, again like fate, again with hidden faces, who accompany him like a funeral choir to his death . . .

I once asked myself what had been the most frightening thing in my life, and I vividly recalled the railway lines at Smolensk during the civil war.

The number of lines was countless. The number of freight trains on them was . . . even more countless. A gigantic bottleneck, in which these dark red snakes, straining after the advancing armies, had been caught.

For the time being they were quiet at Smolensk, but were ready to dash off at any minute.

Like vast long whales, the trains lay in the backwaters of cold rails in the Smolensk sidings.

As I looked down on their backs from the narrow little bridge thrown across their width, their length to right and left was hidden in the distance and

---

5. The text of Eisenstein's treatment is in Ivor Montagu's *With Eisenstein in Hollywood*.

6. General Heinz Guderian (1886–1954) was the commander of the German armored units that rolled against Poland, France, and Russia in World War II.

7. The *oprichniki* were the bodyguard of Ivan the Terrible.

sprinkled with the dust of the distant tracks, disappearing into the darkness. (In the same way, the lights of Los Angeles, a city forty miles long, merging with the mist, disappear endlessly as the circling plane descends. A piercing pain in the eardrums. Throbbing in the temples . . .) Trying to envision this nocturnal mirage of the scaly spines of trains. They move backward and forward through the night, and the switchmen's whistles play hoarsely in the dark, and I think of the far-off night noises in the night scene, on the eve of the bloody Battle on the Ice in *Nevsky*.

No less vast and awful is this park of inanimate and yet mobile monsters when you pick your way down between the rails and under the wheels, in search of your heated boxcar.

In 1920 I lived in a boxcar on a side track. Though I worked in the political administration of the front, the city of Smolensk was so overcrowded that some of us continued to reside in boxcars. In the yards the heated boxcars trundled past with a rattle, out of the darkness back into the dark. The pale rectangles of the open and empty cars passed, like the line of dashes that mark train tracks on route maps.

Hammers knocked against axles, as in Anna Karenina's nightmares. The whistles blared in the dark, and the points switched, jumping over rhythmically, as if in a strange dance. The red light changed to green. The green back to red . . .

But this was not what was most frightening. Not the hours spent at night in searching for your car along miles of silent railroad cars, nor the dreadful heat of the scorching roofs in the midday sun, when you lay there ill. But the tail of a long endless train, dozens and dozens of cars long, moving backward, bearing down on you with the blunt snout of the last car.

The red rear lantern glimmered like a solitary unseeing eye. Nothing to stop it nor hold it back.

How many times during my hours of wandering along the tracks have night monsters of trains sneaked up on me so treacherously, alongside me, scarcely clanking, out of the darkness and back into the darkness! Their implacable, blind, pitiless movement has migrated to my films, now dressed in soldiers' boots on the Odessa steps, now directing their blunt snouts into knights' helmets in the "Battle on the Ice," now in black vestments sliding over the stone slabs of the cathedral, in the wake of a candle shaking in the hands of the stumbling Vladimir Staritsky.

This image of a night train has wandered from film to film, becoming a symbol of fate.

In *An American Tragedy*, this image is first the inertia of the crime, then the course of the soulless automation of justice and law . . .

Later I myself fall into the tenacious clutches of the image, now come alive.

My intention, formed in the autumn of 1943, collapses. The beginning of 1946 reaps the fruit. This is probably the most dreadful autumn of my life. If one does not count two catastrophes: the ruin of *Mexico* and the tragedy of *Bezhin Meadow* . . . Time heals all wounds.

The passage of time smoothes away all unpleasantnesses. In the romanticizing haze of the past, meannesses seem innocent trifles, evils seem unimportant meannesses, abominations no more than modest evils.

But time brings no abatement during my stay in Alma-Ata.[8] Apart from the purely creative satisfaction (not much!) in the work on *Ivan* itself, everything else here is repulsive.

With what composure, without even a pose (in any case, there would have been no one to notice it), I had performed the act of renunciation from everything that remained dear to me in the house on Potylikha!

Twenty years of manuscripts.

Everything concerning my busy path in art these two decades.

Everything that seemed a find, a discovery.

Everything for which I had fought, made myself ill; everything in which I had erred.

And books, books; fragments of life, thoughts about them, quotations not yet transformed in unfinished works.

And thoughts . . . One thought huddles in the corner between these shelves. Another hovers by this table. A third is tasted in the nearness of these shelves. A fourth by others.

Thoughts live within these walls more materially than do books.

It sometimes seems that one can touch them, embrace them, hug them . . .

They are almost three-dimensional.

Perhaps that is why they are so difficult to set down on paper!

In the dreadful *The Confession of a Fool* the mentally ailing Strindberg feels himself to be physically inseparable from the other members of the family, from the furniture, from his surroundings, from the walls.[9]

I, it would seem, go further.

I feel (felt?) like Peer Gynt, physically one with the imagined ghosts of thoughts, not fully thought out, not fully expounded, not fully pronounced, not fully written down . . .

I pass slowly among those invisible inhabitants of my home which stand among the books. There are many of them. A kingdom of the unborn. "Those whose hour has come, are you ready to set sail?"[10]

The author of these dreadful words runs from a ruined castle somewhere in

---

8. The Moscow film industry was evacuated to Alma-Ata, in Kazakhstan, during the early years of World War II. Eisenstein filmed *Ivan the Terrible* there.

9. Much of Strindberg's writing is autobiographical, including the novel *The Son of a Servant* (1886–1887), which explains some of the bitterness found in his works.

10. The quotation is from Maeterlinck's *The Blue Bird*.

Belgium. He casts off into the English Channel in a little rowboat. On his knees is a cage. In it are two bluebirds.

Maeterlinck.

"Are you ready to set off?"

It is Eduard[11] who is asking me this now. He plies back and forth many times from our Sparrows Hills to the distant Kazan Station. He takes everything that is possible. More than that, even. The Germans are strangely silent now. And the car, its lights dimmed, slips easily through blacked-out Moscow.

I walk slowly past the books, a journey past everything I have lived through.

The renunciation has been made . . .

I should like to look at myself from the side.

Instead, I take only five books. Which? As always when setting off for a journey, detective stories.

---

11. Eduard was E. K. Tisse, Eisenstein's cameraman.

Intellectual Cinema

W<small>HEN I WAS NOT TOO YOUNG</small> I fell prey to the Voltairian germ of disrespect for the Supreme Being. This occurred before the Revolution and took a rather aggressive form, since it came after almost hysterical religiosity in my childhood and the cult of mystical feats in my youth. The fault was not so much "Ferney's wicked bawler," that "first poet amongst poets,"[1] who led Pushkin, a young student of African extraction, into skittish atheism. The basic blame can probably be laid on the very ministers of the mystic cults themselves. Or perhaps it is the very balefulness of dogmatism and casuistry that inevitably undermines the essence of emotional passion; that undermines all that in its most mysterious secrecy determines one's adherence to a specific religion.

In my own case "father-hermits and wives immaculate"[2] share their guilt with the catechism — its divisions, paragraphs, and cunning system of questions and answers, calculated not to educate and deepen the foundations of religious passion, but to educate the experienced casuist — a "catechist" in the primary, direct clerical significance of the word.

As is well known, the concept of "catechist" grows unrestrainedly in the fertile fields of the very latest film art.

Father Nicholas Perekhvalsky, my spiritual mentor and guide, was a sumptuous man. Jehovah himself would have envied his graying mane. When at Mass, Father Nicholas, dressed in a silvery blue chasuble and with his arms raised heavenward, stood in a cloud of incense pierced by the slanting rays of the sun. As he performed the sacrament of the Eucharist, the bells, certainly prompted by a mysterious force, pealed from the lofty belfry, and it actually

---

1. The quotations are from Pushkin's poem *Gorodok* (*The Little Town*). The first words refer to Voltaire, who lived at Ferney.

2. The words are from the opening line of another of Pushkin's poems.

seemed that the heavens had opened and grace was pouring out upon the sinful world.

From such moments springs my lifelong weakness for the ornate in religious services: the sunbeams cutting down through the smoke of incense, the standing columns of dust or mist, the luxuriant shocks of priestly hair (from the priest in *Potemkin* to the religious procession in *Ivan the Terrible*), and a passion for sacristies, chasubles, dalmatics, omophorions, and epitrachelions. All these I included in my films. I was attracted to everything of this nature which Anatole France, though he belonged to a different faith, attributed to himself as a "Catholic who ceased to be a Christian."

Such was Father Nicholas during the performance of the Eucharistic rites. For anyone given to flights of imagination he was utterly irresistible. But he presented an altogether different personality during classes in religious instruction. There he would gather his divine beard into his fist, twist it around his chin, toss his great mane, and drive us relentlessly through Christian casuistry, paragraph by paragraph.

"You, there!" he would say, pointing at me with a finger of his free hand. "Let us say that you affirm that God is omnipotent. Right?"

"Right," I would reply cautiously, sensing from the very tone of the question that he was laying a trap.

"You say it's right? Why, then, if He is omnipotent, is it impossible for Him to commit a sin? Omnipotent, and yet it is not in His power to do what any of us great sinners is capable of doing."

Oh, no, Father, you can't catch me that way! I am sufficiently versed in your sophistry to "hit the nail on the head" with a humble expression and inner jubilation: "To sin is a sign of weakness, Father. To be incapable of sin is the great strength of omnipotence."

Father Nicholas would grunt his approval, release his beard from his fist (thus regaining his resemblance to Jehovah), and record in his grade book a fat 5 opposite the name of his most capable student. Little did he realize that, with his convoluted phraseology of ecclesiastical casuistry, he was stifling the profound complexes of the religious passion for "natural" religion.

But the final blow, both insulting and traumatic, was delivered by the resplendent dean of the Riga Cathedral, Archpriest Father Pliss, who presided at the final examination in divinity in our high school.

Seventeen years before this exam he had submerged in the baptismal font a lump of pink flesh, screaming on contact with the water, and gave it the name of Sergei. That, however, did not prevent him from trying to catch me with tricky questions, beyond the scope of the examination.

Father Nicholas watched this game with obvious alarm, for his personal prestige was at stake. Licking their chops, the other commission members enjoyed this unworthy entertainment immensely. One might have thought they were sitting around a card table, though that green-covered one, which seemed to cut their bodies in half, was of entirely different proportions. Like a bridge, it spanned the entire width of the assembly hall.

All the members of the commission were teachers of the Russian language, gathered from all the classes of the school, and all were former seminarians.

This was understandable, for ours was a Baltic province, and the main contingent of the teachers consisted of poorly Russianized Germans forced to teach the mass of Latvian pupils in Russian.

Interesting in this respect are the inner feelings of us, the Russian pupils, amid the mass of Latvians. Nominally, we were colonizers and the owners of their province. Socially, on the whole, we belonged to the bureaucratic, ruling clique of the province. But no doubt because of the democratic circumstances of almost comradely relationships, particularly in regard to the Russians, there was an atmosphere of responsive moral oppression. In this curious paradox of the exchange of the roles of "oppressed" and "oppressors," among the youngsters there was a kind of compensation for the abnormal relationship between their parents.

Be that as it may, these feelings and impressions of colonization experienced "in the flesh" were later to be close and comprehensible to me, a representative of an oppressing class and nation.

This later revelation was no succor when Father Pliss finally succeeded in cornering me on the question of "divine revelation" during the exam. From where I stood on that day, the green baize–covered table, like a bridge thrust in through the parquetry of the assembly hall, seemed to narrow to a ribbon. Then to wire. On that wire I began to flounder helplessly, clutching at Buddhism and Brahminism, hazily known to me by hearsay, for his question was crafty:

"What other peoples — besides Christians — still dispose of the fruits of direct divine revelation?" (That is, direct "access" to great religious wisdom, directly from the "primary source.")

Buddhists and Brahmins didn't help me. I tried to bring in the Dalai Lama. My body wobbled on a tightrope. The venerable monk became transformed into a long-haired, long-necked South American goat. Lama and llama. Father Pliss was shocked. The former seminarians smiled even more broadly. Father Nicholas anxiously dropped his hand onto the flax of his beard. Then Father Pliss maliciously asked in a caressing voice, "And the Jews?"

My God! I had forgotten all about the Old Testament, where the burning bush with its mysterious voice flares inextinguishably, where Moses receives the Tablets of the Law, where prophets storm and castigate . . .

Thus it was that, long after uniting me through the mystery of baptism with the one true faith, Father Pliss, at that graduation examination, sowed in me also the seeds of future atheism.

Still, the Christian virtue of compassion must have been at work to induce this all-powerful conclave not to spoil my report card, for on it, under the heading "Divinity," stood in all its splendor the traditional 5, a must for all top pupils. But this did not deter me from atheism.

Perhaps this digression from my basic theme is too long, but besides explanations concerning myself, it carries a certain general lesson. I notice with astonishment that today's student, freed from the study of religious instruction, reveals the same hostility to the study of dialectics. And I believe this is because, in the process of teaching this almighty shining miraculous method of cognition, the heavy hands of our sophists, catechists, Plisses, and Perekhvalskys are too often laid on it.

Instead of an all-penetrating science, as it was understood and presented by Lenin; a science invoking us to study and reveal its nature and essence everywhere, in everything and over everything ("Begin with the most simple, ordinary, mass-evident, etc., from any premises: the leaves of the tree are green; Ivan is a man; Zhuchka is a dog, etc. Already here, as the genius of Hegel noted, is dialectics . . ."[3]). Instead of this, the boring catechists, pettifogging pedants, and casuists come to the institutes, and in their hands the living spirit of the sorceress Dialectics disappears. All that remains is an indigestible skeleton of paragraphs, abstract propositions, and the perpetual motion of the vicious circle of once-and-for-all chosen quotations.

Their activity (of course, of course — not always, not everywhere and anywhere!) is similar to that on the threshold of Buddhist temples (Aha! So at last the Buddhists have come in handy!), where a similar process is rationalized in the system of prayer wheels. According to this custom the supplicant may, if he wishes, turn a wooden wheel instead of praying himself, and Buddha will benevolently accept this as equivalent to the revolutions of the rosary.

However, this speculation is also rather irrelevant. Incidentally, it is also a certain foreknowledge of the way these catechists of dialectics will pounce on my insufficiently orthodox formulations, or, maybe, on my independent attempts to investigate questions of the methods of art outside the usually accepted norm.

Be that as it may, the "excess baggage" of these pages is needed for the express purpose of explaining my not too respectful attitude toward the founders of the Christian cult.

(In passing it may be worthwhile to recall the sad fact that the epic pathos of, say, the "rural theme" in the cinema, in its direct initial premise, was catastrophically smashed to pieces on the iron grill of prescribed demands of scenario departments and the Chief Repertory Committee[4] for the cinema: "Cooperatives not shown," "weeding campaign not shown," "the work of the

---

3. The quotations are from Lenin's *Collected Works*, Volume XII of the Russian edition.

4. The Chief Repertory Committee was, and remains, the censoring group in the arts. Without its permission, no one in the USSR can produce or perform a play, produce a film, and so on.

Village Soviet is missing," etc., etc. It was thus that noble attempts to embody the pathos of the theme of Socialism, which had alighted upon the face of the earth, withered away at their roots.)[5]

These, then, are the sources that prompted me to seize my opportunity in *October*[6] to attack the very concept of deity by revealing its hollowness. To do this I searched for the most accurate expression of the idea about the splendor of the external aspect and the emptiness of content. The required image came of itself. It lay in the equation of the most richly gilded Baroque Christ and the crude wooden idol of the Eskimos or Giliaks. It is easy enough to photograph each one separately. But how to convey, on film, that they are one and the same? How is it possible by means of cinematography to place that equal sign between them?

Here an early childhood impression came to my rescue. I was completely unaware of it at the time. And the realization of its connection to what I did in *October* came to me much, much later.

In 1940, I happened to acquire the original lithograph of a reproduction that early in my life had captured my imagination.

There are two ways of discovery that can lead us to a long-lasting passion. Either an older friend or a spiritual mentor shows it to us. Or we come on it ourselves. The latter gives rise to a stronger and more enduring passion.

This is what happened to me with Daumier. I discovered him myself quite accidentally. Browsing through my father's books when I was quite young, I came across an album dealing with the Franco-Prussian War of 1870 and the Paris Commune. (I still cannot understand how this album, banned by the tsarist censors, could have found its way into the library of my father, a most faithful supporter and obedient servant of Russian officialdom.) The album provided me to some extent with the first revolutionary impressions to stir my fantasy and imagination: the repulsive image of General Galiffet;[7] the sinister figure of Thiers;[8] the barricades and Versailles; Louise Michel;[9] and the "kerosene maidens."[10] The toppled Colonne Vendôme!

In addition, the album contained many caricatures that sharpened the

---

5. Eisenstein here seemed to be thinking of his work on *The General Line* or *Old and New*, a film made in 1926–1927. In it, he tried to show the socialism in the village in epic form, without the usual documentary description of agricultural activity. (H.M.)

6. *October* is sometimes shown in the United States as *Ten Days That Shook the World*, since it concerns the events written about by John Reed in his book of that name.

7. Gaston de Galiffet (1830–1909) was a general who suppressed the Paris Commune with merciless ferocity.

8. Adolph Thiers (1797–1877) was a statesman and historian. During the Revolution of 1848, he was a moderate. In 1871 he crushed the Commune and was elected president of France's Third Republic.

9. Louise Michel (1830–1905) was one of the leaders of the Commune.

10. The "kerosene maidens" were squads of women revolutionaries who were ready to burn Paris rather than let the Versailles government armies enter the city.

emotional content of events, the full meaning of which I was as yet unable to grasp. (The pungency of caricatures had attracted me even earlier.) I liked André Gill. Cham, not so much; and Bertall, not at all. But my admiration for Honoré Daumier was boundless.

I was so captivated by him that the very, very first book I ever bought of my own choice was a modest monograph on Daumier (a purchase accomplished in conspiracy with my governess, who secreted the needed sum from her expense money). I was ten at the time.

So it goes.

My involvement with Daumier led me to the heroic pages of French caricature at the time of the July monarchy and the Citizen King, Louis Philippe. That heroic period of brilliance which glittered under the rays of the "pear," created by Philipon as a symbolic representation of King Louis Philippe. The king's forelock and sideburns together looked like the silhouette of a pear, which gave birth to that conventional symbol of mockery perceived by Philipon.[11]

This pear theme was repeatedly utilized by old Daumier, too, in his immortal series of widely known caricatures. However, to Philipon also belongs another drawing, subsequently a lithograph, that appeared in *La Caricature* in Number 56, on November 24, 1831, and that I have known from childhood from reproductions.

This is his famous drawing of the court.

Now, when I recall my childhood impression of that print, and what occurred to me as the solution of the image of the deity for my film *October*, I am deeply convinced that one was subconsciously suggested by the other.

Be that as it may, by purely visual means I forged a similar chain of interlocking links, connecting at both ends a crude wooden Giliak idol with the most ornate representation of the deity that I could find among the Baroque monuments of St. Petersburg.

Each juxtaposed image plasticly fuses with the next into an almost complete unity.

The Baroque Christ's semicircle of golden rays almost coincided in its contours with the many-armed Hindu god Shiva, which followed it.

The terrifying image of this god was transformed into another Hindu image, whose silhouette resembled the outline of the cupola of the mosque on Kamennostrovsky Prospekt in Leningrad.

The cupola in its contour coincided with the mask of the Japanese goddess Amaterasu (according to legend, the founder of the Oriental theater).

---

11. Charles Philipon (1802–1862) was perhaps the first to combine journalism and caricature. (Illustrators like André Gill, whose real name was L. A. Gosset de Guines, and Bertall, the pen name of Charles Albert Arnoux, concentrated on lithographs and political drawings.) In 1831, Philipon founded *La Caricature;* four years later, it was suppressed. He also founded *Le Charivari.* Cham (the pen name of Amédée de Noé), Gavarni, Robida, and many other skilled satirists worked with Philipon. The most brilliant was Daumier.

She was replaced by the awesome beak of one of the minor deities of the Nipponese Olympus.

And this, in turn, in tone and pattern, coincided with the Negro religious mask of the Yoruba.

From here to the final Giliak idol it was but two jumps over one of the Eskimo shamans, with its helplessly dangling wooden paws!

And from the screen the idea came across with the clarity of Philipon's sequence, and inevitably provoked laughter.

But the gods punished their offender by inflicting on him a temporary eclipse of reason.

We have already noticed a tendency toward speculation in our author. And although, in the thirties (to be more exact, 1927 to 1928), the street cars already ran on schedule, and there was no need then for this author to go anywhere, for he was editing *October*, both day and night, within the walls of what was then the Cinema Committee's headquarters, and he virtually lived within those walls, yet even here this foolish habit of speculation never left him.

"What precisely has happened?" wondered the author, no longer a young novice but still prone to enthusiasm, as he completed the sequence of the god images.

After all, the "thesis" I had just managed to convert to film form was purely logical, abstract, even, if you please, intellectual.

Ah, is it then possible to achieve direct filmic expression of abstract ideas, of logically formulated theses and intellectual concepts, and not merely emotional phenomena?

Is it possible to do this without recourse to the limitations of plot, storyline, characters, actors, etc., etc.?

It was possible on the stage to construct an emotionally effective "montage of attractions" (using plot development within the individual attraction only as a by-product), so it must be possible to achieve effective montage of *intellectual attractions.*

"Intellectual attractions"!

Birth date — 1928.

Code name: "I-A-28."[12]

Considerations of "economy of energy output" triumph with the emergence of this embodiment of a thesis. Any thesis. Even the most abstract.

God help me! Haven't we just succeeded in doing this with one of the most abstract philosophical themes?

And with great emotional effect on the public, to boot: the audience laughed.

Therefore, it must be possible to construct an entire system of this type of

---

12. "I-A-28" was never published.

filmic expression, to develop a film language capable of making an abstract idea blossom in an emotional way.

Therefore, intellectual cinema is a possibility.

And galloping — as I have done so often — from premises insufficiently explored to unfounded generalizations, I envisioned in perspective the cinema of the future (nothing less, of course) as the intellectual cinema. As an era of intellectual cinematography.

A militant manifesto on the subject was feverishly written.

It was entitled "Perspectives,"[13] of course, and was published in Numbers 1 and 2 of the journal *Iskusstvo* of the People's Commissariat of Education, a journal that seemed to have come into being expressly for the publication of this article. For some reason Anatoly Vasilievich Lunacharsky discontinued it afterward.

The possibilities of this type of cinema are positively limitless. Only this type of film technique is capable of translating into filmic language the philosophical concepts contained in *Das Kapital* by Karl Marx. And it is precisely this theme which is featured in my production plans. Meanwhile, I am off on a trip through Europe and America, carrying in my suitcase the sensational discovery of the principles of intellectual cinema.

The idea is a resounding success and provokes comment.

While certain domestic critics and supporters of naturalism tear "Perspectives" to shreds (because of my attack on a number of semiofficial tendentious slogans of the day, such as the "theory of the real man"[14]), other writers and Western journals could not but welcome a trend that offers the most immediate means for converting abstract philosophical formulae into a dynamic, rich, emotionally expressive art form.

Of the unfriendly critics, I must honestly say that they didn't fully grasp the essence of the problem. I have continued snapping back at them even *post factum.*

But even those who were favorably disposed failed to see that the essential part of the program was to present an idea in emotionally gripping images, equally applicable to any thoughtful and purposeful art expressions. What was controversial and new was the concept of direct blending of the idea into a structure of plastic images that, by means of a definite sequential order (montage), were said to achieve this "magic" effect.

I was not bothered much by polemics. I was more interested in methods; in how this extract of the gods from *October* was the next "intellectual" stage in relation to the "figurative" stage, the leaping lions from the finale of the "Odessa Steps" sequence in *Potemkin.*

---

13. "Perspectives" appears in part in *Film Essays*, edited by Jan Leyda (New York: Praeger, 1968; London: Dobson, 1968).

14. Eisenstein was referring to RAPP, the Revolutionary Association of Proletarian Writers.

And so, the thesis: god = block of wood. That is how the logic builds its premises and conclusions. What exactly did we do?

Between these two distantly linked objects we inserted an unbroken chain of links, embodying the unity of that common chain, to which (for a specific tendentious point of view) these distant links actually belong. . . .

And this way we not only arrived at the implanting of the idea itself — the thesis — but also achieved it with greater emotional effect — an increment.

But . . .

What is that like?

It is like *the reverse process* of that which takes place in the development of thinking from its primitive form to its conscious form, to the form of thinking at the level of "our circle." Indeed, if we open any book on the history of the evolution of thought, we will find in it a very precise definition of this phenomenon. And so the development of consciousness goes step by step toward *condensation*. Thus, the "method" of my intellectual cinema consists of moving backward from a more developed form of expression of consciousness to an earlier form of consciousness; from the speech of our generally accepted logic to a structure of speech of another kind of logic.

I had already met with another structure of thought in studying the Japanese language.

However, the question of hieroglyphs and the similarity of their method with the method of juxtaposition in montage, in its time occupied so much of my attention by its very *mechanism of combination* that I didn't then surmise that that unfortunate language, with its structure and peculiarities, would serve me once more. Instead, I plunged passionately into questions of primitive thinking in general.

A tendency toward generalization — my basic illness — is a kind of sweet malady.

And then there crept up on me a supposition — an apprehension: What if this backward translation of today's level of our consciousness to the forms of consciousness and thinking of an earlier kind is itself the secret not only of my intellectual cinema but of art in general?

Still, at that moment the problem of the "sign" — forward or backward — did not interest me. I was too preoccupied with gathering material, with the analytical disemboweling of the appearances of forms in works of art, to ponder larger themes. However, a more detailed study of this strange "other" sphere of thinking, into which I was delving, went on in tandem.

All around, in Moscow, and particularly in Petrograd, the first mighty flood of Japhetidology bubbled furiously. Step by step, Marr[15] revealed the depen-

---

15. Nicholas Y. Marr (1864–1934), philologist, archaeologist, and member of the Academy, dealt in his work with the formation and evolution of language and its connection with thinking. His Japhetic theory concerned the kinship of the languages of the people of Transcaucasia with a

dence of our thinking on earlier thinking, the relations between both stages and the fundamental significance of the language of the past for problems of contemporary consciousness. His enthusiasm for journeying into the depths of the ages on the hobbyhorse of etymology attracted me first as a diversion, but after a while, sensing something that might be useful, I began delving into that sphere too.

But there is more to come.

During a visit to Paris I glanced into the window of a bookshop on Boulevard St. Michel and was attracted by a tiny book, slightly redder than orange, with the title *La Mentalité Primitive*.[16] I bought it and put it on my table in my hotel in Montparnasse, where it caught the eye of a journalist.

"Are you interested in primitive thinking?" he asked.

"God forbid!" I replied. "I'm about to leave for America and am studying the laws of thinking of cinema sharks!"

Be that as it may, the orange brochure soon grew into a blue three-volume "complete" Lévy-Bruhl, published by Alcan. And that hasn't yet been surrounded by the twelve weighty tomes of the *The Golden Bough* by Sir James Frazer, only because the edition has been sold out, and I haven't the money to search for them in secondhand bookshops. Never mind! Meanwhile, Lévy-Bruhl suffices, and through its pages I make the most dizzying excursions into the secrets of what already takes on the more precise definition of "prelogic."

At the same time I myself am making a no less fantastic geographic trek through those very territories and countries which seem to exist only in unpronounceable names, but not in actuality.

I remember how I laughed over the pages of *The Golden Calf*,[17] so kindly sent to me from my far-off homeland to the far-off tropics, where Ilf and Petrov (alas, no longer with us) enumerated just such geographical designations, whose reality seemed to be only in tongue-twisters. Among those enumerated, outstanding, of course, is that most unreal and most unpronounceable name: Popocatepetl.

Ha, ha!

For I have only to raise my head from the page I am reading to see before my eyes the summit of that snow-white extinct volcano in the blindingly blue tropical sky.

I am in Mexico.

And I am sitting at the foot of this very "verbal abstraction" that has

---

number of languages of the ancient world and the consecutive stages of their development. "Japhetic" was a term he coined, deriving it from Japhet, one of the three sons of Noah, and analogous to the Semitic and Hamitic languages.

16. *La Mentalité Primitive* by Lucien Lévy-Bruhl (1857–1939) was originally published in 1922. An authorized translation was done by Lillian A. Clare.

17. *The Golden Calf* was a Soviet satirical novel by I. Ilf and E. Petrov.

borrowed, it would seem, the virginal accuracy of its slanting sides from those Japanese prints of Fujiyama's countenance, which has bored so many millions.

Popocatepetl is so real that once we nearly crashed into its crater in the tiny plane that carried us to the borders of Guatemala to film a catastrophe resulting from one of the earthquakes so frequent in Mexico.

Curiosity drove us to peer into the extinct crater of the mysterious Popo.

Not checking the contents of our fuel tank, we made an aerial detour up and around.

You should have seen the deadly white faces of the navigator and pilot as, with a choking motor, they whirled us, "gliding," toward the outskirts of Mexico City, just missing the tops of the telephone poles!

I survived to sit at the foot of the volcano, surrounded by the representatives of those very peoples whose system of thinking (for by that time I already knew that this kind of thinking is also called sensuous) seemed so fantastic and unreal in the pages of Lévy-Bruhl or Frazer.

There in dusty Taxco, under a burning sun, the same natives, not having changed for hundreds and hundreds of years, will show me the ruins of a stone house where — in a pause between his pursuits — rested that other hunter for the history of languages, the untiring "great inquisitive," old Humboldt.[18] Around the stone walls of that massive house, on dry stalks, grow leafless, blood-red, five-pointed, velvety, fantastic flowers that seem to call to mind the uniform of that great explorer, decorated with stars. They are called *sangre de toro* (bull's blood), and seem like blood spots in the gray-yellow dust of that part of Mexico.

It is here in *tierra caliente* (burning earth) that I come to know the fantastic structure of prelogical, sensuous thinking — not only from the pages of anthropological investigations, but from daily communion with those descendents of the Aztecs and Toltecs, Mayas, or Huichole who have managed to carry unharmed through the ages that meandering thought. It determined the astonishing traits of that miracle of Mexican primitive culture, as its tribes, to this day, stand beside the cradle of a cultural era that has not yet begun for them.

I spend many days within the sacred fraternity of the *danzantes*, who surged from every corner of Mexico to the national consecration so that, in honor of that most Christian of Madonnas — the Spanish — they can perform, from dawn to dawn, without tiring, their ancient pagan dances.

In the eternal traditions of the matriarchy, this entire "fraternity" is headed by one leader — a tanned, wrinkled, gray-haired old woman. Among the authorizations of our cinema expedition is a certificate from her, with a rosy gutta-percha seal of bloody hearts entwined with a thorny crown. The *danzantes* do not shun us, but share knowledge about themselves with us.

18. Alexander von Humboldt (1769–1859), the German naturalist, traveled through parts of South America, through Cuba, and in Mexico from 1799 to 1804.

In desolate tropical villages I sit with a circle of women who are sorting out, with mysterious murmurings, numberless little dishes made from little local pumpkins. Pinch after pinch of ground black coffee slips into those dishes from hand to hand. They are echoed by a counterflow, in definite proportion, of some kind of locally grown bean — all in the same kind of little dishes. The clang of the little dishes against each other creates the characteristic murmur of this scene, which is otherwise conducted in total silence.

A tedious and exhausting process.

Only very small numbers of bowls can be taken in at a glance; it is difficult to embrace more than three within the field of attention, and one must not forget that the visiting vendor, bringing around coffee, conducts an exchange instantaneously and simultaneously with approximately twelve local women. And there is a strict, ruthless control over that incredibly complex mechanism, beside which double-entry bookkeeping seems child's play.

During this sojourn I accumulate many vivid impressions that bring to life the printed pages of more reliable travelers, such as Von den Steinen and Major Powell — all those doctors, missionaries, adventurers, customs officers, enthusiasts, and colonizers have become living and near. Thus I merge the memories of personal experience with the sources of human culture.

I recall how my friend Paul Robeson (a scholarly philologist as well as a gifted singer and actor) wanted to go further in this respect. Indeed, he wished to enter, for one year of his life, into the primeval state of one of the most primitive peoples of Africa. He wished to submerge himself completely in their customs, morals, languages, and thinking.

The well-known Cushing,[19] whose data are used by Lévy-Bruhl, succeeded in doing this. The data about his personal immersion into the stage of "linear speech" is exceptionally interesting. His original article, "Manual Concepts," in the journal *American Anthropologist*, I discovered in one of the university book repositories in Moscow. It was amazing that for decades its yellowing pages had remained uncut. No one had shown the slightest interest or need to delve into the depths of the history of consciousness!

Robeson, however, didn't succeed in carrying out his intentions. His active participation in the events and struggles of Spain completely swallowed up his life for a number of years. Ultimately, he preferred to use his wide, powerful shoulders in helping move humanity forward to a brighter future, rather than doing research into the depths of his primitive past.

Honor and glory to him!

Only, all the same, it is somewhat a pity . . .

Now I am absolutely at home in this hitherto mysterious and incomprehensible sphere.

---

19. Frank H. Cushing (1857–1900), an American ethnologist, lived for five years among the Zuñi Indians of New Mexico.

The last meeting: a book by Marcel Granet, *La Pensée Chinoise*. (That very same incomparable black giant Paul recommended it to me in grateful acknowledgment of my having initiated him into the teachings of Marr.) How fascinating! This happened on the very first evening of our acquaintance, the day he arrived in Moscow.

Thus is the circle of acquaintanceship completed in a singular fashion. "Chinese thinking," but good heavens — that is the very thing I couldn't overcome, the cramming of the Japanese language! Both this and the former language in its external speech have preserved that very same sensuous linguistic canon of prelogic, with which we ourselves speak when we talk to ourselves — our internal speech. (Such internal speech captivated me, in its own way, somewhat earlier, so far without any direct relationship to these problems. The pure research aspect was to excite me later.)

The year that gave birth to the idea of intellectual cinema was the year that I became acquainted with Joyce's *Ulysses*.

What is so fascinating in *Ulysses*?

There is the inimitable sensuousness of the text (surpassing by far the organically felt beauty of my beloved Zola). There is the "asyntaxism" of Joyce's writing, overheard in the very origins of that internal speech which each of us speaks in his own way, and which only the literary genius of Joyce thought of as a possible foundation for the writing of literature. Indeed, in the linguistic kitchen of literature, Joyce occupies himself with the same thing I rave about in relation to laboratory researches on cinema language. Yet Joyce had predecessors. He names them himself: Dostoyevsky, for the substance of internal monologues; and Edouard Dujardin,[20] for the techniques and manner of writing, a style peculiar to internal speech (*Les Lauriers sont Coupés*, 1887). That same Dujardin is drawn in one of the most luxurious posters of Toulouse-Lautrec: *Le Divan Japonais*, advertising that very popular center of entertainment. In the center of the poster is a black silhouette of the dancer Jane Avril in ordinary clothes. On the left, in the corner, with her head cut off by the upper part of the poster — but nevertheless infallibly recognizable — is the star of the Divan Japonais, Yvette Guilbert, performing her songs. Two double-bass necks. A wineglass. And in the right corner is Dujardin, a dandy in a top hat. With a monocle. His silky beard merging with his motley-colored scarf. A dashing twist of the curved handle of his walking stick. He's stroking his sensuous lips lovingly; his eyes are indifferent to Yvette but are steadily fixed on the waist of Jane.

So the figure of Dujardin in an odd way links pioneering work in the sphere of the internal monologue with two persons whom, above all, I wanted to meet in Paris, James Joyce and Yvette Guilbert!

---

20. Edouard Dujardin (1861–1949) was a French journalist and writer often associated with the Symbolists.

Meeting Joyce . . .

But he is no longer among the living! And at any new meetings I shan't have to worry over sad details of our last farewell.

He bids me good-by in the narrow corridor-entrance to his bright little apartment (I still remember the striped wallpaper of the little corridor, the white matt alternating with the shining white). He is a tall, slightly stooping man; a man almost without a front — so sharply outlined is his profile. He has reddish skin and thick grizzled hair. When I see him standing there, he is for some reason waving his hand strangely about, as if rummaging in the air.

Somewhat surprised, I ask him what the matter is.

"Well, somewhere here must be your overcoat," replies Joyce, probing the wall.

Only as I write this do I realize how weak his vision had become in relation to the surrounding world. This external blindness no doubt influenced that particular sharpness of inner vision with which, in addition to the wonderful means of internal speech, the inner life of *Ulysses* (and *A Portrait of the Artist as a Young Man*) is described.

And now I am terribly embarrassed.

With great sincerity, Joyce asks me to show him my films, since he has become interested in the experiments in the language of cinema that I am carrying out on the screen (just as I am fascinated by his kindred researches in literature).

Before we part, Joyce autographs a copy of *Ulysses* for me, and when I return home and open the cover of the book, I see on the first page some almost indecipherable marks and the date (November 30, 1929), obviously drawn from memory. (Perhaps that's why he went with the copy into the next room, where he fussed around for a long time over just three words of his dedication, of which two were the name and surname, and third the city — Paris!) And so I myself, like a blind man, have spent a whole evening with an almost blind man, not noticing, not sensing, not seeing his affliction! . . .

I am rescued from my embarrassing situation by the third interlocutor. This is a rather suspicious Russian with a lackey's physiognomy.

No doubt an émigré. But perhaps a spy. It seems so natural to put on an overcoat with his help! Joyce has engaged him in order to learn the Russian language.

Joyce tells me that his next work following *Ulysses* will reflect linguistically the birth of different languages from general chaos and will be written in a fusion of undifferentiated linguistic poetry. The Russian language will be needed in that fusion.

This very production is *Work in Progress*, and the even voice of Joyce reads for me a fragment from it ("Anna Livia Plurabelle").

"But was Joyce indeed blind?" some attentive and benevolent female reader will say here, and I stress female, for only a female reader will pay attention to it.

Calm down, female reader.

I said, "The voice of Joyce," not "Joyce."

For it is his voice that reads it . . . from a record on the gramophone, which Joyce is winding.

"Anna Livia Plurabelle" had not long ago been published as a tiny booklet in a separate edition, and this fragment Joyce had recorded.

As I listen, I follow the articulated text on a giant meter-wide sheet of paper, filled with gigantic lines of gigantic letters.

It was by these tables of enlargements from the miniature pages of the little book that Joyce, with difficulty, reinforced his memory when making the disc.

By exaggerated dimensions of the miniature pages of the miniature booklet fragment!

How in character that is with the author! How in tune with that magnifying glass with which he scans the microscopic convolutions of the mysteries of literary language! How symbolic for the path of his roaming along the winding inner movement of emotion and the inner structure of internal speech!

Calligraphy

SURELY THE SLIGHTLY Nietzschean title of the article "Beyond Acting and Nonacting" (*Kinogazetta*, 1927), for example, was characteristic of the age. Examine its beginning: "Of two who are fighting, it is the third who is usually right. The acting film and nonacting film have now entered the ring to do battle. But right is on the side of a third. On the side of the *beyond-acting* film . . ."

This uses the very conception of "beyond-acting" cinematography; that is, cinematography that stands on principles outside the petty row between the "story-makers" and the "documentalists." Indeed, the concept of the nonacting cinema was synonymous at that time with documentary cinema.

Beyond-acting cinema spoke of the fundamental freedom and universality of the new cinematography. A cinematic method whose aesthetics were not based on a reworking of the materials from other arts (acting or nonacting methods) would stem above all from aesthetics that arise from fundamental ideological conceptions — a method that would rework the material of actuality and design, that would be equally acceptable and compatible, equally worthy of inclusion in a synthesis of film process with film spectacle.

Another characteristic conception of that era was my theory of intellectual cinema, which grew from the experience of *October* following a path from the image of the lions in *Potemkin* to the play of concepts in this film (gods, Kerensky on the staircase, etc.). Although the emotionalization of intellectual concepts was my thesis here, the very designation ("intellectual") placed this school of cinema beyond the bounds of emotional cinema, if not altogether, then at least beyond the bounds of what was then generally accepted as emotional cinema. (And it is no accident that the watershed era passes between emotion and intellect, as if echoing the initial traumatic situation of the author's life. Book learning, outstripping learning acquired by experience and the senses!)

And it is surely interesting that only a few months ago, by way of a chance biographical note on this question in my life history, I came across this very notion in choosing for the dust jacket (and frontispiece of the corresponding part of the book about *Potemkin* for foreign publication) a sixteenth-century engraving, picked out long, long ago, showing a monk, a follower of Cardinal Nicholas,[1] gazing out "beyond the stars." I chose *Beyond the Stars* as the title for this, having film stars in mind, and meaning that the book is concerned with all problems of the cinema, apart from the stars and the direct human (in this primitive sense of the word) participant in the film.

Regarding "man" again, it is interesting that the presence of the human (very human!) basis interests me in its "not yet human" stage. That is, in all those spheres and beginnings where man is present in art in a way that is *hidden*, not yet manifest. For I am most interested in man when, by the rhythms of his feelings, he is present in the design of a work of art. The "self-portrait" interests me in the stage of the pot[2] (as a pattern of oneself and a receptacle for one's food and drink). I am captivated by the Chinese landscape metaphor, in which a flower is not only a flower but at the same time an allegory of the beloved (giving it a special tension and quiver of lyricism). And it is the Chinese, too, who take my breath away with their portraiture of living natural phenomena, in the various styles of calligraphic strokes. In this regard I quote Lin Yutang, from the book *My Country and My People*. (The first book of his that I read was *The Importance of Living*.[3] I read it rather late, when I was already quite well acquainted with China, Mei Lan-fang,[4] and the researches of Marcel Granet.) Lin Yutang's books are imbued with the irresistible, fascinating aroma of the ancient East. It sometimes seems that the ironic, slightly skeptical, and eternally patient spirit of the old reveler and great sage Lao-Tse has migrated to Lin Yutang, who is so amazing when he talks of the traditions and antiquities of China, and so absurd and childishly helpless when he tries to interpret the fate of modern China, the role of Chiang Kai-shek, or the essence of the Chinese civil war:

> As this art has a history of well nigh two thousand years, and as every writer tried to distinguish himself by a new type of rhythm or structure, therefore, in

1. Nicholas of Cusa (1401–1464), a German theologian who became a cardinal and later a bishop, was a philosopher and mathematician. He anticipated Copernicus in theorizing that the earth rotated and that it revolved around the sun.

2. In his article "Nonindifferent Nature" (published in Volume III of the Russian edition of his collected works), Eisenstein posited that in the first stages of the evolution of the art of pottery, the vessel was not only used as a receptacle for food and liquids, but was the earliest means of human portraiture. Later, the making of human portraits was separated from the making of pots, and the pot retained only its utilitarian function.

3. Lin Yutang (1895–1976) wrote *My Country and My People* (1936), *The Importance of Living* (1937), and many other books. He was trained as a philologist.

4. Mei Lan-fang (1893–1943) was the great Chinese actor of the classic stylized theater who played only female parts. His troupe visited Moscow in 1933, and Eisenstein and Tretiakov were enthusiastic spectators. All of us Eisenstein students had to go to see his performances. (H.M.)

calligraphy, if in anything, we are entitled to see the last refinement of the Chinese artistic mind. Certain types, such as the worship of beauty of irregularity or of a forever toppling structure that yet keeps its balance, will surprise the Westerners by their finesse, all the more so because such types are not easily seen in other fields of Chinese art.

What is of significance to the West is the fact that, not only has it provided the aesthetic basis for Chinese art, but it represents an animistic principle which may be most fruitful of results when properly understood and applied. As stated, Chinese calligraphy has explored every possible style of rhythm and form, and it has done so by deriving its artistic inspiration from nature, especially from plants and animals — the branches of the plum flower, a dried vine with a few hanging leaves, the springing body of the leopard, the massive paws of the tiger, the swift legs of the deer, the sinewy strength of the horse, the bushiness of the bear, the slimness of the stork, or the ruggedness of the pine branch. There is thus not one type of rhythm in nature which has not been copied in Chinese writing and formed directly or indirectly the inspiration for a particular "style." If a Chinese scholar sees a certain beauty in the dry vine, with its careless grace and elastic strength, the tip of the end curling upward, and a few leaves still hanging on it haphazardly and yet most appropriately, he tries to incorporate that into his writing. If another scholar sees a pine tree that twists its trunk and bends its branches downward instead of upward, which shows a wonderful tenacity and force, he also tries to incorporate that into his style of writing. We have therefore the "dry-vine" style and the "pine-branch" style of writing.

It seems to me that calligraphy, as representing the purest principles of rhythms and composition, stands in relation to painting as pure mathematics stands in relation to engineering or astronomy. In appreciating Chinese calligraphy, the meaning is entirely forgotten, and the lines and forms are appreciated in and for themselves. In this cultivation and appreciation of pure witchery of line and beauty of composition, therefore, the Chinese have an absolute freedom and entire devotion to pure form as such, as apart from content. A painting has to convey an object, but a well-written character only its own beauty of line and structure. In this absolutely free field, every variety of rhythm has been experimented upon and every type of structure has been explored. The Chinese brush makes the conveyance of every type of rhythmic movement possible, and the Chinese characters, which are theoretically square but are composed from the oddest elements, present an infinite variety of structural problems which every writer must solve for himself. Thus, through calligraphy, the Chinese scholar is trained to appreciate, as regards line, qualities like force, suppleness, reserved strength, exquisite tenderness, swiftness, neatness, massiveness, ruggedness, and restraint or freedom; and as regards form, he is taught to appreciate harmony, proportion, contrast, balance, lengthiness, compactness, and sometimes even beauty in slouchiness or irregularity. Thus the art of calligraphy provides a whole set of terms of aesthetic appreciation which we may consider as the bases of Chinese notions of beauty. [Lin Yutang, *My Country and My People.*]

The quotation from Lin Yutang was not a "first revelation." Many years earlier, through actual experience, I had become acquainted with the secrets of Chinese calligraphy.

At that time, 1920, I was studying Japanese and had learned to inscribe the letters. The affinity of the stroke and the rhythm of Eastern drawing and calligraphic inscription, which permits the harmonic interweaving of both in pictures, so that the drawing and the calligraphic dedication are compositionally inseparable, struck me even then.

A little picture depicting a horse, "taken" from the aspect of the crupper, illustrates, by the manner of the stroke, the affinity of calligraphic inscription and the run of line in free drawing. The stroke for a drawing is classified in exactly this way, according to style, in strict accordance with the subjects they are intended to summarize. The folds of clothes are drawn with different kinds of strokes from those used for mountain slopes, and the stroke for drawing running water differs sharply from that with which the outlines of clouds are caught.

I read and reread *The Importance of Living* in — 1941!

The first summer of war is already past.

The mire of autumn has already begun.

During bombing one can no longer go down into the trenches surrounding our building on Potylikha.

One can no longer doze on the earth, looking up at the play of searchlights in the night sky over Moscow.

The neighbors are put out by my imperturbable snoring.

"How can you sleep at such a time?"

I reply that sleeping on the earth is, of course, most natural for man, for countless millions of people in the course of countless centuries have done it.

But now autumn has come, with its cold and its downpours.

I am too lazy to go down.

The building empties at the first sound of the sirens.

Doors are banging in the empty apartments. They have not been locked for fear of fires and incendiary bombs, which might fly into the apartments.

Abandoned cats wander from flat to flat.

There are more empty apartments every day.

More abandoned cats.

Moscow is being feverishly evacuated.

Thousands of Muscovites are daily migrating from Byelokamennaya and Pervoprestol'naya to the Volga, and beyond the Volga into the depths of Asia.

The roar of aircraft, flying in wave after wave, exactly on course over our building in Potylikha (the vast film studio served as a constant reference point for raids from the direction of Mozhaisk) does not allow one to fall asleep.

Unwillingly, you listen to the far-off explosions beyond the Moscow River, or in the region of the Kiev Station, or the Circle Railway Bridge, which separates us from the city.

Somewhere there is the sound of aircraft.

Somewhere the thunder of explosions.

If you look out through a crack in the blackout curtain, you can see in the distance and to the right and left the trembling glow of fires . . .

How fine to die for one's country!

But how vital to live for it!

Monkey Logic

GALOSHES SQUELCH.
Give a sucking sound.
Stick in the mud and come off one's feet.
The mud is a mixture of sodden clay and the first snow.
An utterly deserted zoo in Alma-Ata.
Steppe eagles with ruffled feathers on their heads, resembling my companion's aunt.

Hornless deer with great, black, moist eyes, like those of my companion himself (the director Kozintsev).[1]

A bear marching pointlessly up and down.

An amazing snow leopard whose dreadful tail reacts to our slightest movement. He is like a fat, hairy, gorged snake. The whole body is lazily motionless. The eyes are now closed . . . now suddenly open in all their greenish-gray unfathomableness. In the depths is the barely visible second hand of the vertically narrowed pupil.

The leopard — absolutely motionless beneath the roof of its cage.

Only the very end of its tail reacts nervously, tirelessly, to our every movement.

The snow leopard is like the Japanese military attaché at the Red Army parade on Red Square.

Bushido, the Samurai code of honor, did not permit a Japanese of the selected caste (and later the tradition applied generally to all the Japanese) to

---

1. Gregory Mikhailovich Kozintsev (1905–1973), the Soviet film director and producer of the famous Russian *Hamlet,* was also the author of *Our Contemporary William Shakespeare* (New York: Hill and Wang, 1967; London: Dobson, 1967).

show a facial reaction to anything at all. Ergo, the Japanese attaché's face was stone.

But now a new type of fighter comes sweeping across the sky.

The face is motionless.

His hands are behind his back.

But heavens, what is happening to those hands!

They flutter behind his back like doves, concealed in yellow gloves.

Like the snow leopard's tail.

In complete immobility the eyes are fixed on us.

The next day I send Misha Kuznetsov[2] to study the leopard's eyes for his part of Fedka Basmanov. Kuznetsov's gray eyes are most suitable for it, and he must be able to capture the leopard's look.

We proceed farther into the zoo. We enter a covered building.

The sharp smell of urine.

A black Great Dane.

A flock of green parrots.

Pelicans.

A doglike smell from the lion.

A mouselike one from the tiger.

We approach the monkeys.

The baboons are separate . . .

I throw a piece of carrot.

A monkey stops searching for fleas and, without taking its eyes off the carrot, leaps down in three jumps.

A piece of white paper to one side of the carrot attracts its eye, for a white impression is sharper than a dull orange one. The carrot is forgotten.

The monkey goes over to the piece of paper.

But now, somewhere nearby, there is a sharp screech and the characteristic, shrill chattering of teeth. The monkey turns away from the paper toward the cry, and its eyes light on a swaying branch, for a moving object is more attractive than a still one.

A jump — and the monkey has already caught hold of the branch.

Up above, the monkey's mate has begun to squeal, and the monkey once more obligingly searches its mate's coat.

A live mate, of course, is still more attractive than a moving object.

The branch, the paper, the carrot are forgotten.

There is only one difference between me and the Alma-Ata monkey.

I too jump from object to object as soon as my memory turns up a new one.

But unlike the monkey, I sometimes return to the initial one.

---

2. Misha Kuznetsov acted in *Ivan the Terrible*.

Mi Tu

THE LITVINOVS[1] HAD A DOG, but it was not Litvinov who loved it. The terrier was loved by Madame Ivy Walterovna Litvinova and by the children.

Of course, strictly speaking, a dog has no place in these notes at all. If I were as rigorous as old Goethe, who left his post as director of the Weimar Theater because they permitted a dog to be led on the stage, thus defiling the great boards, I would now have to give up writing and be offended at myself.

Offended that I allowed a tousled terrier into such a serious work as this; a dog that is not even mine.

Still, the entry of dogs into my writing is not without precedent. Kachalov's dog turned up in my writing in the form of a quotation from Yesenin when I was defining the effectiveness of a subject according to what can be achieved by training dogs.

Training, as is well known, is the use of existing reflexes for the purpose of establishing new conditioned reflexes. Those subjects are effective which act on the specially deep, inborn reflexes. (The chase acts on the hunting instinct if the point of view is the hound's, or on the instinct of survival if you look at it from the point of view of the hare.)

The Litvinovs' dog enters these pages for a less profound reason if you look at it casually, but a far more important one if you look into its essence.

What brings the dog here is its strange name: Mi Tu. I have not gone into the linguistic labyrinth of this name's origin, nor do I know the exact tran-

---

1. Eisenstein was referring to the family of Maxim Maximovich Litvinov (1876–1951), former Soviet minister of foreign affairs. His wife was an Englishwoman, the former Ivy Low. They were the grandparents of Dr. P. Litvinov, who was arrested and exiled in 1968 for demanding freedom of speech and of demonstration in the Soviet Union.

scription. Is it a French Mi Tou, a Chinese Mi-tu? It has always sounded English: Me too.

And in this transcription it has always made sense, quite definite sense: "Me too and me too."

The formula "Me too" is one of the basic formulae of my work. To be more exact, one of the dynamic impulses of my work. One of the innermost springs driving me now, as in the past, to do a great, great deal.

And so: "Me too" — "Us too!"

Self-Abasement

AMONG THE STORIES, legends, plays that I not only liked, but that formed a series of notions, desires, and "ideals" in my youth, are three that had a deep influence on me.

The first is not even a story or legend, but just a thought, possibly from Marie Corelli's *The Sorrows of Satan*, possibly from one of Victoria Cross's novels (the author of *Six Chapters in a Man's Life*). The thought is that philosophy is like cocaine — it kills the feeling of joy, but also delivers one from the feeling of pain.

The second, picked up somewhere very early and impressing me deeply, was some legend from, I think, a Persian folk epic about a certain herculean man who had had from his childhood a calling to accomplish something exceedingly great. In order to achieve his destiny, he did not permit himself to waste his strength. He saved it so that it might reach its full potential. One day he went to the market and was jostled by the tanners. "Kiss our feet and lie in the dirt of the market so that we may walk over you," they shouted, mocking him.

Our hero, preserving his strength for the future, obediently spread himself out in the dust beneath their feet.

This happened to him three times.

Later, the hero reached manhood, gained full use of his unprecedented strength, and accomplished all the unprecedented heroic deeds required of him. But it was the episode with the tanners, the unprecedented self-control and sacrifice of everything, even his self-respect, to further the achievement and realization of what had been prescribed and ordered from the beginning, that completely captivated me.

This motif shows through clearly in my works.

In the unrealized part of the scenario of *Alexander Nevsky*, when the Tartar horde moves threateningly against Russia, after the defeat of the Germans at Lake Peipus, Nevsky the victor rushes to meet the horde. There he passes meekly between the cleansing fires before the Khan's royal tent and kneels humbly before the Khan himself, winning time by his humility for building up strength so that this enslaver of our land might also with time be overthrown, though not by his own hand, but by the sword of his descendant and follower, Dmitri Donskoi.

On his way back from the horde, the poisoned prince dies, looking before him at the distant plain of Kulikova. Pavlenko and I had our saintly warrior, on his way home, make a little detour from the historic route actually taken by Alexander Yaroslavich in returning from the horde to his hearth and home, which he did not manage to reach.

A hand other than mine drew a red pencil mark after the scene about the defeat of the Germans.

"The scenario finishes here," the words were passed on to me. "Such a fine prince could not die!"[1]

But if the saintly prince was not brought to his knees by me, in the name of a higher aim, Ivan Vasilievich the Terrible did not escape that fate. The victor of Kazan, immediately after the flight of glory — the beating of kettledrums, against a background of racing clouds, rises over the erupting thunder of the guns, and in the next scene ascends one more high step of glory — lowers himself, crushed and meek, to the golden hems of the boyars' coats, tearfully imploring them not to divide Russia after the approaching demise of the Russian state's first crowned autocrat, now shaking in a fever . . .

In my own personal, too-personal, history I myself too often perpetrated this heroic deed of self-abasement. And in my personal, too-personal, innermost life, perhaps somewhat too often, too hurriedly, even almost too willingly and also . . . as unsuccessfully.

However, I have also, like Ivan, managed to cut off heads sticking out of fur coats; the Terrible Tsar and I have pressed the proud gold hems together, accepting humiliation in the name of our most passionate aspirations.

And often, after lifting up the sword over another's head, I have brought it down not so much on his as on my own.

The third impression was gleaned from George Bernard Shaw's *Chocolate Soldier* during my tender, romantic, and heroically inclined years. By its pitiless irony, the play cooled my ardent and youthful craving for pathos. Afterward for my whole life I shouldered the heroic-pathetic yoke of screen "canvases" in the heroic style.

My visit to Shaw in London in 1929 culminated in his sending me a radio telegram, which, reaching me in mid-Atlantic on my way to the United States,

---

1. The red pencil was wielded by the party censor, probably Stalin himself. (H.M.)

invited me to make a film of the *Chocolate Soldier*,[2] "on condition that the text is kept full and in completely undistorted form." This proposition was a great honor, coming from a man who had previously refused, for any amount of money, to give anyone the rights to make a film version of his works. Just as with Maxim Gorky, another great writer, whose propositions to film his work were turned down by me.[3]

And here, naturally, there begs to be included a description of my trip to Gorky,[4] to see Gorky, in order to hear the scenario, which he wanted to see made by my hands.[5]

And until his death (I saw him several times after this), the old man did not forget or forgive me this outrage.[6]

---

2. Based on *Arms and the Man*.

3. Eisenstein wrote "turned down" in English.

4. The city where Gorky lived, which was named after him, was formerly Nizhni-Novgorod.

5. This was in 1934. The script was titled *Criminals*.

6. Eisenstein also wrote "outrage" in English. Indeed, the turning down of the most prized writer in Stalin's stable could not have been more of an outrage to those in power at a time when Eisenstein's status was at its lowest. (H.M.)

History of the
Close-up

A LILAC BOUGH.

White and full blossomed.

Its succulent greenery of leaves bathed in a dazzling shaft of sunlight.

It bursts into the room through an open window.

Sways over the windowsill.

It returns to me now — the first memory-impression from my childhood.

The close-up!

A close-up of a white lilac bough swaying over my cradle.

Yet it is no longer a cradle. It is a little white four-poster with nickel-plated balls and a net stretched between the posts to keep me from falling out.

I am past the cradle age. I am perhaps three or four. I am with my family during the summer on the coast of Riga at what is now Maiori but was then known as Maiorenhof.

The white lilac, in a slanting beam of sunlight, peeps into my window.

It sways close above me in the wind.

My first conscious impression — a close-up.

So my consciousness awoke under a lilac bough.

For many, many years, I dozed off beneath such a bough. A bough embroidered in silk and gold thread on a three-paneled Japanese screen.

I do not recall when the screen was first placed by my bed. But it now seems to me that it had always been there.

The embroidered bough was in full bloom, bent under the weight of its flowers. Tiny birds perched upon it, and far in the distance, beyond it and through it, was a Japanese landscape.

Small huts. Clumps of reeds. Little bridges spanning streams. Sharp-prowed boats, drawn with a couple of brush strokes.

The lilac bough was no longer simply a close-up.

The bough became a foreground plane, with the distant vista seen through it, so typical of Japanese composition.

Thus, before my discovery of Hokusai, before I fell under the spell of Edgar Degas, I became exposed to the enchantment of the foreground composition.

In this composition a small detail in the extreme foreground is given such scale as to dominate the depth of the entire pictorial plane.

I now believe that those two lilac boughs, the real and the artificial, fused two conceptions into a single vivid impression: the concept of the close-up and the concept of foreground composition.

And when, many years later, I began to search for the historical predecessor of the film close-up, I found that I did not direct my search to portraits or still lifes with their isolated images. Rather, I became fascinated by how a single element within the total organic structure of a painting begins gradually to push its way to the foreground plane. How, out of the general landscape composition, where it is frequently impossible to distinguish the falling Icarus[1] or Daphnis and Chloe, the figures in full size begin first to approach the foreground and then gradually come so near that they are cut by the very edge of the picture, as in El Greco's *El Espolio (The Disrobing of Christ)*, and then leap three centuries — to the French Impressionists under the powerful influence of Japanese prints.

Two Edgars carried on for me the tradition of foreground composition: Degas and Poe. But Poe was first.

The vivid impression of the painted Japanese bough evidently determined the intensity of my reaction to the story of how Poe looks through the window and suddenly sees a gigantic monster crawling over the peaks of a distant mountain range. Later, it becomes evident that it is not a monster of prehistoric dimensions, but a modest cricket, crawling across the windowpane.[2] The optical superimposition of the dominant foreground on the distant mountain range creates the frightening effect. It is instructive to note that Poe's fantasy could not have come from immediate impression. The human eye is not capable of simultaneously focusing on both the extreme close-up of a foreground object and the sharp outlines of the mountain range in the distance. Only a camera lens (a 28 mm) can accomplish this. This lens can do another marvelous thing — it can distort the foreground by exaggerating its size and shape.

The combined impact of both the white lilac bough and the extremely graphic description in Poe's terrifying story has, in some ways, determined my most effective and most expressively realized foreground compositions.

Those skulls and monks, the masks and merry-go-rounds, from the "Day of Death" in my Mexican film.

---

1. Eisenstein referred to the painting by Brueghel.
2. Actually, in Poe's story "The Sphinx," it is a death's-head moth crawling on the window.

The white lilac bough becomes the white skull that dominates the foreground plane.

And the horror of Poe's tale translates itself into the cluster of black-robed monks in the background.

These elements taken together are perceived as the Catholic asceticism of the Jesuits, imposing the iron heel of fire and blood upon the sensual splendor of the tropical beauties of Mexico.

The merry-go-rounds of the "Day of Death" repeat the same tragic theme ironically.

Here more white skulls are brought into the foreground, and in such an extreme close-up that they become almost tangible.

But the skulls are made of papier-mâché: they are masks of skulls.

Beyond them, in full scale, the merry-go-rounds and the vertical wheels of laughter spin around, flashing into view through the empty eye sockets of the masks, making them wink, as though to say that death is nothing but a hollow-carton contraption, through which, all the same, will ever blow the whirlwind of life.

Another good example of the effective juxtaposition of two images within one frame is the profile of a Mayan girl placed against the entire Chichén Itzá pyramid, and I had been quite involved with this type of composition earlier, especially during my work on *The Old and the New*.

The incomparable compositions of the other Edgar — Edgar Degas — and those of Toulouse-Lautrec, which at times are even more extreme in their structure, again bring us into the sphere of purely plastic creation. But the very interweaving of descriptive impressions and of purely visual impressions had quite a special significance for me. This is undoubtedly what gave me the first feel of the connecting link between painting and literature, when both are seen in equally plastic terms. Here were the beginnings of the realization that it is possible to read Pushkin visually — plastically and filmically,[3] and, when an example is needed in the English language, John Milton also.

Deeper involvement with Pushkin, and later with Gogol, too, strengthened the feeling of that connection. For in Poe we see what, in essence, is a visual scene, described in exact visual detail, almost as an optical phenomenon; then in Pushkin we find a description of an event or situation accomplished with such absolute precision and fidelity as to make it possible for us to re-create for ourselves the almost total visual image that our poet saw passing before his eyes. I say "passing" deliberately, because this dynamic concept is well within the possibility of literary description, though not available to the fixed immobility of the picture canvas. That is why the quality of *moving pictures* in Pushkin's

---

3. See "Montage 1938" in *Film Form*. "Pushkin: Film Editor" was published posthumously in the Russian journal *Iskusstvo Kino* in 1955.

compositions could be so clearly perceived only with the advent of cinematography.

Tynyanov[4] in his writings noted the concrete character of Pushkin's poetry — that his lyrical poems are not an exercise in the use of stylized lyrical formulae, but are always a record of truly lyrical "moods of the soul," of emotional states that have an actual source and are firmly rooted in reality.

The study of Pushkin's poetry (and prose) reveals a similar precision in the description of realistic visual images, which can be re-created, made to exist again, by following his descriptions. Indeed, it is sheer joy to transpose Pushkin's descriptions into montage sequences of changing film-frame images, each following the other. It is a delightful experience, because step by step you observe how the poet himself saw and sequentially revealed an entire event. (Examples: The end of *The Bronze Horseman*,[5] *Istomina, Prisoner of the Caucasus, Count Nulin*. The appearance of Peter I. These are from the sphere of montage.)

No less amazing is Pushkin's "micromontage," the relationship of different elements within a single frame. For Pushkin, this is paralleled by the placement of words within a single phrase. And if we take it as a rule that the placement of words governs their position in relation to the foreground plane and to the depth of the "frame" (which is natural), then almost every phrase written by Pushkin corresponds to the strictly prescribed pattern of plastic composition. I say "pattern of composition," because word placement determines the major and most decisive factor in composition: the rational correlation and juxtaposition of plot elements and other values within the picture frames. This "determinative skeleton" can be clothed in a variety of individual pictorial solutions. It allows anyone who undertakes to transpose literary description into plastic forms to interpret it in his own way while remaining completely faithful to the author's original concept. As in any aspect of direction, this determinative skeleton defines the premises and delineates the limits of creative interpretation of any author's work.

The Chinese, without a doubt, provide the most striking examples in this area. The unity of their pictorial and literary description springs equally from the initial visual perception and its specific features, investing both areas of description with amazing originality of detail and form.

Just as Pushkin's word order stimulated my ideas beyond first impressions, so the general study of Pushkin proved to be a step in the direction of audio-visual counterpoint. For in the process of creating a visual equivalent of Push-

---

4. Yuri Tynyanov (1894–1943) was a literary critic and a novelist. He was a leading member of the Formalist movement. At one time, Eisenstein thought of making a film of Tynyanov's historical novel about Pushkin.

5. See the visualization under Eisenstein's direction in *Cinema as a Graphic Art* by Valdimir Nilsen (London: Newnes, 1937).

kin's word order, very often the intonational and melodic flow is interwoven into the phrase itself. The melodic line is so distinct and coincides so closely with the word representation of the scene that sometimes it appears to be the outline of dynamic elements, or the *mise en scène* of actions, or the fixed relationship of all the elements within the field of vision. (Example: the cannonballs in *Poltava*.) From this it is but one step to the point where concrete objects as such disappear, leaving behind only the outline and the characteristic texture of their own intonational pattern.

The melody of poetry leaps into music, and we face the problem of how to create audiovisual unity from the various combinations of the elements of sight and sound.

It still fascinates me to recall all the different roads and crossroads I took to approach the central problems that excited me in different areas of my creative work.

The sweet poison of audiovisual montage came later.

In the silent film, I was concerned with montage and the role of the close-up. It is interesting, however, to note that even back in the days of the silent cinema, I frequently searched for ways of conveying the element of sound by purely plastic means.

I remember, in 1927, while filming the Winter Palace on the night of the October Revolution (for my film *October*), I tried to find pictorial means to create the impression of the shots from the *Aurora* reverberating through the palace. The echo rolls from hall to hall until it reaches a room shrouded in white slipcovers, where, wrapped in their winter coats, the ministers of the Provisional Government await the fatal moment — the establishment of Soviet power. By a previously determined rhythmic pattern rising in and out on the empty halls, I tried to capture the pulsating rhythm of the echo throbbing through them.

I was more successful with the well-remembered sequence of the crystal chandeliers tinkling through the palace in response to the machine-gun rattle out on the square. Here, in addition to the visual and dynamic equivalent of the trembling crystal pendants, there was the association supplied by the object itself. More methodologically interesting, of course, was my attempt to catch a pictorial equivalent of the echo! The close-up in the form used by the silent film — already differentiated from the general background, having ceased to be related to the background, but in itself completely abstracted *pars pro toto* — was, to me, also linked with live impressions years before I began to work even in the theater.

The close-up of a synonymous sequence — as a possible element of pure tempo combinations — to me was linked with a real sarabande of noses and eyes, ears and hands, tucked-in sashes, earrings, and headdresses with interwoven flowers and ribbons.

Day vision in the sense of "being awake" is profoundly different from night vision in the sense of seeing in your sleep. In normal day vision the interweaving of details and the general scene is so harmonious that it requires either a keenly developed special knack — the eye of the Pathfinder or his grandnephew Sherlock Holmes — or an unexpectedly sharp stimulation of one's own attention if one is suddenly to distinguish the scattered islands of close-ups within this harmonious whole.

One needs a special, analytically trained eye to pick out the details; a special mental faculty for synthesis is required if one is to be able, among the various data of visual analyses, to spot the crucial detail, the characteristic detail, the detail within the fragment of the whole, capable of conveying the idea of the whole.

It is interesting that in dreams the whole and the part are somehow so harmoniously intertwined that both are equally notable.

Dostoyevsky gives us the best illustration in a conversation between Ivan Karamazov and the devil, where "higher aspirations" and "the last button on the shirt front" are mentioned side by side. (Here too Leo Tolstoy comes to mind — equally brilliant in vast battle scenes and in unexpected details, like the stray curls on Anna Karenina's neck.) It is said that such things are seen in dreams by quite ordinary people; that is, by the kind of people for whom, when awake, the "whole" certainly appears as a somewhat cluttered, complex, and undifferentiated picture.

But the most interesting are the intermediate states: neither dream nor reality.

The leap from one state to another, as it were, splinters both this and the other harmony: fragments of perceptions or impressions of things become tossed around like dice and shuffled like a pack of cards.

It was in one of these in-between states that I saw the sarabande of close-ups mentioned above. It was not a dance on "the bald mountain."[6] In fact, it was not on any mountain. But on a well-trampled square facing some mighty log houses somewhere near Kholm in the former Pskov Province.[7]

---

6. The reference is to Moussorgsky's symphonic fantasy *A Night on Bald Mountain*.

7. The scene is in *Alexander Nevsky*.

Images

I SEE BEFORE ME whatever I am reading about, and whatever I imagine comes into my head with extreme clarity. Evidently the combination of a very large store of visual impression, a sharp visual memory with a considerable training in "day-dreaming" is natural to me. All that I remember or think about seems to pass before my eyes in visual images, like a film. Even as I write, my hand almost outlines the contours, the drawings of an unbroken stream of visual images and events. These impressions, sharply visual, beg with painful intensity to be reproduced.

At one time, the only means (both as object and subject) of such reproduction was myself. But more recently for this purpose I sometimes have had at hand a good three thousand assistants, "man-units," raising city bridges, squadrons of ships, herds of horses, and fires. Still, a certain touch of "relatedness" remains, and in order to quiet down, I often find it quite sufficient to re-create the all-inclusive visual image that is disturbing me, though not in all its details. This, of course, largely determines the special visual intensity of my *mise en scène*.

Often this acts as a barrier against other expressive elements, which do not manage to get onto such an intensive creative path as that which is subordinated to the visual side of my works.

Music, especially that of Prokofiev and Wagner, enters also into the visual category in this way; or would it be more correct to call it sensual rather than visual? Not in vain do I expend so much ink on paper and inspiration on film in searching for ways of fixing the commensurability of the visual and the aural. But on the other hand, am I so wholly dedicated to questions of sensual thinking and sensual bases of form?

Words and subtext — they are what often remain for me out of the focus of sharpened attention.

The disproportionate intensity of my interest in various elements of composition and structure is undoubtedly evident. Even so, I prefer such a "disequilibrium" to the classical severity of balanced elements, and am ready to pay for the delight of excess and sharpness in one field with losses and incompleteness in another. But do not mistake me: this does not at all mean that the audiovisual primacy in my works is a preference for form over content, as some idiots might think.

The audiovisual image is the extreme limit of self-revelation outside the basic motivating themes and ideas of creative work . . .

Meeting with Magnasco[1]

HOW DID I FIND OUT about Van Gogh and come to love him? Was it in the Shchukin Museum?

I was taken there for the first time (on the second or third day after my arrival in Moscow, I should add) by one of my Moscovite friends, who was crazy about Gauguin.

I have never especially liked Gauguin.

With the exception of the *Yellow Christ*, which I knew from the reproduction in Tugenkhold's book on French painting.[2] I borrowed the book to read when I was in Gatchina, serving in military construction in 1918, and afterward made off with the book. The reproduction was not in color. I saw Gauguin in color much later and was very disappointed. I had supposed his range of colors to be quite different: a piercing chrome against a background of ultramarine and cobalt with the white spots of the Breton women's headwear. In fact, the color of the *Yellow Christ* turned out to be a sort of *fraise écrasée* of spherical rosebushes, the jaundice-yellow body of Christ, the indeterminate tone of the landscape. This occurred after I had already used the actual drawing of Christ's figure for all the crosses and crucifixes in *Ivan the Terrible*. The upward flight of the crucified figure's arms, the turn of the head, and the face twisted in grief were just what I needed, and I ran my Alma-Ata colleagues off their feet in order to get hold of a reproduction.

Matisse did not entice me.

Picasso intrigued.

---

1. Alessandro Magnasco (1667–1749) was a painter of genre scenes.

2. The book is *Fransuskoe Iskusstvo i ego predstaviteli* (*French Art and Artists*) by Y. A. Tugenkhold (St. Petersburg, 1911).

Van Dongen's[3] strange big-eyed women attracted. But Van Gogh captivated. Meyer Greffe[4] traveled to Spain to pay homage to Velasquez and suddenly came across El Greco. Velasquez vanished, and only the captivating master from Toledo remained. And my passion for El Greco began in almost the same way.

There are pictures that become so hackneyed through reproductions that it is impossible to look at the originals. Such is the fate of almost everything in the National Gallery in London, where one seems to be walking through the pages of Muter,[5] Werman,[6] and other such herbaria, where *chef d'oeuvres*, too perfected and finely finished, are reproduced in "long shot" and described boringly, dryly, and unintelligibly. When you see them in real life, they appear to be enlarged color reproductions of the illustrations familiar to you in books.

It is impossible to look at Titian's *Birth of the Milky Way*.

It is difficult to look at Holbein's *Emissaries* with the distorted-perspective picture in the foreground.

It is impossible to look at the Greeks in the period of their heyday.

And the eye finds no rest even if it turns to the Egyptians inhabiting the British Museum.

The searing incompleteness of Mexican plastic art, the sketchiness of Peruvian pots and vessels, the displacement in the proportions of Negro plastic art — these are what my generation has liked. Thus, only *Pope Paul with His Nephews* attracts me (and attracts me greatly!) out of Titian's works. And I walked through the National Gallery, gazing blankly, half-asleep.

The impression created by the Louvre as a whole is inseparable from the Galeries Lafayette and Maison Printemps,[7] the masquerade in Magic City or the *bal couture* in the Opéra. Amid this crush of people and pictures, jostling one another in something akin to a flower market or railway station, the isolated Ingres (*Madame et Mademoiselle Rivière*), Daumier (*Grispin et Scapin*), portraits by Clouet[8] sparkle blindingly; the rest, including *Mona Lisa*, dissolve into a sort of mirage of sunspots, figured murals on ceilings, sweating tourists, shuffling feet . . .

---

3. Kees van Dongen (1877–1968) was a Dutch-born French Fauvist.

4. Meyer Greffe (1867–1935) was a German art critic.

5. Richard Muter (1860–1909), a German art critic, was author of the five-volume *History of Painting*.

6. Karl Werman (1844–1933), a German art critic, wrote the six-volume *History of Art of All Times and Peoples*.

7. The Galeries Lafayette and the Maison Printemps are leading Parisian department stores.

8. Eisenstein may have been referring to any member of a family of Flemish-French painters of the late Renaissance: Jean Clouet (fl. 1500), his son Jean (1485?–1545), and his son François (1510?–1572). The oldest was court painter to the Duke of Burgundy. The others were painters to King François I.

El Greco's *The Agony in the Garden of Gethsemane* burst piercingly out of the dull halls of the National Gallery in the same way.

The cherry-colored robe cuts the green like a razor.

Each color by itself.

No running into each other, no smoothing over by a general softening tone.

No, the colors ring out like fanfares.

Form, mocking the academicism of bodies and robes, is built up by the cutting surfaces of tone, across which run traces of brush strokes like veins.

Figures soar up, bend, twist . . . surpassing Van Gogh's poplars in a vortex of movement.

Magnasco . . . in Odessa.[9]

Noisy Deribasov Street.

Pruzhiner's sign PRIMUS REPAIRS.

Smell of cats and fried "feesh."

Smoothly laid paving stones of the roadways.

White aprons of the janitors, who had just been provided with badges by order of the City Soviet.

Red plush and black velvet legs of uncomfortable armchairs in hotel rooms.

Cotton curtains.

Dust and a dry wind.

I am spending a few days in Odessa on my way to Yalta, but it is not the Odessa, throbbing with the life of fountains, that we shot at the time of *Potemkin*. It is not the Odessa of crowds thronging down the steps. Nor the Odessa that streamed in thousands through the streets to Vakulinchuk's tent. The Odessa that strolls through the mists to the port.

Now I am alone in Odessa. Alone with my foreboding about the unpleasantness of *Bezhin Meadow*.

Slender little trees along the pavements.

The ruins of Sakhalinchik.[10]

Old inhabitants mutter of splendid commissionaires who once stood at brothel doorways.

The silent duke at the top of the deserted steps.[11]

Solitude.

A pale yellow building with gray columns.

---

9. Eisenstein was filming in Odessa (for the third time) from August to October 1936, during the production of *Bezhin Meadow*. (H.M.)

10. Sakhalinchik was the thieves' quarter and red-light district of Odessa.

11. The reference is to the statue of Armand Emmanuel du Plessis, Duc de Richelieu (1766–1822), an émigré who served in the Russian army during the Napoleonic era and who, from 1803 to 1814, was governor-general of the Novorossisk Region and governor of Odessa. After the restoration of the French monarchy, he was chief minister to Louis XVIII. His monument stands on the highest platform of the Odessa steps, made famous by the film *Potemkin*.

The dead port of Odessa.

How dead Odessa must be, how great the depression, to bring me to this two-story building! To bring me to this typical provincial museum displaying gold-lined cups and teapots from incomplete Empire services, a few Karelian birch trees, forged copies of minor pictures, rouged breasts, and darkened landscapes on vast canvases brought in from surrounding estates.

In Novgorod is the local museum where one could see *The Italian Comedy* by Benois and Borisov-Musatov;[12] in Pereslavl, beside the brass Buddhas (they were made here, then taken to Mongolia, from where they were brought back as rarities!) were gouaches and watercolors by Serebryakova;[13] in Alma-Ata's artistic appendix to the Darwin Ethnographic Museum, alongside two-headed calves and "portraits" of nomad tents, were Serov and Dobuzhinsky . . .

In Odessa, just as unexpectedly, I came across Magnasco.

Who had brought these two little dark canvases of monastic life?

How had the works of this master strayed into Odessa, wandering beyond the bounds of common recognition and textbook acceptance, into the ranks of the generally accepted clientèle of art history? I had not known the name Magnasco and had never before seen his pictures, but I made a careful note of the name so as not to forget.

No doubt these were copies or variants. Today I know that he often repeated his subjects, and it is even known that he was forged. Then I took Magnasco into my own hands. And not in vain.

With Magnasco it often seems as if El Greco's figures have become even thinner, their ecstatic fracturing still more sharply fractured. With Magnasco a movement was no longer the movement of a figure, caught by a brush, but the independently mannered movement of the brush, hurriedly masked by the bones and flabby bodies of ascetics, by outstretched arms, by refined hands and long fingers. At times it seems that these florid and affected flourishes have transplanted themselves into monastic vestments in order to warm their scampering tails, loops, knots, and intersections around the hearth.

Christ Helping Peter from the Water could have been by El Greco — by Honoré Daumier.

Beggars and Street Singers by Jacques Callot, *Company in a Garden* by Goya or Longhi.[14] Goya's *Inquisition* is a crib from *Lesson in Milan Cathedral*.

Magnasco's possessed monks seem to join with El Greco and Goya, with Goya and Daumier, into a single chain.

Goya, Daumier, Callot, Longhi: all are names dear to me.

---

12. Victor E. Borisov-Musatov (1870–1905) was a Russian painter influenced by the French Impressionists.

13. Zinaida E. Serebryakova, born in 1884, was a Russian painter who moved to Paris in 1927 and remained there until her death, in 1967.

14. Giuseppi Longhi (1766–1831) was a Venetian engraver.

And many of Magnasco's pictures have been hidden under these names, except for Daumier, for many years.

Magnasco — born in 1667. Magnasco — dead in 1749.

Magnasco — interesting to me because, more than El Greco, it was Alessandro Magnasco's monks who stylistically determined the appearance and movement of my Ivan the Terrible, Cherkassov.

The Keys of Happiness

*S*ANIN BY ARTSYBASHEV, *The Anger of Dionysus* by Nagrodskaya, Lappo-Danilevskaya's novels, Verbitskaya's *The Keys of Happiness*.[1]

An entire epoch in literature. An epoch reflecting the complete loss of any stability in that stratum of the intelligentsia which had not come over to the revolutionary movement. In the years these books came out, we were still too young to read all this. We knew of them by hearsay, by the debates among adults, by snatches of arguments in connection with their publication, more by the titles and by the names of the authors. How long ago that was! How much water under the bridge! How the face of Russia is transformed! How Europe is carved up anew! How the world is changed over these decades!

How strange it is to see a photograph of Madame Lappo-Danilevskaya,[2] and to remember her as a participant in the front-line troupe of the Western Front Political Directorate in 1920, when I myself worked as a scene designer and painter in Minsk. How unexpected to realize that one can see the son of the author of *The Keys of Happiness*, Verbitskaya, daily on the stage of the Moscow Art Theater in *Anna Karenina* or *The Enemies* by Gorky.

Almost as strange as realizing that Matisse, a "museum name" for so long, is still alive. Almost as strange as realizing that it is only two years since Edvard Munch[3] died. Munch, the Scandinavian forerunner of Expressionism — a movement that blossomed before our eyes, and then long ago sank into obliv-

---

1. Artsybashev, Nagrodskaya, Lappo-Danilevskaya, and Verbitskaya were popular Russian novelists of the early 1900s.

2. The photograph referred to was published in a 1946 issue of the Russian illustrated weekly *Ogoniok*.

3. Matisse died in 1954. Edvard Munch, the Norwegian painter born in 1863, died in 1944, two years before Eisenstein wrote this.

ion beneath the layers of Constructivism and Surrealism, which replaced it long ago and, in their turn, long ago left the stage.

Evreinov's three-volume work, *Theatre for Oneself*, arose from the turbulent vortex of those same prerevolutionary and prewar years, and one of the books contained model scenarios of plays for this theater without audiences, without critics, without auditoriums.

One of these scenarios was called *Trying on Deaths*. It suggested that the reader should, by making a small incision in the blood vessels on the side of the arm while in a warm bath (under the control of a hidden friendly doctor, and to the distant sounds of a harp), experience the delightful sensations of the dying Petronius[4] when he cut open his veins. Or, it was suggested, by heaping up flowers one could experience the first feelings of death by perfume . . .

Contemporaries explained that *The Keys of Happiness* was so titled because it was about the springs, the sources, that give birth to streams of happiness. In a similar fashion, as is well known, the title *Dead Souls* can be read in two ways: concerning the dead taxpayers, in whom Mr. Chichikov trades, or the unfeeling souls of his clientèle, the representatives of Russia's landowning class. *The Keys of Happiness* has just such another "hidden" meaning, apart from "the springs"; a quite cynical meaning, that in the arena of love there is an exact correspondence to the above-mentioned entertainment of Evreinov's *Trying on Deaths*.

During my childhood the Keys of Happiness were a kind of lottery. They stood in a row of other such amusements at charity bazaars, like hoops that had to be thrown over poles with prizes hanging from them, or little balls that had to be thrown into suspended colored bags containing gingerbread and lollipops.

On a little table was a box.

A locked box.

Twelve keys lay beside the box, but only one could open it, and each key cost a rouble. If you opened the box, you received its contents as a prize. Ten roubles, perhaps.

The box might open on the first attempt. The box might open on the second, the third. Often it was the twelfth key, and the winner was out of pocket. In the book, Madame Verbitskaya subjects her heroine to such an ordeal in the search for love, but Madame Verbitskaya's heroine is not left out of pocket.

The Keys of Happiness are not only a method of searching for love. In considerable measure, the Keys of Happiness are also a method of searching in art. A method most applicable in those turbulent stages of its development, when new resources or new techniques, not yet assimilated or mastered, suddenly appear; new means of expression, new methods of creating an effect.

---

4. Petronius, Roman satirist of the first century A.D., author of the *Satyricon*, and member of Nero's court, on hearing that he had been sentenced to death, enjoyed a feast and opened his veins, to die surrounded by friends.

Where to search for an approach? How to find the right ways? Where to discover the key that can open the casket, full of wonderful new secrets and resources?

Of course, one could simply break it open.

One might justifiably dub as "housebreakers' art" much that has been done with dialogue and music in the sound film, when the theater has simply shamelessly broken into cinematography. And the same thing is happening now with the color film, which has been broken into not so much by painting as by oleography.

The other way is that of fitting keys, the way of the Keys of Happiness. For one can have a very clear outline of one's own desires, a very exact set of equations, which should give you the unknown x of new resources, and a very exact idea of the formula by which the solution should be expressed. But the step from these abstract conceptions, however precise for the realization of them in practice, sometimes lies across unbridgeable gulfs of difficulties for mastering the specific characteristics of the new area of creativity.

The real keys of happiness should concern several of those right, but more often wrong, keys with which we have been attacking the Pandora's box of color cinema.

Color (1)

COLOR. PURE. BRIGHT. Ringing. Resounding.

When did I fall in love with it? Where?

Perhaps it was in Vologda or, to be more exact, in Vologodskaya Province. To be still more exact, in the little town of Vozhega, where I had been tossed by the civil war.

Blinding snow, and on that snow: peasant women. And on the peasant women: short, copper-colored sheepskin coats with braid, and felt boots.

Between the coats and the boots: a strip of woolen jumper in mercilessly colored vertical stripes — violet, orange, red, green.

An interruption: white.

And again: blue, yellow, mauve, scarlet. All the colors worn, faded, moth-eaten.

A quarter of a century later these images are still beside me in the pillow on a wicker chair; in the tablecloth on a table. And with them is interwoven the no less merciless stripes of Mexican serapes burning with the inexhaustible heat of the tropics, as their background sparkles with crystals of white frost.

Carnivorous pink interweaves light blue. Yellow links green. Brown runs in zigzags, separated by white stripes from deep indigo.

Perhaps the once pure colors of ikons were a prelude to barbaric joy from the pure color of Vologda jumpers. Perhaps the strident chorus of live pink flamingoes, against the blue background of the Gulf of Mexico, completes chords struck in The Hague's Van Gogh Museum — the color vortex of the Arles canvases of the great madman with the amputated ear.

It makes no difference. The green square of the tablecloth in the lemon-colored room is flooded with sunlight.

The dark blue teapot glows among the red cups.

The gold Buddha gleams against the azure paint of the wall.

The orange and black binding of a book rests against the green and gold brocade of the round table.

I am always among such swatches of color. My rooms are ringed tighter and tighter in an inescapable Vologda jumper of vertical colored stripes by the book spines on my wall shelves. Gold beside crimson.

Deep blue, white, white, orange.

Red, light blue, orange.

Red, light blue, green.

Red, red, white again.

Black.

Gold . . .

How dull when blue and yellow pencils do not blaze on the desk; when the red pillow with green stripes is not on the blue divan; when the dressing gown does not blind with its many colors; when no yellow stripes run across the curtains, intersecting blue, cutting across scarlet . . .

When the Philippine ribbon, with its many embroidered colors, lies snaking across the Uzbek garment I am pleased. When the embroidered Mongolian pattern is spread across the dull red background of the wall, it amply displays the whiteness of the Mexican cardboard emblems of the Day of the Dead and the black Morisco masks, with their bloody wounds.[1]

---

1. The Moriscoes were Spanish Moors, and the Arab (Moorish) influence in Spain was carried to the New World during the age of Spanish expansion and exploration.

Three Letters
on Color

I BEGAN TO WRITE THESE "memoirs" when I was still in the Kremlin Hospital, bedridden, scarcely able to stir, and with the sole basic aim of proving to myself that I actually had had a life . . .

Later, I gradually began to see my writing as a series of exercises in style. No, more than that. Rather, that this was a training in relaxed writing and would give me the ability to set down directly in written form every thought, every feeling, every image that entered my head, losing almost no time in any sort of intermediary processes, unburdening myself straight onto paper.

Another little motive loomed "behind the scenes": to give myself the freedom and opportunity to spill onto paper the whole agglomeration of associations that arise in me with painful immediacy on the slightest pretext — indeed, without any pretext at all.

So for several months I gave myself full rein, and so far (up till today) I have discovered the following: a certain relaxed descriptiveness has been achieved, an irresponsibility regarding what is being written has been *fully* achieved, and, on a good day, output has reached thirty-four pages of manuscript (that is something in the region of a printed quire) at a single sitting.

On the other hand, I have utterly wrecked my "serious writing" style.

I have found no relaxation of style, but have slipped into a fatal, unrestrained verbiage in all directions, away from the immediate and actual topic.

On color, three letters[1] were conceived (prior to my illness) as an addendum to "Nonindifferent Nature."

"Three Letters on Color."

"Attack on the Cypresses" — an exposé of a fundamental tackling of the

---

1. The first of the three letters was called "An Attack on Cypresses" and dealt with the theory of color in cinematography. It is in the Eisenstein archives in Moscow. The second, "Keys to Happiness," became part of his autobiography. The third, "The Unsent Letter," was, in fact, never written. Its basis was to be an actual letter sent to Yuri Tynyanov at the end of 1943, shortly before Tynyanov's death, on December 20, 1943, at Perm. (Eisenstein, in this section, was uncertain of the place.) In that letter, Eisenstein described the origin of his conception of a film on Pushkin, in which

problem of color. *Andante héroïque.* "The Keys of Happiness" — a *scherzo* on the theme of *les tribulations* of the practical realization of these lofty intentions. And the third article, "The Unsent Letter," composed from the letter to Tynyanov, which was actually never sent.

After it was written I got news of this fine master's agonizing death in a hospital (in Orenburg?) during the evacuation. I wrote from a mountain sanatorium near Alma-Ata, beneath apple trees sprinkled not with the snow of spring blossoms, but with real snow. I was resting there during the winter, and had read the third part of Tynyanov's *Pushkin* in *Znamya.*[2]

Quite recently, someone who had been in the same ward with him told me the details of the last days of his life, when Tynyanov could no longer lie down but sat doubled up, with his knees hunched to his chest, suffering incredibly. The last time I saw him was in 1939 in the Central Executive Committee building, from which I took him away after we had both received decorations from Mikhail Kalinin,[3] who passed away just a few days ago.

Tynyanov could scarcely walk (I almost carried him to the car), but he told me that my *Mexico* was really an outstanding picture . . .

A ghastly detail: Tynyanov, doubled up on his bed, holding a giant crab's red claw in his hand.

The hospital extremely short of supplies. The patients fed with a consignment of giant crabs, sent by accident to the town from the Far East . . .

I shall not digress here about crabs.

I shall not recall my first encounter with them in childhood, in Houlgate, off the Norman coast, where there are mountains of dead crabs with orange-red bellies upturned, left on the rocks of the coves after the tide has receded so far that it seems only a dark green stripe somewhere near the horizon.

I shall not begin to recall them here, for recalling them would inevitably lead me to my seven-year-old friend, little Jeanne. (At that time in Trouville I was eight and little Jeanne knew me only in my bathing costume. Once I met her, not in the morning — when, side by side, we caught little lobsters and shrimps every day — but later, respectably dressed, and little Jeanne passed me by, without recognizing in this neat boy the little friend with whom she splashed through pools in the mornings.)

Recalling little Jeanne would lead me to recall the big waves. The colossal and impetuous waves of the Atlantic, with which the ocean in a wide sweep advances, stroke after stroke, during the incoming tide, with shattering rollers

---

he was to develop, in practice, his theory of color cinematography. But, of course, the film was never even begun. His first essay, "Pushkin and Cinema — A Preface," was written in 1939 and is published in Volume II of the Russian edition of his works. In his essay "Montage," in the same volume, is a section called "Pushkin — Film Editor."

2. *Znamya* (*Banner*) was a monthly literary journal published in Leningrad.

3. M. Kalinin (1875–1946) was president of the USSR from 1923 to 1946.

sweeping up the emptying beach. Woe to anyone who lingers, loiters, daydreams, or simply does not notice the movement of the waters!

One moment, there is the smooth surface of the beach, with little pools of warm water with starfish or a family of shrimps. Suddenly arises a fathom of sinister green, in a blue tide of salt waters.

A little white figure in a light, knitted bathing costume is paddling among the shrimps. The ocean's treacherous bluish-green rollers are already creeping round him in a wide curve. A few more seconds and the gray-haired crests, the rearing ridges of ocean waves, will be roaring down on each other . . .

And had it not been for someone's strong hands at the last moment; had it not been for the speed of their muscular legs in making off to the safety of the distant strip of sand that the tide could not reach, little Jeanne would not have met her little friend anymore, and that once white little boy would not be sitting here now and would not be aimlessly scribbling in pencil on a packet of white sheets of paper, swallowed up in a flood of memories . . .

Tynyanov died. The letter was never sent.

The letter was about my wish to present Pushkin's life in color cinema. Pushkin, Pushkin the lover, in Tynyanov's conception, which was developed in *A Nameless Love*. The captivating story of the poet's secret love for the wife of Karamzin. In the early part of the novel, the passion is stated far more sharply and inspiringly than in the last part, where it seems that the hand is hurrying to write the last pages, afraid that it will not manage to finish them.

Apart from this, my letter was full of ideas about the color resolution of the film.

The letter was a rough draft. And that gives me the right to rework it, in the direction of a more detailed setting out of the color conception of the film, resolvable in color.

However, it seems that I have wrecked my way of writing for all time. The two introductory lines to what became, instead of the second article, "The Keys of Happiness," an independent, verbose "page of recollections," have themselves grown into a whole memoir fragment.

And their sole purpose was to serve as an introductory note, explaining the derivation of the following pages.

Begun as "a couple of words" of introduction to "the second letter on color," they have become anything you please, except what they were intended to be, and now instead of an *Anhang*[4] to "Nonindifferent Nature," they lie in a heap of *freie Einfalle*,[5] presumptuously called "Memoirs"!

They are, though, more than anything else, about the associations, leading images, impressions, and recollections of previous works that I went through to find a resolution to the scenes of the feast in *Ivan the Terrible*.

---

4. A supplement.

5. A free association of ideas.

Color (2)

I DON'T KNOW WHETHER you call everything that led me to my first work on color luck or even a lucky accident. But the chain of accidents is indisputable, and it was this chain which led to the work itself. Indeed, the combination of the unexpected and accidental determined the solution of the actual problems of color.

Color in cinematography has occupied me for so long that I consider the whole stage of my work in black-gray-white cinema to be work in the field of color and, in the field of color, limited to a spectrum of single-tone values. Work on color itself has also occupied me for quite a long time, though only, it is true, from that time when it seemed that the technical problem had been finally solved.

There are different sorts of pioneers. Some engage in the development and elaboration of technical resources and engage in work to perfect the very latest technical phenomena. There were such enthusiasts for sound at a time when sound did not yet allow an independence from the picture and a combination at will with the picture. There were such enthusiasts for mastering color when it demanded an unparalleled quantity of light, an optic cube, and three films of different tones, running through a single projector, in order to catch on the screen, in a sort of crude, multihued confetti, colors without nuances, tones without semitones, and the colors of reality distorted beyond recognition.

I am not this type of pioneer in any way. I am not attracted by research having, as a starting point, the perfection of reproducing a soprano, which is at first in no way distinguishable in sound cinema from a hoarse tenor. For I consider that, before the beginning of real research, there must be an assurance that a clear recording of a piano and an unexceptionable sound of a violin is technically possible from the screen. Only from this moment can real research into the field of sound-visual counterpoint begin. Without this, nothing can be accomplished in the aesthetics of audiovisual cinematography.

It is the same with color.

My first almost incoherent project for a colored film (*Giordano Bruno*),[1] and the first color film to be conceived in detail (*Pushkin*), were laid on the shelf as soon as it became clear that the necessary techniques were still at such an infantile stage that not a single resolution of the problem of form could be guaranteed.

The next theme, *Ivan the Terrible*, turned out to be one in which the largest part of its first two-thirds was in a color scale achievable by black and white cinematography: traditional white, gray, and black with the richest variety of textures, from the metallic gleam of brocade of various qualities and appearances, through material and cloth, to the soft play of furs, including the whole gamut of shades of furry surfaces from sable and fox to wolf and bear, brown in the coats and white in the carpets and counterparts.

I saw the first examples of colored cinematography a very long time ago.

These were the hand-tinted Méliès fairy scenes: an underwater kingdom, where bright yellow warriors in armor hid in the jaws of greenish whales; where blue and pink enchantresses were born from the sea foam.

Soon after this, films in natural colors appeared.

I no longer remember by what system and what technique, but they began to be shown at one cinema in Riga from about 1910 or 1912. This cinema in Werman Park had the resounding name of Kino-Kultura, which in no way prevented it from showing, after these colored "scientific shorts," week after week, serial after serial of *Fantomas* and *Vampires*.

The color subjects were short, with an overall pinkish tinge, and showed the yachts' white sails skimming across the blue sea, various fruits and flowers in various colors being selected by girls who had fiery red or straw-yellow hair, and the spring tilling of the fields.

My own first steps in using color were the well-known, hand-tinted red flag in *Potemkin*, and the lesser-known montage of short pieces of film, sharply and variously dyed, in the scenes around the milk separator and the bull's wedding in the film *The General Line*.

The actual question of production in color arose in 1939, in connection with the fact that work on the film *Ferghana Canal* had fallen through and (as I then put it) "Tamerlaine had been excised" from me.

I had conceived of the film about the Ferghana Canal as a triptych about the struggle for water: blossoming Central Asia with a wonderful irrigation system in antiquity. Then the power of man over water is lost in Tamerlaine's fratricidal massacres and campaigns. The desert sands gain the upper hand.

---

1. In 1939–1940, Eisenstein proposed a film on Giordano Bruno (1548?–1600), the Roman philosopher who had a great influence on Spinoza, Leibnitz, Hegel, and others. Bruno, who championed Copernican cosmology, was forced to leave the Dominican order and was eventually burned at the stake by the Inquisition. The film never went beyond the proposal stage.

The poverty of the sandy wastes under tsarism. A fight over an extra drink of water from the irrigation ditch, in the place where there had once been the most complete irrigation system in the world. And, finally, the miracle of the first collective exploit, the building by Uzbekistan's collective farmers of the Ferghana Canal, bringing wealth and prosperity to Socialist Central Asia on an unprecedented scale.

For reasons unknown to me, the filming of the first part of the triptych fell through on the very eve work was to start. Then the whole composition hung helplessly in the balance, and soon the entire work fell through.

I began the staging of *Walküre* in the Bolshoi Theater.[2] I dedicated the whole of the last scene, "The Magic Fire," to research in combining elements of Wagner's score with changing tinted lights on stage. Notwithstanding the extremely limited technical resources and very imperfect color and lighting equipment on the Bolshoi stage, and the extremely poor possibilities for varying the light's palette of the play of fire, the color interpretation of "Wotan's Farewell" was resolved most convincingly. It is from this, perhaps, because of the quite accidental cancellation of the shooting of the Ferghana film, that there began a chain of regular accidents which led me to practical work on color.

Children ask: "Why a lamp?"

"So that one can ask in the same way: "Why *Walküre?*"

"Because 'because' begins with a *b*." It is difficult to give a more meaningful answer, initially.

Walküre, probably the most unexpected and instant decision in my whole career, was in answer to a telephone call from Williams and Samosud,[3] who for some reason had decided to tempt me with this production.[4]

Their temptation was completely successful. I could not, of course, resist "The Ride of the Valkyries." But this seemingly accidental and incidental work now entered with an iron necessity into the resolution of the sound-visual question, which had had me in its grip since the practical sound-visual work on *Alexander Nevsky*. It was that work which crowned what the composer Meisel and I had done long ago in musical experimentation for *Potemkin*. (If you do not count the still earlier experiments in the same direction in the Proletcult Theater.)

However that may be, I received almost simultaneously with my work on Wagner a proposition to engage in serious work on color in color cinema. Of course, as one should have expected, the proposed theme was put forward

---

2. Eisenstein was asked to produce *Die Walküre* at the Bolshoi as part of Stalin's concessions to Germany during the period of the Nonaggression Pact, but the production was taken off the stage when Germany attacked the Soviet Union on November 21, 1940. It has never been revived.

3. Peter V. Williams (1902–1947), leading designer of the Bolshoi Theater, was an Honored Artist of the RSFSR. Samuel A. Samosud (1884–1964), artistic director of the Bolshoi from 1936 to 1943, was a People's Artist of the USSR.

4. Eisenstein, of course, was fully aware of the reason and could not say no. (H.M.)

because of its natural "colorfulness." The thematic material most colorful (and at the same time most ideologically interesting and acceptable to the "leadership") was described in the most glowing colors (!) as the theme of — Giordano Bruno.

Italy, you know . . .

Renaissance costumes . . .

Fires . . .

Two other themes came with this one at the same time. One turned up by itself and was Colonel Lawrence[5] and the Muslim revolt in Asia . . .

The figure of Lawrence as a psychological problem could not fail to excite any reader who knew not only *Revolt in the Desert,* but also the dreadful inner confession of nihilism, of spiritual bankruptcy, and Dostoyevskian despair with which the story of Lawrence's military adventures is permeated in the fuller account, his *Seven Pillars of Wisdom.* It is true that color here plays, for the time being, only the minor role of the green banner of the Prophet and the green turbans of the chieftains. And then how wonderfully Lawrence describes the old woman from one of the Arab tribes, who, never before having seen blue eyes, asked the blue-eyed intelligence officer if it was the sky shining through his eye sockets. The green turban, though, is not so much from the colonel's works as from an English novel on a similar theme. Indeed, for a greater freedom in handling the material, the film would have to be not too factually biographical, and the scene of the action would have to be different, the no less popular base of operations for the secretive colonel — Iran.

The other theme was history again.

They unfailingly sought the colorful past on the borders of the Middle Ages and the Renaissance. This theme, still on the basis of the colorfulness of the costumes, was brought to me, like a slipper in the mouth of a fox terrier, by one of the readers for the Committee for Cinema Affairs.

The theme was . . . the plague.[6]

Why the plague?

Why not cholera? Why not smallpox or typhus?

However, this theme captivated me, though only briefly, not for its colorfulness, but for quite a different reason: a single graphic sketch. Because this presented an opportunity to base the film on the way in which, as the plague spread, that "colorfulness" so dear to the heart of the leadership was steadily devoured by black . . .

From another point of view, with other material, this same theme of the devouring of the sensual (and brightly colored!) wealth of life by mortifying

---

5. Eisenstein planned, in 1940, to make a film from a scenario by L. R. Sheinin about Lawrence of Arabia.

6. In the Eisenstein archives in Moscow is a note to the Committee for Cinema Affairs, written in 1940, proposing a film called *Battle with the Plague.* It was never made.

petrification excited me. This was the way in which I resolved the central part of the drama about gold, in the projected film (and finished scenario) of Blaise Cendrars's novel *Sutter's Gold*.

I originally wanted to make this fictionalized biography of Captain Sutter at the Paramount studios in America. I wanted to express the disastrous role of the gold strike on Sutter's California lands, the destruction and ruin of his fertile estates and of him, through the vivid impression made on me by the California gold dredgers still at work today.

Those mountains of waste being disgorged today, as in Sutter's day, from the half-devastated gold fields lie over the fertile green of the surrounding fields. The blossoming orchards, fields, pastures, and arable land die beneath the gray, soulless layer of stone. The rampart of stone moves implacably, ceaselessly, unrestrainably, over the green, pitilessly crushing beneath it the living shoots of life to ratify the hunger for gold.

The Gold Rush of 1849 lured to California hundreds of thousands of those seeking the precious metal that so greatly exceeds in worth the labor spent on it. It is difficult to force oneself to join in experiencing this madness of people seized by gold fever. Yet by means of a small sample that I myself have experienced, I can easily imagine what a typhoon, what a hurricane, what a madness of passion, this elemental pursuit of gold must have been.

Once, considerably later, in the Kabardino-Balkarian Republic, I happened to be in a place in the mountains where gold had just been discovered.[7]

A narrow gorge.

A little stream.

A few primitive, rickety gold-washing machines.

My companion and guide (as you may imagine, he was one of the top comrades in the republic's NKVD!) stooped down and scooped up a few handfuls of muddy soil.

The clod of earth was laid in a tin basin.

The earth was carefully washed away in the rhythm of the rocking basin.

And suddenly one could see a few grains at the bottom.

Gold!

It seemed that the earth shook beneath your feet, that it was about to open its bowels and exude suddenly through its muddy brown surface, overgrown with clumps of turf, millions of scarcely visible grains of gold dust — gold!

It is easy to imagine people flinging themselves upon this earth, people trying to embrace it, drunk with this contact with wealth scattered beneath the soles of their boots; people ready to kill the owner of feet that dared to tread on this sea of gold, concealed beneath the dull topsoil; people ready to wash away

---

7. In September 1933, Eisenstein went to Kabardino-Balkaria for a month. While there, he actively participated in a conference on architecture and presented a project for remodeling the republic's capital, Nalchik.

this immoral and lasciviously rich earth with the hot blood of any competitor who dared encroach on the invisible and scattered grains of gold . . .

The feet of thousands of such madmen trample Sutter's land, thousands of hands rip it up and turn it over; the teeth of thousands of people, who have come running from all corners of the world, are ready to fasten on each other's gullets, to get any little scrap of land bearing in its bowels that strange harvest of pale yellow metal.

Captain Sutter's blossoming paradise of California orchards and fields is trampled underfoot and crushed by dirty hordes greedy for gold.

And Sutter is ruined . . .

But the proud old man launches thousands of lawsuits against the invading horde — thousands of actions in answer to the willful trespass and occupation of his land.

It was in California that the town of San Francisco had grown in a few years from a little mission named after St. Francis.

It had grown unexpectedly and in a strange way.

The bay had become choked with a herringlike mass of barges and ships, clustering at any possible mooring.

The ships had dropped anchor and remained at anchor forever.

The spaces between the ships became crisscrossed with gangways and later filled in with sand.

Shacks arose on the decks.

Single story. Then two. Three.

The holds became cellars.

The decks joined together into streets and side streets.

The invasion of decks and holds covered the surface of the bay as the mountains of waste covered the green meadows, as the mysteriously whispering sand covers the once green paradise (now a Central Asian salt marsh).

Suddenly one man, vigorous and decisive, throws out a challenge to this town of boats and barges which is clutching tenaciously, like an octopus, on to the shore and surrounding hills in a rash of settlements.

And now a new flock descends on California in a cloud. This time a black flock.

A lawyer's costume in the 1850s consisted of a long frock coat and a tall top hat, shaggy, like those we know from portraits of Lincoln and his fellows in the legal profession.

Thousands of black frock coats and top hats, like flocks of crows and ruffled black steppe eagles, descend on San Francisco, for an unprecedented struggle is impending — the struggle of a whole town against one man.

And the third flock, black and awful, silhouetted against the yardarms and lamps, in the coastal fog and blackness of the California night, spreads out over Captain Sutter's once blossoming and fruitful land in a third layer.

The black flock — real . . . magnetic.

Where, how, and in what circumstances today, or certainly before the war, could one see dozens and even hundreds of black top hats, wandering among old, low buildings, disappearing into the twilight, and suddenly outlined in the yellow rays of a candle falling on them through little barred windows? Can there really be such a place, not just in Daumier's lithographs, but in real life, where you can see such a fantastic sight?

There is. Indeed, there is.

You will not see beards or whiskers under the top hats, it is true. Perhaps just some fluff on an upper lip, because the wearers are not overburdened in years. The eldest of them is probably not yet twenty. Still, the mysterious twilight conceals the age in these figures' overall silhouette, and the figures of the younger, really juvenile, top hat wearers in these back streets, and the mysterious tricks of the light, deepen the fantasy still further, for they seem to be gnomes who have escaped from Hoffmann's works, or the strange inhabitants of Edgar Poe's dreadful stories.

And in fact they are really just kids.

Not kids, though, but boys, the sons of privileged English families who have the means to send their children to study at Eton.

I did not mention neighboring Windsor Castle, and round, white wing collars and striped trousers, for you would long ago have guessed who and what the subject was!

Having looked over Windsor Castle, the repository of Leonardo's notebooks and Holbein's drawings, my friend Professor Isaacs (with red side whiskers and bowler, and the ever-present umbrella in his hand) took me to visit neighboring Eton. The first link in the system of English upbringing, which, by its regimen, discipline, and spirit, molds frail, degenerate, overfed, and spoilt boys into stern, soulless, and cruel gentlemen, who do not proclaim that they are the masters of the world, as do the less prudent Germans, but who firmly believe that they are, and who act implacably and persistently for the glory of Britannia, Queen of the Seas.

In the cold rooms of Oxford and Cambridge, clad in Tudor and pre-Tudor stonework, in the refectories, the tops of whose walls are lost in the gloom, in the lofty church naves, but also in the fine laboratories for physics, chemistry, and electromagnetism, that type of gentleman is produced whose first blueprint is to be found in the paradoxical silhouette of the Eton boy in his top hat. And in the third link in his career, which leads almost unfailingly from Eton via Oxford or Cambridge to Parliament, the now fully formed gentleman exhibits to the world the extraordinary spectacle of the immutability of British politics of the Cadogans,[8] quite independent of whether Labour or Tory has been placed at the helm of power by the chance play of the keys of luck at the ballot boxes . . .

An avalanche of black, that devouring color, has sat in the circle of my

---

8. The Cadogan family has contributed statesmen to Britain for generations.

favorite conceptions for a very long time. From time to time it is fed by new interlacing impressions: the trip to Windsor, a page from Cendrars's novel, the mountains of waste near Sacramento, and even by the flock of black razorbill vultures in Mexico, circling above the carcasses of horses that have fallen in the bullring and been dragged out into the back yard.

Black vultures sit sedately on the fence surrounding the bullring's back yard in Mérida, the capital of Yucatán.

They wait . . .

However, Giordano Bruno, Lawrence, and the plague quickly make way for another candidate on the agenda of my projected works.

This hero is almost mathematically calculated.

This was how, I think, by the interference in the orbits of other heavenly bodies, the planet Uranus was calculated long before it was seen with the eye aided by a powerful telescope.

But what did they begin to make with the coming of sound in the cinema?

Biographies of musicians.

And what will they make with the coming of color?

Biographies of painters.

What should not be made with the coming of sound and color in cinema?

Neither the one nor the other!

What should be made?

Not the first nor the second.

A third!

Not the biography of a painter, not the biography of a musician, but the biography of . . . a poet!

So the idea of making a film about Pushkin was born.

I intend to dedicate the third letter on color to other and, of course, basic and decisive motives of my project. "The Unsent Letter" will tell, in a concrete example, how I see the composition, complete in conception, of an integral color film. Here I shall say only that, for the time being, Pushkin shares the fate of the plague, Bruno, and Lawrence. It lies in the archive section devoted to "Projects."

From the field of practical color work comes news that color film is still not ready. The technical problems of color are still unsolved. Color is not yet an obedient tool in the hands of the craftsman or researcher, but a menacing and ferocious tyrant. It not only burns the actors' costumes and melts their make-up in the floods of the many powerful light units; it also is a scoundrel, hardening the very heart of the color conception; it is a boor, trampling underfoot the nuances of color perception; it is a lazy good-for-nothing, unable in any measure to keep up with concepts of color, with color fantasy, with the flight of color imagination.

Then came *Ivan*.

Then came war.

And then, later, victory.

And a flood of color abomination came gushing from defeated Germany's cinematography.

But double-emulsion color film came too.

And now begins a new chain of accidents, catching up, after the war, the chain of prewar plans regarding color.

Of course, the actual longing for color grows directly from work on sound-visual counterpoint. For only color, color, and again color, is fully able to solve the problem of measuring and reducing sound values to a common unit of sound.

Once, enthusiastically greeting the coming of sound to cinema, I wrote most condescendingly about color and three-dimensional cinema as being unable to contribute anything fundamentally new in the field of cinematographic form. (Pudovkin and Alexandrov signed the declaration "On Sound Cinema" together with me.[9])

There was then merely an anticipation of the possibilities of audiovisual counterpoint in cinema, and the picture at that time had only just begun to strain toward a development into sound. Now, the practice of audiovisual cinematography is a concrete contribution to the development of cinema. And sound, striving to be realized in visual form, struggles powerfully in the black and white limitation, which holds back its urge to a complete fusion with the picture. The higher forms of organic affinity of the melodic pattern of music and of tonal construction of the system of succeeding color shots are possible only with the coming of color to cinema.

However, from general phrases down to business; from a program to action; from proclamations to practice. From tirades to the history of the sad and funny, depressing and gratifying, exciting and gladdening, but often distressing ups and downs on the paths of actual color work on two reels in the second part of *Ivan the Terrible*!

Is there anything here that is not accidental?

There is the fact that Sergei Prokofiev left Alma-Ata before I did. And it was impossible to shoot the feast in *Ivan the Terrible* and the dance of the *oprichniki* without having the music already composed and recorded. That fact forced us to move the shooting of the feast and dance to Moscow. More than that, Prokofiev was unwell and, what with the necessity of finishing *War and Peace* and *Cinderella,* did not find time that summer to give me the necessary score.

Autumn was approaching; winter was not far off. The studio had been standing ready since the summer, but the score was held up.

At that time, a conference on color was held at the Cinema Club in Moscow.

There is no more dismal spectacle than arguments and discussion about something that no one has yet actually held in his hands. The emptiness of the discussion was irritating, but the free supplement to it made one still more

---

9. The declaration can be found in *Film Form.*

angry. It was a showing of examples of color work by the Americans, Germans, and those few brave souls who attempted, by forcing the Soviet prewar double- and triple-emulsion system to show off, to boast that we too could show on the screen "the wretched wealth of finery" and "the false blush of a cheek."

Anger is a marvelous creative stimulus. But suddenly, among all this imported banality of chintz balls, a documentary film appeared on the screen. A documentary shot in color: *The Potsdam Conference*. This film's color is awful in parts. In some places the faces are brick-colored, in others, violet. Green is the color of an onion omelette or the color of mold on old copper coins. Two thirds of the spectrum are impossible. No! Perhaps, a half. But here on the screen is a series of the inner apartments of Cecilienhof(?);[10] and among them certain rooms.

A blinding red carpet covers the whole area of the screen.

A row of white chairs with red upholstery cuts across at a slant.

Red exists!

Moreover, the Chinese Pavilion at Sans Souci is shown in a few shots.

Once, when looking over Potsdam, I saw it, along with other relics of Friedrich II's reign. The gilt Chinese figures also come across successfully. What is more, the reflections on them of the surrounding green and white marble steps are also successful.

There is red.

And gold works.

Black, of course.

If one can assume that light blue might work . . . one might perhaps risk trying it.

The studio for Ivan the Terrible's feast has been ready since summer. The feast must burst explosively between the dark scene of the plot against the tsar and the gloomy scene of the attempt to kill him. Why not have this explosion . . . in color?

Color will enter in an explosive dance of colors, and will fade toward the end of the feast, imperceptibly flowing into black and white photography . . . into the tone of the tragic, accidental death of Prince Vladimir Andreyevich at the hands of the murderer, sent by his mother to kill the tsar.

How much this would be in my style and to my taste!

First, in the previous color episode let the black of the cassocks flow onto the gold of the *oprichniki*'s caftans,

the *oprichniki* (black in their caftans) onto Vladimir (golden in his regalia),

then, like a black flood, the whole mass of black *oprichniki* inundates the interior of the cathedral, in which Vladimir, helpless, pathetic, and yet calling out for their pity, gulps with a scarcely audible moan in the dark night of the cathedral's womb,

among the black figures and their still blacker shadows . . .

---

10. The query in the text is Eisenstein's own.

Unity

IF I WERE A DETACHED researcher, I should say of myself: it seems as if this author is obsessed once and for all with a single idea, a single theme, a single subject.

I would say that everything that he has conceived and done, not only within particular films but throughout all his projects and films, is always and everywhere one and the same.

I would note that the author uses different eras (the thirteenth, sixteenth, and twentieth centuries), different countries and peoples (Russia, Mexico, Uzbekistan, America), different social movements and processes within the upheavals of particular social forms, almost unfailingly as the changing masks of one and the same face. That this face is the embodiment of the ultimate idea of the achievement of unity.

In Russian revolutionary and socialist material this problem of unity is national-patriotic (*Alexander Nevsky*), state (*Ivan the Terrible*), mass collective (*Battleship Potemkin*), socialist-economic (the collective farm theme of *The Old and the New*), communist (*Ferghana Canal*). On foreign soil such unity is either the same theme, modified in corresponding national aspects, or the shady and, without exception, tragically hued reverse side of the same theme, setting off the positive theme of the whole opus just as, for example, the basic bright patriotic theme of *Nevsky* is set off by the gloomy episodes of the Germans' reprisals at Pskov, which stood for the unity of Russia.

Such are the tragedies of individualism, planned during our Western tour, *An American Tragedy*, *Sutter's Gold* (the paradise of primitive patriarchal California, destroyed by the curse of gold — exactly in the moral and ethical system of General Sutter himself, the opponent of gold), *Black Majesty* (about the Haitian hero of the revolutionary liberation struggles of the Haitian slaves against the French colonialists, about the fellow fighter of Toussaint L'Ouverture, who became the Haitian emperor, Henri Christophe, and who fell because of his individualistic alienation from his people).

Ferghana Canal is again a hymn to collectivist unification in Socialist work, which alone is able to constrain the forces of nature, water, and sand (which were given free rein by the human carnage of Tamerlaine's Central Asian warriors, and with the fall of whose state the desert's triumph began), and to overthrow nature's enslaving yoke, under which the peoples of Asia languished, in addition to their enslavement by tsarist Russia.

Finally, *Que Viva Mexico!*, this history of the change of cultures, presented not vertically (in years and centuries), but horizontally (as the geographical coexistence of the most diverse stages of culture), for which Mexico is so amazing, in that it has a province (Tehuantepec) that has a matriarchal society next to provinces that almost achieved Communism in the revolution of the first decade of this century (Yucatán, Zapata's program, etc.). And, as a central episode, it had ideas of national unification: historically, in the joint entry into Mexico's capital of the united forces of Pancho Villa the northerner and Emiliano Zapata the southerner; and in terms of subject, the figure of the Mexican woman moving, with the same care for her man, from group to group of the Mexican troops, all fighting each other, torn with the contradictions of the civil war. She seems physically to personify the image of a single, nationally united Mexico, opposing foreign intriguers who try to dismember the nation and set its separate parts against each other . . .

P.S., P.S., P.S.

OF COURSE, A P.S.!

On November 2 of this year there occurred a tearing of the heart muscles and a hemorrhage. (Infarction.) By some inexplicable, foolish, and pointless wonder I remained alive.

By all the laws of science I should have died.

But for some reason I survived.

Therefore, I consider everything that happens to be a postscript to my own biography.

P.S. . . .

And indeed who at the age of forty-eight had to read this about himself: *"Un des plus fameux metteurs en scène de son temps . . ."*[1]

The monthly publication of the *Institute des Hautes Etudes Cinématographique*, Paris, 1946, in the section "Critique des Critiques" concerning *Ivan the Terrible*. Or "La Revue du Cinéma," October 1, 1946:

". . . La présentation d'un nouveau film d'Eisenstein suscité le même étonnement que ferait nai la création d'une nouvelle pièce de Corneille. On c'est tout appliqué a donner au cinéma une histoire qu'a force de traiter les metteurs en scène de classiques il semble qu'ils soient d'un autre age . . .

"On pardonnerait volontiers Eisenstein d'être encore en vie s'il s'était content de refaire Potemkine *ou* la ligne Générale. *Mais* Ivan le Terrible *vient bouleverser toutes les idées saines et simples que la critique avait facilement dégagés de l'étude des grandes auteurs du muet . . ."*[2]

I assume that they would have begun to write about me in this manner, at best, when I was seventy, and figured that I simply would not live that long!

And here it is when I'm forty-eight . . . P.S., P.S., P.S. . . .

---

1. "One of the greatest directors of his time."

2. "The appearance of any film by Eisenstein arouses as much amazement as would a new play by Corneille. There have been so many attempts to give the cinema a history that it has begun to seem as if the directors of the classical cinema lived in another age . . ."

"Eisenstein would be willingly forgiven for still living, even if he remained content with repetitions of *Potemkin* and *General Line*. But *Ivan the Terrible* upsets all the sound and simple ideas that criticism has elicited from studying the great masters of silent cinema . . ."

Chronology of Eisenstein's Life and Works

1898

January 10. A son, Sergei, is born to Mikhail Osipovich Eisenstein, a civil engineer and architect, and his wife, Yulia Ivanovna (*née* Konetsky), in the city of Riga.

1906

In Paris, Eisenstein sees his first film.

1908

Autumn. Eisenstein enters the first-year class of the Riga Municipal High School.

1912

Eisenstein attends a performance of *Princess Turandot* at the K. N. Nezlobin Theater. In later years he considered this performance to have been decisive in his choice of profession.

1915

May 2. Eisenstein receives his certificate of graduation from the Riga Municipal High School.

May 30. Arrives in Petrograd to enter the Institute for Civil Engineers.

September. Eisenstein is admitted to the first-year class of the institute.

1917

February–March. Eisenstein becomes a member of the city's militia in the Narva section of the First Precinct. Passes examinations for the second year at the institute.

Spring. Is called up for military service and enrolls in the School for Ensigns of the Army Corps of Engineers. The corps is sent to the front in August.

Summer–Autumn. Eisenstein publishes his first caricature, "The Militia Introduces Order," in the *St. Petersburg Gazette;* submits to the periodical *Ogoniok* a caricature of

Kerensky; and makes the first tentative sketches for scenery, costumes, and make-up for Italian masked comedies.

1918

January. After the disbanding of the School for Ensigns of the Army Corps of Engineers, Eisenstein returns to the Institute for Civil Engineers.

March 18. Volunteers into the ranks of the Red Army and is made a technician in the Second Army Corps of Engineers of the Petrograd District (subsequently the Eighteenth Army Corps of Engineers).

September 20. Leaves Petrograd for the Northeastern Front with a squadron of the Eighteenth Army Corps of Engineers.

September 24. The squadron arrives at Vozhega, Vologda District. Eisenstein joins the Sixth Regular Army in the Third Division of the Second Army Corps of Engineers.

No definite dates. Eisenstein makes sketches for the scenery of Mayakovsky's *Mystery Bouffe.*

1919

January–February. Eisenstein takes an active part in the productions of the Communist Club of Vozhega as director, stage designer, and actor.

March 6. Moves from Vozhega to Dvinsk.

June 22. Eisenstein is transferred to the First Division of the Eighteenth Army Corps of Engineers, with the rank of technician.

June. During his travels, Eisenstein occupies himself with developing the principles of theatrical presentation, making sketches for scenery and costumes for medieval miracle plays and Shakespearean plays, and reading theatrical literature.

July 1. Eisenstein arrives at Kholm, Pskov Province.

August 1. Appointed to the post of junior works superintendent in the First Division of the Eighteenth Army Corps of Engineers.

First half of November. Is transferred to Velikie Luki as assistant to the chief of the Construction Department, Second Army Corps of Engineers.

November–December. At Velikie Luki, Eisenstein takes an active part in the theatrical activities of the local cultural-educational club, and makes the acquaintance of the painter and all-around man of the theater, K. S. Eliseyev.

1920

January. Eisenstein works on designs of scenery and costumes for the productions of *The Twin* by A. T. Averchenko, *The Looking Glass* by F. M. Sluchainy, and *Marat* by A. Amnuel.

February 9. Amateur performances of *The Twin, The Looking Glass,* and Gogol's *The Lawsuit,* produced by Eisenstein, are presented at the Velikie Luki Garrison Club by the Eighteenth Army Corps of Engineers. In *The Twin,* Eisenstein also participates as actor, playing the role of a man with eyeglasses.

Second half of February. Eisenstein organizes a drama studio at the Velikie Luki Garrison Club and becomes the permanent director of the ensemble.

March–May. Prepares sketches for scenery and costumes for the following plays: *The Fourteenth of July* by Romain Rolland, *Georges Dandin* by Molière, *The Good Hope* by G. Heijermans, and others.

May 25. Travels from Velikie Luki to Polotsk in connection with his assignment to the Army Engineers.

June 27. At Polotsk, Eisenstein is transferred to the Theater Department of the Political Section of the Western Front.

July 1. Leaves Polotsk for Mogilev, where he tries to establish a model theater for the front.

July 11. Arrives at Smolensk, where he assumes the post of scene designer in the Theater Department of the Political Section of the Western Front.

August 4. Eisenstein moves to Minsk. Is the scene designer for the theatrical ensembles at the front. In addition to his principal duties, he is engaged, along with Eliseyev, in the task of decorating agit-prop trains.

September 27. Arrives in Moscow following demobilization and is assigned to the General Staff Academy to study Japanese.

October 8. Enrolls as a student of the eastern branch of the General Staff Academy.

October 20. Is appointed to the post of director of the Scene-Design Section of the First Proletcult Workers' Theater.

October 23. Begins work on the scenery, costumes, and make-up for the production of *The Mexican,* based on Jack London's story.

November 8. Is appointed to the post of director of the Art Section of the First Proletcult Workers' Theater.

End of November. Leaves the General Staff Academy.

December. In addition to his duties at the First Proletcult Workers' Theater, Eisenstein occupies the post of director of the Scene-Design Section of the Central Arena under the Proletcult Central Committee, and teaches (later performs the duties of administrator) in the Proletcult stage-directing workshops. (Among Eisenstein's students are M. M. Shtraukh, G. V. Alexandrov, and J. S. Glizer.)

1921

April 13. Eisenstein is confirmed as a member of the theatrical collegium of Proletcult's Central Arena.

April 29. Eisenstein, under the supervision of V. V. Tikhonovich, begins a director's analysis of L. N. Andreyev's play *King Hunger* and undertakes the preparation of designs for scenery, costumes, and make-up.

May 3 and 18. A performance for the Moscow art world, and the première of *The Mexican,* in a production by V. S. Smyshlayev and Eisenstein, takes place at the First Proletcult Workers' Theater.

August. Eisenstein begins teaching a course on the art of the theater, given for the Red Army men of the Kremlin garrison.

September 15. Eisenstein enrolls as a student at the State Higher Directors' Workshops, under the direction of V. E. Meyerhold.

November 15. Eisenstein begins work on the play *Enough Simplicity in Every Wise Man*, based on the play of A. N. Ostrovsky, as revised by S. M. Tretiakov, in a production by the First Proletcult Workers' Theater.

November–December. Eisenstein, together with S. I. Yutkevich, works on the production of two plays: Shakespeare's *Macbeth*, and *The Good Treatment of Horses* by B. Z. Mass.

1922

January 5. Première of the slapstick comedy *The Good Treatment of Horses* at N. M. Foregger's theater workshop, designed by Eisenstein and S. I. Yutkevich and produced by Foregger.

January. Eisenstein begins work at Meyerhold's Theater Workshops on designs for scenery and costumes for George Bernard Shaw's *Heartbreak House.*

April 25. Première of the production of *Macbeth* at the Central Educational Theater of TEO, Glavlitprosvet (Chief Literary Educational Organization), designed by Eisenstein and S. I. Yutkevich and produced by V. V. Tikhonovich.

First half of June. Eisenstein is director of Proletcult's TEO.

Autumn. Leaves Meyerhold's Theater Workshops. Engaged as director of the Moscow Proletcult traveling troupe.

November 24. Première of Sukhovo-Kobylin's *The Death of Tarelkin*, produced by Meyerhold at the State Institute of Theatrical Arts. Eisenstein is assistant director.

1923

March. Eisenstein makes his first film, *Glumov's Diary.* As a special feature, this film was shown with Ostrovsky's play *Enough Simplicity in Every Wise Man.* Subsequently, under the title of *Proletcult's Spring Smiles*, it was included in Dziga Vertov's documentary *Spring Cinema Verité.*

April 2. On a gala night at the Bolshoi Theater, in commemoration of the twenty-fifth anniversary of Meyerhold's stage activity, Eisenstein presents for the first time the fragment *Joffre Prepares for Battle*, from Ostrovsky's play *Enough Simplicity in Every Wise Man.*

April 22 and 26, May 8. First performances of *Enough Simplicity in Every Wise Man* in Eisenstein's production at the First Proletcult Workers' Theater.

May 20. Eisenstein publishes an article entitled "Montage of Attractions" in *LEF*, Moscow.

May 21. First showing of the film *Proletcult's Spring Smiles*, included in Dziga Vertov's *Spring Cinema Verité.*

September–October. Eisenstein is occupied with the production of S. M. Tretiakov's play *Do You Hear, Moscow?* at the First Proletcult Workers' Theater.

November 7. Première of *Do You Hear, Moscow?*

December. Eisenstein begins work on the production of S. M. Tretiakov's play *Gas Masks.*

1924

March 4 and 6. First performances of *Gas Masks* at the Moscow Gas Works.

March 29–31. Eisenstein participates in the re-editing of the film *Doctor Mabuse*, directed by Fritz Lang and distributed in the Soviet Union under the title of *Pozolochennaia gnil (Gilded Decay)*.

June. Eisenstein, together with G. V. Alexandrov, starts work on the scenario of the film *Strike (Stachka)*.

July–October. Work in progress on the scenario and shooting of *Strike* in Moscow and its environs.

November. Editing of *Strike*.

December 4. Eisenstein breaks with Proletcult. (A series of his "open letters" concerning the reasons for his break was published in 1925.)

December. Eisenstein, having completed the work on *Strike*, works on the development of the scenario for the film *Red Cavalry (Konarmiia)*, after transferring his activities to the Moscow branch of Sevzapkino (Northwestern Cinema Organization).

1925

January 21. A discussion of *Strike* takes place at the club of the Moscow plant Krasnaya Kuznitsa (Red Forge).

March 31. A notice appears in the *Cinema Gazette*, stating that Eisenstein will not produce *Red Cavalry* at Sevzapkino and that he is beginning the shooting of a film about the year 1905, at the first Goskinofabrika (State Cinema Studios).

April 28. *Strike* is released to appear on the screen. Its first public showing is at the motion picture theater Kolizei (Coliseum).

April. Eisenstein publishes an article called "The Materialistic Approach to Form," about the film *Strike*.

June 4. On the occasion of the twentieth anniversary of the 1905 Revolution a commission of the Presidium of the Central Committee of the USSR passes a resolution concerning Eisenstein's production of the film *The Year 1905*, based on the scenario of N. F. Agadzhanova-Shutko.

Beginning of July. Eisenstein begins shooting *The Year 1905* in the suburbs of Moscow.

End of July–beginning August. Shooting of *The Year 1905* in Leningrad.

August 11. Eisenstein publishes the article "Method for Producing a Workers' Film."

August 24. Arrives at Odessa for the shooting of *The Year 1905*. Here is crystallized the concept of the film later called *The Battleship Potemkin*.

October 26. The International Exhibition of Decorative Arts in Paris awards Eisenstein the Gold Medal for the film *Strike*.

Beginning November. Shooting at Sebastopol of *Potemkin*.

November 23. Eisenstein returns to Moscow and commences the editing of *Potemkin*.

December 21. First showing of *Potemkin*, at the Bolshoi Theater, at the gala session in commemoration of the twentieth anniversary of the 1905 Revolution.

December 25. The Commission of the Presidium of the Central Committee of the USSR, set up for the commemoration of the 1905 Revolution, accepts the film *Potemkin*.

End of 1925. Eisenstein begins work on the scenario of the film *Jungo*, based on a treatment by S. M. Tretiakov.

1926

January 18. Potemkin is released for the screen.

March 18. Eisenstein and E. K. Tisse arrive in Berlin at the behest of Goskino to learn about the latest development in cinema technique and about the methods employed by German film directors.

April 18–26. Eisenstein and Tisse return to Moscow.

May 10. Eisenstein and Tisse lecture at ARK (Association of Revolutionary Cinematographers) about their trip to Germany.

May. Eisenstein and Alexandrov begin work on the literary scenario of the film *The General Line.*

June 5–20. Eisenstein and Alexandrov work on the director's scenario of *The General Line.*

June 22. Eisenstein publishes an article entitled "Béla Forgets the Scissors," part of his running debate with Béla Balász.

End of June. Eisenstein publishes "Five Epochs," in connection with the production of *The General Line.*

July 7. The Council for Cinema Affairs of Glavpolitprosvet submits a favorable review of the literary scenario for *The General Line.*

July 21. At the Moscow film studios of Sovkino (State Film Organization), Eisenstein meets Mary Pickford and Douglas Fairbanks, who, on behalf of United Artists, invite Eisenstein to come to Hollywood.

September 1. Sovkino proposes to Eisenstein that he begin work on the scenario for a film commemorating the tenth anniversary of the October Revolution.

September 27. Contract is signed with Sovkino for writing the scenario for *The General Line* and for shooting the film from October 1, 1926, to February 1, 1927.

November 7. Eisenstein and Alexandrov begin work on an outline treatment of the film *October.*

November 18–19. Eisenstein leaves for Baku to shoot *The General Line.* En route he does some shooting at Rostov-on-Don.

December. Shooting of *The General Line* in the Mugansk steppes and in the northern Caucasus.

1927

January 16. Eisenstein returns to Moscow and, after an interruption in the work on *The General Line,* starts work on the film treatment and shooting script of *October.*

February 5. The film treatment of *October* is discussed and approved at a meeting of the administration of Sovkino.

March 11. Eisenstein's film group arrives in Leningrad to shoot scenes for *October.*

April 13. First shooting of *October* in Leningrad.

June 14. Beginning of the filming, in Leningrad, of the *October* episode "Attack on the Winter Palace."

September 7. Eisenstein begins editing *October.* The filming in Leningrad is continued by Alexandrov and Tisse.

1928

March 14. October appears on the screen.

March 15–21. Eisenstein participates in the proceedings of the All-Union Party Conference on Problems of Cinema. He drafts an address entitled "To the Party Conference, on Problems of Cinema, from a Group of Film Directors."

May 12. Eisenstein is appointed instructor of a course in directing at the State Technical School for Cinematography (GTK, or Gosvdarstvenny Tekhnikum Kinematografii, later the GIK).

June 20. Resumption of the shooting of *The General Line*, which had been interrupted in connection with the work on *October*.

July 19–20, Eisenstein, Alexandrov, and V. I. Pudovkin publish "The Future of the Sound Film. A Statement."

August 10. Eisenstein publishes an article entitled "The Unexpected Meeting Point" (about the Kabuki theater).

September 14. Stefan Zweig calls on Eisenstein during his visit to the USSR.

October 23. The GTK Instructional and Research Workshop is inaugurated, with Eisenstein as director.

October. Eisenstein publishes an article entitled "I-A-28" ("Intellectual Attraction of the Year 1928").

November. Shooting of *The General Line* completed.

1929

January 12. Eisenstein, in collaboration with Alexandrov, publishes "An Experiment Comprehensible to Millions," an article about *The General Line*.

February 14. The General Line approved at an expanded meeting of Sovkino.

March 4. Eisenstein publishes "Perspectives," an article formulating the theory of "intellectual cinema."

April 18–May. There is additional shooting of *The General Line* in the northern Caucasus and at the Gigant State Farm near Rostov-on-Don.

August 19. Eisenstein, Alexandrov, and Tisse are sent abroad to study the technique of foreign cinematography.

August 25. Eisenstein is in Berlin.

September 3–7. Eisenstein's party attends the Congress of Independent Cinematographers at the castle La Sarraz, in Switzerland, as guests of the congress. Eisenstein delivers a lecture.

September 10, 16, and 17. In Zürich Eisenstein gives a series of lectures entitled "Russian Cinema and My Creative Work." After the third lecture at the Forum cinema theater, in Zürich's working-class district, Eisenstein is forbidden to appear in other Swiss cities.

September 19. Eisenstein broadcasts over the Berlin radio a talk on Soviet films.

September–October. Meets George Grosz and Luigi Pirandello in Berlin.

October 7. The General Line appears on the screens of the Soviet Union.

October 13. Eisenstein delivers a lecture in Hamburg, at the Society of National Film, called "Russian Cinema and My Creative Work."

October 20. Eisenstein makes another appearance in Hamburg, in the city's largest cinema theater, to present a lecture on Soviet cinema.

October. He gives a lecture at the Berlin Psychoanalytical Institute on the problem of human expression.

Early November. Eisenstein visits Belgium.

November 18–19. Eisenstein gives lectures in London on cinematography. He meets George Bernard Shaw.

November 29. Leaves London for Paris.

December 3. Returns to London.

December 7–9. Eisenstein is in Cambridge. On December 8 he lectures at the university on the general problems of the theory of cinema.

December 13. In London, at the Society for Cultural Relations between Great Britain and the USSR, he gives a talk entitled "Film Production in Soviet Russia."

Public showing of the film *The General Line* in Paris, attended by the creators of the film.

December 30. In Antwerp, at the Society for Cultural Relations with Russia, Eisenstein delivers a lecture called "Understanding the Art of Cinema."

1930

January 19. Eisenstein gives a lecture in Amsterdam, at the Niederland–New Russia Society, called "Contemporary Films and Sound Films."

January 26. Meets Albert Einstein in Berlin.

January 29. Arrives in Brussels from Berlin.

January 30. At the university in Brussels, gives a talk called "Intellectual Cinema."

February 3. Leaves Brussels for Paris.

February 17. At the Sorbonne, Eisenstein gives a lecture entitled "The Principles of the New Russian Film."

February–April. In Paris, meets Louis Aragon, Abel Gance, James Joyce, Paul Eluard, and Jean Cocteau.

March 14. Receives notice from the police prefecture in Paris, denying him continuation of his stay in France. A number of left-wing bourgeois newspapers protest the expulsion of Eisenstein.

April 1. His stay in France is extended to April 26.

April 21–30. Negotiations with Paramount concerning an invitation for the Eisenstein party to come to Hollywood.

April 30. Signing of contract with Paramount for Eisenstein's work in Hollywood.

April. Tour of France, accompanied by Léon Moussinac.

May 6. The American consulate in Paris issues a visa to Eisenstein for a visit to the United States.

May 8. Eisenstein and E. K. Tisse leave France for the U.S. on the liner *Europa*.

May 12. Eisenstein and Tisse arrive in New York.

May–June. Eisenstein, with great success, delivers lectures on the general problems of the theory of cinema, and about Soviet cinema, at Columbia, Harvard, University of Chicago, Princeton, Yale, and other universities.

June 16. Eisenstein arrives in Hollywood.

June 18–24. He meets Charlie Chaplin, Upton Sinclair, Theodore Dreiser, and Walt Disney.

June 27. Hollywood's reactionary elements, headed by a Major Pease, demand the expulsion of Eisenstein from the U.S. because he is a Communist.

August 4. Eisenstein delivers a lecture, "Cinema in the Soviet Union," at the University of California.

August 21. Eisenstein gives an address at a banquet in his honor at the Academy of Motion Picture Arts and Sciences, in Hollywood, of which he is elected a member.

September 17. Eisenstein participates, in Hollywood, in a discussion on wide-screen films.

September. In accordance with an agreement with Paramount, Eisenstein, together with G. V. Alexandrov, begins the directorial treatment of the scenario for the film *An American Tragedy*, based on the novel by Theodore Dreiser.

Up to October 22. Participates in the proceedings of the Convention of Sound-Film Technicians in New York.

October 22. Delivers an address, in Hollywood, at a banquet of the Society of Cinema Technicians.

October 23. Paramount breaks the contract with Eisenstein.

Beginning November. Eisenstein's party tours the United States.

November 18. The Department of Labor denies the Eisenstein party further permission to remain in the United States, and requests its immediate departure.

End of November. Eisenstein's party, in agreement with Soyuzkino and the Russian-American Joint Stock Company (Amkino), decides to shoot a film on Mexico. Upton Sinclair undertakes to finance the filming.

December 5. The Eisenstein party crosses the U.S.–Mexican border.

December 11. The Mexican government issues a permit for the shooting of the film *Que Viva Mexico!*

December 14. First filming of a bullfight in Mexico.

1931

January 16. The Eisenstein party flies from Mexico City to Oaxaca, where it films the scene of an earthquake. Within forty-eight hours, this film is shown throughout Mexico.

February–December. The Eisenstein party is engaged in shooting *Que Viva Mexico!* all over Mexico.

1932

First half of February. Eisenstein helps organize an exhibition of the works of D. Siqueiros in Mexico.

February 17. The Eisenstein party leaves Mexico for the USSR via the U.S. The party is detained at the border. Eisenstein requests special permission from Washington for entry into the U.S.

February. Twelve senators, backed by American public opinion, protest the delay in the government's issuing a visa for Eisenstein's admission to the United States, and demand that it be issued.

March 16. The Eisenstein party, having obtained permission to enter the U.S., leaves Mexico by car. Its route is from Laredo to New York, by way of New Orleans and Washington.

Second half of March. Eisenstein delivers a lecture on the theory of cinema and on Soviet cinema at a Negro college and at a Negro Baptist church in New Orleans.

Beginning of April. The Eisenstein party arrives in New York.

After April 7. The Eisenstein party leaves for home aboard the *Europa*.

May 9. The Eisenstein party returns to the USSR.

August–December. Eisenstein works on the scenario for the comedy *MMM*.

September 29. Eisenstein delivers a lecture, "Theater and Cinema in Europe, U.S.A., and Mexico," at the Moscow Theater Workers' Club.

October 1. Eisenstein is confirmed as chairman of GIK's Department of Film Directing.

October 25. Eisenstein leaves for Soviet Armenia and Georgia to deliver a lecture on his trip abroad and for consultations on scenarios.

December. Returns to Moscow.

End of year. Publishes an article entitled "Through Revolution to Art — Through Art to Revolution."

1933

March. Begins work for VGIK (Higher State Institute of Cinematography) on a program of theory and practice of directing.

March. The scenario for the comedy *MMM* is accepted for production by Soyuzfilm (the All-Union Trust for Production of Artistic Films).

May. Eisenstein completes a projected program for VGIK on the theory and practice of directing, and begins work on *Directing*, a book based on his lectures given at the institute.

June. Eisenstein commences work on the scenario for *Moscow*.

July 3. Publishes an article entitled "Moscow Through the Ages" (about the forthcoming film *Moscow*).

July 29. Is confirmed as a director at the Moscow studio of Soyuzfilm.

1934

March 9. Eisenstein publishes "Fascism, Germany Cinema Art, and Real Life. An open letter to Doctor Goebbels, German Minister of Propaganda."

April–July. Eisenstein prepares for the production of N. A. Zarkhi's play *The Second Moscow* for the Theater of Revolution, now the Mayakovsky Theater. (This work is interrupted by the accidental death of Zarkhi.)

May 24. Eisenstein publishes "Eh! Concerning the Purity of Cinema Language."

June. Eisenstein is present at Gorky's meeting with some workers of the Soviet cinema, at which Gorky reads his scenario about homeless waifs.

August 4. At the all-Moscow meeting of writers, Eisenstein is elected a delegate to the First Congress of Soviet Writers.

August 17–September 1. Participates in the proceedings of the First All-Union Congress of Soviet Writers.

September. Publishes "The Average of Three (1924–1929)," an article commemorating the fifteenth anniversary of Soviet cinema.

End of September. Visits Yalta and Odessa to familiarize himself with the work of film studios there.

December 23, 26. Meets Paul Robeson when the latter arrives in the USSR, and gives an introductory address at a concert-soirée at Domkino, the Cinema Workers' Club, Moscow.

1935

January 8. Eisenstein delivers a lecture at the First All-Union Conference of Cinematographic Workers.

January 11. In accordance with a resolution of the Central Committee of the USSR, Eisenstein is awarded the title of Honored Worker of the Arts of the RSFSR.

March 12. Eisenstein meets Mei Lan-fang, the Chinese classic actor.

March–May. Eisenstein is working on the shooting script of the film *Bezhin Meadow,* based on the scenario of A. G. Rzheshevsky.

Beginning of July. Eisenstein arrives at Kharkov for the shooting of *Bezhin Meadow.*

October. Eisenstein, together with I. E. Babel, begins work on the final version of the shooting script of *Bezhin Meadow.*

1936

May 22. Eisenstein participates in a conference of the Central Committee of the Young Communist League concerning children's films.

August 22. Eisenstein resumes shooting *Bezhin Meadow* in Odessa and Yalta, after revising the scenario.

November 11. Eisenstein returns to Moscow.

1937

January 17. Eisenstein is appointed professor of film direction at VGIK.

March 17. By order of the Chief Administration of Cinematography, work on the production of *Bezhin Meadow* is suspended.

April. Eisenstein publishes an article entitled "The Errors of *Bezhin Meadow.*"

August–September. Eisenstein, together with P. A. Pavlenko, begins work on the scenario and composition of the shots for the film *Alexander Nevsky.*

September 26. Eisenstein writes a letter to the Presidium of the First Congress of the Union of Cinema Workers, under the heading "In Lieu of an Address."

December 31. The Chief Administration of Cinematography authorizes the preparation of the shooting script from the *Alexander Nevsky* scenario.

No definite date. Eisenstein publishes "Patriotism — My Theme." (A revised version of the article was published posthumously in 1956.)

1938

February 18. Eisenstein arrives at Novgorod to collect material for *Alexander Nevsky*.

March–May. Works on a study entitled "Montage 1938," an analysis of the laws of montage.

April 29–May 18. Eisenstein is in Pereslavl-Zaleskii to collect historical material, study the surroundings, and select a location for the shooting of *Alexander Nevsky*.

June. Beginning of the shooting of *Alexander Nevsky* at the Moscow film studios and in Pereslavl-Zaleskii.

November 4. The film group of *Alexander Nevsky* is awarded the Red Banner for excellence for completing the filming ahead of schedule.

November 9. Alexander Nevsky is examined by the Committee for Cinematography and approved.

November 25. Première of *Alexander Nevsky*.

November–December. Eisenstein is preparing to produce a new film entitled *Perekop*, based on the scenario of A. A. Fadeyev and L. V. Nikulin.

December 1. Alexander Nevsky is given public distribution.

No definite date. Eisenstein writes "The Film-Novel *We the Russian People*" by V. V. Vishnevsky (published posthumously in 1956).

1939

January–March. Eisenstein is working on the director's scenario of *Perekop* and on an article entitled "The Structure of Things."

February 1. By order of the Presidium of the Supreme Soviet of the USSR, Eisenstein is awarded the Order of Lenin.

February 17. During the presentation of the awards at the Kremlin, Eisenstein delivers an address on behalf of the recipients.

March 23. The Higher Testimonial Commission awards Eisenstein the learned degree of doctor of arts (without his defending his dissertation).

June 8. Eisenstein is elected a delegate to the All-Union Congress of Cinema and Photo Workers.

Middle of June. Eisenstein, in collaboration with E. K. Tisse, begins collecting material for a new film entitled *The Great Ferghana Canal* (scenario by P. A. Pavlenko).

June 23. Eisenstein and Tisse arrive in Tashkent.

Middle of June. Eisenstein returns to Moscow from Central Asia after inspecting the area of the projected canal and familiarizing himself with Kokand, Samarkand, and Bukhara.

July. Eisenstein works on the shooting script for *The Great Ferghana Canal*.

August–middle of October. Takes sample shots of *The Great Ferghana Canal*, in the area of the Ferghana Canal.

End of October. Work on *The Great Ferghana Canal* is interrupted. Eisenstein returns to Moscow.

End of December. Eisenstein produces Wagner's opera *Die Walküre* at the Bolshoi Theater.

No definite date. Eisenstein works on the study of "Pushkin the Film Editor."

1940

January. Eisenstein publishes an article about A. P. Dovzhenko, "The Birth of a Master."

February. Eisenstein delivers a lecture, "Problems of Dramaturgy and Directing of Soviet Historical Films," at a symposium of cinema workers concerned with problems of the historical film.

March 12. Eisenstein begins work on an article entitled "Embodiment of Myth."

March. Eisenstein works on a project for a film about Pushkin.

May 15. Writes the first autobiographical fragment, "A Topic Inexhaustible."

May 28–June 3. Eisenstein prepares a rough draft for the scenario *The Beilis Affair*, based on the play by L. P. Sheinin.

June. Eisenstein publishes an article called "Again on the Structure of Things."

July–August. Eisenstein works on the articles entitled "Vertical Montage," the second part of a study on the laws of montage.

September. Begins work on the literary scenario for the film *Ivan the Terrible*.

October 13. Eisenstein is decorated with an anniversary medal in commemoration of twenty years of Soviet cinematography.

October. Is appointed artistic director of Mosfilm.

November 21. The première of Eisenstein's production of *Die Walküre* at the Bolshoi Theater.

1941

February 1. A plenary session at Domkino is dedicated to the fifteenth anniversary of the film *Potemkin*.

March 15. In accordance with a decision of the Council of People's Commissars of the USSR, Eisenstein is awarded the State Prize (First Degree) for *Alexander Nevsky*.

July 3. Eisenstein broadcasts a talk, "The Patriotic War of the Soviet People," to the United States.

August 7. Eisenstein, in the capacity of artistic director of the Moscow film studios, is thanked by the government for the successful work of the studio under wartime conditions. He is made a member of the editorial board for the production of wartime documentary and newsreel films.

October 6. Eisenstein is released from the duties of artistic director for the duration of his work on *Ivan the Terrible*.

October 14. The film studios are evacuated to the city of Alma-Ata.

November–December. Eisenstein completes the work on the literary scenario for *Ivan the Terrible*. Begins work on an article entitled "Dickens, Griffith, and Ourselves."

1942

January–July. Work in progress on the director's scenario for *Ivan the Terrible*.

November. Eisenstein completes an article entitled *PRKFV*, on S. S. Prokofiev (published posthumously in 1956).

No definite date. Eisenstein writes a preface to the American edition of his articles on the theory of cinema.

1943

April 22. Shooting of *Ivan the Terrible* begins.

September 25. Eisenstein is temporarily relieved of his teaching load at VGIK in connection with the return of the institute to Moscow.

December 26. The Committee on Art Affairs approves the assembled rushes of *Ivan the Terrible*.

No definite date. Eisenstein works on an article called "Charlie the Kid," about Charlie Chaplin (translated by Herbert Marshall and published in *Sight and Sound*, the British Film Institute's journal).

1944

January–June. Continuation of the shooting of *Ivan the Terrible*.

July 26. Eisenstein returns to Moscow from Alma-Ata.

September 5. Is made a member of the Artistic Council of the Committee for Cinema Affairs.

September 10. Writes an essay called "About Myself."

October 28. Preview of the first part of *Ivan the Terrible*.

December. The first part of *Ivan the Terrible* is accepted by the Committee for Cinema Affairs.

1945

January 20. Première of the first part of *Ivan the Terrible* is held at the Udarnik Cinema, with an exhibition of costumes.

February–March. Eisenstein publishes a series of articles about the work on *Ivan the Terrible*.

April 6. Eisenstein's radio broadcast about the work schedule for *Ivan the Terrible* (Part II).

April. Completes an article entitled "Twelve Apostles" (published posthumously in 1950).

June 19. Eisenstein is made a member of the editorial board of the journal *Iskusstvo Kino* (*Cinema Art*).

September–December. Eisenstein works on *Ivan the Terrible* (Part II).

October 1. Eisenstein again occupies the post of professor in the Department of Film Direction of VGIK.

No definite date. Eisenstein works on a study entitled "Nonindifferent Nature."

1946

January 26. Decision taken by the Council of People's Commissars of the USSR to award Eisenstein the State Prize (First Degree) for *Ivan the Terrible* (Part I).

February 2. Eisenstein is confined at the Kremlin Hospital, after suffering a heart attack.

May–July. While at the Kremlin Hospital, and later at the Barvikh Sanatorium, Eisenstein writes his memoirs.

November 23. Eisenstein is presented with a medal "for heroic labor during the Great Patriotic War of the Soviet People."

December 14. Eisenstein completes the final autobiographical fragment, entitled "P.S., P.S., P.S."

1947

June 19. Eisenstein is appointed director of the Cinema Section of the Institute of Art History of the USSR Academy of Sciences.

October. Completes an article entitled "Thirty Years of Soviet Cinematography and the Traditions of Russian Culture" (published posthumously in 1949).

No definite date. Eisenstein works on a study called "Pathos," on a number of essays collectively entitled "People of a Certain Film, Ivan the Terrible" (published posthumously), and on the study "Stereocinema." He continues work on an article about color cinema.

1948

February 10. Eisenstein writes his last article, "Color Cinema," in the form of a letter to L. V. Kuleshov. It was never finished. The incomplete article was published posthumously in 1956.

February 11. Death of Eisenstein.

February 13. Eisenstein's interment at Moscow's Novo-Devichie Cemetery.

Appendix:
Eisenstein's "Hope of the Future"

Students of his Directors' Faculty at the Higher State Institute of Cinematography, Moscow, 1931–1935

Abramov: Russian-Jewish. Representative of Soviet Export Films in London.

L. Altzev: Russian. Died in Ashabad earthquake. Director at Moscow Film Studios. Former Soviet Export Film representative in Canada.

Kira Andronnikova: Wife of the famous Russian-Jewish writer Boris Pilnyak. Both were arrested and imprisoned in the Gulag, and her son was adopted by the Georgian film director Shengalay. Kira eventually was released but died of the privations endured in the prison camps. Director at the Moscow Children's Film Studios.

Harry Aslanyan: Armenian. Assistant to A. Dovzhenko; later, director at the Dovzhenko Film Studios in Kiev.

Y. Fradkin: Russian-Jewish. Died with Kishmishov in the Home Guard. Director at Moscow Film Studios.

Victor Ivanov: Ukrainian-Jewish. Former locomotive engineer. Director at the Dovzhenko Film Studios, Kiev.

Yasha Kacheriyan: Armenian. Director of documentary films, Erevan Film Studios.

Valya Kadochnikov: Russian. Director at Moscow Film Studios. Died of "natural" causes. Eisenstein, whose favorite he was, bitterly mourned his death and accused the Communist Party of inhumanity and neglect.

Vartan Kishmishov: Armenian. Former GPU guard. Killed in the Home Guard defending Moscow during the Second World War. Director at the Moscow Film Studios.

Jay Leyda: American. Did not complete the course or graduate. Later, translator of Eisenstein's works and professor of cinema.

Grisha Lifschitz: Russian-Jewish. Tank commander and war hero. Director at the Dovzhenko Film Studios, Kiev, and worked at Ukraine TV studios. Died of heart failure.

Herbert Marshall: English. Graduated as feature film director in 1935. Later, film and theater director, author, and broadcaster in radio and TV. Professor emeritus at Southern Illinois University. Translator of Eisenstein's works.

Vladimir Nizhny: Russian. Chief assistant to Eisenstein at the film institute. Author of *Lessons with Eisenstein*, translated by I. Montagu and J. Leyda.

Sigismund Novrotsky: Polish. Director at the Dovzhenko Film Studios, Kiev.

Constantine Pepinashvili: Georgian. Honored Artist of the Georgian Republic. Director at the Georgian Film Studios, Tbilisi.

R. Y. Perelstein: Russian-Jewish. Brother of Eisenstein's widow, Pera Attasheva. Died of sickness.

F. Phillipov: Russian. Director at the Moscow Film Studios.

Masha Pugachevskaya: Former Red Cavalry woman under General Budyenny. Married to high-ranking Red Army officer. He was executed, and she disappeared in the Gulag. Director.

Isaac Schmidt: Russian-Jewish. Left the institute to become a leading caricaturist and artist of the Soviet Union. Emigrated to Israel; died in Austria.

Joseph Skliut: Russian-Jewish. Scriptwriter. Eventually appointed secretary of the club of cinema workers, Dom Kino, Moscow.

Tsoi: Korean. Played a lead in Dovzhenko's film *Aerograd*. Later arrested and sent to the Gulag. Director of eastern theater in Siberia.

M. A. Velichko: Russian. Died in studio accident, 1962. Director at the Moscow Film Studios.

Acknowledgments

This work is probably the most revealing of all Eisenstein's writings, because it is a kind of diary written when he was aware of how near death he was. Of course, he never dreamed it would be published in his lifetime or Stalin's — and it wasn't. It appeared in the first volume of his *Selected Works*, published sixteen years after his death. Volume I also contained other material, which I have not included in this book. Some of the material has already been published in English translation, but not the autobiography.

Actually, I completed this translation ten years ago, and it should have been published long since. But, alas, an English publisher held it up for all those years, continually promising its imminent publication. The delay has been an embarrassment to my reputation and work, for I had planned to do three volumes from Eisenstein's *Selected Works*: Volume I, *The Autobiography;* Volume II, *Montage;* and Volume III, *Nonindifferent Nature*. They were all held up by the nonappearance of the announced Volume I. In the meantime, the last two volumes, translated by me and Roberta Reeder, have been completed for publication.

I have spoken of Sergei's widow, Pera Attasheva, in my preface. I wish to extend special thanks and my deep gratitude to so many of those around her who helped in the days of her final sickness: Valya, Veda, and Naum, as well as many others.

Many friends and colleagues have helped me in my work on this translation. Mr. Tony Wraight volunteered to do the preliminary work of breaking the soil of the original. Pera Attasheva's sister Zina Voynow had done some draft translations of a few chapters, which she handed over to me to use as I wished. They were made from the original serialization in the Russian magazine *Znamya* and were not the complete form, later published in the *Selected Works*.

On the editorial side, I have had the help of three graduate assistants in the Center for Soviet and East European Studies in the Performing Arts of Southern Illinois University. First, my thanks to Mr. Samuel Sorgenstein, who, under my general supervision, did the first checking of the translation, particularly sources, dates, and quotations in Volume I, and translated the Chronology.

My graduate assistants, Mr. Ron Levaco and Miss Marilyn Hengst, each helped in checking and researching. The final checking was completed by Mr. Michael Rose and Mr. M. A. Nicolson. My typists, Mr. David McGan, Miss Carolyn Poole, and Mrs. Jane Keyes, who were also S.I.U. students, had quite a job trying to read my final corrected manuscript and struggling with the fantastic array of foreign names and spellings.

Finally, of course, I owe much to Southern Illinois University — to its president emeritus, Dr. Delyte W. Morris; its former chancellor, Dr. Robert MacVicar; the former chairman of the Theater Department, Dr. Archibald McLeod; and their staffs.

In fact, special thanks are due to Dr. McLeod, for it was he who first invited me to S.I.U. as a Distinguished Visiting Professor, on the suggestion of my old friend Professor Mordecai Gorelik. Thanks are also due to the S.I.U. Office of Research and Projects, which provided some financial support for the typing. Without the university's setting up the Center for Soviet and East European Studies in the Performing Arts, with its premises, equipment, staff, and myself as its director, the completing of such a monumental task would have been far more onerous than it has been, for the second and third volumes were even more difficult than the autobiography.

The support of such a scholarly enterprise is one of the reasons for the existence of universities.

Through all the trials and tribulations of this project, my wife, Fredda Brilliant, has been my major help and support — not only moral but practical, including assistance with the final editing of the manuscript. To her, my love and gratitude.

— Herbert Marshall

Index

Abd-el-Krim, 14
Adler, Alfred, 159
Afrosimov (engineer), 39, 42
Agadzhanova, N. F. (Nooneh), 81–83, 163
Aksyonov, I. A., 76
Albert, Bishop of Riga, 17
Alexander Nevsky, ix, xiv, xv, 8, 35, 36, 197, 225–26; "Battle on the Ice" in, 198; bridge scene in, 65, 66; and problem of unity, 259; prologue to, 72; sound-visual work on, 251
Alexander II, 158
Alexander III, 27, 88
Alexandrov, Douglas, 163
Alexandrov, Grisha, x, xvii, 48, 53, 99, 124, 136, 142; *The Market of Lust* (with Eisenstein), 163; "On Sound Cinema," 257
Allandi, Dr. (French politician), 91–92, 93
Altzev, L. (director), xx
Alvarez delVayo, Julio, 81
Amelang sisters, 41, 43, 50
American *Film Index*, 8
American Tragedy, An, see under Dreiser, Theodore
Andronnikova, K., xxi
Antheil, George, 80, 191–92
Anthony Adverse (H. Allen), 171–72
Aragon, Louis, 120, 121

Arliss, George, 195; *Old English*, 195–96
Army Corps of Engineers, School for Ensigns of, 54, 58, 66, 85
Artsybashev, M. P.: *Sanin*, 241
Auriol, Jean Georges, 137
Averchenko, A. T., 51
Avril, Jane, 213

Babanova, Maria I., 160
Babel, Isaac E., xi, 162, 163; *Maria*, 163
Bachman (Hollywood supervisor), 156
Bakst, L. N. (Léon), 188
Balász, Béla, 137
Balzac, Honoré de, 146; *The Fatal Skin*, 117; *La Comédie Humaine*, 116
Bancroft, George, 154
Barbusse, Henri, 138
Bardèche, Maurice, 44
Barnum & Bailey Circus, 78
Barrymore, John, 166
Basch, Victor, 106, 107
Battleship Potemkin, xiii, xv, 8, 65, 104, 110, 155, 202; book about, for foreign publication, 217; color used in, 250; first screening of, 84–86; image of lions in, 216; musical score for, 87–88, 251; "Odessa Steps" sequence in, xiii, 208; première of, 80; and problem of unity, 259; rhythm in, 49; success of, 81
Baum, Vicki: *Grand Hotel*, 126, 147